REPRINTS OF ECONOMIC CLASSICS

ENGLAND AND AMERICA

ENGLAND
&
AMERICA

A
COMPARISON
OF THE SOCIAL AND POLITICAL STATE
OF BOTH NATIONS

[EDWARD GIBBON WAKEFIELD]

[1834]

REPRINTS OF ECONOMIC CLASSICS

AUGUSTUS M. KELLEY · PUBLISHERS
NEW YORK · 1967

First Published 1834

(New York: Harper & Brothers,
No. *82 Cliff-Street*, 1834)

Reprinted 1967 by
AUGUSTUS M. KELLEY PUBLISHERS

Library of Congress Catalogue Card Number
66-21699

PRINTED IN THE UNITED STATES OF AMERICA
by SENTRY PRESS, NEW YORK, N. Y. 10019

ENGLAND

AND

AMERICA.

A

COMPARISON

OF THE SOCIAL AND POLITICAL STATE OF

BOTH NATIONS.

NEW-YORK:

PUBLISHED BY HARPER & BROTHERS,

NO. 82 CLIFF-STREET.

1834.

PREFACE.

The following pages are intended for publication in America as well as in England. They have been written with two objects in particular : first, to lay before Americans a sketch of the political condition of England, and before the English an explanation of some peculiarities in the social state of America ; secondly, to point out the means of removing those causes which are productive of great evils to both countries.

For the satisfactory performance of such a work, powers are required which the author does not possess ; command of language, a style calculated to engage the reader, and a name which should give to every statement or suggestion the weight of authority. But on the other hand, he has had peculiar motives for examining the condition of America, and he is so far partly qualified to treat upon that subject ; he believes also that he is enabled to make Americans comprehend the state of England, which hitherto has been described to them only by Englishmen, writing, not for America, but for England. The English and Americans know very little of each other's affairs. Now, the present writer has looked at America with English eyes, and at England with American eyes. It was a consciousness of this advantage, that prompted him to undertake the task of describing to each nation the chief social peculiarities of the other.

Another advantage which the writer fancies that he possesses over many Englishmen and Americans who might

have written on these subjects, is the want of any patriotic
prejudice in favour of either country—of any motive for
concealing or perverting the truth. His opinions, he believes, have been formed, and are stated, without affection
or fear. Plain-speaking must nearly always be disagreeable to somebody ; and in this case it will offend many, because large classes, both in England and America, are
mentioned without any regard for their selfish interests,
their mean passions, or even their honest prejudices.

The following Notes are not to be considered as so many
discussions on distinct subjects ; but each of them is more
or less connected with all the others. In fact, they all relate to the social state and political economy of England
and America.

What, it may be asked, has the political economy of England to do with that of America, or that of America with
that of England ? What relation can there be between the
political prospects of the English, and the origin, progress,
and prospects of slavery in America ? To such questions
these Notes supply an answer. Comparison is the easiest
way to truth. In many cases, the Americans and the English may have an equal interest in the same subject, though
they may have very different objects in view. Of this common interest with different objects, the subject of colonization is a good example. Admitting that the three elements of production are land, capital, and labour ; supposing that the chief social evils of England are owing to a
deficiency of land in proportion to capital and labour, and
those of America to an excess of land in proportion to
capital and labour (whatever great advantages she may
owe to a sufficiency of land), in that case, the Americans and the English have a common interest in understanding the art of colonization, though the object of the
Americans should be to have less, and that of the English to have more, of one of the elements of wealth. So,

also, if it be for the interest of the English to buy cheap corn of the Americans, and of the Americans to buy cheap manufactured goods of the English, the two nations have a common interest in the repeal of the English corn-laws and of the American tariff. In every subject treated of in these Notes, the Americans and the English have more or less a common interest.

The statements and arguments contained in these Notes might have been supported by reference to numerous authorities; but, though the writer wished, for his own sake, to adopt that course, still he was afraid that, by doing so, he might render his work too formal. To one book, however, he has referred pretty often; Mr. Stuart's Three Years in North America; a production which may be termed a storehouse of facts concerning the United States. If Mr. Stuart had seen fit to develop the causes of the facts which he has collected, to give reasons for the chief social peculiarities of America, these Notes, or at least such of them as treat directly of the United States, would not have been published.

CONTENTS.

NOTE I.

THE WEALTH OF ENGLAND.

NOTE II.

MISERY OF THE BULK OF THE PEOPLE.

NOTE III.

UNEASINESS OF THE MIDDLE CLASS.

NOTE IV.

COINCIDENCE OF OVERFLOWING NATIONAL WEALTH, WITH THE UNEASINESS AND MISERY OF INDIVIDUALS.

NOTE V.

POLITICAL PROSPECTS OF THE ENGLISH.

NOTE VI.

FREE TRADE IN CORN, AS A MEANS OF ENLARGING THE FIELD OF EM-PLOYMENT FOR ENGLISH CAPITAL AND LABOUR.

NOTE VII.

CLOSE RELATION BETWEEN THE FOREIGN CORN-TRADE OF ENGLAND AND THE FOREIGN TRADE OF CHINA.

NOTE VIII.

MEANS OF EXTENDING FREE TRADE TO THE WHOLE COAST OF CHINA.

NOTE IX.

SOME SOCIAL PECULIARITIES OF THE AMERICANS.

NOTE X.

ORIGIN, PROGRESS, AND PROSPECTS OF SLAVERY IN AMERICA.

NOTE XI.

APOLOGY FOR THE AMERICAN TARIFF.

NOTE XII.

THE ART OF COLONIZATION.

APPENDIX.

No. I.

No. II.

No. III.

NOTE I.

THE WEALTH OF ENGLAND.

First signs of wealth observed by a foreigner—Proofs of wealth in London —In the country—Superior enjoyments of the English—Large proportion of the English who enjoy much wealth—Immense capital invested —Abundance of capital ready to be invested—Overflow of capital—Causes of the great wealth of England—Combination of power—Division of capital and labour a cause of poverty—Effects of combination of productive power on the agriculture, manufactures, and commerce of England— Some conclusions from the principle, that production depends on the degree in which men help each other—Constant progress of wealth and civilization in England.

An American citizen visits the continent of Europe, and on his way home passes some time in England. Here he finds the roads in every direction far better than any he has seen before, and he sees more of them on a given space than in France or America. The cross-roads are kept in far better order than those of any other country. By the side of nearly all the great roads, he sees, for the first time, a well kept foot-path. In many places, the foot-paths across fields are as dry, and smooth, and trim as walks in pleasure-gardens. All the carriages on the road are stronger and lighter, more useful and sightly, than those to which he is accustomed ; and the vast number of those carriages strikes him with astonishment. The strength and beauty of the horses, the quality and neatness of their harness, and the very whips with which they are driven, excite his wonder. The uncommon speed with which he travels raises his spirits and inclines him to look favourably at every thing. He exclaims, what magnificent crops— what beautiful meadows—what fine cattle and sheep—what skill and care in the mixture of wood, arable and grass lands—what noble trees—what regularity and neatness in the fences ! even the ditches and gate-posts are admirable ! The mansions are palaces, the farm-houses mansions, the merest village of cottages has an air of peculiar comfort ; while the number of those mansions, farm-houses, and villages gives to the country the appearance of a scattered town. But then the towns : many of them are so extensive, the houses in them are so well built, the shops have such

a display of rich goods, the streets are so well paved, and
contain so large a proportion of good houses ; these towns
are so full of well-dressed people, that each of them might
be taken for a city.   Even the smallest towns appear like
sections of a wealthy capital ; and the number of towns,
large and small, is so great that, together with the great
number of good houses by the road side out of town, one
seems to be travelling all day through one street.   This,
the foreigner imagines, must be the most populous road in
England ; there must be something peculiar in this part of
the country which attracts rich people.   By no means.
He is told that, so long as fourteen years ago, the length
of the paved streets and turnpike-roads of England and
Wales was about twenty thousand miles ; and he soon
learns that nearly all the great roads show marks of wealth
like those which he has so much admired.   He therefore
supposes that the wealth of the country must bear a very
large proportion to that of the metropolis ; but on this point
he is undeceived on reaching London.   Here the crowd is
so great, the objects which attract his attention are so many
and so different, that, for a while, he is bewildered and
incapable of arranging his thoughts so as to draw conclusions from what he sees.   At length he begins to observe
methodically, and to compare his observations with those
which he has made in other great cities.   Until now he
has conceived New-York or Paris to be the place in which
the greatest amount of wealth was enjoyed by a given
number of people ; but he is now convinced that the inhabitants of London obtain a greater quantity of things
necessary, useful, or agreeable to man, than the inhabitants
of any other city in the world.   The quantity of flour and
meat consumed, in proportion to people, he finds not much
greater in London than in Paris, and even less than in
New-York, where the working classes live better than in
London ; so also the proportion of looking-glasses he knows
to be greater in Paris, and the proportion of rum drank
to be greater in New-York than in London ; but he cannot
doubt that, on the whole, more good things are enjoyed in
London, by a given number of people, than any where else
out of England.   It is not in his power, indeed, to compare
the quantities or values of all necessary, useful, or agreeable
things enjoyed in London, with the quantities or values of
such things used in other great cities ; but he is convinced
of the superior wealth of London by the same mode of
observation which has satisfied him that the people of

New-York drink more rum, and the people of Paris own more looking-glasses than the people of London. In London one meets with every thing the immediate produce of agriculture, such as meat, bread, sugar and tea, of the very finest quality. Of manufactured objects used in London, scarce one can be mentioned which is not brought to greater perfection than similar objects used in other capital cities, while the variety of such objects is yet more striking. The fittings and furniture of a third-rate house in London are of a better quality than those of a palace in France or Germany; the doors and windows answer their purpose better; the chairs are stronger, lighter, and more convenient to sit upon; the tables, if not more useful, are far more beautiful; the glass is more transparent, the knives cut better, the fastenings of all sorts, the corkscrew and the toasting-fork, are better suited to their purpose, and composed of superior materials. In every London house, excepting those of the poorest order, one finds many useful and agreeable objects which are either scarce or unknown in Paris, New-York, and Vienna. The inhabitants of London pay, it has been reckoned, about 50,000*l.* a year,—being the fourth of 200,000*l.* which the nation pays,—for what? for blacking advertisements—that is, for the facility of choosing between different kinds of blacking. The number of kinds of horses used in London, though very striking to a foreigner, is less remarkable than the forethought, pains, and skill required for making each variety—the Lincolnshire dray horse, for example, the Cleveland coach horse, the high-bred nag, the cob, and the trotting hackney—so obviously distinct from all the others. The variety of carriages, whether for business or pleasure, and the fitness of each sort for its peculiar purpose, whether that purpose be determined by the weather, by the fortune of him who owns the carriage, or the business of him who uses it,—are equally deserving of admiration. At night, when other great cities are in darkness, all London is brilliantly illuminated; nay, the beautiful gas lights extend for some miles into the country, in all directions. The pavements of London—but the list of examples might be continued through a volume. Still, the foreigner is less surprised at the quantity, variety, and perfection of useful and agreeable objects used in London, than at the great proportion of the people who enjoy in abundance the most perfect of those objects. That the houses of the high aristocracy should be large, fine, and richly furnished, is nothing strange; but the houses in many quarters which the aristocracy despise, are as large, fine, and well furnished as those of the most aristocratic quarters. The best houses, for instance, in Bloomsbury, Finsbury, and Lambeth, and in such villages or suburbs as Highgate, Hornsey, Tottenham, Hackney, Peckham, and Clapham, though a lord would disdain to live in one of them, are as large, fine, and well furnished, as those of Mayfair, or of such aristocratic villages as Roehampton and Wimbledon. The shops, too, in many of those "low" quarters, though stocked for the supply of persons engaged in some industrious pursuit, are as full, and as rich, as those of Bond-street or Regent-street. The number of carriages, also, kept for pleasure in those despised quarters greatly exceeds the number of such carriages kept by the high aristocracy in and about London. In the quantity and quality of good things which he uses, in his own dress, and that of his family, in his table, furniture and books, or in whatever mode of expense he may prefer, a prosperous lawyer or merchant is not far behind the richest duke ; and the number of rich people in London who pursue an industrious career is very much greater than the number of rich lords. But it would be improper to measure the wealth of a society by the enjoyments of its richest members alone. Dividing the inhabitants of London and Paris into the same number of ranks with respect to the consumption of wealth, every London rank enjoys more good things than its corresponding Parisian rank. A second-rate merchant in London spends at least twice as much a sa second-rate Parisian merchant ; a third-rate London advocate spends, perhaps, three times as much as a first-rate Parisian advocate ; a fourth-rate London attorney spends six times as much as a second-rate Parisian notary ; a physician in London, a surgeon, a dentist, a tradesman of whatever description, a servant from the butler to the scullion, a mechanic in whatever line, a porter, or a common labourer, spends more, and in most cases a great deal more, than one of a corresponding rank in the Parisian scale. But this is not all. In London there are more first-rate merchants, lawyers, and tradesmen *in proportion* to second-rate ones, more second-rate ones in proportion to third-rate ones, and so on all down the scale. In a word, turn which way you will, London abounds with proofs of its enormous wealth.

Thus the foreigner is apt to fall into another error ; to imagine that a very large proportion of the wealth of England is collected in London. He is undeceived again by visiting some great provincial towns of different descriptions, such as Bath, Liverpool, and Leeds. Each of these resembles a large section of the metropolis; Bath being like Marylebone, Leeds like manufacturing Southwark, and Liverpool like the commercial Tower Hamlets. In point of size and general character Liverpool bears some resemblance to Bordeaux or New-York, and Leeds to Lyons; but in America there is no town like Leeds, nor, either in America or France, any town like Bath. England abounds with such towns as Bath—mere pleasure towns, they may be called—such as Leamington, Hastings, Margate, Cheltenham, and Brighton; with more of the same kind, though of smaller extent, such as Tunbridge Wells, Worthing, Harrowgate, Aberystwith, Southend, Lowestoft, and Sidmouth. Of towns like Leeds, while in the United States there is not one, and in France but few, there is in England a number without end, such as Macclesfield, Sheffield, Nottingham, Coventry, Birmingham, and Manchester. Of towns like Liverpool, though there be several in the United States, there are many more in the United Kingdom, while neither in the United States nor in France are there any towns of a mixed character, like Norwich and Glasgow. Again, neither in France nor in the United States are there any great provincial capitals like Edinburgh and Dublin. But after all, that for which, in respect to towns, England is most distinguished,—even more so than for the number and size of her pleasure towns,—is the vast number and great size of her smaller provincial capitals, which are neither seaports nor the seats of manufactures; such as York, Canterbury, Gloucester, Exeter, Shrewsbury, Reading, Colchester, and Bury St. Edmund's. And now, further, let the wealth of any English town whatsoever, be compared with that of a town of the same character in any other country. With a single, and no doubt very important exception, England has greatly the advantage. In the United States every labourer, not being a slave, obtains more and better food, more and better clothes, as well as a better lodging, than a labourer of equal skill in England. Without any further exception, the inhabitants of English provincial towns enjoy a greater quantity and variety of good things, approach nearer to the inhabitants of the capital in respect to the consumption of wealth, than people of a similar rank in the provincial towns of other countries. A merchant of Liverpool or Bristol, a manufacturer of Bir-

mingham or Leeds, be he first, second, or third-rate, in-
dulges in expenses for his house, his table, the education
of his children and the amusement of his family, which,
to think of only, would frighten a Bordeaux merchant,
or Lyons manufacturer of the same rank. What a French
provincial doctor spends in a year, would not keep an
English provincial doctor in equal practice for three
months. Country attorneys in England get and spend, on the
average, ten times as much as French country attorneys.
Common tradesmen in all English country towns, bakers,
butchers, cheesemongers, and linen-drapers, as well as mechanics, such as carpenters, builders, and glaziers, live
much better than a similar class of people in Paris; they
have more rooms to live in; their rooms are better furnished; they, their wives, and children are better dressed;
they find it more easy to obtain comforts and indulge in
luxuries. Surely there are fifty country towns in England
which contain a good inn, that is a comfortable innkeeper,
for one French country town that contains a passable inn,
held by a man who does not live so expensively as the
keepers of most English alehouses. That English town is
reckoned poor in which there are not some shops that would
be considered good in the best quarter of London; and
there are hundreds of towns in England, in which you can
purchase almost every thing that is commonly for sale in
London. The number of booksellers' shops in the provincial
towns of England, and the stocks which they contain, present a very striking contrast with the number and stocks of
French booksellers' shops out of Paris. In the number and
quality of horses and carriages kept for pleasure, English
country towns surpass, very far indeed, French country
towns of equal magnitude. Every town in England, that at
all bears the character of the capital of a district, possesses
a circulating library, such as would be called good in Paris
or New-York; while most of such towns, as well as many
small towns, and indeed rural parts, miles away from any
town, have the inestimable advantage of a book club. No
English town containing 10,000 inhabitants is without foot
pavements or gas lights; while many towns, with less than
5,000 inhabitants, are as well paved and well lighted as the
finest quarter of London. In their literary and scientific
institutions, such towns as Liverpool, Leeds, and Birmingham, appear to surpass the metropolis, allowing for the difference of numbers; and in this respect they obviously
excel, beyond comparison, French or American towns of

like magnitude. Another proof of the general diffusion of wealth in England, is the large proportion of the sums invested by savings-banks, which is subscribed out of London; the whole fund, amounting to about 14,000,000*l.*, and subscribed by persons little above the condition of labourers, being a proof of the wealth of England. But finally, the most striking proof of the wealth of the English, all over England, is the facility with which, in any part of England, funds are raised for any undertaking that offers the least chance of profit. It is to this point, especially, that I would draw the attention of Americans.* Though thousands of millions have been spent in rendering England the most habitable country in the world, in making bad land good, on fences, farm buildings, roads, bridges, canals and docks, on the opening of mines, the building of manufactories and warehouses, not to mention houses, still it appears as if thousands of millions would be forthcoming for similar purposes, if there were but room for carrying such purposes into effect. Abundance of CAPITAL invested, and ready to be invested, is the most marked, nay the peculiar, characteristic of England. By guessing at what it would take to put France, or one of the American States, into the same condition as England, with respect to the improvement of land, to farm buildings, roads, bridges, canals, wharves, docks, manufactories, warehouses, and machinery, &c., we may form some idea of the degree in which the fixed capital of the English exceeds that of the French or Americans: and yet the French or Americans, who have invested so small a capital in comparison with that invested by the English, have far less than the English ready for investment.† Money makes money, says the proverb; which, translated into the language of modern science,

* " The great public work in this part of the United States in which the people are engaged, is the canal between the Chesapeake and the Ohio rivers, that is, between Georgetown and Washington on the one hand, and Pittsburgh on the western side of the Alleghany ridge on the other. This prodigious work, which is now in progress, is estimated by General Bernard, at about twenty-two millions of dollars. The sum of fifteen hundred thousand dollars, subscribed by the citizens of Washington, Georgetown, and Alexandria, on the Potomac, *has been obtained from Dutch capitalists*, the house of Messrs. Crommelin, of Amsterdam."—*Three years in North America, by James Stuart, Esq.* vol. ii, page 62.—*Third Edition.*

† " The canal (at Louisville), is two miles in the length, cut out of the solid rock, and in some places forty feet deep, and is of sufficient width to allow the largest class of steamboats to pass. Dry docks are to be constructed for the repairing of steamboats. *There is at present a want of funds* ; but the work is so far advanced that there is no risk of its not being completed."—*Stuart*, vol. ii, page 290.

means that capital creates capital.   In America, where
there is so much room for the investment of capital, because
so little capital has been invested, innumerable works, holding out the certainty of large profits, are projected, but for
want of capital are not begun; while in England, where,
by reason of the vast masses of capital already invested,
there seems but little room for the profitable investment of
more, millions accumulate so rapidly, that funds are never
wanted for even the most hazardous undertakings.   How
to obtain capital is the question in America ;* what to do
with their capital is the puzzle of the English.   In this difficulty the English build Waterloo bridges, which yield no
profit, send goods to be sold in distant countries at less than
prime cost, squander millions on South American speculations, lay out immense sums in the purchase of foreign securities, and lend money, by tens of millions at a time, to
North American States, South American anarchies, and
European tyrants, great or small.   If the wealth of a society
depend on the proportion which capital bears to numbers,
then it is clear the English are the richest people in the
world.

What are the causes of the enormous wealth of England?
This question has never been answered to the satisfaction
of Americans ; who, descended from the English, using
their language, able to use their knowledge, paying fewer
taxes than the English, cultivating a much more fertile soil,
and as well protected, to say the least, in the enjoyment of
property, cannot perceive, in the reasons usually given for
the peculiar wealth of England, any circumstance peculiar
to the English.   This question I propose to examine, with
a view to show, here, why the English are so much richer
than the Americans ; and, further on, how the Americans
might become as rich as the English, if not richer.   The
question is of no little importance to the English themselves,
and is full of the deepest interest to all new societies, like
the American States, and the English colonies in America
and Australia.

All wealth being the produce of industry, it is evident
that the wealth of a society must depend on the degree in
which the productive powers of industry are improved by
that society.   What are the greatest improvements in the
productive powers of industry ; improvements, I mean, beyond that simple exertion of power, which in two indi-

* The State of Louisiana has lately borrowed a great sum of the English.

viduals of equal strength, working separately in the same way, would raise equal amounts of produce? Adam Smith has said that the greatest improvement in the productive powers of industry is *division of labour;* others have dwelt on the great effects of *machinery;* and some again have taken pains to show, what is self-evident, that the productive powers of industry are greatly increased by *the use of capital.* Unquestionably capital, machinery, which is capital, and "division of labour," tend to increase the quantity of produce in proportion to the number of hands employed; but none of these improvements are primary causes, as some of them, and especially "division of labour," have been considered by political economists; each of them, on the contrary, though an immediate cause, is the effect of some antecedent cause. One cannot use capital merely by wishing to use it, nor can a single workman practise "division of labour;" but the use of capital and "division of labour" result from some anterior improvement. What, then, is the first improvement in the productive powers of industry, that improvement on which others depend?

In the most simple operation of industry,—in that, for example, which savages perform when they hunt for subsistence,—two persons assisting each other would obtain more game in a given time than two persons hunting each by himself without concert; just as two greyhounds, running together, will kill more hares than four greyhounds running separately. The very first improvement, therefore, in the productive powers of industry, seems to be not division, but combination of labour. Several individuals, by combining their labour, procure more food than they want: behold the second stage of social improvement; the society has obtained a capital. The possession of capital leads to the institution of property: it also leads to the division of employments. Some members of the society still co-operate in the production of food; others in making instruments which facilitate the production of food; and between these two parties an exchange takes place of their respective productions: commerce has begun; the power of exchanging, on which, all economists agree, depends the division of employments. But now, as food is produced with less and less labour, the wants of the society increase, and a still further distribution of employments takes place: some build houses, some make clothes, and some become dealers. Thus far it is plain every step in civilization, every improvement in the productive powers of industry, including distribution of employments, has rested on concert or combination among all the members of the society.

But, thus far, all the members of the society are supposed to possess equal portions of capital. Such a state of things, if it were to last, would not admit of much further improvement in the productive powers of industry. No man would find others willing to employ his capital for his advantage as well as their own, rather than their own capital for their own exclusive advantage : no man, consequently, would have a motive for accumulating more capital than he could use with his own hands. This is to some extent the case in new American settlements, where a passion for owning land prevents the existence of a class of labourers for hire ; and where, consequently, half the crop is sometimes left to rot upon the ground. In the next place, so long as the capital of the society was equally divided among all, it would be impossible to undertake any of those works which require the employment of many hands and a fixed capital. It would be quite impossible, for instance, to build a ship or a bridge ; for, even if a sufficient number of workmen to admit of. that division of employments which takes place in building a ship or a bridge, should possess the right sort of capital, and a sufficient quantity of it to enable them to wait for distant returns, by what means could that scattered capital be combined ? and how could the profits be divided ? Only, it would appear, by the institution of a joint stock company ; a contrivance for the combination of capital in particular works, which is used only in the advanced societies. Mankind have adopted a much more simple contrivance for promoting the accumulation of capital, and the use of capital, when required, both in large masses and in a fixed shape : they have divided themselves into owners of capital and owners of labour. But this division was, in fact, the result of concert or combination. The capitals of all being equal, one man saves *because* he expects to find others willing to work for him ; other men spend *because* they expect to find some men ready to employ them ; and if it were not for this readiness to co-operate, to act in concert or combination, the division of the industrious classes into capitalists and labourers could not be maintained.

A baker and a tailor, who deal with each other, are said to divide their labour : if they did so in reality, each of them would make both the bread and the clothes which he wanted, and there would be no intercourse between them.

Co-operating, dealing with, depending on each other, they combine their labour: it is the employments which they divide; and, what is more, the division of their employments results from the combination of their labour. The two men divide the whole work, which is to be performed by their united labour for their common advantage. The workmen of a pin-factory are said to divide their labour: if they did so in reality, each of them would make all the parts of a pin. As it is, each pin is the produce of many persons' *united labour;* many persons whose labour is united in order that the work, which it is to perform, may be easily divided among them. In this case, also, division of employments is an effect of combination of labour. In what case is a work divided among many, without combining the labour of those who are to perform the work?

But it may be said that this is a question of terms merely; that though there be a marked difference between the work performed and the labour which performs it, still, as either labour is divided among the several parts of a work, or the several parts of a work are divided among several labourers, it is indifferent whether we say division of work or division of labour. If so, by what terms are we to express that minute division of labour which takes place among the cottiers of Ireland, the small farmers of France, and most free settlers in new colonies: a state of things, under which each labourer works by himself, and for himself only, with no larger capital than his own hands can employ, without exchange, or nearly so, and producing, even in the most favourable case—that of the settler—not much more than enough for his own subsistence. If this be a dispute about terms only, how are we to express that combination of labour on an English farm, or a tobacco plantation in Virginia, which enables the English workmen or American slaves to raise so much more produce than they could possibly consume? The reader who may take the trouble to find an answer to these questions, will, I cannot help thinking, perceive, that "division of labour" is an improper term as commonly used; and, what is of far greater consequence, that the use of this improper term has kept out of sight the first great improvement in the productive powers of labour, namely, combination of power.

As for building a ship or making a road, so in the manufacture of pins, it is necessary to employ a large capital. A large capital, applied to one purpose, may be said to be combined. A minute division of capital, such as takes

place among the small farmers of France, the cottiers of
Ireland, and most settlers in new colonies, is as unfavourable to production as the minute division of labour practised
in those cases.

Combination of capital and labour, or combination of
productive power, seems to be of two distinct sorts; *first,*
that general combination which, if there were no restrictions
on trade, would render mankind one vast co-operative
society; general combination, on which depends that general
distribution of employments, or division of work, under
which some men grow tea, some dig for metals, and others
build ships, some are farmers, some manufacturers, and
others merchants; *secondly,* that particular combination,
on which depends the use of large masses of capital and
labour in particular works, and the most beneficial division
of those particular works.

Turning to the sources of the wealth of England, her
agriculture, manufactures, and commerce, it will be seen
that all these display in the highest degree the advantages
of both sorts of combination of power.

First, as to agriculture. No part of the population of
America is exclusively agricultural, excepting slaves and
their employers, who combine capital and labour in particular works. Free Americans, who cultivate the soil, follow
many other occupations. Some portion of the furniture
and tools which they use is commonly made by themselves.
They frequently build their own houses; and carry to
market, at whatever distance, the produce of their own
industry. They are spinners and weavers; they make
soap and candles, as well as, in many cases, shoes and
clothes for their own use. In America, the cultivation of
land is often the secondary pursuit of a blacksmith, a miller,
or a shopkeeper. In France a similar division of capital
and labour takes place among several employments, though
not to the same extent. The number of proprietors of land
in France is supposed to exceed 5,000,000; the number of
separate holdings or pieces of land is known to be about
10,000,000. But even supposing that, on the average, each
proprietor owns two separate pieces of land, still it does
not follow that two pieces of land are generally cultivated
by one person. On the contrary, while the large properties
are generally divided into several distinct farms, it does
not very often happen that two or more of the smaller properties are united under a single farmer. Consequently,
after making a liberal deduction for land which is not culti-

vated, the number of farmers or cultivators, not being hired labourers, probably exceeds 5,000,000. It is further estimated, that the number of agricultural labourers who work for hire amounts, with their wives and children, to about 5,000,000. Of these, however, not above two-fifths, 2,000,000, can be men. If the number of farmers be 5,000,000, and of farm-servants 2,000,000, there must be 3,000,000 farmers who employ no labourers at all. Suppose each of the remaining 2,000,000 farmers to employ one labourer, the agricultural capital and labour of France would be divided into 5,000,000 parts, of which three-fifths would be the smallest fractions into which capital and labour can be divided, and the remaining two-fifths would consist of fractions only twice as large as the smallest. Since, however, some farmers employ more than one labourer, more than 3,000,000 farmers cannot employ any labourers; and it thus appears probable, that three-fourths, at least, of the agricultural capital and labour of France are cut up into the smallest possible fractions, into single pairs of hands, and portions of capital such as one pair of hands can use. Limiting the smallest fractions to three-fourths of the whole, the remaining quarter will consist of 1,250,000 capitalists, having among them 2,000,000 labourers. If 750,000 of these capitalists employ two labourers each, 500,000 employ about one labourer each; and for each of them, who is supposed to employ more than two labourers, an addition must be made to that number, each of whom employs only one labourer. "Il faut habiter un pays," says a modern French writer,* "où tout le monde est propriétaire, pour se faire une idée juste des inconvéniens et du malheur du *morcellement* infini des biens territoriaux." The mischief lies, however, in the division, not of the land, but of the capital and labour employed on the land.

One of the evils resulting from the *morcellement* of agricultural capital and labour in France is, that the farmers and farm-labourers of that country, like those of the United States not being slave owners or slaves, do not confine themselves to one pursuit. In England, on the contrary, a farmer is, generally speaking, nothing but a farmer, and an agricultural labourer works nowhere but on the farm. The English farm labourer is a miserable wretch, no doubt, because he obtains but a very small share of the produce

---

* M. de Bonald (1826), quoted by Professor M'Culloch in note XIX. (Division of Property by Will) of his edition of Smith's Wealth of Nations,

of his labour; but this is a question, not of distribution, but of production. In England, the agricultural class seems to have come to an understanding with the other classes, to separate its employment from those of the manufacturer and dealer. Except in some of the wildest and worst cultivated districts, the practice, which is so common in France and America, of spinning wool by those who keep flocks, is gone quite out of fashion. Whatever manufactured object or mechanical work is required on an English farm, is procured at some shop in the nearest town, or performed by some mechanic who lives in the town. The mixed produce of American or French agriculture is, for the most part, sold in the nearest market, by those who raise it to those who consume it; while in England there is between the producers and consumers a distinct class of dealers, subdivided again into particular classes, such as cattle jobbers, dealers in corn, in hops, and in wool. An English farmer seldom deals, even with his own labourers, for any part of the produce of his farm; he pays for their labour with money, which they lay out, either directly in the nearest town, or through the medium of village shopkeepers. Thus the farmer and his men are occupied almost exclusively with the business of the farm.

English farming is also remarkable for a peculiar refinement in the distribution of employments, according to various circumstances of soil and climate. The county of Kent is somewhat more congenial to the growth of hops than the neighbouring county of Sussex; the Sussex farmer, therefore, abstains from growing hops, even for his own use; the beer which his family drink is made of hops grown in Kent. There are some districts especially fit for the growth of natural and artificial grasses for fattening cattle; and the farmer of such districts is seldom a cattle-breeder, but purchases lean cattle from jobbers, who have purchased them from farmers in districts best suited to the breeding of cattle. Though the inhabitants of Norwich require a great deal of cheese, yet the farmers thereabouts do not attempt to supply that demand. Their land is less suited to dairy-farming than the land in Cheshire, from which county comes great part of the cheese consumed in Norwich; while there are towns again in Cheshire which obtain the greater part of their flour from distant spots peculiarly suited to the growth of corn. Examples without end might be cited of this division of agricultural employments, which seems to be carried to a much higher pitch in England than in any other country. In France and the United States, though much greater differences of climate occasion a more marked separation of some agricultural employments,—such as the production of sugar in the southern states for the use of the northern states, and of oil in the south for the use of the north of France,—still a French or American cultivator generally seeks to raise whatever can be raised on his own land, which he either wants himself, or for which there is any demand in his own neighbourhood. The division of agricultural employments in England is all the more remarkable, because in England the differences of soil and climate are not very remarkable.

The advantage which England derives from confining her agriculturists to agricultural pursuits, and, in various parts of the country, to that particular mode of agriculture best suited to each district, becomes manifest in the superior skill of her farmers. The corn-growers of Essex, Suffolk, and Norfolk, the hop-growers of Kent and Worcestershire, the sheep-farmers of Sussex and Hampshire, the dairy-farmers of Gloucestershire and Cheshire, the cattle-breeders and cider-growers of Devonshire and Herefordshire, the breeders of horses in Lincolnshire and Yorkshire; all these, and many more which it would be tedious to mention, apply to their several pursuits a wonderful degree of knowledge, forethought, and calculation. It is rather a science than an art which each of them pursues; storing up the facts which come to his knowledge, and from a knowledge of those facts adopting, as a system, that mode of proceeding from which he expects the most beneficial results. Thinking of the pains which an English farmer takes in draining and manuring his fields, in the disposition of his land for various crops, in the selection of seeds, in the use of the best instruments, in keeping up or improving his fruit trees, in the management of his working cattle, in maintaining a peculiar and perfect race of cattle or sheep, and in subdividing the work performed by his united labourers, one might venture to call him a philosopher; though the term would excite ridicule in England, where science is almost as much despised in the abstract as in practice it is industriously cultivated.

But the superior knowledge of English farmers would be of little avail—it could not have been acquired indeed—if their capital and labour had been cut up into small fractional parts, as happens generally in France and America. In agriculture each farm is a particular work.

The most striking characteristic of English farming is the combination of capital and labour in particular works. Even in England, those districts in which the farms are largest, and in which each farmer employs the largest capital and the greatest number of labourers, are known to produce more, in proportion to the hands employed, than those less civilized districts in which the three elements of production, land, capital, and labour, are divided into smaller portions. But agricultural capital and labour are more combined in those parts of England, where the lowest degree of combination occurs, than in those parts of France or America (slave plantations excepted) which are distinguished for the highest degree of combination. In order to observe in the United Kingdom the bad effects of that division of capital and labour which takes place in France or America, one must travel to Ireland, where, in some districts, the separate fractions of capital and labour are almost as numerous as the cultivators. Well-informed Frenchmen are satisfied that the division of capital and labour in their country will, if it be carried much further, reduce the agriculture of France to a cottier system, like that of some parts of Ireland, under which the produce of industry is scarcely more than sufficient to feed those who work. In America, truly, the smallest fraction of capital and labour obtains a considerable produce ; but then it should be remembered that in America the chief element of production, the land, is not divided into small pieces as in France and Ireland. Hereafter I shall have occasion to notice the causes and effects of the division of capital and labour in America. Recurring to the agriculture of England, the large farms of that country exemplify the proverb—union is force. The most scientific of English farmers, if he were to apply his knowledge to the cultivation of a single field, would not raise a much greater produce than the most ignorant of Irish cottiers. The great extent of his farm allows full scope for the exercise of his superior knowledge. That of which he has a superior knowledge, is the art of cultivation on a large scale : and for the practice of this art, capital and labour in proportion to land are indispensable. Holding a large farm, and employing capital and labour in proportion, he is able to wait for distant returns, to pursue the best course of crops, to adopt improvements which at first bear the character of experiments, to employ many hands in one field, at one time, in one work, and when it is required, for a considerable period of time without intermission; finally is able to make that distribution of employments among his labourers, which, after combination of labour in single works, is the greatest improvement in the productive powers of industry. The results are obvious. By means of drainage and manure, an immense extent of land in England which was once sterile, now possesses the highest degree of fertility; and in every part of the country the fertility of land is carefully preserved. In France, on the contrary, the practice of exhausting the natural fertility of land is general, while in America it may be described as almost universal.* But the grand result of the superiority of English agriculture is, that while in France about two-thirds, and in America probably three-quarters, of the people are employed in agriculture, more than two-thirds, it is believed, of the people of England, are fed by the agricultural industry of less than one-third. The greatness of England, notwithstanding laws which forbid her manufacturers to exchange the produce of their industry for the surplus food of other countries, is incomprehensible to a foreigner until he observes the excellence of her agriculture. That excellence consists in raising from a given extent of land, without impoverishing the land, and with a given number of hands, a far greater produce than results from the labour of the same number of hands, on the same extent of soil, in any other part of the world.†

Less than one-third of the people being engaged in agriculture, more than two-thirds are set free, as it were, to follow other pursuits. Of these a considerable proportion are engaged in manufactures. The vastness of the produce of English manufacturing industry, in proportion to the number of hands employed, may be roughly estimated by three separate considerations: first, the power of tens of millions of men is obtained from steam, which produces without consuming; secondly, notwithstanding a load of English restrictions on trade, the English are, by

* The causes of the exhaustion of land in the United States are explained in the note on the Origin, Progress, and Prospects of Slavery in America.

† " No one will presume to say that the agriculture of France is nearly as well improved as that of Britain—that it is not indeed a hundred years behind ours, and yet while there are more than two-thirds of the people of France employed in this inferior cultivation, less than one-third of our people suffice to carry on the infinitely superior system of cultivation adopted in this country. It is in this single circumstance that the great superiority of our domestic economy over that of the French chiefly consists."—*Professor M'Culloch's Edition of Smith's Wealth of Nations—Note XIX.* vol. iv. page 475.

means of their manufactures, the greatest commercial
people in the world; thirdly, notwithstanding heavy taxation and the high price of food in England, objects of English manufacture are so cheap as to drive out of any market,
where fair competition is allowed, similar objects made any
where but in England.

As in agriculture, so in manufactures, every improvement in the productive powers of industry may be traced
to general and particular combination of power, leading to
general and particular division of employment.

The same complete division of employments, which
makes the English farmer nothing but a farmer, makes all
the English people who are engaged in manufactures nothing
but manufacturers.   Further, while in France and America
the capital of one man is frequently divided among several
different manufactures, the attention of the English manufacturing capitalist is confined almost exclusively to a
single object.   Thus the English manufacturer is, as such,
a man of single purpose, " a man with one idea."   Hence
that earnest, unremitting and successful pursuit of improvement, which is conspicuous in every branch of English
manufacture.

Another peculiarity in English manufactures seems
worthy of remark; I allude to the congregation in one
place of vast numbers who are engaged in the same branch
of manufacture.   In some cases, no doubt, the main seat
of a particular fabric is determined by natural circumstances, such as abundance of coal or iron, or falling water:
in other cases it appears to have been settled by accident.
In every case, however, that congregation of numbers engaged in the same pursuit, by promoting the interchange
of many persons' thoughts on one all-engrossing subject, by
exciting the inventive powers, by preventing a fortunate
discoverer from monopolizing the use of his invention, and
above all, by stimulating competition, must have had a large
share in the progress of improvement.

The great effects of particular combination are still more
plain.   For the success of some fabrics, a high and constant
temperature is required.   This could not be obtained by
any one of a number of small manufacturers: it is easily
obtained by him who employs a large capital, and collects
a great many people under one roof.   There is scarcely
any fabric of which the produce in proportion to the hands
employed, is not greatly augmented by the use of steam
power; but it is of the essence of steam power to give
effect to the labour of united numbers.   The general use

of steam power in England depends, therefore, on the combination of capital and labour in particular works. The distribution among many hands of the several parts of a particular work is greatly facilitated by the congregation of many hands under one roof. In England, accordingly, all the most flourishing manufactures are carried on in large factories, with large capitals, and by a great number of hands, brought together for the purpose of distributing among them the several parts of each work. Those manufactures which are conducted by small fractions of capital and labour, such as the silk works of Spitalfields and the lace works of Buckinghamshire, are rapidly perishing : that is, they are in the course of being superseded by the use of large factories ; those which have been mentioned, by the large silk factories of Macclesfield and Manchester, and by the large lace factories of Nottingham and Tiverton. Universally, indeed, throughout all the branches of English manufactures, as in all of them there is an obvious tendency to improvement, so in all of them one observes a tendency to increased combination of capital and labour in particular works.

The commerce of England, both domestic and foreign, exhibits, like her agriculture and manufactures, a high degree of combination of power, both general and particular. The whole commercial work performed by the people of England is so admirably distributed that one might imagine it to be under the control of a single will ; while no particular operation languishes for want of sufficient force to carry it on. In vain might the state of New-York have projected the Erie canal, if a supply of labour for completing it had not been obtained from Ireland : that great work was performed by Irishmen, and could not have been performed with American free labour, which, for reasons to be stated hereafter, can seldom be used in combination.* The peculiar skill with which the English

---

* "The truth is," says Captain Basil Hall in a letter to Mr. Wilmot Horton, published by the latter, "that there is no hired labouring class, properly so called, in any part of America, *excepting where the ground is tilled by negro slaves :* I mean that there is no class of men who support themselves *permanently*, by wages derived from labouring in the service of others. There is, in fact, no labour to be had for hire, of such a sort, at least, as to produce *permanently* a return greater than the wages which such hired labourer requires. I speak now of agricultural labour ; and I may say that it is almost an axiom in those countries, that *there is no productive labour in the fields of a new country, except that which results from the sweat of the proprietor's own brow.* Canals and other casual public works, and other menial service of the cities, and even the smaller towns, must, of course,

apply capital and labour to the business of exchange, might be proved by a thousand facts : four of the most remarkable will suffice for this general notice. First, while in France or America, the prices of the same commodity are often very different at different but not very distant places, all over England prices are nearly always on a level : secondly, it is estimated that the rail-road between Manchester and Liverpool saves 600,000*l.* a year on the cost of carriage for goods and passengers between those two towns only : thirdly, the best informed persons concur in supposing, that twenty-nine thirtieths, at least, of the currency of the northern manufacturing districts consist of bills of exchange, which, though they circulate with much greater ease than silver or gold, cost next to nothing : fourthly, the foreign and domestic bills of exchange payable by bankers in London, which often amount to some millions in one day, instead of being presented for payment each bill to the house on which it is drawn, are all carried to the same spot, where a general exchange of bills takes place among the several houses ; and in this way, one clerk from each house performs in an hour or two, and without any money, a work which, if each bill had been presented to the house on which it was drawn, would have required the labour of several clerks, from all the houses, during many hours, and the use of some millions of money.

This brief notice of the sources of England's wealth shows why that wealth is so great in proportion to the number of people who enjoy it ; and the more the subject shall be examined, the more plainly, I feel assured, will it appear, that, in all countries, the produce of industry must be in proportion to the degree in which capital and labour are combined and employments are divided. But it may be said that this is an idle speculation, leading to no conclusions of practical utility ; that, whether or not the great wealth of England be owing to combination of power, the English will continue to pursue that course which they find so productive ; and that other nations will not follow their example one day sooner in consequence of perceiving the causes of their wealth. To meet such observations, I offer the following conclusions, derived from the principle that, as respects the produce of industry, union is force.

be done by hirelings ; but I must again and again remark, that it is the characteristic feature of all kinds of labour in those countries to be for the time only."

"The workmen employed (in making a road in New-York State) are chiefly Irish."—*Stuart*, vol. ii., page 492.

1. I have said that combination of power appears to be of two distinct kinds, general and particular, leading to two distinct kinds of division of employments. But this distinction has been drawn merely for the purpose of explaining a principle not hitherto noticed. Considering the operation of industry throughout the world as one great work, it will be seen that all the parts of the work, from so great a part as the growth of tea in China, to so small a one as the making of a pin's head in England, are productive in proportion to the degree in which men help each other. Here then we perceive exactly, how war between nations, and restrictions on trade, interfere with the productions of wealth; how friendly intercourse among different nations, by promoting concert or combination, on which depends division of employments, adds to the general powers of industry; how facilities of communication among different countries, and in each country, promote the increase of wealth; how a new road or canal enables more people to live in comfort; and how millions owe all their enjoyments, nay, their very existence, to the institution of the post for letters.

2. From considering the increase of productive power derived from combination, one perceives how various tenures of land in different countries, and in the same country, influence the production of wealth. Three examples will suffice. The poverty of French agriculture,—the large proportion of the people of France who are engaged in agriculture, leaving but a small proportion for other pursuits,—is owing to the law of division, which at a Frenchman's death cuts up his estate into portions as numerous as his children. In Ireland, again, it is the minute subdivision of land, which causes a minute subdivision of capital and labour, and renders the produce of agricultural industry, in proportion to the hands employed, so much less than that of the same kind of industry in England. Lastly, a history of colonization would show, that all new colonies, having a vast territory at their disposal, have prospered or languished according as the governments by which they were founded took care, or neglected, to dispose of the land to be colonized with a view to combination of power among the colonists. In the case of the last colony founded by England, the greatest pains were taken to disperse the colonists, to cut up their capital and labour into the smallest fractional parts, whence a miserable failure with all the

elements of success : but on this subject I have to dwell at length in another place.*

3. By ascertaining how much the productiveness of English industry depends on the most artificial combination of labour and division of employments; by perceiving the extreme complication of the machine which produces the wealth of England, and the close dependence of all its parts upon each other, the English may learn the peculiar evils which any serious political convulsion would inflict on them.

After exhausting the language of admiration in a description of the actual wealth of England, one might suppose that in this respect the English could make no further progress. This would be a mistake. It would be hard to name a single instance of the wealth of England, which does not exhibit, at this present time, a tendency to improvement. Though of late years the roads of England have been reckoned the best in the world, yet on every great road, and many cross-roads, some striking improvement is now taking place. Though the carriage and foot pavements of English towns have long been celebrated as perfect, yet these are, as well in country towns as in London, in the course of being greatly improved. The number of good houses in London, and of people who can afford to keep a carriage, astonishes a foreigner; yet in every direction new houses of this class are in the course of being built; and no soooner are a hundred of them finished, than they are all occupied, and each of them has a carriage at the door. In ninety-nine out of a hundred old streets, all over England, you will find new houses greatly superior to those by their side. The difference in point of utility and appearance between old houses which are pulled down in London and those which take their place, is, universally, almost as great as the difference between the old and new London bridges; a difference which is striking to the English themselves, and is grateful even to such of them as, hating innovation, love to talk of the wisdom of their ancestors. But a catalogue of those objects, which exhibit the actual progress of improvement in England, would comprise nearly all that is necessary, useful, or agreeable to Englishmen: it would include every useful or ornamental art, from the great arts of printing, architecture, engineering, painting, and sculpture, down to the lowest

* Note XII.

occupation of human industry ; besides the whole list of
sciences, from the most important, such as chymistry,
medicine, and government, down to the meanest department of human knowledge.   In England, improvement is
everywhere.   In England, advancement from good to
better is a universal principle.   Where all this will end,
who will venture to predict?   Sober imaginations are con-
founded by observing the very rapid progress which
wealthy and civilized England is at this time making in
wealth and civilization.

NOTE II.

MISERY OF THE BULK OF THE PEOPLE.

Who are the bulk of the people—Misery of the bulk of the people a favourite topic in England—Proofs of misery—What is a pauper—Factory children—Irish wages—Increase of gin-shops—Cheapness of English children—Murder of Parish apprentices—Other trades in pauper children—
Climbing boys—Prostitutes—Cheapness of women—Degradation of the
common people—The common people are too cheap to be happy.

AMONG our wise ancestors the bulk of the people was
slaves, as is still the case in Russia and the southern states
of North America.   In modern states, which deserve to
be called civilized, a part of the people consists of the
labouring class; that is, a class, whose only property is
their labour, and who live by the sale of that property to
the other classes.   The proportion which the labouring
class bears to the other classes, is very different in several
of the most civilized modern states.   In the northern states
of the American Union, it may be doubted whether so many
as a tenth of the people would fall under the description of
hired labourers.*   In France, the *morcellement* of land has
converted a very large portion of the people into the class
of proprietors of land.   Deducting from the remainder

* " Although it is not a general practice for gentlemen in Mr. Verplanck's
situation in this part of the United States, in which I mean to comprehend
the populous parts of New-York, Pennsylvania, and New England, to
be thus actively employed in agricultural operations, I mean actually to
work with their farm-servants, nothing is more common in the United States,
taken as a whole, than for proprietors to work in the field at the same occupation as their servants."—*Stuart*, vol. i., page 460.

the class of capitalists, those who live on government an-
nuities, soldiers, and indeed all who do not labour for wages,
the labouring class, properly so called, will not be estimated at more than a third of the whole population.   In
Ireland, the cottier system takes a great majority of the
people out of the class of hired labourers, and turns them
into something between capitalists and workmen. In Spain
and Portugal, if these may be called civilized nations, the
class of people who sell their labour, who live by wages,
seems to be very small indeed.   In some of the Italian
states, hired labourers bear a small proportion to the other
classes.   On the continent of Europe, the proportion of
hired labourers appears to be greatest in Holland.   But in
England, where the system of large farms is established,
where a great part of the population is engaged in manufactures, and where, in every department of industry, a
complete separation has taken place between capitalists
and workmen, the labouring class compose the bulk of the
people, the great body of the people, the vast majority of
the people,—these are the terms by which English writers
and speakers usually describe those whose only property
is their labour.

If there be one subject in particular upon which Englishmen love to dwell, it is the misery and degradation of the
bulk of the people.   Every year that melancholy subject
forms the matter of numerous petitions to the legislature, of
many speeches in parliament, of discussion at public meetings in all parts of the country, of some large volumes, of
innumerable pamphlets, and of frequent, one might say
constant, remarks in nearly all newspapers, and in all political magazines.   There are some cheap newspapers,
writen expressly for the labouring class, which treat of
scarce any thing else ; and the political sect called Owen-
ites talk of nothing else.   But the writers of these cheap
newspapers, and these sectaries, differ from writers and
speakers of the conservative or tory party only as to the
way of curing the misery of the bulk of the people.   The
Standard newspaper, Blackwood's Magazine, and the Quarterly Review, all high tory journals, dwell on the prevalence of misery with as much zeal as the Poor Man's Guar-
dian, and other radical publications.   Mr. Owen, Mr. Car-
lisle, and Mr. Cobbett do not appear more anxious than
Mr. Sadler and Dr. Southey to remove the misery of the
working classes.   Mr. Sadler, who, by-the-way, has written
a large book on the causes and remedies of pauperism,

lately declared in the House of Commons that the working classes in England are white slaves. It was a tory bishop who first called the attention of the House of Lords to the fact, that Englishmen are harnessed to carts like cattle. Mr. Wilmot Horton, after Mr. Sadler the most industrious writer and speaker on the subject of pauperism, who lately delivered a course of lectures on that subject at the London Mechanics' Institution, was a member of parliament, a privy counsellor, and a tory. Concerning the misery and degradation of the bulk of the people of England, men of every order, as well as every party, unite and speak continually; farmers, parish officers, clergymen, magistrates, judges on the bench, members on either side of both houses of parliament, the king in his addresses to the nation, moralists, statesmen, philosophers; and, finally, the poor creatures themselves, whose complaints are loud and incessant.

Of comprehensive words, the two most frequently used in English politics are distress and pauperism. After these, of expressions applied to the state of the poor, the most common are vice and misery, wretchedness, sufferings, ignorance, degradation, discontent, depravity, drunkenness, and the increase of crime; with many more of a like nature. The measures which have been gravely proposed as remedies for the misery of the English working classes amount to at least nineteen; namely, a fall of rent; the conversion of tythes to the use of the poor; more protection for home manufactures; the repeal of the corn laws; abolition of the poor laws; correction of the poor laws; poor laws for Ireland; spade husbandry; home colonization; gardens and cows for the poor; abolition of the national debt; other modes of lessening taxation; a more liberal expenditure by the government; more paper money; emigration; universal suffrage; moral restraint, or promiscuous intercourse; and property in common, or rather no property at all. Each of these specifics is earnestly recommended by its partisans, and as vehemently opposed by the partisans of nearly all the others; but on two points nearly all parties agree. They concur in describing as excessive the evil which it is their object to cure, and in expressing their solemn belief that, unless a remedy be found for it, some dreadful convulsion must ensue. Upon the latter of these points I shall have to remark in another place; the former is the proper subject of this note.

There are proofs without end of the misery of the bulk

of the English people. The late insurrection of the peasantry of the south of England, and the modern practice
of burning farm-produce, are universally attributed to the
misery and discontent of those unfortunate beings. If the
English had been a martial people, those forlorn men, once
roused as they were, would either have destroyed the
classes whom they consider their oppressors, or have perished in a servile war. White slaves they have been
properly called. It was some of this class whom a bishop
described as being harnessed to carts like cattle. In
America, too, they harness men to carts; but then they
treat them as valuable cattle; give them plenty to eat;
shelter them from the weather; keep them in good heart;
and bring up their little ones in clover. English slaves are
harnessed to carts, and ill-fed, ill-clothed, ill-housed, and
variously ill-treated into the bargain. American slaves
live longer than their masters, while English slaves die
prematurely of hunger, wet, cold, and sorrow. In America
the increase of slaves, in one way only, that is, by births,
is more rapid than the increase of free people in three
ways—by births, by the emancipation of slaves, and by
immigration: and the proportion of slaves being a hundred
years old is 1 in 1400, while the same proportion of whites
is 1 in about 14,000; showing a difference of ten to one in
favour of the longevity of slaves. The peasant of the south
of England suffers nearly all the evils, but enjoys none of
the advantages, of slavery. He is not a freeman, nor is he
a slave; he is a pauper. What a pauper is, Americans
may learn from the following description of the " bold peasantry of England," which I extract from one of the countless pamphlets on pauperism lately written by Englishmen.

" What is that defective being, with calfless legs and
stooping shoulders, weak in body and mind, inert, pusil-
lanimous, and stupid, whose premature wrinkles and furtive
glance tell of misery and degradation ? That is an English
peasant or pauper ; for the words are synonymous. His
sire was a pauper, and his mother's milk wanted nourish-
ment. From infancy his food has been bad, as well as
insufficient; and he now feels the pains of unsatisfied hunger nearly whenever he is awake. But half-clothed, and
never supplied with more warmth than suffices to cook his
scanty meals, cold and wet come to him, and stay by him,
with the weather. He is married, of course; for to this
he would have been driven by the poor laws, even if he
had been, as he never was, sufficiently comfortable and

prudent to dread the burden of a family. But, though instinct and the overseer have given him a wife, he has not tasted the highest joys of husband and father. His partner and his little ones being like himself often hungry, seldom warm, sometimes sick without aid, and always sorrowful without hope, are greedy, selfish, and vexing; so, to use his own expression, he 'hates the sight of them,' and resorts to his hovel only because a hedge affords less shelter from the wind and rain. Compelled by parish law to support his family, which means to join them in consuming an allowance from the parish, he frequently conspires with his wife to get that allowance increased, or prevent its being diminished. This brings begging, trickery, and quarrelling; and ends in settled craft. Though he have the inclination, he wants the courage to become, like more energetic men of his class, a poacher or smuggler on a large scale; but he pilfers occasionally, and teaches his children to lie and steal. His subdued and slavish manner towards his great neighbours shows that they treat him with suspicion and harshness. Consequently he at once dreads and hates them; but he will never harm them by violent means. Too degraded to be desperate, he is only thoroughly depraved. His miserable career will be short: rheumatism and asthma are conducting him to the workhouse, where he will breathe his last without one pleasant recollection, and so make room for another wretch, who may live and die in the same way. This is a sample of one class of English peasants. Another class is composed of men, who, though paupers to the extent of being in part supported by the parish, were not bred and born in extreme destitution, and who, therefore, in so far as the moral depends on the physical man, are qualified to become wise, virtuous, and happy. They have large muscles, an upright mien, and a quick perception. With strength, energy, and skill, they would earn a comfortable subsistence as labourers, if the modern fashion of paying wages out of the poor-box did not interfere with the due course of things, and reduce all the labourers of a parish, the old and the young, the weak and the strong, the idle and the industrious, to that lowest rate of wages, or rather of weekly payment to each, which in each case is barely sufficient for the support of life. If there were no poor laws, or if the poor laws were such that labour was paid in proportion to the work performed, and not according to a scale founded on the power of gastric juice under various circumstances,

these superior men would be employed in preference to the
inferior beings described above, would earn twice as much
as the others could earn, and would have every motive for
industry, providence, and general good conduct. As it is,
their superior capacity as labourers is of no advantage to
them. They have no motive for being industrious or prudent. What they obtain between labour and the rate is
but just enough to support them miserably. They are
tempted to marry for the sake of an extra allowance from
the parish : and they would be sunk to the lowest point of
degradation but for the energy of their minds, which they
owe to their physical strength. Courage and tenderness
are said to be allied : men of this class usually make good
husbands and affectionate parents. Impelled by want of
food, clothes, and warmth, for themselves and their families,
they become poachers wherever game abounds, and smugglers when opportunity serves. By poaching or smuggling,
or both, many of them are enabled to fill the bellies of their
children, to put decent clothes on the backs of their wives,
and to keep the cottage whole, with a good fire in it, from
year's end to year's end. The villains! why are they not
taken up? They are taken up sometimes, and are hunted
always, by those who administer rural law. In this way
they learn to consider two sets of laws—those for the protection of game, and those for the protection of home manufactures—as specially made for their injury. Be just to
our unpaid magistrates! who perform their duty even to
the shedding of man's blood, in defence of pheasants and
restrictions on trade. Thus the bolder sort of husbandry
labourers, by engaging in murderous conflicts with game-
keepers and preventive men, become accustomed to deeds
of violence, and, by living in jails, qualified for the most
desperate courses. They also imbibe feelings of dislike, or
rather, of bitter hatred, towards the rural magistracy, whom
they regard as oppressors and natural enemies; closely resembling, in this respect, the defective class of peasants
from whom they differ in so many particulars. Between
these two descriptions of peasantry there is another, which
partakes of the characteristics of both classes, but in a
slighter degree, except as regards their fear and hatred of
the rural aristocracy. In the districts where paupers and
game abound, it would be difficult to find many labourers
not coming under one of these descriptions. By courtesy,
the entire body is called the bold peasantry of England.
But is nothing done by the " nobility, clergy, and gentry,"

to conciliate the affection of the pauper mass, by whose toil all their own wealth is produced? Charity! The charity of the poor laws, which paupers have been taught to consider a right, which operates as a curse to the able-bodied and well-disposed, while it but just enables the infirm of all ages to linger on in pain and sorrow. Soup! Dogs'-meat, the paupers call it. They are very ungrateful; but there is a way of relieving a man's necessities which will make him hate you; and it is in this way, generally, that soup is given to the poor. Books, good little books, which teach patience and submission to the powers that be! With which such paupers as obtain them usually boil their kettles, when not deterred by fear of the reverend donor. Of this gift the design is so plain and offensive, that its effect is contrary to what was intended, just as children from whom obedience is very strictly exacted are commonly rebels at heart. What else? is nothing else done by the rural rich to win the love of the rural poor? Speaking, generally, since all rules have exceptions, the privileged classes of our rural districts take infinite pains to be abhorred by their poorest neighbours. They enclose commons. They stop footpaths. They wall in their parks. They set spring-guns and man-traps. They spend on the keep of high-bred dogs what would support half as many children, and yet persecute a labouring man for owning one friend in his cur. They make rates of wages, elaborately calculating the minimum of food that will keep together the soul and body of a clodhopper. They breed game in profusion for their own amusement, and having thus tempted the poor man to knock down a hare for his pot, they send him to the tread-mill, or the antipodes, for that inexpiable offence. They build jails, and fill them. They make new crimes and new punishments for the poor. They interfere with the marriages of the poor, compelling some, and forbidding others to come together. They shut up paupers in workhouses, separating husband and wife, in pounds by day and wards by night. They harness poor men to carts. They superintend alehouses, decry skittles, deprecate beer-shops, meddle with fairs, and otherwise curtail the already narrow amusements of the poor. Even in church, where some of them solemnly preach that all are equal, they sit on cushions, in pews boarded, matted, and sheltered by curtains from the wind and the vulgar gaze, while the lower order must put up with a bare bench on a stone floor, which is good enough for them. Everywhere they are ostentatious in the display of wealth and enjoyment; while, in their intercourse with the poor, they are suspicious, quick at taking offence, vindictive when displeased, haughty, over-bearing, tyrannical, and wolfish; as it seems in the nature of man to be towards such of his fellows as, like sheep, are without the power to resist."

In the parishes of the north of England the system of pauperism has not been so generally established. This difference is commonly attributed to the prevalence of manu-factures in the north. But then, the misery of the labour-ing class employed in manufactures, though different in some respects from the misery that attends the pauper system, is equal to it in degree, if not more obvious and deplorable. Last year a mass of evidence was laid before parliament, touching the condition of children employed in factories, which describes a system of torture, compared with which the treatment of American slaves appears truly benevolent. When this evidence was published, the whole press of England repeated, day after day, that the worst kind of slavery exists in England. Children of tender years, it was shown, babies they would be called in Amer-ica, are shut up in factories during 12, 14 and 16 hours every week-day, and there compelled to work incessantly, or as hard, at least, as their slight frames will permit, and for wages which but just satisfy their ruined appetites. The pale cheeks, parched lips, swoln stomachs, deformed limbs, and melancholy looks of these little wretches will be easily imagined. They die off with strange rapidity; but the places of those who perish are instantly filled, and a frequent change of persons makes no alteration in the scene.

To remedy this evil a law is proposed, to fix within some limit dictated by common humanity the number of hours during which children shall be employed in factories. But let us suppose that a law should be passed, of which the humanity would not appear extravagant, to forbid altogether the employment of young children in factories. The con-sequence of such a law must be, that the parents of chil-dren who had been employed in factories would no longer be able to support those children. No parent, no mother, who has the means of supporting a child at home, sends it to be worked to death in a factory: unless we are to sup-pose, what has, indeed, been asserted by some, that the working class in the manufacturing districts are so deeply degraded as to sell their children's labour, or lives, deliberately for the sake of gin.   Not believing this assertion, though it may be true in a few cases, it appears to me that the only choice of the parents lies between two evils; on the one hand the factory, with its probable result, death by disease, of which the progress is hardly perceptible; on the other, immediate, palpable starvation at home.   Such a law as I have supposed would deprive the parents of this choice, would compel them to suffer that evil which, since they seek to avoid it, they appear to consider the greater of the two. I make this remark, not to disparage the humanity of those who would pass laws for the mitigation of English slavery, but for the purpose of explaining, that the misery of these factory children results from the misery of their parents : they are all miserable, fathers, mothers, and children.

Though the remote causes of their misery form the sub-ject of endless controversy, its immediate cause seems as plain as that two and two make four.   Their only property is their labour.   They take this property to market.   They find the market overstocked with labour : there are more sellers than buyers.   The sellers, in order to live, undersell each other, till they reduce the market-price of their pro-perty to what political economists call the minimum of wages,—to that sum, namely, which will barely supply the labourer with necessaries according to his estimate of what is necessary.   In every condition of life an Englishman's estimate of what is necessary rises above that which is formed by people of the same rank in most other countries. To a European labourer, clothes are necessary : to a Hin-doo labourer they are not.   The necessary clothes of an English labourer are better than those of a French labourer. An English workman considers bread necessary ; an Irish workman is content with potatoes.   If, therefore, the Eng-lish markets of labour were confined to Englishmen, and if, above all, pains were taken to raise still higher the Eng-lish labourer's estimate of what is necessary, the minimum of wages in England would probably become sufficient to support all labourers in a state of decency and comfort. But the English markets of labour, and especially those of manufacturing labour, are not confined to Englishmen : they are full of Irish labourers, who fly from Ireland to escape death by famine.   These, whose estimate of necessary wages is a hovel, rags, and potatoes, by underselling the English workman, by consenting to work for the lowest wages that will support life, compel the English labourer to adopt the same course, and thus reduce the general minimum of wages to a wretched pittance. The Irish workman is content with his wretchedness; the English workman is not. Here lies the only difference between them. The discontent of the English, if properly encouraged, might soon lead to a higher minimum of wages, were it not for the competition of the Irish. It is the competition of Irish labour which ruins the manufacturing population of England. In some difficult manufactures, truly, where the labour of the barbarous and easily satisfied Irishman would not be worth having at any price, we find a rate of wages, high when compared with that which always attends Irish competition. But improvements in the use of steam power, rendering the work performed by man's labour more simple and easy, have lately diminished, and will still further diminish, the number of those difficult manufactures, which already must be considered as exceptions to the general rule. In English manufactures, the general rule is Irish wages.

English work and Irish wages! " Peter Moreau," says P. L. Courier in his Village Gazette—" Peter Moreau and his wife are dead, aged twenty-five years. Too much work has killed them; and many besides. We say—work like a negro, like a galley slave: we ought to say—work like a free-man." I say, work like a Lancashire weaver. There is no such work in France or America, even among slaves; all day long, from Monday morning till Saturday night, week after week, and year after year, till the machine is worn out. Talk of negroes and galley slaves: American slaves, or convicts in New South Wales, are fat and happy compared with very many free-born Englishmen. By-the-way, it happens, not rarely so as to be matter of wonder, but so often as to pass unnoticed, that Englishmen commit crimes for the purpose of becoming galley slaves in New South Wales. They do not keep their purpose secret; they declare it loudly, with tears and passionate exclamations, to the magistrate who commits them for trial, to the jury who try them, and to the judge who passes sentence on them; and all this is published in the newspapers, but so often that no one exclaims—Great God, am I in merry England! Well may judges on the bench talk of the misery and degradation of the people!

Of this misery and degradation, there are some who say the cause is gin: it may be so, but let us see. Every one remarks the increase of gin-shops. In all those parts of Leeds or Manchester, and of London too, where the poorest people live, there you find, in almost every dirty street, not one, but several fine houses, handsomely stuccoed, curiously painted, ornamented with plate-glass and polished brass ; in the windows, placards inviting custom by such expressions as "mountain dew," and "cream of the valley !" inside, great barrels of spirits gayly painted and disposed for show, carved mahogany, and more polished brass, with men and women, smartly dressed, smiling welcome to all who enter. The doors of these splendid dens are carefully hung so as to fly open with a touch and shut in an instant ; whether for the convenience of those dram-drinkers who are ashamed of their taste, or to give to the concern an air of mystery, which pleases the ignorant, Messrs. Thompson and Fearon can best tell. These gentlemen, who, being rich, are highly respectable, keep the largest gin-shop in England—in the world. It is situated (I mention this as a guide to Americans visiting London) on Holborn Hill, near to Saffron Hill ; a quarter in which Irish wages prevail and pawnbrokers abound. Here gin is served by young women dressed up like the *belle limonadiere* of a Paris coffee-house, and the establishment in all its parts is nearly as fine as *Verey's* or the *Café de Paris.* There is another great gin-shop, not much inferior to it, a little further to the west, adjoining the gate of Gray's Inn ; two or three close by in Chancery Lane ; and twenty or thirty not far off. In half an hour you may visit a hundred. What a contrast between the finery of the shops and the beggarly appearance of the customers ! Among these are few really old people ; but then plenty of the young people appear very old. Livid cheeks, deep wrinkles, blood-shot eyes, brown teeth, or white gums without teeth, skin and bone, shaking hands, sore legs, creeping palsy, a hacking cough, rags, filth, and stench ; these are marks by which to know the regular gin-drinker. Nine out of ten of all who may enter the finest gin-shop in Manchester of a Sunday morning, will show one or more of these marks ; counting women, boys, and girls, as well as men, but not the children, who, of course, are only beginners. In some great towns of the north, they have low counters and small glasses on purpose for the small children : in London the children stand on tiptoe to pay for half a glass of gin ; but London will improve. As to gin-shops, London is improving most rapidly, both in number and in finery ; every week, almost every day, producing a new gin-shop. fitted up with spring doors, plate-glass, carved mahogany or rose-wood, and polished brass ;

all more "elegant," as they say in America, than the gin-
shops which sprung up the week before. But the quarter
of London in which the greatest increase of fine gin-shops
has lately taken place, is Spitalfields and its neighbourhood.
I have said before, that the silk manufacture of Spitalfields
is perishing. The most zealous enemy of gin-shops does
not pretend that the increase of gin-shops in Spitalfields has
ruined the Spitalfields manufacture; but the ruin of the
Spitalfields manufacture may have caused the increase of
gin-shops in Spitalfields. This is my humble opinion,
founded on the considerations which follow.

Generally, a man understands his own affairs better than
other people understand them for him. The common
people of London have a saying, lately adopted, but now
proverbial—" To live, be a pawnbroker, or keep a gin-
shop." Here the increase of gin-shops is explained in ten
words. Pawnbrokers and keepers of gin-shops depend on
the common people : the common people are distressed, that
is, they find it hard to live : their distress drives them, first
to the pawnbroker, and then to the gin-shop; they pawn
their goods to purchase—what, poison? yes, in the long
run, but for the moment, oblivion of their misery. Misery
to the common people is wealth to pawnbrokers and
keepers of gin-shops. The common people are very miserable, therefore the demand for gin is very great ; therefore the profits of selling gin are very high ; therefore gin-
shops increase.

This conclusion is supported by some who take pains to
know the sentiments of the common people, and who
earnestly advise them to abstain from gin ; I mean members of the Temperance Societies, Quakers for the most
part, diligent in works of benevolence, gentle, patient, per-
severing, not proud, but feeling with the poor as well as for
them. These, addressing the common people in friendly
and common language, say—" Believe us, it is a mistake to
suppose that gin will keep the cold out of your stomach.
The more gin you drink, the more will you feel cold in
your stomach. What warms you to-day will not have that
effect a month hence : by-and-by, in order to feel warm,
you must double the quantity. But twice the quantity, as
soon as you are used to it, will not make you feel warm.
The more you drink, the more you must drink in order to
feel warm. At last, no quantity will warm you ; your
stomach will be destroyed, and you will die of drinking gin
to keep the cold out of your stomach." This is all very

true ; and it shows how well the Quakers understand those feelings of the common people which lead to dram-drinking. Cold in the stomach! but neither the Spitalfields weavers, nor their friends of the Temperance Societies, suppose that cold is matter which enters the stomach. Cold in the stomach is a figurative expression, meaning either hunger or despair, or both. " Sir," says a Spitalfields weaver, in reply to his friendly adviser, " all that you say is true. The more gin we drink, the more we want; but also the less we drink gin, the more we feel the want of something else. Give us bread, meat, beer, and fire ; then we should feel warm without gin. I am not begging: we are all ready to work. I work, God knows, morning, noon, and night : work, work, work ; we have plenty of that. If we did not work we should die outright. But what does our work bring? work and hunger, work and cold, work and sorrow. I get about fourteen shillings a week, out of which there's rent to pay—we can't lie in the street,—and clothes to find, such as they are,—but we must be covered ; what remains for fire and food among six of us, four children, their mother, and me? Enough to starve upon, and that is all. The children cry for bread ; they must wait: their mother cries because they cry ; she is sick with crying and what not, and wants some tea; she must want. In cold weather we all shiver for want of fire : the children and their mother may lie in bed to keep themselves warm ; but I, hungry and cold, must work on. I do work ; and when I drink gin, it is to keep myself from going mad. I allow it—my wife drinks gin sometimes, and the children, too, poor things, now and then, to pacify them. If you were as poor as we are, sir, and had to work as hard as I have, without hope, you would be apt to learn that gin is bread, and meat, and fire, and hope, all in one. Without gin, I should not have heart to work ; and we must all go to the poorhouse, or die, for the poorhouse is choke full, and the rates are not paid. We say cold in the stomach ; but we mean hunger in the belly and despair in the heart. Gin cures both for a time ; but it kills, you say. Well, we can but die, with gin or without ; and life such as ours, without gin, is worse than death." Just so : those who frequent gin-shops best know why. The gin-shops in Spitalfields are many and magnificent, because the trade of Spitalfields is going to ruin. In other parts of London the poverty of the common people enriches pawnbrokers and keepers of gin-shops. At Manchester, Bolton, and Blackburn, the cause of gin-shops is Irish wages. Verily, the life of the bulk of the people of England is worse than death.

In the slave-states of America, a strong, healthy boy or girl is worth about 50*l*. In London, on the gates of poor-houses, one reads—"Strong, healthy boys and girls, with the usual fee; apply within." With, not for, the usual fee: you do not pay the fee to obtain a boy or girl; but the parish officers pay you for taking one. The usual fee in London is 10*l*.; so that in America you pay five times as much as you receive in England. To be sure, the boys and girls in London are neither strong nor healthy: the notice on the workhouse-gates says that they are both, to invite customers, just as the keepers of gin-shops placard their windows with "mountain dew" and "cream of the valley." But a little, a very little care and kindness would make the English children as strong and healthy as young negroes in America. It is not, therefore, the difference of strength which causes the difference of value between young people in Kentucky and young people in London; nor can it be the difference of colour: on the contrary, one might suppose that a white boy or girl would be worth more than a black one, instead of being, so to speak, worth 10*l*. less than nothing.

Ah, but, says a "respectable" Englishman, the young Americans, who cost 50*l*. each, are born in slavery; the others are free-born English children. The buyer of an American child can do what he likes with it: the English children are merely bound apprentice for a term of years, and the parish pays with each of them an apprentice-fee, as a recompense to the master for teaching them his trade. The magistrate is a party to all the indentures of apprenticeship; he requires the child's consent; he cancels the bond if the child is ill-treated. English children are protected by our glorious, our inimitable constitution, which makes no difference between rich and poor: it is absurd to compare English apprentices with American slaves.—I answer: it is the whole press of England, not I, that calls English children white slaves; but, not to dispute about words, let us come to facts. In the reign of George III., one Elizabeth Brownrigg was hanged for beating and starving to death her parish apprentices. About three years ago, another woman, Esther Hibner by name, was hanged in London for beating and starving to death a parish apprentice. In both these cases, the constitution, the law, which makes no difference between rich and poor, interfered on behalf of a pauper-girl : but when ? not before the girl was murdered, but after.   Does the law interfere to prevent the murder of parish apprentices ?—this is the question.   The evidence in the case of Esther Hibner proved, that a number of girls, pauper apprentices, were employed in a workshop : that their victuals consisted of garbage, commonly called hog's wash, and that of this they never had enough to stay the pains of hunger ; that they were kept half-naked, half-clothed in dirty rags ; that they slept in a heap, on the floor, amid filth and stench ; that they suffered dreadfully from cold ; that they were forced to work so many hours together that they used to fall asleep while at work ; that for falling asleep, for not working as hard as their mistress wished, they were beaten with sticks, with fists, dragged by the hair, dashed on to the ground, trampled upon, and otherwise tortured ; that they were found, all of them more or less, covered with chil-blains, scurvy, bruises, and wounds ; that one of them died of ill-treatment ; and—mark this,—that the discovery of that murder was made in consequence of the number of coffins which had issued from Esther Hibner's premises, and raised the curiosity of her neighbours.   For this mur-der Mrs. Hibner was hanged ; but what did she get for all the other murders which, referring to the number of coffins, we have a right to believe that she committed ?   She got for each 10*l.*   That is to say, whenever she had worked, starved, beaten, dashed, and trampled a girl to death, she got another girl to treat in the same way, with 10*l.* for her trouble.   She carried on a trade in the murder of parish apprentices ; and if she had conducted it with moderation, if the profit and custom of murder had not made her grasp-ing and careless, the constitution, which protects the poor as well as the rich, would never have interfered with her. The law did not permit her to do what she liked with her apprentices as Americans do with their slaves ; oh no. Those free-born English children were merely bound as apprentices, with their own consent, under the eye of the magistrate, in order that they might learn a trade and be-come valuable subjects.   But did the magistrate ever visit Mrs. Hibner's factory to see how she treated the free-born Englis hgirls ? never.   Did the parish officers ? no.   Was there any legal provision for the discovery of the woman's trade in murder ? none.   That woman has not traded in murder during the last three years ; but why not ? because

she was hanged three years ago: but what hanged her?
the glorious constitution, or the number of coffins?   Plainly,
the number of coffins; that is, the impunity, the security
with which she had murdered; the forlorn state of her apprentices; the utter neglect of them by parish officers,
magistrates, laws, and constitution.

Since Mrs. Hibner was hanged, the inimitable constitution
has been greatly altered, but not with respect to parish apprentices.   You still read on the gates of London poor-houses,
" strong, healthy boys and girls, &c. ;" and boys or girls
you may obtain by applying within, as many as you please,
free-born, with the usual fee.   Having been paid for taking
them, and having gone through the ceremonies of asking
their consent and signing bonds before a magistrate, you
may make them into sausages, for any thing the constitution will do to prevent you.   If it should be proved that
you kill even one of them, you will be hanged: but you
may half-starve them, beat them, torture them, any thing
short of killing them, with perfect security; and using a
little circumspection, you may kill them too without much
danger.   Suppose they die, who cares? their parents? they
are orphans, or have been abandoned by their parents.
The parish-officers? very likely indeed, that these, when
the poor-house is crammed with orphan and destitute children, should make inquiries troublesome to themselves;
inquiries which, being troublesome to you, might deprive
them of your custom in future.   The magistrate? he asked
the child whether it consented to be your apprentice; the
child said " yes, your worship;" and there his worship's
duty ends.   The neighbours? of course, if you raise their
curiosity like Esther Hibner, but not otherwise.   In order
to be quite safe, I tell you, you must be a little circumspect.
But let us suppose that you are timid, and would drive a
good trade without the shadow of risk.   In that case, half-
starve your apprentices, cuff them, kick them, torment
them till they run away from you.   They will not go back
to the poor-house, because there they would be flogged for
having run away from you: besides the poor-house is any
thing but a pleasant place.   The boys will turn beggars or
thieves, and the girls prostitutes: you will have pocketed
10*l*. for each of them, and may get more boys and girls on
the same terms, to treat in the same way.   This trade is as
safe as it is profitable.

In England there are many charitable institutions for
assisting orphan and destitute children.   One of them, at

the head of which I observe the name of Lord Grosvenor, informs the public that London contains, at all times, 15,000 orphan or destitute children, houseless, prowling about the streets, and supported by begging or robbing. By dint of zeal, advertisements, and public meetings, this society has, I believe, found means to provide for 20 of these children. Of the 14,980 which remain, how many are run-away parish apprentices? A committee of parliament might easily learn; but parliament represents only the payers of poor-rates, to whom an exposure of the truth would not be agreeable. Great things, however, are expected of the reformed House of Commons. Should they wish for information on this subject, I hereby undertake to put them in the way of learning, for certain, that one-fourth, at least, of the boys under fourteen years of age, who pass through the prisons of London, are run-away parish apprentices.

The American reader must not suppose that London is the only place in England where free-born boys and girls may be obtained with the usual fee of 10*l.* for each. In all great towns the parishes get rid of destitute children in this manner; and in most of them the usual fee is 10*l.* for each child. In rural parishes the usual fee is from 5*l.* to 7*l.*; a difference explained by the smaller proportion which in rural parishes destitute children bear to the rates, whence less anxiety on the part of the rural overseer to get rid of destitute children.

In all England there cannot be less than five millions of chimneys. Suppose that on the average each chimney is swept twice a year, and that a fifth of the whole number are swept by machinery. If so, something like what I am going to describe occurs eight million times every year in England. A chimney requires to be swept, and the master sweep attends, with a little boy. He fastens a blanket across the fireplace to prevent any soot from falling into the room. Now watch the child. Trembling, he draws a black bag over his head and shoulders; the master grasps him by the arm and guides him to the fireplace: he disappears up the chimney. Now watch the master. He is motionless, his head on one side, listening attentively. Ask him a question: "hush" is the answer, with his finger on his lips. Presently a low, indistinct moaning is heard in the chimney. "William," says the master, putting his mouth to the edge of the fireplace, and speaking in a brisk, cheerful tone, "that's right, William." Another moan: and then "I say, William—brush it well out, I say." Down comes a quantity of soot, and the child is heard scraping the sides of the chimney. Presently, silence ; and then moaning again. " William," exclaimed the master, " I say, Bill, you've almost done, ha'nt you ?" No answer; the child's head being, remember, in a thick bag: but the brush is heard once more, and the master holds his tongue. Silence again; and the moan of the child returns. This time the master shouts—" Bill, Bill, I say, Billy, how do you get on ;" and so till the end of the work; whenever the child cries, or is silent, his master shouts to him, " Billy, I say, Billy, my lad." This is a mild case, without oaths, threats, or blows. Ask the master why he tormented the half-smothered boy by speaking to him while his head was in the bag up the chimney: he will say, " for no reason that I know of." Believing this answer to be false, you press for another, when the master says, " We always speak to 'em when they're up the chimney, for fear they should run sulky and stick." Run sulky and stick ! droop, faint, and die of suffocation. Examine the boy when he comes from the chimney. If his knees and elbows are not raw and bloody, they are covered with horn like the knees of the mountain goat ; his face, neck, and breast are wet with the water that flowed from his eyes, which are red with inflammation; the veins of his temples are swoln into cords; and his pulse is at high fever mark. In a word, he has been tortured.

Every climbing-boy suffers great pain every time he mounts a chimney ; and a good half of the climbing-boys in England are parish apprentices, free-born, consenting, recognised by the constitution, engaged in learning a trade which, as men, they could not follow, if by chance they should grow to be men. Of those parish apprentices who become thieves, a great many have first been climbing-boys, tortured several times a day as long as they would bear it. This, also, with the power to examine unwilling witnesses, might be abundantly proved.

In England, any one who belongs to the ruling class may be irreligious and immoral without so much punishment as disgrace. The titled concubines of royalty have been envied by numbers of their sex, and honoured when they appeared in public ; a lord high-chancellor, who keeps the king's conscience, may also keep a mistress, or more than one, without incurring the slightest odium ; any man of fortune may change from prostitute to prostitute without forfeiting any of the high respect which is paid to him as a man of fortune:

no one, in short, suffers any thing by encouraging prostitution, provided he can afford the expense. Women, on the contrary, whose poverty drives them to sin against religion and morality—prostitutes for bread—are regarded with that sort of scorn which a Turk expresses when he says—" dog of a Christian !"   The English show profound respect for their devil, in comparison with the way in which they treat their women of the town.   For these, such epithets as wicked, vile, nasty, such terms as slut, strumpet, wretch, are too good: you must not mention them at all in public, and you cannot allude to them in a book without staining your pages.   Recommend that they should be treated like fellow-creatures, as in the Netherlands : if you are not prosecuted for blasphemy, many will say that you deserve to be hanged.   In America or Holland, if you strike a woman of this class, she will take the law of you : in England, her evidence might be rejected, or at all events would not be believed.   " Gentlemen of the jury," the counsel of the accused would say, " this charge rests on the evidence of a common" (meaning poor) " prostitute : faugh ! my res—pec—table" rich) " client is already acquitted."   I do not pretend that such a speech was ever made, but assert, admitting the hypothesis to be absurd, that if, by chance, a respectable Englishman were prosecuted for assaulting a woman of the town, then this would be the way to get him acquitted.   The English constitution recognises parish apprentices, but not poor prostitutes.   Prostitution is one thing ; the prostitutes another.   The laws and customs of England encourage prostitution, but do not even protect the prostitutes.   At the royal theatres, for instance, which are managed by the king's servants, there are grand saloons, built expressly for the encouragement of prostitution : but I cannot hear of any law or regulation, like those which subsist in France and Holland, intended to provide for the health, the personal security, and the decent behaviour of this unfortunate class.   The laws and customs of England conspire to sink this class of Englishwomen into a state of vice and misery below that which necessarily belongs to their condition.   Hence their extreme degradation, their troopers' oaths, their love of gin, their desperate recklessness, and the shortness of their miserable lives.

But how, considering the very great mortality to which they are subject, shall we account for their vast numerical proportion to the other inhabitants of England ?   In France, and more especially in Holland, women of the town are frequently reformed, married, and respected in their new condition. In England, where the mere idea of a reclaimed prostitute, married and respected, would shock the least fastidious, prostitution means speedy death. English women of this class, or rather girls, for few of them live to be women, die like sheep with the rot; so fast that soon there would be none left, if a fresh supply were not obtained equal to the number of deaths. But a fresh supply is always obtained without the least trouble : seduction easily keeps pace with prostitution or mortality. Those who die are, like factory children that die, instantly succeeded by new competitors for misery and death. One cannot prove, indeed, by statistical tables, that the proportion of girls of the town is greater in England than in other countries, because in England any deliberate inquiry concerning this class would be considered shameful; nor are statistical tables required : the fact speaks for itself, is proved by the swarms of prostitutes to be met with in every town, and in every quarter of the great towns. To prove this, statistical tables are not more necessary than to establish, what no one denies, that in England there are more splendid mansions and gin-shops than in any other country. But the cause; what is the cause of this excessive number of prostitutes, notwithstanding so wonderful a rate of mortality?

One cause of this evil is, of course, an excessive demand for prostitutes. That demand is occasioned principally by a custom now prevalent among the English middle classes; the custom of abstaining from marriage, the custom of celibacy, vulgarly speaking; of "moral restraint," in the language of political economy. This cause is explained in the next note : the other causes, the inducements to a life of prostitution, are explained by the following story.

Some out-of-the-way people founded a refuge for prostitutes; a charity of which the object was to reclaim a small number of public women. One day a girl applied for admission to this retreat, saying, "I am out of work, cold, hungry, tired, houseless, and anxious to be saved from evil courses." She was dismissed, not being qualified; so the story goes. This story may not be true; but most Englishmen have laughed at it in private. The story passes for a good joke; and its currency proves two things; first, that the few English with bowels of compassion for prostitutes are ridiculed as eccentric; and next, that the English themselves consider poverty the main inducement to a life of prostitution. In America, where no class practises "moral restraint," the demand for women of the town is very small, and, such as it is, arises principally from the sojourn of foreigners in seaport towns; but if that demand were doubled by a sufficient increase of foreign visiters, it would not be supplied; because in America every girl can readily obtain an honest livelihood.   In America, you may travel a thousand miles, taking the towns in your way, and not meet a prostitute: in England, you cannot walk a mile upon pavement without meeting hundreds.   In America, it is as difficult for householders to get women-servants, as in England for women-servants to get places.   In America, prostitution is a choice seldom made; to English women, thousands every year,—it is a dire necessity.   In order to reclaim the prostitutes of England, you must first find employment for them, which would be the harder task of the two; and when this was done, there would be as many as before.   Not vice and misery, Mr. Malthus, but misery and vice is the order of checks to population.   Charity, virtue, happiness! these are English words still, but the meaning of them appears to have settled in America.   I wonder that emigration is not more the fashion, and wish that Mrs. Trollope would write a book on the domestic manners of the English.

In England, the increase of crime is a common subject of lamentation.   About a hundred and twenty thousand of the people, it is reckoned, are always in jail; besides convicts, transported to comfort by way of punishment, and debtors looking through prison-bars for the means of paying their creditors.   In England, the increase of fine jails is nearly as striking as the increase of gin-shops.   The new jails, one in every county, and in some counties several, would be thought grand in America; noble buildings of beautiful brick-work or handsome masonry, with imposing fronts, bearing chains, emblematical, carved in stone.   In Lancashire the magistrates boast, that their county jail is very like Windsor Castle, the finest of palaces.   The increase of fine lunatic asylums, also, may be noticed here; since it has been lately ascertained that there are more mad paupers, in proportion, than mad people of any other class, except governesses.   Poor-houses, gin-shops, mad-houses, jails; one almost sees them grow in numbers and magnificence, with the increase of paupers, parish-apprentices, drunkenness, and crime.   In England, those who compose the bulk of the people are too cheap to be happy.   If their condition be such that it must be worse before it can be better, the crisis is coming.

NOTE III.

Who compose the aristocracy—Particular distresses of the middle class—
Uneasiness of farmers—Of manufacturers—Of dealers—Low profits—
Uneasiness of professional men—Of several classes possessing the common run of knowledge, or superior knowledge—Of persons having fixed
incomes and families—Primary cause of prostitution—Domestic life
among the English middle class.

In America, it is a common mistake to suppose, that the
English aristocracy consists entirely of the nobility, squires
of good estate, wealthy churchmen, and highly-paid public
servants. The aristocracy means the privileged class.
Except the privilege of being born to make laws, there is
none in England that money will fail to procure ; and even
that one, any man, having abundance of money, may obtain
for his unborn, first-born son. A judge, a bishop, or a secretary of state, does not consider the trouble of his vocation
a privilege ; his privileges consist of money, patronage,
power ; the respect, the adulation, the devotion of his inferiors. In England, with plenty of the first of these privileges, you have all the others in abundance. Any Englishman, being very rich, would find it hard, if such a whim
should take him, to avoid the respect, the adulation, the devotion of numerous parasites. Not the man, but the wealth
is worshipped. The man may be ignorant, stupid, selfish,
dishonest, in every way worthless ; but if he have £50,000 a
year, he will have fifty, nay, five hundred devoted friends, telling him continually that he is wise, just, generous, all over
noble. Poor lords, though of Norman descent, are very little
esteemed, and would be quite despised, but that as hereditary legislators they commonly obtain a good deal of the
public money. The money is given to them avowedly for
the purpose of maintaining their dignity. On the other
hand, money will purchase the reputation of Norman descent. Mr. Thistlethwaite, whose father wore wooden
shoes and made a million by cotton-spinning ; Mr. Thistlethwaite, who has purchased a mansion called Thistlethwaite
Hall, intends, when he obtains a peerage, to take the title
of Thistlethwaite and Vermont (his mother's name was

Greenhill), in order to make it be believed that he descends in the female line from the Norman lords of Vermont : and this will be believed, religiously, on account of the million of money. In short, there is nothing that the English will not do to please him who can dispose of a great deal of money, either his own or that of the public. All rich Englishmen, therefore, belong to the aristocracy quite as much as any duke, minister, or archbishop; not excluding tradesmen, provided they be called great, like Calvert the great brewer, Baring the great stockjobber, Crawshay the great iron-founder, Mellish the great butcher, and Morrison the great draper. Still, one cannot draw a very distinct line between the aristocracy and the class next below them. I thought at one time of counting among the aristocracy all who are called respectable; but respectability has various meanings in England; with some it means to keep a carriage, with others a gig. I have it—the privileged class consists of those who, whenever they are wronged, or would injure, can buy law without depriving themselves of any other costly luxury; those, in short, who, be their rank what it may, have more money than they know how to spend. Captain Basil Hall calls them the spending class.

After these comes the middle or uneasy class. Uneasiness, according to Johnson, is care, trouble, perplexity. By the uneasy class, I mean those who, not being labourers, suffer from agricultural distress, manufacturing distress, commercial distress, distress of the shipping interest, and many more kinds of distress, of which the names and descriptions have appeared over and over again during the last fifteen years, in the journals of parliament, in pamphlets without number, and in all political publications, quarterly, monthly, weekly, and daily. In English politics, the word distress is used more frequently than any other comprehensive word, except pauperism. Distress, applied to any particular class, signifies the trouble, care, perplexity of that class, but not that the trouble, care, and perplexity are unequal, or confined to any one set of people; for each distress has lasted fifteen years, and all the distresses together make permanent general distress. This steady national distress is attributed to causes more numerous than the several distresses of which it is composed; to transition from war to peace; to the admission of foreign corn; to restrictions on the admission of foreign corn; to taxation; to diminution of the public expenditure; to inadequate production; to over-production; to change in the currency;

to free trade, and restrictions on trade ; to political economy, and the blunders of practical men ; and, finally, to rotten boroughs.   For an evil attributed to so many causes, it was natural that numerous methods of cure should be proposed. Accordingly, the business of English politicians, for about fifteen years, has been to devise remedies for general dis- tress or particular distresses.   Some of these specifics will be noticed hereafter, and especially reform of parliament, from which the uneasy class expect the most happy results; but here the many alleged causes, and supposed remedies of distress are alluded to, merely with a view to show that the distress itself is real, extensive, severe, not imaginary, as some of the spending class assert, nor confined, as in former periods, to the idle and thriftless.   In fact, the uneasy class consists of three-fourths, or rather perhaps nine-tenths, of all who are engaged in trades and professions, as well as all who, not being very rich, intend that their children should follow some industrious pursuit.   The proof of this assertion is very easy.

There are some English farmers, though but few, so rich as to be called great ; and these do not belong to the uneasy class.   Even these, however, complain of low profits.   But if he whose farming capital is, say, 30,000l., grumbles because his annual profit is only two and a-half per cent, or 750l., what must be the state of that farmer whose capital is only 5,000l. ? Supposing his profits to be equal to those of the great farmer, his annual income is only 125l. ; not so much, allowing for the difference of prices, as the income of a common labourer in America.   Anywhere in America, a farming capital of 5,000l. would return a profit of fifteen per cent. ; so that taking the common rate of farming profit in England to be two and a-half per cent., the American farmer possessing 5,000l. enjoys an income equal to that of the English farmer possessing 30,000l. But the common rate of farming profit in England, during the last fifteen years, has not been so much as two and a half per cent. : on the contrary, the rate of loss has been considerable.   Impossible ! cries a bigoted political econo- mist ; that is impossible, because if farming profits had sunk very low, capital would have been withdrawn from agriculture, and employed in other pursuits of which the profits were higher.   But what if the profits of other pur- suits were not higher ?   Political economists frequently suppose the case of low profits in a particular trade : surely, what takes place in one trade, may take place in all.

But be this as it may, there can be no doubt that in England, of late years, many farmers have employed capital with a high rate of loss. Hundreds, thousands have lost their whole capital, while all, with the exception of those whose capital were so large that they could save out of very low profits, have lost more or less. The number of farmers, it might be supposed, has been diminished by the total or partial ruin of so many : not at all. A farmer was ruined; had the landlord any difficulty in letting his farm ? On the contrary, the ruin of a farmer has generally occasioned wonder at the anxiety of other farmers to pay as high or a higher rent for the ruinous farm. Except during a few years before the close of the last war, the competition for English farms was never more keen than it has been during the long period of agricultural distress. There are very many farms which have ruined two or three tenants since 1815. No one pretends that the rent of farming land is lower; every one knows that it is much higher, reckoned in corn or cattle, than at any former time, except just before the peace ; and at this time high rents are, by some, supposed to be the cause, or at least one cause, of agricultural distress. The distress continues without diminishing the number of people who are distressed. As one farmer is ruined, another takes his place ; but the change of persons, as with children who are worked to death in factories, makes no alteration in the scene. I do not say, that all the farmers, or all farmers who begin with moderate capitals, are ruined in a few years, and succeeded by others to be ruined in like manner ; but every year sees the ruin of many farmers of moderate capital, whose places are instantly filled ; and all farmers, except only those who have very large capitals, are constantly on the verge of ruin ; in a state of care, trouble, and perplexity.

As in agriculture, so in manufactures ; with this difference, however, that the proportion of great capitals to moderate or small ones being much larger in manufactures than in agriculture, the proportion of manufacturers who suffer trouble and perplexity is much less than among farmers. There are many manufacturers, each of whom employs a capital of more than 100,000*l.* These might be content with a low rate of profit ; they are discontented, but they are not care-worn, troubled, and perplexed, like those smaller capitalists, to whom a low rate of profit brings ruin, or, at least, the constant dread of ruin. The number of manufacturers who have been ruined since the peace, is perhaps as great as the number of farmers who have been ruined in the same period. But has the amount of capital employed in manufactures decreased? On the contrary, it has increased rapidly and steadily ever since the peace. Has the number of master-manufacturers decreased? On the contrary, it has increased, though in a less proportion than manufacturing capital; this difference being explained by the constantly increasing proportion of large capitals to moderate or small ones. In other words, supposing the whole number of master-manufacturers to have been doubled, the number of those, each of whom employs above 100,000*l.*, may have been quadrupled. But how could this be, with a constant and universal low rate of profit? I have endeavoured to answer that question in the next note. Here it must be admitted, that ever since the peace, the common rate of profit in English manufactures has been extremely low; that a great deal of capital has been employed with loss instead of profit; that many of the owners of capital so employed have been ruined; and that at this time a very low rate of profit condemns all manufacturers of small or moderate capital to uneasiness, trouble, and perplexity. Great manufacturers, who possess immense capitals, must not be counted among the uneasy class.

In the commerce of England, since the peace, a low rate of profit has produced the same effect as in agriculture and manufactures. Great merchants, merchants who employed very large capitals, have complained of very low profits, and frequently of loss; an immense number of merchants, having only small or moderate capitals, have been ruined; and all owners of moderate or small capitals employed in commerce are in a state of uneasiness. In commerce, which admits of more speculation than manufactures or agriculture, the loss of capital has caused uneasiness, and even misery, to numbers who owned very large capitals, and who, impelled by the low rate of profit to seek out new channels of trade, have employed their capitals in glutting distant markets, and been ruined by such speculations. But has the total ruin of these great capitalists, and of a much larger number of small capitalists, diminished the number of merchants, or the amount of capital employed in trade? On the contrary, the increase of commercial capital has kept pace with that of manufacturing capital, and the number of merchants with the number of manufacturers. Millions, tens of millions of English capital have been thrown away since the peace in supplying distant markets with goods at less than cost price, and in other speculations, such as working, or pretending to work, the mines of South America; but whenever capital was in this way abstracted and lost, its place was immediately filled ; or rather so large a waste of capital seems not to have caused even a temporary vacuum. Where all the capital came from, how it was so rapidly accumulated, is a question; but that commercial capital has been produced faster than it was thrown away, is a plain fact, about which there can be no dispute. The number of merchants employing large, moderate, and small capitals, is very much greater than it was fifteen years ago ;* more business is done ; new channels of trade have been opened and filled : yet the profits of commercial business are now so low that only the most wealthy merchants are at ease ; all the others are troubled, perplexed, uneasy, always on the verge of bankruptcy.

With retail dealers, there is the same complaint of low profits, the same uneasiness as with farmers, manufacturers, and merchants. Until of late years most retail trades were conducted by persons of small or moderate capital. Of late years, however, very large capitals have been embarked in several retail trades. The owners of these large capitals act on the maxim—much business with small profits is as good as little business with large profits. They are satisfied, and as each of them possesses a large capital they may well be satisfied, with low profits. But nothing is better established than the tendency of all capitals, and especially of all capitals employed in the same business, to an equal rate of profit. It was impossible, therefore, that retail dealers of small capital should obtain high profits while great capitalists engaged in the same retail trade were satisfied with low profits. Still, a general low rate of profit in retail trades must not be considered as an effect of the employment of large capitals in retail trade. On the contrary, large capitals have been employed in retail trade, though, first, because the agricultural, manufacturing, and commercial fields were fully occupied, still, secondly, because the fulness of the retail field offered to the great capitalist some advantages over the small one ; such advantages as being better able to wait for distant returns, as

* In a late debate on " Distress" in the House of Commons (1833), Mr. Grote, member for the city of London, a great capitalist, and a very accomplished gentleman besides, referred to the increase of names in the London Directory as a proof that the number of traders had increased.

being able to buy when the market price was low, and to sell when it was high. The owners of a large capital can save when the owners of a small one cannot. The owners of a large capital engaged in retail trade have increased their capitals, notwithstanding a low rate of profit: a low rate of profit has ruined many retail dealers of moderate or small capital, and at this moment condemns all such dealers to great uneasiness. In London, and throughout England, retail dealers of moderate or small capital complain of dulness of trade, stagnation of trade, and so forth. Do they buy and sell less than formerly? on the contrary, except in special cases, which fall out of the general rule and might be explained by some special circumstances, they do more business than formerly : the profit, not the business, is less. And further, more of them do business: in all towns without exception, the number of retail dealers is greater that it was at the close of the war; and in most towns the increase of retail dealers has kept pace with that striking increase of houses which has been noticed before. As in manufactures and in wholesale trade, so in retail business, the number of persons who suffer trouble and perplexity has greatly increased with the uneasiness occasioned by a low rate of profit.

How a low rate of profit renders the middle class uneasy, I will now try to explain.

The rate of interest is a pretty sure criterion of the rate of profit. During the last war, the rate of interest was very high. The lenders and borrowers of money practised numerous tricks for evading the usury laws. One trick, practised by noblemen who borrowed large sums, was to give the lender a seat in parliament besides legal interest. Ever since the peace, the common rate of interest has remained below five per cent. Four per cent. has been a common rate for large sums, which the borrowers were entitled to hold for a fixed number of years. In other cases, where the lenders exacted repayment within a short period, three per cent., two and a half per cent., and at times even two per cent. has been the ordinary rate of interest. Now let us suppose, though merely for the sake of illustration, that during the war the ordinary rate of profit was twenty per cent., and that since the peace it has been five per cent. If so, during the war, which lasted near thirty years, the income of him who employed a capital of 10,000*l.* was 2,000*l.* a year, and has been, since the peace, 500*l.* a year ; if so, the incomes derived from all capitals have,

since the peace, been only one-quarter of what they were
during the war. It would follow, that the means of every
man engaged in business, agricultural, manufacturing, or
commercial, wholesale or retail, his means of existence, of
supporting his family, of educating and establishing his
children, and, above all, of contending against unfavourable
accidents, such as bad seasons, changes of fashion, and the
bankruptcy of his debtors; his power for doing all these
things, has been less by three-quarters since the common
rate of profit was five per cent. than when twenty per cent.
was the common rate of profit. The difference may be
more or less than from twenty to five per cent.; at all
events, it is very considerable. But with a smaller power
for doing certain things, as large, or a larger power has been
required. In every branch and rank of industry, every one
conceives that a certain expenditure is necessary to maintain his rank, or as he might call it, his respectability. The
amount of expenditure which makes an Englishman respectable, in whatever condition or rank, has not been much less
since the peace than during the war; the education of
children has not been much cheaper, while the desire to
give children an expensive education has greatly increased;
the desire or obligation to establish children in the world is
the same as before, while the difficulty of accomplishing
that object is much greater, since beginners in trade require
a much larger capital than formerly to obtain the same
income as formerly; unfavourable accidents happen as
before, while bankruptcies, complete or partial, are more
frequent than ever. All those, therefore, whose incomes
are derived from the employment of capital, except great
capitalists, who can easily save out of diminished incomes,
have smaller means of meeting heavier calls. Their existence is a continued struggle with difficulties. How to
make the two ends meet, which way to turn, how to provide for one claim without neglecting another, how to escape ruin, or at least what they consider degradation, how on
earth to manage for their children; these are the thoughts
which trouble and perplex them. The anxious, vexed, or
harassed class, would be a better name for them than the
milder term which I have used. These are the people
who in classes, or altogether, keep up the cries of agricultural distress, manufacturing distress, commercial distress,
distress of trade, and national distress.

Distress is not confined to those who employ a material
capital. The learning, skill, and reputation, united, of a

professional man, may be called his capital. Great professional capitalists, those who possess all at once great
skill, great learning, and a high reputation, still make
large incomes ; but none of those whose learning, or skill,
or reputation is small, make enough to live upon. The
very high prizes of the bar and the church have always
led to a keen competition in these professions ; so that at
all times there has been a large proportion of barristers
without briefs, and of clergymen eager to obtain a miserable
curacy ; but at this time the proportion of briefless barristers is greater than ever, as well as the number of clergymen eager to be curates. And, at this time, not only the
bar and the established church are crowded with hungry
competitors; but also every dissenting church, the attorney's
branch of law, and all the branches of the medical and surgi-
cal professions. Nay, full, overflowing as are all these professions, the number of young people who hope to live by
them is far greater than ever ; witness the crowds of
students in the inns of court, of young men every year
admitted to practise as attorneys, of clerical students in the
universities and dissenting schools, and of students in the
schools of medicine and surgery. It seems impossible that
a third of them should ever live by the pursuits which they
intend to follow ; for even now two-thirds of the persons
engaged in those careers live by snatching the bread out
of each other's mouths. Two-thirds, therefore, at the
very least, of professional men, may be reckoned among the
uneasy class.
    To these must be added a swarm of engineers, archi-
tects, painters, surveyors, brokers, agents, paid writers,
keepers of schools, tutors, governesses, and clerks. The
occupations of some of these classes permit the employment of a material capital. Engineers, for example, or
architects, who employ a material capital, must be excluded
from this list ; since whatever has been said of farmers,
manufacturers, and merchants, applies to them. Such of
them as employ a large capital increase their fortunes with
small profits ; such of them as employ a small or moderate
capital live in trouble and vexation. Some few also must
be taken out of this list, who, without employing a material
capital, are distinguished for learning, skill, and reputation
united. There are some painters, now and then there is a
paid writer, who make large incomes ; but the great mass
of these two classes, those who supply the ordinary, one
may say the necessary, demand for pictures and composition, are miserably poor. But was not this always the

case? Without a doubt; the poverty of painters and authors is proverbial; moreover there can be no doubt, that the aggregate of money earned by English painters and authors since the peace has been very much greater than during any former period of equal length; but during the last fifteen years the proportion of poor painters and authors has greatly increased; and never was it so great as at this moment. Since the invention of printing and the general spread of education, the common run of knowledge has always been held cheap; but now, in England, it is the cheapest of all commodities, except Irish manual labour. It is not, however, the smallness of the incomes earned by a swarm of educated people that strikes one so much, as the vast number of competitors for those very small incomes; the hungry crowd of expectants watching to oust the beggarly crowd in possession. What condition of life is more detestable than that of an English governess? In England, where poverty is a crime, governesses, young, beautiful, well-informed, virtuous, and, from tne contradiction between their poverty and their intrinsic merit, peculiarly susceptible, are generally treated as criminals; imprisoned, set to hard labour, cruelly mortified by the parents and visiters, worried by the children, insulted by the servants; and all for what? for butler's wages. Yet take up any London newspaper, any day in the year, and you shall find in it a string of advertisements for the hateful situation of governess. There is an institution in England, of which the object is to provide for decayed governesses, by means of a small yearly subscription from those who are not yet worn out; and the title of this benefit club is the "Governesses' Mutual *Assurance* Society." Last year, a newspaper, which is read principally by the aristocracy, by Captain Hall's spending class, noticing the club in question, proposed that it should be called "the governesses' mutual *impudence* society." This blackguard joke was uttered to please whom? the readers of the newspaper in which it appeared; a class who employ governesses, a class to whom, in that very newspaper, numerous advertisements for the situation of governess are continually addressed. An eminent English physician, whose wife had been a governess, states that, of the inmates of madhouses, the largest proportion consists of women who have been governesses. Yet for this dreadful and shabbily-paid office of governess, there are, judging from the newspapers, more candidates, in proportion to places, than for any other disagreeable employment: not, however, that one observes any lack of candidates for other subordinate employments which require the common run of knowledge, or even superior knowledge. They talk much in England of superabundance of labourers, meaning common workmen; but these are not more redundant than governesses, keepers of schools, and clerks of every description.

Superabundance is a relative term. Considering the superabundance of capitalists, in proportion to the means of employing capital with profit, and of professional men in proportion to the demand for their services, there is a reason why, of necessity, the subordinate classes should be redundant: because the fields for the employment of capital in agriculture, manufactures, and trade, and for the employment of professional learning and skill, being quite full, there is no room in those fields for the progeny of the subordinate classes; while the grown up children of capitalists and professional men, who are either ruined, or can but just make the two ends meet, instead of following the careers of their fathers, increase the competition for subordinate employments. But is there less room for the subordinate classes, than there was fifteen years ago? Positively, no; relatively, yes. Subordinate employments are far more numerous than they were fifteen years ago; but then, throughout the fifteen years, the classes wanting subordinate employments have increased more rapidly than the demand for their services. Suppose the field to have been doubled, the cultivators have been quadrupled: with a greater field than ever, never was there such a want of room.

Among the uneasy class must be included, finally, a large body of people whose incomes are fixed, whose means of existence are not subject to the rate of profit or the demand for professional and subordinate services,—landowners, sinecurists, public servants, and owners of government stock. Great landowners, great sinecurists, highly paid public servants, and great stockholders, belong to the spending class, together with great farmers, manufacturers, merchants, tradesmen, and lawyers. The owner of 10,000 acres of land, Lord Ellenborough with a patent income of 10,000*l.* a year, the lord-chancellor with an income lately cut down to 14,000*l.* a year, or the stockholder who receives 5,000*l.* or even 2,000*l.* a year in regular half-yearly payments at the bank, has no reason to complain of distress. Nor indeed has any one, apparently, whose income was fixed during the war, and has been much increased by an alteration in the value of money. Nevertheless, many thousands of people, enjoying fixed incomes, suffer deep anxiety; anxiety caused by the distress of those classes whose incomes are not fixed: I mean landowners, sinecurists, public servants, and fundowners, whose fixed incomes are not large, and *who have children to provide for.* What is to become of the sons and daughters? No man likes that his son should fall, or his daughter marry, into a circle much inferior to his own; especially in England, where this sort of degradation, like absolute poverty, is disgraceful, if not criminal. Every Englishman of property, moreover, likes that his eldest son should inherit nearly the whole of his property. What then, when there is property, must become of the younger sons and the daughters? What of all the children, where the property is only for life? The father must save: good; but the moment he proceeds to invest his savings, he feels the low rate of profit.and interest. During the war he could, with a little management, have obtained ten, twelve, perhaps fifteen per cent. for his money: now, no one pays five per cent. with good security. He consults his banker as to the best mode of investment. " Upon my word," says the latter, " I cannot advise you: the funds are so high, and so likely to fall through political agitation, there is so much money with so much distress and discontent, that we know not what to do with our money. I have 100,000*l.* in that drawer; and if you will tell me of a better place for it, I shall be very much obliged to you."* He is troubled, therefore, to fix on a mode of investment, and when the choice is made, annoyed because the interest is so low. But he cannot save enough to prevent the degradation of his children, without incurring degradation himself; without losing caste by a great diminution of expenditure. His savings, therefore, when invested in the best way, that is, in an insurance of his life, whereby he reaps the benefit of low profits in the shape of a low premium, are but just sufficient to provide a

* "In the money market, the greatest torpor and want of enterprise prevail. There has probably never existed a period at which so little employment for capital, at once safe and profitable, has presented itself; and it is quite evident, that unless some change takes place, capitalists are on the point of being forced into some wild and dangerous schemes, that must be attended with ultimate loss, by the mere impatience of letting their money lie idle. Whatever the cause of the low rate of interest may be, reflecting men look at it with much alarm, especially as it has now been of long continuance; and if some legitimate employment for capital does not soon offer, we may expect soon to see a new influx of foreign loans and joint-stock schemes."
—*City Article of the Times.* *October* 10*th,* 1832.

maintenance for his wife and children after his death. What are the sons to do when grown up, or if grown up? The army? —pay for a commission; and then, unless you belong to the spending class, look on promotion as hopeless. In the navy, candidates for promotion are quite as redundant as in the army. The church?—buy a living, or else your son must struggle, and may struggle in vain too, with a host of needy competitors for miserable curacies. The law, medicine, trade?—all full, overflowing; while the last, whether agricultural, manufacturing, or commercial, requires a large capital, or it will bring uneasiness, perhaps bankruptcy. A place under government?—yes, perhaps, if you are the parasite of a great man. I say perhaps, because the class of parasites wanting places has greatly increased of late, like all the other classes, while the number of places is become somewhat less. At best, your son will obtain but a small place; all the great ones, both at home and in the colonies, being kept for young people of the spending class. At any rate, the pain of being a parasite brings you within the uneasy class. There was a way, indeed, by which a man of moderate or small income could obtain places for his sons without cringing to any one; by connecting himself with a rotten borough, as alderman, bailiff, returning officer or crier; but the glory of rotten boroughs has passed away; and, if reform should go no further, only the spending class and their parasites will obtain places under government.

But if a man of fixed income, his income being small or moderate, be troubled to provide for his sons, how to provide for his daughters is a more perplexing question. The first, no, the second point, is to get them married; the first point is to prevent them from marrying into a lower, which commonly means a poorer, rank than that in which they were born. The first point is generally effected during childhood, when every day, and almost every hour of the day, something happens to impress them with a fear of such degradation as attaches to imprudent marriages. The second purpose, being subject to the first, becomes extremely difficult. If the girl had a fortune, she would belong to Captain Basil Hall's spending class; we suppose her to have no fortune except beauty, tenderness, modesty, and good sense. Who will take her as a wife, that she will take as a husband? She may by chance, or rather her mother may, by dint of great toil and management, catch one of the spending class; but this would be an exception to the general rule. The general rule with the daughters of men of small income, whether fixed or not, is a choice between celibacy and marriage with one of the uneasy class. Now, a great proportion of young men in the uneasy class dread marriage, unless there be fortune in the case, as the surest means of increasing their embarrassment. This is one of the most important features in the social state of England. Among the middle class, among all classes except the highest and the lowest, "moral restraint" is a confirmed habit. Hence immorality without a parallel in any other country. This is the cause of that exuberant prostitution which shocks an American. Another effect of "moral restraint" among the middle class is, that a great proportion of the females in that class are doomed to celibacy. One may well say doomed. Custom forbids them to practise that sort of "moral restraint" to which their brothers resort without disgrace ; and custom is stronger than walls and bars. In this case, it has more power than the strictest discipline of a convent. But why do the English, Americans, French, Dutch, and Germans regard with horror the legal institution of celibacy? On account of its unnatural cruelty. Well then, in England, a certain state of political economy, pride, or prudence, and custom, occasion more unnatural suffering than the villanous theocracies of Italy and Spain. The proportion of English women who pine in celibacy, is far greater than that of Spanish or Italian women who languish in convents ; and the English women suffer more than the others, because, living in the world, they are more in the way of temptation, more cruelly tantalized by their intercourse with happy wives and mothers. There is not in the world a more deplorable sight, than a fine brood of English girls turning into old maids one after the other; first reaching the bloom of beauty, full of health, spirits, and tenderness; next striving anxiously, aided by their mother, to become honoured and happy wives ; then fretting, growing thin, pale, listless, and cross; at last, if they do not go mad or die of consumption, seeking consolation in the belief of an approaching millennium, or in the single pursuit of that happiness in another world, which this world has denied to them. The picture may displease, even because it is correct. This, Americans, you whose domestic manners an English woman holds up to the ridicule of her countrywomen; this is a faithful sketch from domestic life among the English middle class.

The misery of the working class of Englishmen is not, perhaps, at this time, much greater in degree than at former times, or so great as the misery of the bulk of the people in

most other countries, except America.   In this respect, the
difference between the past and the present seems to be ;
first, that with the increase of population there are more
people to be miserable, not more in proportion, but more
absolutely ; and secondly, that, with the increase of knowledge, one learns all about that misery which was formerly
concealed from the happy classes.   But the great uneasiness
of the middle class in England is a new state of things ;
unexplained, and at first sight unaccountable, if one reflects
on the vast and rapidly increasing wealth of the English
nation.   Competition for wages is, plainly, the immediate
cause of misery among the working class : but what
occasions that severe competition among people of capital
and education, that snatching at each other's means of existence, which renders the life of the English middle class
one struggle with difficulties ?   This question is examined
in the following note.

NOTE IV.

COINCIDENCE OF OVERFLOWING NATIONAL WEALTH WITH THE UNEASINESS AND MISERY OF INDIVIDUALS.

Theories of the English economists—A dream of Robinson Crusoe's island—
The field of production an element of wealth—Argument with the economists—Argument with the Archbishop of Dublin—America and England,
as to the field of production—Cases of various proportions among the elements of production—Peculiar case of England—As wealth increases,
many individuals are less rich—Moral and strictly political effects of the
various proportions which the field of production bears to capital and
labour—Peculiar effects in the peculiar case of England.

ACCORDING to certain theories of the English political
economists, it is quite impossible that my account of the
wealth, uneasiness, and misery of the English people should
be true.   Those philosophers would say—If the capital of
England be so much greater in proportion to people than
that of other countries, wages must be higher in England
than elsewhere ;* for " wages depend on the proportion
between population and capital."*   Again, if the middle

* " Universally then we may affirm that, other things remaining the same,
if the ratio which capital and population bear to one another remains the
same, wages will remain the same ; if the ratio which capital bears to population increases, wages will rise ; if the ratio which population bears to

class suffered from the low profits of stock, the labouring class would enjoy high wages ; and if the labouring class suffered from low wages, the capital of the middle class would yield high profits ; since " the profits of stock depend upon wages, rise as wages fall, and fall as wages rise."† This is called reasoning *à priori*, and though very sound and profound, no doubt, to those who understand it, is sadly puzzling to common intellects. Let us try, however, to make it out.

The English people have accumulated a far greater capital than the same number of people ever possessed, or dreamed of possessing, since the world began : they have so much capital that they know not what to do with it : though during the last half century they have squandered, wasted, utterly thrown away, more capital than most nations possess, they still possess more capital than they ever possessed before. Abundance of capital, in proportion to people, always produces high wages. Therefore, wages are much higher in England than they ever were among any other people, or at any previous time among the English people. Aristotle would not have quarrelled with the syllogism, and that great logician and economist, the Archbishop of Dublin, will find no fault in it, logically speaking. But there must be an error somewhere, since the conclusion is directly at variance with a known fact. Let us try again.

1. When capital is less in proportion to people, wages are lower ;

2. The proportion of capital to people is far less in America than in England ;

3. Therefore, wages are far lower in America than in England.

The logic is still good ; but the conclusion is again directly at variance with a known truth ; the fact being, that wages are far higher in America than in England. Wherein lies the error ? in one of the propositions, but in which of them, my lord ? I put the question to the archbishop, and to Mr. Mill, who, like his grace, is a great economist and logician.

capital increases, wages will fall. From this law, clearly understood, it is easy to trace the circumstances which, in any country, determine the condition of the great body of the people."—*Mill's Elements of Political Economy*, page 44, 3d edit.

* Mill's Elements of Political Economy, Section *Wages*, p. 41, 3d edit.

† Mill's Elements, Section *Profits*, p. 71, 3d edit.

"It must at once be seen," says Mr. Ricardo, that " profits would be high or low, exactly as wages were low or high. * * * * * There could be no rise in the value of labour, without a fall of profits."

Now for the question of profits; according to the economists.

1. When profits are high, wages are low;
2. In America, profits are very high;
3. Therefore, in America, wages are very low.

Again,—

1. When wages are low, profits are high;
2. Wages are very high in America;
3. Therefore, profits are very low in America.

Or thus,—

1. When profits are low, wages are high;
2. In England, profits are very low;
3. Therefore, in England, wages are very high.

And again,—

1. When wages are low, profits are high;
2. Wages are very low in England;
3. Therefore, in England, profits are very high.

Deuse take the conclusion! it always comes wrong, which ever way one looks for it. I had been puzzling myself to get over a difficulty in political economy by means of logic, when growing more and more confused, I at last had the good luck to fall asleep. Good luck, I say, because during my sleep I had a dream, which explained to me why profits and wages, both together, are so low in England and so high in America. This was my dream :—

I was shipwrecked and cast into the sea. I heard the shrieks of my shipmates who were drowning, and felt the pain of having my own head struck against a rock. My next impression was less disagreeable. I found myself alone, but quite well, in Robinson Crusoe's island, walking up the green slope from the creek to the cave. Robinson came out by his ladder to meet me, and said with a smile— " Welcome! countryman." For my part, I embraced him tenderly, as an old and very dear friend. Presently, Friday ran up to us, and though he made me laugh by bowing very low and kicking up his legs, backwards, one after the other, expressing respect and joy at the same time, still I could not help shaking hands with him also, the faithful creature. Robinson asked me to take something after my voyage; but I, not to be behind him in politeness, seeing that he was in a hurry to show me all his fine things, said—" Not at present, thank you; I should like to see your improvements." Hereupon he led me, first to his crops, which had a most creditable appearance; and then within the enclosure, where I admired his goats, the tools which had cost him so much trouble, and the great store of provisions and seeds which he had laid up.   At length, we sat down to a very respectable dinner of fish and roasted kid ; chatting as follows during the meal.

Dreamer.—Altogether, Mr. Crusoe, you seem quite at your ease.

Robinson.—Why, yes, blessed be God ! but I have had my trials. It was a sore trial when I was obliged to sow the seed that I would fain have eaten, and when I had no Friday to help me ; but 1 have been very comfortable since I got before the world, with a good stock of seeds, tools, and goats : nay, since I lighted on Friday, I have lived like a gentleman, quite at my ease, as you say.

D. You are a capitalist now, Robinson ?

R. Capitalist ! what is that ?

D. Why, seeds, tools, and goats are capital ; and as you possess these, you are a capitalist.   Friday works ; you direct him, and give him a share of the produce : Friday is a labourer.

R. A labourer ! yes, he works ; a share ! he takes what he pleases.

D. Of course, high wages of labour, eh ; and high profits of stock also, or you would not be so much at your ease, Mr. Robinson Crusoe.

R. I have forgotten some of my English.   High wages of labour, high profits of stock ! what are they ?

D. In this island, high wages mean, that you can let Friday take what he pleases without stinting yourself ; and high profits mean, that Friday takes what he pleases without stinting you. Friday's labour, with the aid of your seeds, tools, and goats, produces plenty for both of you.

R. Yes—but hark ! man Friday ! friend ! down upon your knees ! here's another earthquake !

And sure enough it was a terrible earthquake ; for though it hurt none of us and did not last a minute, when we recovered ourselves and passed from the cave, through the enclosure, and over the outer fence, behold, every part of the island was covered with water, except the rock which formed the cave, and about half an acre of land in front of us.   Robinson and his man knelt again, and returned thanks to God for having preserved our lives ; while I stood by, distressed to think of what would become of them with only that half acre of land. Crusoe's calmness and resignation were quite admirable.   Rising, he embraced

Friday, saying—" The Lord giveth and the Lord taketh away ; blessed be the name of the Lord !" Poor Friday, however, began to cry; and I felt disposed to keep him company, when Robinson pointing to the enclosure said—" We have plenty left, food for a year, seeds, tools, and goats ; capital, sir, I think you called them ?"

" But what," asked I, " is the use of capital without a field to employ it on ? Your goats will be starved, and with no more than this little bit of land you will be unable to use half your tools, or a quarter of your seeds."

Robinson looked rather blank at this, but said—" We must do with less ; there will be less for Friday and less for me, but enough, I hope, to keep us alive."

" Low wages and low profits," said I ; " but that is a shocking state to be in. Cannot you set Friday to make, with the things that are left from your wreck, instruments and ornaments for some neigbouring savages, who have more food than they know what to do with ? In that way, if Friday were expert and industrious, you might be better supplied than ever."

" Our neighbours," answered Robinson, " would make food of us if they could."

" Oh !" said I, " I had forgotten that restriction on trade. Well, you cannot enlarge your field of production in that way, and it is a sad affair ; but I know what the English political economists would advise ; for Friday's sake, at least."

" Political economists !" exclaimed Robinson, " who are they ?"

" They are," I replied, " a new sect, and have set up a new god, which is called capital, and which they worship devoutly."

" The wicked idolators ! but what would they advise ?"

" Only for Friday's sake, mind, in order that his wages might be higher, they would advise you to increase your capital."

" What ! when I have already more than Friday and I shall know how to use ?"

" Yes ; with abundance of capital, they believe, wages are sure to be high."

" And my share, the profits I think you called it, how is that to be made high ?"

" By diminishing your capital, so that wages may be low ; for, say they, when wages are low, profits are sure to be high."

Here Robinson laughed so loud that I awoke; saying
to myself—The only way in which Robinson and his man
could get back to high profits and high wages, would be
by getting back the land that they have lost.

By this dream I was led to observe, that the modern
economists, in treating of the production and distribution
of wealth, have overlooked the chief element of production;
namely, the field in which capital and labour are employed.
They have written volumes on capital and labour, and the
effect of the various proportions which these may bear to
each other, but have scarcely noticed the field of production; and this but incidentally when explaining what they
conceive to be the nature of rent. In their theory of rent,
indeed, they show, that as capital increases on a limited
field of production, it is employed with less and less productiveness, whence the inference might be drawn that in
such a case profits must become lower and lower; but
of this the modern economists say not a word. In fact, to
have drawn such an inference would have placed them in
an awkward position; since in order to support their views
of the omnipotence of capital without regard to the means
of investment, they have fallen upon Adam Smith for saying,
that "the mutual competition of capitalists naturally tends
to lower profit." Instead, therefore, of showing the effects
which arise from various proportions between capital and
the field of production, they have taken some pains to
establish that there are not any such effects; that the effects
which Adam Smith supposed to arise from an increase of
capital in proportion to the field, or from a decrease of the
field in proportion to capital, have never existed, save in
imagination of their great master. How far they are
right or wrong, is a question of great importance to the
English.

Bring all the people out of France into England; would
that make any difference in English profits and wages?
None, Messrs. Mill and M'Culloch would say, provided
the French should bring all their capital with them. But
what could they do with their capital in a field which is
already quite full? Employ it, would be the answer, in
manufactures, and so get food from other countries.
Good, I reply, if there were no corn laws; but that means,
increase the field of production, lay hold of foreign fields,
in proportion to the increase of capital and people in England. Field of production they would say, we acknowledge
no such term; capital is all in all.

Well, then, suppose that only the capitalists of France should come to England, with all their moveable property; what effect would that have on English profits and wages? Wages, according to the economists, would rise; and, through the rise of wages, but not otherwise, profits would fall. But in what way would this increase of capital raise wages? By causing, would be the answer, a greater demand for labour. Truly, if the new capital were invested productively, but not otherwise; and how should it be invested productively, or even at all, when already the capital of England is so great, in proportion to the means of productive investment, that it overflows into France* and other foreign fields of production? Nonsense! I hear them exclaim, capital and production are synonymous. Let us try them again.

Suppose the sea, for three hundred miles east and west of England, to be turned into excellent land, and that every one were at liberty to take as much of it as he could cultivate in the most productive way, that is, with the greatest combination of power, according to the English system of farming. What effect would that have on profits and wages? Answer not rashly; but think of America. Messrs. Mill and M'Culloch, answering devoutly towards the god of their idolatry, would say—No effect at all, provided the proportion between capital and population remained the same. Well, gentlemen, let us suppose that the proportion between capital and population were not altered for some time; that a great mass of capital which is now lying idle, or about to fly abroad in the shape of foreign loans and distant speculations, were employed in cultivating the new land and turned into food, which is capital; would not the effect be, supposing always that the mass of capital now idle and so to find employment were very great indeed; in that case, I say, would not the effect be a great increase of the demand for labour and a general rise of wages? They must answer —yes. Yes, gentlemen, in that case the mere conversion of one sort of capital into another sort, without any increase of the quantity, would produce higher wages. Let us suppose, further, that the new land were of so good a quality that the gross produce of all capital employed on it should be sufficient to replace that capital, to pay high wages, and to leave high profits for the capitalists; in that case, bearing in mind that the extent of the new land is six hundred

* Some large iron works, and considerable manufactures of cotton and lace, in France, are carried on with English capital.

miles square, would not capital be withdrawn from pursuits in which the profits are low, and employed in cultivating this very productive land? and would not the effect be a general rise of profits? Inevitably, they must admit. Then the case may be supposed in which wages and profits, both together, would rise without any increase or decrease of capital.

Supposed, yes, they might say, but you suppose a miracle. And you, gentlemen, do not you illustrate all your doctrines, true or false, by supposed cases? But I will soon come to the practical case: meanwhile, one more question with regard to this miracle. Suppose that the eight hundred millions which have been thrown away, in creating your national debt, had been saved, had not been wasted abroad, and were lying idle in any shape you please; or rather, for a much lower draft on the imagination will serve my turn, suppose that the mass of English capital actually either lying idle, or invested with very low profit, were sufficient, when employed on this new and very product- ive land, to create a demand for more labourers than Eng- land could supply without delay; and that, consequently, labourers, tempted by the prospect of high wages, should immigrate from Ireland and France. In that case; no in- crease, mind, but merely a conversion of capital is supposed; in that case, an enlargement of the field of production, a mere increase in the productiveness of capital, would have caused a change in the proportion between capital and labour, would have made the labourers more in proportion to capital. Here, you see, is a cause antecedent to your great first cause, the proportion between capital and labour: and observe, further, that the effect produced by enlarging the field of production, namely, an increase of labourers, might have no effect at all on the rate of wages; or rather that wages might rise while the number of labourers was in- creasing, provided the amount of capital lately idle, and now used productively, were more than sufficient to employ the increasing body of labourers.

In America, profits and wages both are high, without a miracle. In America, the land is so good, it returns so large a produce to capital and labour, however unskil- fully employed, that all who cultivate it obtain plenty, like Robinson and his man in the first part of my dream; the share of the masters being called high profits, and that of the servants high wages. Moreover, the good land in America is so plentiful, that no one is forced to employ his capital or labour less productively than in agriculture. Consequently, all the capital employed in America yields high profits and high wages ; the high profits and wages of agriculture being spent in giving high profits and wages to capitalists and labourers engaged in other pursuits. The productiveness of all capital and labour is very great, and does not decrease with the increase of capital and labour ; because, however rapid that increase, it is accompanied by a corresponding increase of the very productive field. The continued high profits and high wages of America, then, appear to rise from the large proportion which, in America, the field of production continually bears to capital and labour.

In England, on the contrary, the field of production is limited, first by nature, and next by the corn laws, which decree that the people of the United Kingdom shall have no bread but that which is grown in the United Kingdom. This limited field, moreover, is so full of capitalists, that these, by competing with each other, reduce profits to a very low rate ; and so full of labourers, that these, by competing with each other, reduce wages to a very low rate. If it were not for this severe competition among capitalists, a greater difference than actually exists between the prices of English and American corn would show the vast difference between the natural fertility of land in England and land in America : if it were not for this severe competition among labourers, English labour, which from the mode in which it is employed is so much more productive than American labour, in proportion to the number of hands, would be better paid, instead of being far worse paid than American labour. In England, both classes, capitalists and labourers, are fighting for room. Consequently, it may be said that, in England, low profits and low wages are owing to the small proportion which the field of production continually bears to capital and labour.

But, the Archbishop of Dublin might say ; but low profits and low wages, together, have occurred in England before now, when the proportion of capital and labour to the field, as you call it, was much less than it is at present. How could that have occurred if, as you say, profits and wages depend on the proportion which capital and labour bear to the field of production ? Further, the cases have often happened of low wages with high profits, and high wages with low profits. Such cases are at variance with your theory.

No, my lord ; nor do I say that profits and wages depend solely on the proportion which capital and labour bear to the field of production.   But I will try to explain my theory after the fashion of the economists: begging such readers as find this note dull to pass on to the next, where they will find some urgent reasons for turning back to this one.

Capital pays labour, and labour uses capital.   Between these, therefore, there is an intimate relation.   The proportion, also, which these bear to each other, is always of some importance; because, whatever the produce of industry, the division of that produce between the two classes who raise it, is regulated by the number of labourers in proportion to the capital employed.   I say employed, because capital which cannot be employed, which lies idle for want of employment, is as if it did not exist.   When labourers are few in proportion to capital for which there is employment, the labourer exacts a large share of the produce, which leaves but a small share for the capitalist; and when capital is small in proportion to labour, the capitalist can reserve a large share of the produce for himself, leaving but a small share for the labourers.   So far the political economists; and so far both profits and wages depend on the proportion between labour and capital.   But all this relates to nothing but the division of the produce.   A far more important question remains—what determines the amount of produce to be divided ?   Suppose the shares *fixed* at half and half: now double the produce.   Profits are doubled and wages are doubled; the capitalist who got ten per cent. now gets twenty per cent.; the labourer who got two shillings a day now gets four shillings a day.   Messrs. Mill and M'Culloch would contend that wages had not been altered; but your friend Mr. Senior, and you, my lord, would say that wages had been altered in amount, though not in share.   Still, with this remark you would rest satisfied; and concerning the effect on profits of doubling the produce of industry, you would say nothing.

Now I venture to suggest, that the mere division of produce between capitalists and labourers is a matter of very small moment, indeed, when compared with the amount of produce to be divided ; that, whether the capitalist obtain three-quarters and the labourers one-quarter, or the labourers three-quarters and the capitalist one-quarter, the grand question is, how much do the two parties divide between them ?   By discussing the question of shares only, all that we can learn is, how one party may gain by the other party's loss ; by discussing the question of amount, we may discover what is that state of things most beneficial to both parties.   By dwelling altogether on the former question, we make bad blood between the two classes ; telling the capitalist that he must suffer unless his labourers be miserable ; assuring the labourer that his sufferings arise from his master's prosperity : by examining the latter question we may prove that masters and servants have one and the same interest ; that, as there is a state of things bad for both parties, so is there a state of things good for both parties. And this latter question is of vast practical importance to the English at this present moment ; when, as I have endeavoured to show in the succeeding note, there is every prospect of a desperate struggle between the two parties, who have been set against each other by being told, that the welfare of either party is incompatible with the welfare of the other.

The productiveness of industry depends upon, first, the agency of nature, that is, the natural quality of the land from which subsistence is derived ; secondly, upon combination of power for distribution of employments, which, for shortness, may be called skill.   But these two regulators of production have a tendency to act in opposite directions. When a people cultivate land of very great natural fertility, and without limit as to space, so that the people may increase without resorting to inferior soils, they have no inducement to employ their industry in the most skilful way. On the contrary, they are strongly impelled to cut up their capital and labour into small distinct fractions.*   America is the example, where the produce raised by a given amount of capital and labour, though sufficient to yield high profits and high wages, is not equal to a fourth, perhaps, of what the same amount of capital and labour would produce on the same land, if employed with English skill.   To proceed at once to the other example, a produce sufficient to feed the actual population of England, could not have been raised in England without the greatest skill in the application of capital and labour.   As population increased in a country naturally steril and of limited extent, industry was applied with more and more skill to the cultivation of land ; and the increase of skill counteracted the decrease of natural productiveness when capital was applied to waste land of inferior quality, or more capital was used on land already cultivated.

But though greater skill counteract the growing necessity of employing capital and labour with less and less assistance from nature, still, in the long run, the produce obtained with

---

* See note on the origin, progress, and prospects of slavery in America.

the maximum of skill and the minimum of natural fertility, will not be more than sufficient to afford inducements for continuing the work of production. The amounts of produce, indeed, raised by equal capitals will be very different, because land varies in natural fertility and in circumstances of position, such as vicinity to manure and a market; but, as those who cultivate land of superior quality or position, must pay to the owners of such land, as a premium for being allowed to use it, all the excess of produce above what suffices to replace capital with ordinary profits (they must do this, because others would do so if they would not), the whole produce to be divided between capitalists and labourers is, notwithstanding the greatest skill, reduced to the minimum.

The land, therefore, from which a society derives its food, constitutes its field of production; and the productiveness of capital, subject to the temporary effect of increasing skill, depends on the proportion which capital bears to the field in which it is employed.

With this introduction, the four following cases will describe all the common conditions of society which exhibit different rates of profit and wages.

First. The case in which capital bears a large proportion to labour, and a small proportion to the field of production. The United States and some new colonies are the examples. In this case, wages are high in share and in amount; profits being, though low in share, high in amount.

Secondly. The case in which capital bears a large proportion to labour, and also a large proportion to the field of production. High wages and low profits will be the result. This was the case in France towards the close of the last war, when the conscription had rendered labourers scarce : more than once, it has been the case in England after a pestilence.

Thirdly. The case in which capital bears a small proportion to labour, and also a small proportion to the field of production. Low wages and high profits will be the result; the produce divided being great, but the labourers' share small. This is the case of nearly all countries in which, with superabundance of labourers, there is plenty of room for the employment of more capital without any decrease of productiveness. Bengal is a good example, where wages are two-pence a day, and the rate of interest twelve per cent.

Fourthly. The case in which capital bears a small proportion to labour, and a great proportion to the field of production. This case gives low profits and low wages also; the whole produce of industry to be divided among the producers being reduced to the minimum. France may be an example of this case.

But these are common cases. The present case of England differs from all of these, in as much as we cannot say that English capital bears a small proportion to English labour; seeing that, in consequence of the very high proportion which English capital bears to the field of production, great masses of capital lie idle, are invested unproductively, that is, wasted, and are exported to other countries, not taking with them a corresponding amount, or any amount, of English labour. The same thing appears to have occurred formerly in Genoa, Venice, and Holland.

The case of England differs from all other actual cases in a very important particular. Political economists have described three states of society, the progressive, the stationary, and the retrograde. They call progressive that state of society in which both capital and the field of production increase as fast as population can possibly increase; so that profits and wages, both being constantly high, whatever the division of produce, the people increase as fast as possible. They call stationary that condition of society in which there is no further room for the productive employment of industry, in which case, profits and wages are constantly as low as possible. They call the retrograde state of society that in which, generally from moral causes, the field of production constantly decreases; in which case, not only are profits and wages constantly at the minimum, but every year some capitalists are reduced to the state of labourers; and, yet the labouring class becomes less and less numerous. The Venetian republic, when she lost the trade between Europe and Asia, was an example of this case: was not Holland in political convulsions another?

There appears to be a fourth state of society, which may be called stationary as to profits and wages, but which is progressive as to the amount of capital, the extent of the field for employing industry, and the number of people. The field, the capital, and the people, may increase; yet if the enlargement of the field be not more rapid than the increase of capital, no alteration of profits will occur; nor any alteration of wages, unless the field be enlarged and capital be increased, at the same time, more rapidly than people shall increase.   Though, in such a state of society, both capitalists and labourers will increase in number, though new means of communication will be opened, though fresh towns will arise, though the increase of population and of national wealth may be striking, nevertheless the rate of profits may still be low, the rate of wages but just sufficient to permit an increase of labourers, the majority of capitalists in a state of uneasiness, and the whole body of labourers miserable and degraded.   This has been the case of England since 1815. War ceasing, great masses of capital were no longer wasted every year, but were accumulated in England; new channels of investment were opened; the number of capitalists was visibly augmented; signs of increasing wealth appeared in all directions; but as the field of production was not enlarged so rapidly as capital increased, more and more competition among capitalists led to the lowest rate of profit, and made the condition of the greater number worse than that of the smaller number. So with respect to the labouring class; with the peace, which removed one check to the increase of people, came great improvements in medicine, which removed other checks; and the common people increased faster than the means of employment for increasing capital.   In a word, both the capital and the people increased faster than the field of production was enlarged.   This change of the proportion between two of the elements of production and the third or chief element, explains the coincidence of enormous, nay, of rapidly increasing national wealth, with the uneasiness of the middle class and the misery of the bulk of the people.

The moral and strictly political effects of the various proportions which the field of production bears to capital and population, must now be briefly considered.

In the progressive state of society, capital has a tendency to an equal distribution among all the people. In America, notwithstanding high profits, individuals seldom accumulate large fortunes.   Though the produce divided between the capitalist and the labourer be large, the labourer takes so great a share that he soon becomes a capitalist.   Under this most progressive state of society, therefore, the increase of capital is divided, pretty equally, among a number of capitalists increasing at the same rate as the capital; so that while none are compelled to work as servants through life, few, even of those whose lives are unusually long, can accumulate great masses of wealth. Moreover, in such a state of things, the independence and self-respect of all begets a love of equality, and thus conduces to the equal distribution of the capitalist's wealth among his children; so that an individual seldom inherits the savings of many generations, or even the bulk of his father's property. In this state of things, there is no idle class, no spending class, as Captain Hall has remarked, no adoration of wealth, no oppression of the poor, no reason for political discontent. This appears to be the happiest state of society consistent with the institution of property.

In those states of society which are either retrograde or stationary, as well as in that peculiar state which, though advancing in the aggregate of wealth, gives low profits and low wages, wealth inevitably accumulates in a few hands. Wages being extremely low, the great body of the people are unable to save; and profits being extremely low, small capitalists consume the whole, or nearly the whole, of what remains to them after replacing their capital. Some, indeed, appear to be employed in diminishing their capital. Mr. Mill has incidentally supposed the case, in which none but large capitalists should be able to save, or even to live, on the profits of capital; in which society should consist only of labourers and great capitalists.* These last, whose consumption is small when compared with the returns of their large capitals, even with very low profits, are able to accumulate in proportion to the amount of their wealth. In the next place, when the common rate of profit is low, the small capitalist is apt to be ruined by fluctuations in trade, which are the periods of harvest to the great capitalist, who can wait to buy when the market price is low, and to sell when it is high. When, too, the common rate of profits is low, great capitalists are not always subject to the law of competition. In some operations, such for example as the distillation of spirits, porter brewing, tanning, and the publication of a daily newspaper heavily taxed, the amount of capital required is so large, and the time when a return may be expected so distant, that no small capitalists can undertake one of them with a prospect of advantage. Such operations can be conducted only by the owners of large

---

* " In proportion as capital is attended with less and less of annual return, the owners of capital have less and less income. If the income from capital be continually diminished, in process of time *none but the owners of large masses of capital will derive from it the means of subsistence.*"—*Mill's Elements of Political Economy,* page 61, 3d edit.

capitals, who thus establish monopolies whereby they obtain profits somewhat above the common rate. Again, when wages and profits are low in consequence of the large proportion which capital and people bear to the field of production, a part of the produce of industry falls to the owners of land, both as landlords and capitalists; a class who, speaking generally, disdain the pursuits of industry, and who in most countries have made laws for the descent of land, and of capital fixed on land, which promote the accumulation of wealth in a few hands. When, further, low wages and low profits condemn the bulk of the people to want, and all small capitalists to distress or vexation, wealth obtains such inordinate respect and so many advantages over and above what wealth will purchase in any market, that slavishness on the one hand, and pride on the other, become habitual. And to these evils must be added, the corruption of idleness, grasping and gambling habits, which lead to dishonesty among the middle class, and savage discontent among those who are without hope. Thus the retrograde or stationary condition presents at the same moment gorgeous palaces and wretched hovels, complete idleness and incessant toil, high mental cultivation and the most barbarous ignorance : it cannot but produce a general corruption of morals, nor end, sooner or later, but in violent political convulsions.

Not only the coincidence of misery and uneasiness with enormous wealth, but all the most striking social peculiarities of England may be traced to a superabundance of capital and population in proportion to the means of employing capital and labour. Nay, it might perhaps be shown, by reference to history, that the decline and fall of empires have, in great measure, been owing to the excess of two of the elements of production over the third ; which disproportion throws great part of the national wealth into the hands of an idle class, producing an extreme inequality of conditions, and therefore an extreme corruption of morals, with pride, insolence, and cruelty on the side of the wealthy few, discontent and recklessness on the part of the suffering many ; and resulting, finally, in jealousies, divisions, commotion, and civil wars, which dry up the very springs of national greatness.

NOTE V.

POLITICAL PROSPECTS OF THE ENGLISH.

Retrospect—The constitution of 1688—Its merits and defects—Maintained by corruption—Populace subservient to the ruling class—Effects of knowledge—On the middle class—On the poor—History of the late change in the constitution—New constitution obtained by the physical force—New constitution described—Not likely to last—Dangers in the prospect of change—Democracy or worse, apparently inevitable—Dangers of democracy—Possible means of avoiding the probable evils of change—Christian legislation—Means of improving the physical condition of the bulk of the people, and of removing the uneasiness of the middle class.

IN order to take a just view of the political prospects of the English, we must look back a little ; besides observing carefully by what means was brought about that peaceful, but very difficult political change, that most pregnant revolution which has just taken place in England.

The theory of the English government, as settled by the revolution of 1688, was this :—three powers in one power ; the king one power, the lords one power, and the commons one power ; but the power of the king, of the lords, and of the commons, is all one, co-existent and co-equal : the king powerful, the lords powerful, and the commons powerful ; and yet there are not three powers, but one power. And in this trinity, none is afore or after the other, none is greater or less than another ; but the whole three powers are co-existent together and co-equal. Nevertheless, though all laws must have the consent of king, lords, and commons, the king cannot originate any laws, nor the lords any laws relating to taxes ; while the king is the sole executor of the laws. But the king can do no wrong ; his ministers, alone, being responsible for his acts. Furthermore, the king's power descends from father to son ; as does that of the lords ; and the king can create lords without any limit as to number. Lastly, the commons represent the whole nation, save the king and lords, in parliament assembled.

This is the theory of the English constitution, as settled in 1688. The practice of that constitution has been as follows.

Since no operation of government can be conducted without money, the commons, who hold the public purse, have been omnipotent. They have possessed the power to make whatever laws they pleased, and to compel the execution of such laws in whatever manner they pleased. What things they have done by the exercise of that power, or left undone by abstaining from the exercise of it, is quite another question, depending on the motives by which they were actuated. They may have chosen to agree with the king and the lords, or occasionally to disagree with them, to enlarge or curtail the royal functions, to restrict or extend popular rights; but, whatever may have been their inclinations, whatever their acts, they have never wanted power to do as they pleased.

This is the first great difference between the theory and practice of the English constitution. The next is, that the commons, instead of representing the whole nation, save the king and lords, have been partly self-elected, partly nominated by individual lords, and partly chosen by certain bodies of the people. The rights of self-election and of nomination were bought and sold like an estate, and descended along with estates; while the open elections were so costly to the candidates that none but rich men could be chosen. The whole power, therefore, of the English government resided in a few hundred men, who had the inclination and the wealth to buy seats in the House of Commons, either for themselves or their dependents. That government has been called the oligarchy of boroughmongers.

Seeing how this oligarchy was constituted, its motives for doing certain things, and for leaving other things undone, become plain enough. This would have differed from all other oligarchies, if the main object of its members had not been to share among themselves the emoluments and distinctions of government. Monarchy being a costly form of government, requiring a great outlay to maintain the dignity of the crown, opens a wide field of emolument: the English boroughmongers, therefore, have always been strongly attached to the monarchical form of government. Titles of honour are among the distinctions enjoyed by a governing class, and it is natural that he who has himself delighted in a title of honour should wish to transmit it to his posterity: the English boroughmongers, therefore, have always been fond of an hereditary nobility. But a mere title, such as lord, or three-tailed bashaw, or blue buttoned mandarin, would not be much esteemed unless there were attached to it, not only real power, but also the appearance of power. Now, of the English boroughmongers a good proportion were peers, who exercised real power by means of their dependents in the House of Commons; but, as this was, as far as possible, to be concealed from the nation, they could not appear to exercise power without a legislative assembly of their own : the English boroughmongers, therefore, have always warmly approved of a noble chamber, in which the appearance of making laws should descend along with titles of honour. As wealth was the source of each man's power in the government of boroughmongers, each boroughmonger wished that his wealth should go down to his posterity undiminished : hence the profound attachment of English boroughmongers to entails and the law of primogeniture. But rich men, like poor men, have daughters and younger sons : how was the rich boroughmonger to provide for these without diminishing his wealth? Out of the public purse, over which, either by sitting in the House of Commons, self-elected, or by means of his dependents who sat there, he exercised a large share of control. Boroughs were dear and elections very costly : a snug borough cost near 100,000*l.*, and one man has spent 100,000*l.* on one county election : how were such vast sums to be recovered ? The public purse was always at hand. Hence one learns why the English people, who according to the theory of their constitution were all represented by the House of Commons, have, in practice, been so heavily taxed by that assembly.

Oligarchy and faction are almost synonymous terms; first, as every oligarchy is a faction, and next, as oligarchies have always been divided into opposing factions. From 1688 to 1830, the whig and tory factions of the English oligarchy ruled by turns, one in and the other out, as the force of either party prevailed in the House of Commons. But their struggles for emolument and distinctions, instead of weakening the government, added considerably to its strength. The party that was out commonly found fault with the party that was in, took up national grievances and made great professions of public virtue : whence, as one party was always out, the nation always imagined that a portion of the legislature was singly devoted to the national welfare. When the party that was out became the most powerful in the House of Commons, and therefore got in, the king appeared to side with that party, and the nation rejoiced in a patriotic monarch. Now and then, one faction was strongest in the commons' house and the other in the lords' house, whence differences between the two houses, which gave to the lords' house an air of independence; an occasional appearance which assisted in holding the nation to the constitutional faith. Such differences, however, could never be serious or of long duration, because the faction which ruled in the commons could always exercise, in the king's name, the power of creating peers. At other times, the king disagreed with the ruling faction and dissolved the House of Commons, when a grand election struggle took place between the two parties; but whichever party bought the greater number of votes in the new House of Commons, became master of the government, or rather the government itself; so that, though the king occasionally exerted a will of his own, his independence was but momentary. A dissolution of the House of Commons was always called an appeal to the nation: thus, whenever the king exerted an independent will, the nation appeared to do so likewise; thus an occasional difference between the king and the ruling faction, by giving an air of independence to the king, and an air of power to the people, tended to preserve the nation's belief in the reality and beauty of the constitution. When a petty disagreement occurred among the three estates, the nation admired the beautiful balance of the constitution; and when such a disagreement ceased, the beautiful harmony of the constitution was the thing to be admired. By such fictions and phrases, the real oligarchy of boroughmongers was made to pass for an inimitable mixed government, the envy and admiration of surrounding countries.

And in truth this counterfeit mixture of monarchy, aristocracy, and democracy, was the best government ever established in Europe. Though the powers of government rested in the hands of a few, those few owed their power to wealth, and any one who could acquire great wealth might help to govern. The qualification for the enjoyment of power being wealth, it was natural that the government should take great care of the wealthy. Moreover, as at all times many of those who governed had lately sprung from an inferior class, it was natural that they should sympathize with a class or two below them. The English government, accordingly, ever since it became an oligarchy of boroughmongers, has provided better than any other government of Europe for the security of property and persons.

Security of property! personal safety! What more could be asked of any government? Not much; for these are the chief ends of government. Why then were the English dissatisfied with their glorious constitution? why have they lately made another of a very different character? These questions will be answered by stating in what respect, chiefly, the constitution was not a good one; secondly, by describing the means of its preservation; and thirdly, by showing how the force on which it depended was gradually destroyed.

The old English constitution gave security to property, with safety to persons, according to a scale, by which the security and safety were bestowed in proportion to wealth. Justice was made exceedingly dear. Thus, though there was justice for all who could buy it, there was none for those who could not; and among those who could pay for it, there was most for him who could pay most. As between two persons of equal wealth, law was justice, though dear; as between two persons of unequal wealth, law was injustice. In the attack and defence of persons and property, law, miscalled justice, favoured the richer party, whether he attacked another wrongfully or defended his own right; and was, to the same extent of course, unfavourable to the poorer party, whether he were right or wrong. Down the scale of wealth, there was an active principle of wrong, and up the scale of wealth, a defensive principle of right. He who was at the top of the scale could injure the others, who could not injure him; those who were at the bottom of the scale could not injure the others, but might be injured by them. These were the principles on which the old English constitution afforded protection to persons and property. Recollecting how much the happiness of man in society depends on the administration of law, it will appear that in this respect the old English constitution was a very bad one.

That constitution bestowed upon superior wealth many privileges, some hurtful to the majority and in themselves odious, others odious merely as privileges bestowed upon wealth. Under that constitution, the rich alone could obtain the higher emoluments, distinctions, and other gratifications of power; could receive titles of honour; could make laws in the House of Commons: could enjoy or give places, and receive or bestow pensions; could administer rural laws, after making them; could manage roads at the public expense, and stop roads convenient to the public; could build, fill, and govern jails; could keep game, shoot other people's game, and transport other people for shooting their game; could be married in a particular way, and be divorced from

their wives ; could have their children educated at a particular place at the public expense ; could appoint religious
teachers ; could fix rates of wages, saying to the poor—
" You shall marry, and you shall remain asunder : you who
are married shall not live together ;" with many more privileges, so far of a like kind as to be obviously unfair.
What privilege, indeed, is free from injustice ? Whichsoever
of these privileges was most hurtful to the nation, all of
them were calculated to excite hatred towards the privileged
class ; and though that curious machine, the constitution,
would have been less productive, would not have worked,
perhaps, without them, they were very proper to bring
about a revolution sooner or later.

The existence of every government of the many by a
few must depend upon some kind of force, wherewith to
secure the obedience of the many. The most common
force of government has been a body of guards, assisted by
a body of spies. This, however, was not the force of the
old English constitution, which, out of regard to the liberty
of the subject having property, was always opposed to
standing armies and political police. The force of the old
English constitution was corruption ; an engine of great
power, and one admirably fitted in this case to the machine
that it was employed to work. The oligarchy, which under
the name of a mixed government was set up in France
eighteen years ago, has been worked by an engine of this
sort ; but not well. In material mechanism, simplicity is a
great merit ; in political machinery, having for object to
keep many in subjection to a few, the grand point is complication. In the French oligarchy, there was a sad want
of entanglement ; and then the French corruption was all
of one sort, obvious to the most careless observer. In
France, political corruption was a species of force ; in
England, a genus, comprehending many species. Of that
kind of corruption which was unique in France, namely,
expenditure of public money by the government, there was
plenty in England ; but this, great as it appears when compared with the expenditure of other governments, seems
small when compared with the great mass of jobs and
monopolies by which it was assisted. Small, however, as
it appears in this point of view, it was mighty by the manner of applying it. The public income of France was
divided among the public servants on these two erroneous
principles ; first, that every one should work for his pay ;

secondly, that all public servants should be paid sufficiently. The principles, on the contrary, which directed the public expenditure of England, were, first, that many should be paid who did not work at all; secondly, that those who worked least should be paid the most, and those who worked most, the least. The churches of the two countries give a good example of the operation of these opposite principles. In the French church, none were idle; all the hard working clergy received comfortable incomes; and the income of a bishop was not more than seven or eight times as much as that of a curate. In the English church, large incomes were given to clergymen who seldom entered a church, and never either a pulpit or a cottage; the hard working clergy were kept in a state of want; and the income of many a bishop was equal to the united incomes of three or four hundred curates. Thus, in the French church, there were no great prizes by which strong and ambitious spirits might be attached to the established order of things; nor were clergymen of moderate disposition and talents urged, either by poverty or the hope of riches, to curry favour with the ruling class. The strong and ambitious spirits of the French church, accordingly, instead of supporting the Hartwell charter, spared no pains to overturn it, while French clergymen of moderate disposition and talents were content to vegetate, comfortably indifferent touching questions of government. Now turn to England: here the most able and ambitious of the clergy, desiring either to keep or obtain great prizes in the church, supported the constitution with all their might, while clergymen of moderate temper and abilities could obtain comfortable incomes only by siding with one or other of the state factions, and zealously supporting the constitution, to which both factions were equally attached. The contrast is remarkable, and helps to explain why the charter of William III. lasted a hundred and twenty-five years longer than the charter of Louis XVIII. It does but help, however, towards this explanation; as the clergy of England did but help to support the constitution. The two principles of sinecures, and of much pay for little work and much work for little pay, were adopted in every department of the public expenditure; in the military and civil branches of the army and navy, and the distribution of prize money, in the administration of law, in public education, in the diplomatic service, in the collection of the revenue, in all public offices, and in the management of the colonies, not forgetting Ireland.   Thus a great body of the people were induced, some by the desire of gain and some by the fear of loss, to stand by the glorious constitution. If none had been paid who did not work, and all who worked had received moderate but sufficient pay, those who were able and ambitious might have longed for a change, and the remainder might have wanted a motive for zeal in support of things as they were.   Inequality is the soul of political corruption.

But the corruption depending on a judicious outlay of public money in the way of pensions and places, was small when compared with that which arose out of jobs and monopolies. This distinction may be drawn between a job and a monopoly, that the one is a direct, the other an indirect, robbery of the public.   Under the old English constitution, the public was robbed directly by several classes of jobs; jobs in respect to contracts for supplies, loans, and public works, victualling jobs, slopping jobs, scrip jobs, building jobs, harbour, road, bridge, and canal jobs, and other jobs of the same class without end; the effect of each of these jobs being, that the government paid more than would have sufficed if the contracts had been submitted to open competition; that the difference between the necessary and actual expenditure was so much public plunder bestowed on friends of the glorious constitution.   Next, there were more palpable jobs;—such as when crown lands were sold or let for much less than their value, when the government purchased land for more than its value, when grants of public money were made to reward, in name, public services, in reality devotion to the constitution; when public works were undertaken, either useless or hurtful to the public, or when commissioners were appointed to perform certain acts, and handsomely paid for doing nothing.   All these are but a sample of the jobbing that took place under the old English constitution.   Now observe, if the whole of what was stolen from the public, by means of all these jobs, had been spent honestly in the public service, the constitution would have wanted the zealous support of a great band of robbers, delighted with the present and fearful of change.   Really, the old constitution is to be admired more for its roguery than its profusion.

Next come monopolies; and, first, monopolies of trade, exclusive power to deal with particular countries or in particular articles, such as of late years, the East India Company, the Bank of England, the West India planters' monopoly of the British market, and the corn monopoly of the landlords, which is the greatest of all: secondly, monopolies of quite another kind, such as that of the bar, which bestows on a particular class the privilege of pleading in the courts, and that which almost forbids a barrister even to practise in certain courts unless he can afford to pay for chambers in certain spots, where, of course, chambers are extremely dear; that other monopoly of the law by which 1,200*l.* must be paid as an apprentice fee for liberty to practise in some very important courts;* the military monopoly arising from the system of purchasing commissions, and very many more of which a naked list would fill several pages. The principle of monopoly seems to be:—gain with one hand and lose with the other; you rob me, and I rob you. Englishmen who gain by those monopolies in which they had a share, lost by others in which they had no share. But the gain was manifest, while the loss was imperceptible: there was the pleasure of robbing, without the pain of knowing that you were robbed. So much for individual feeling; but now observe the political influence of monopolies. Of the loss, which was hidden, no one took note; but the gain was felt, joyfully felt, and attributed, with gratitude, to the inimitable constitution. Adding to the long list of simple jobs and pure monopolies, a multitude of establishments, half job, half monopoly, such as corporations enjoying exclusive privileges, holding lands, levying taxes, administering charities, and bestowing offices, one begins to understand the power of that corruption which moved the old English constitution. It works well! George Canning used to exclaim: countless plunderers responded,—it works well!

But corruption was not the sole support of the borough-monger's oligarchy. Wherever there exist only two classes, as in Russia and the slave-states of America, the ruling class despise the slaves, and the slaves hate their rulers. The wise ancestors of Englishmen and Americans lived in such like enmity towards each other, when their habitations consisted only of huts and castles. But as a middle class grows up, the highest and lowest classes generally conspire to injure those by whom they are separated. England, ever since the revolution, presents a striking instance of combination between the aristocracy and the mob for the

* The courts which relate to marriage and the descent of personal property.

purpose of harming the middle class. Until the late peace, the physical force was always subservient to the ends of the ruling class; as when mobs assembled to the cries of "no popery," and "church and king," when the poor delighted in a victory over their "natural enemies," the French jacobins. The old English constitution worked well, as long as it was supported by the physical force. How this support was obtained, is not a mystery. For above a century, at least, after 1688, they who composed the physical force, the bulk of the people, were kept in a state of profound ignorance. Closely resembling working cattle, so far as knowledge goes, they were patient under oppression, as the horse, through ignorance of his own strength, submits to the spur. To obedience they added reverence. A lord or a bishop, a rich squire or beneficed clergyman, a rich contractor or stockjobber, residing in his mansion, surrounded by a park, or when in London still in a mansion, surrounded by mansions, seldom met the poor but on occasions of show or excitement, when a display of his wealth, and of the respect paid to him by the middle class, led the ignorant poorest class to regard him as a demigod. Thus elevated above the crowd, he could treat them with familiarity, and yet preserve their respect, while airs of condescension, from one so raised, were grateful to those so abject. Rank and wealth, accordingly, were higher recommendations to mob popularity than learning and virtue. In the next place, with regard to property, the great cause of jealousy and contention among men, an English aristocrat of the last century was supposed, by the grossly ignorant poor, to derive his wealth from any source but their labour; and he did actually divide among the poor a portion of the money which he obtained from the public purse. A general election used to cause a fall in the funds, by the sale of stock for the purpose of bribing, in one shape or other, all poor electors in the kingdom. Add to this the fiction, by which a good many poor men appeared to exert a voice in choosing the House of Commons, the drunkenness, license, and riot which the ruling class encouraged at elections, the sham of humility and good-fellowship by which the candidates used to cajole the populace; taking all these things into account, the only wonder is, that the poor, ignorant, degraded mass should ever have had a will of their own.

We have now to see how the force on which the constitution depended, was gradually destroyed.

It is not so very long since old Englishwomen were burnt for witchcraft, to the great satisfaction of everybody, save the old women. Why do they no longer burn old women in England? Because, in the course of a little more than a century, public opinion respecting witchcraft has undergone the greatest change. The same thing has happened with respect to dear justice, privileges, jobs, monopolies, and the *prestige* of aristocracy. To examine fully when this change of opinion began, and by what steps it proceeded, would carry me too far; but a few remarks on the subject may not be unacceptable to Americans.

Fifty years ago, instruction was confined to a portion of the highest class. The middle class, indeed, could read and write; but their reading did not extend beyond divinity, novels, the racing calendar, Moore's prophetic almanac, and, now and then, a newspaper adapted to their ignorance. As for any interchange of ideas by means of writing and printing, they never thought of such a thing; or rather they would have thought it presumptuous, if not unnatural, in them to form ideas upon subjects of general interest. Except when one of their narrow superstitions was attacked, as, for example, their fear of popish supremacy, they left all public questions to the nobility, clergy, and gentry, whom alone they supposed capable of understanding such matters. They ate, drank, attended to their business, went to church, horse-races, and raree-shows, stared and wondered when a great man passed, and believed that the whole public duty of man consisted in honouring the king and loving the rest of the royal family. The great French revolution entirely changed their character. When they saw that men of their own class in a neighbouring country had undertaken to govern, their slothful and slavish propensities gave way to political excitement. The very horrors which succeeded the French revolution, had an excellent effect on them; setting them to think, read, and even write on public questions, and, forcing them, above all, to look into the condition of their inferiors. During the long war that followed, some of them sided with the aristocracy, and some wished success to that revolution against which the war was directed; but all of them took an earnest part in public affairs. Every public question was now discussed by them, and for them too by their superiors, who wanted their assistance. Books, magazines, pamphlets, and newspapers came to be reckoned necessaries of life: and the quality of these improved with the greater demand for them. At length, towards the close of the war, when a new generation had grown up, the middle class were better instructed than the highest class, and the charm of aristocracy was gone. Individual Englishmen still revere the distinction of title, still bow and cringe to any one of superior rank; but the English, in general, have lost all reverence for nobility in the abstract; just as each individual, who shares in a monopoly, would preserve his own particular means of robbing the public, while all, including monopolists, loudly condemn monopolies in general. During the war, however, while profits were high, while among the middle class almost every man's condition improved year by year, a great majority of that class sided with the government, and was opposed to any change in the constitution. But with the peace came low profits, all sorts of particular distresses and general distress. Thirty or forty millions a year, instead of being squandered in foreign subsidies and distant campaigns, were accumulated at home. As the national capital increased, the now intelligent middle class became more numerous, in proportion to the other classes; but as capital was invested with less and less profit, the state of each individual among the middle class became more and more uneasy. Thus every year produced a great increase of the strength, and the discontent of the middle class. Touching politics, distress has two very different effects; straining men's attention to their own concerns, and yet disposing them to wish for change in public affairs. In this case, for a long while at least, those who compose each distressed class, when they could think of any thing but how to make the two ends meet at the close of the year, attended only to such public questions as were interesting to their own class in particular. In examining the petitions presented to the House of Commons between the battle of Waterloo and the expulsion of Charles X., it is curious to observe how few, of those which came from the middle class, asked for reform of parliament. Relief from distress was the prayer of the greater part of those petitions; agricultural distress, manufacturing distress, commercial distress, and, at last, the distress of the nation. These petitions were utterly neglected; for the spending class, represented in the House of Commons, felt no distress. In the end, the middle class, thus insulted as well as uneasy, came to suspect that there was some radical fault in the constitution.

A more important effect of the French revolution on the

English middle class was the disposition which it produced in some of them to improve the condition of the bulk of the people. The slaves of a neighbouring country had revolted, and had acted as slaves in revolt will always act. The ferocious animals of Labruyère, " male and female, spread over the country, black, livid, naked, and sun-burnt, fixed to the earth which they stirred and turned with inconceivable obstinacy, having an articulate voice, and showing, when they stood upright, a human face, creeping at night into dens, and living on black bread, water, and roots ;" these despised brutes had proved what Labruyère had only asserted doubtingly, namely, that they were men and women. But what kind of human beings ! Devils, they were called, in human shape, wretches, miscreants, monsters. Till then, the English had not suspected that more, a good deal, than half the people, were miserable and dangerous, like starving wolves. Long before then, indeed, Defoe had shown that the condition of the labouring class was as bad in his time as it has ever been since ; but who cared ? Out of evil cometh good. The burnings, drownings, and massacres by which the French populace proved their humanity, led to humanity, in the other sense, among the English middle class. Selfishness, being scared, was turned into benevolence. It now became an object with the middle class to improve the physical and moral state of their inferiors. But by what means ? This question was not so easily settled. After much discussion, during which some proposed one thing, some another thing quite different, and some strove to prove, by reference to history, that the attempt must fail, it was agreed that education should be tried. The ruling class, however, and the great among the clergy in particular, set their faces against this mode of proceeding. What ! teach the slaves that they were men ! it was a jacobinical project. All the ploughmen would want to be clerks, and the journeymen weavers gentlemen. Who would work, slave for the great, cringe to them, bow down and worship them ? Instruct all the people, and we shall have helps instead of servants ; teach all men to respect themselves as men, and then what man will be valet to another man, pull off his clothes, and scratch his back when required ? No, no—teach the people this, but not more ; to honour and obey the king and all that are put in authority under him, to submit to their governors and spiritual pastors and masters, to order themselves lowly and reverently to all their betters, to labour for their own living (say nothing of ours), and to do their duty in that state of servitude into which it has pleased God to call them. All this teach them, but no more, unless you would turn the world upside down. Such in substance was the language held up by the ruling class (it would be easy to quote chapter and verse for it) when some of the middle class proposed to instruct all the people. But they were not satisfied with pointing out the danger of educating the populace; those who sought to instruct the poor they charged with revolutionary principles, and put a mark on them as jacobins and levellers. Thus many, who wished well to the education project, were deterred from assisting it. A few, chiefly Quakers and other sectaries, persevered, and established a limited number of schools for poor children, on the plan suggested by Joseph Lancaster. The inventer of the system of Mutual Instruction wished that no Christians, except Catholics, should be excluded from his schools by religious scruples; wherefore, though he used the Bible as a school-book, it was without note or comment. The high church party now changed their tone. Christian charity required that so great a blessing as education should not be withheld from the poor. And then the hypocrites established schools on the Lancasterian plan, vowing that one of themselves, a Dr. Bell, had brought the system of mutual instruction from India. In their schools, however, which they called national, they added note and comment to the Bible; that is, they taught the church of England catechism, which makes slavishness the first duty of man. But this device of the aristocratic clergy was of no avail. Instead of confining instruction, as was intended, to those who should be brought up lowly and reverently to the pastors and masters of the tythe church, it piqued the dissenters, who now took more pains than ever to teach reading and writing, at least, to those whom the clergy did not teach. In the tythe schools, after all, more than this was not taught. The result of all the teaching put together is, that about half, perhaps near three-quarters, of the English poor can read, and a tenth part of them write. The writing was of no use to them, nor the reading either, maybe, except as a step. For absolutely nothing was done by any class of teachers to improve the physical condition of the poor. No pains were taken to assist them in turning their limited knowledge, or rather their means of knowledge, to the best account. Religious tracts were given to them in abundance, but nothing else. In all other respects, what they should learn by means of reading was left to chance. Even had it been otherwise, if the greatest pains had been taken to put useful knowledge in their way, how should they have profited by the boon? they who were condemned to incessant toil and severe physical want. They learned, consequently, little more than what the antijacobins had foreseen that they would learn, to be thoroughly discontented with their lot, and to believe that their misery was owing to bad government. This faith may be true or erroneous: it took root firmly in the minds of the English working class; and from that time forward the physical force of the nation was at enmity with the constitution.

Having stated why and how the English became disposed to alter their constitution, I proceed to describe the manner of the change.

The admirers of the old constitution say, that it had a peculiar knack of adapting itself to new circumstances; the pliability, the elasticity of the constitution, they call this alleged virtue. Probably the constitution had become stiff from age; but at all events, it did not adapt itself to the new opinions with respect to it, which having sprung up with the French revolution, were checked by the war with revolutionary France, and have grown steadily and rapidly ever since the battle of Waterloo. Those who managed the constitution obstinately resisted every proposal for altering the venerable machine. But from the moment when a good many people thought of changing the constitution, it no longer worked pleasantly. Instead of only two factions struggling for the management of the constitution, which both factions revered, there arose a third faction, bent on overturning tories, whigs, constitution, and all. For many years the reform party was divided into three parties; first, those who attacked the constitution itself; secondly, those who attacked the power which worked the constitution; thirdly, those who attacked both the constitution and the power. The first class, nicknamed Radicals, consisted, for the most part, of work-people in the towns, and was by far the most numerous; the second class, called Liberals, was composed principally of clever men, belonging to the ruling class, and warmly attached to the constitution, but who, lending an ear to the public outcry against jobs and monopolies, thought that they could stretch the constitution to the length of their liberal opinions without even altering its shape; the third class, self-called Utilitarians, comprising, when that name was first heard, not so many perhaps as five hundred individuals, were content to speculate, to reason in the abstract, on all questions of government, taking care, however, that their speculations should be published. It would be hard to say which of these classes of reformers was most dangerous to the constitution. The radicals, very numerous and always contemplating the use of physical force, were highly dangerous ; for though they were kept down by the physical force of the government, many an accident might any day have given them the advantage. It seems well to observe here, that ever since the poor of England were taught to read, the English have found a standing army absolutely necessary. The liberals were very dangerous, because, not conscious themselves, nor suspected by others, of intending any harm to the constitution, they grubbed at its foundation, blind and unseen, like moles. And the utilitarians were not less dangerous ; for by exposing the fiction of three equal powers, balance, and harmony, the injustice of dear laws, the uselessness of privileges, the iniquity of jobs, and the follies of monopolies, they took the very best method of bringing the constitution into contempt. But whichever of these three classes of reformers was most dangerous to the constitution, no sooner did the whole body of reformers acquire some importance, than there occurred a confusion of parties among the ruling class such as may never perhaps be thoroughly understood. Old whigs now leaned to toryism ; young tories to liberalism ; along with the remainder of the whigs, who happened to be out at the time ; while some whigs declared for parliamentary reform, and a portion of the tories took the title of conservatives, meaning that they would defend the old constitution in all its parts against all its enemies. In short, public opinion forced a new question into the House of Commons : it was no longer which shall be in, the whigs or the tories ? but shall the constitution be altered or shall it be preserved ? From that moment the constitution could not work well ; it was in fact altered, or had begun to break in pieces. Nothing could have saved it but such a war as had saved it before.

At length unconstitutional opinions gained a majority of the House of Commons; and the fact was made known when that house, on the death of Lord Liverpool, chose that George Canning should become prime minister. Canning, who had been devoted to the constitution, was now a liberal. His appointment was received with shouts of applause by all classes of reformers, while the conservatives groaned in

fear and anger.   Still, as yet, the government had performed
no act in accordance with the new opinions of the nation.
Canning, who well understood his mission, began by some
liberal measures with respect to foreign countries ; but the
conservatives were not blind to this mode, however indirect,
of attacking their beloved constitution : they fell upon Canning and killed him.   Then came the Goderich ministry,
mixed and liberal, like that of Canning, but wanting an able
chief to keep together its heterogeneous materials : for
want of a better, it lasted some months, but disjointed and
despised ; and was then broken up, partly by the intrigues
of the conservatives, and still more by its own cowardice
and stupidity.   One fine morning, the prime minister was
not to be found ; when the king, surprised no doubt at the
strange working of the constitution, charged his friend,
Arthur Duke of Wellington, to form a ministry.   Many
supposed that the constitution was saved.

By habit, and perhaps by instinct, Wellington was a pure
conservative.   He had been used to power, he delighted in
power, and valued the constitution as it gave power to a
few over the many ; but that a mere soldier, so ignorant
and even illiterate, should have understood the nature of
that most complex machine, it is very difficult to believe.
At all events, he humoured the liberal House of Commons,
by taking some liberal colleagues, and soon struck the constitution a mortal blow.

By that constitution, no aboriginal Irishman, that is,
Catholic, could become a member of the House of Commons.
A vacancy having taken place in the representation, as it
was called, of an Irish county, the aborigines of that
county met, and in defiance of the law elected a native
Irishman.   What was to be done?   Thirty years sooner,
the armed Protestants, that is colonists, of Ireland, aided by
an English army, would have settled the question in double
quick time ; and Wellington, an Irish colonist, a soldier who
had once governed the native Irish on the spot, would have
been the man of all others to put down such a rebellion by
force of arms.   The Irish, who as a people, seem deficient
in courage, would probably have submitted to force, as they
had often submitted before to a handful of English soldiers ;
but this time there was something to manage in England ;
a thing that never was managed by force.   Public opinion,
acting on the House of Commons, had disposed that assembly, as any corporal might see, to sympathize with the Irish
rebels.   The temper of the House of Commons putting a
massacre of the Irish out of question, there remained for

Wellington only a choice of evils; on the one side, concession to rebels and a repeal of the law which excluded
Catholics from parliament, with a certainty that that great
monopoly-job, the English church establishment in Ireland
would be next destroyed ; on the other side, resignation,
loss of power, with the certainty that some other minister
would ere long carry a Catholic relief bill. Wellington
decided like a brave and ambitious man, as he is. All at
once he became more popular than Canning had ever been.
Himself had declared shortly before, that he must be mad
to think of being prime minister. To what special in-
capacity he referred we cannot tell: though all, save the
conservatives, agreed with him at the time, he now became,
except with the conservatives, the most humane, the most
liberal, the wisest of men. The conservatives had looked
to him for saving the constitution. When, therefore, he led
so outrageous an attack upon it, they were ready to devour
him ; but they could not break his heart, which is rather
hard, as they, aided by him, had broken poor Canning's,
which was of a fine texture. Nay, he converted the greater
part of them to his own views by saying—Support me, or
resign; and as for the remainder, they were so few that he
thought he might safely despise them : a mistake, as it
turned out.

However, a relief bill was passed, large, complete, not
open to an objection from the revolutionists, except as it excluded from parliament, for one year, that popular Irishman,
whom the natives had elected against law. This personal
clause, being attributed to the spite of an underling, a violent
anti-catholic, who had supported the bill to keep his place ;
mean as this clause was, it did not detract from Wellington's
popularity. Humane, liberal, wise, when he proposed the
bill, he was now the greatest statesman of his age or any
age ; he had won a civic crown more durable than his
martial laurels ; his name would go down to posterity as
one of the greatest benefactors of his country and mankind.
These are some of the terms in which his grace was
thanked for his part in the first obvious blow given to the
old English constitution.

Revolutions are terrible, but in one point of view seem
better than great political changes conducted without
violence. After a revolution comes peace ; after a great
peaceful change comes, very often, revolution. The leaders
in great but peaceful political changes are, commonly, unwilling actors, who act from necessity, all their opinions

remaining unchanged ; who yield this, merely to preserve that ; and who, therefore, proceed without regard to consequences ; as if the single concession were to be a final measure, were to have no consequences. It was just so with those who managed the repeal of the Irish slave-code.

A breathing time followed that act ; a pause, during which England was governed, not by a constitution, but by the individual Duke of Wellington. If his grace had not been blinded by his flatterers, he would have seen from the popularity of the once hated Canning, from his own popularity, and above all, from the confidence which the nation reposed in him, the resolute, slashing reformer ; from all this, I say, he would have perceived the absolute necessity of moving on with the work of reform. The reformers, giving the field-marshal credit for common discernment, believed that he would move on, and thought it wise to let him alone; the House of Commons appeared to have abandoned its functions to a dictator ; some of the conservatives merely sulked ; and some, not knowing what to do, called out, for what ? for a reform of the House of Commons.*

Rulers and nations have often deceived each other, but never so completely as the English people deceived Wellington, and Wellington deceived the English people, for some time after the passing of the relief bill. Wellington thought that the people were entirely satisfied with what had been done ; and the people doubted not that Wellington was hatching some grand plot against the constitution. An accident suddenly opened the eyes of both parties.

At the end of 1830, the French constitution, which had never worked well, stopped entirely for a few days. The French king and the citizens of Paris came to blows; the king being beaten, was driven away ; his cousin, after giving some faithless promises to alter the constitution, was appointed king ; and then the constitution of Waterloo, slightly altered, creaked on as before.

The new French king, and the French whigs, call this a glorious revolution; but it did not occupy a fortnight, and it ended in no greater change than would have happened if the old king had died in his bed without male issue. On the face of it, therefore, one can see nothing that should have produced a great sensation in England ; still less

* An article in the Quarterly Review, published just *before* the expulsion of Charles X., and when the question of reform in parliament seemed to possess no interest for Englishmen, exposed very ably some of the greatest defects of the House of Commons, as a legislative assembly.

such violent political excitement as actually occurred.   As respects England, what new political principles were brought to light by the Parisian "three days?"   The right of resistance to tyrants? no, for that principle was acknowledged, nay consecrated, by the oligarchy of borough-mongers.   The right of tax payers to vote taxes, which was the principle of the American revolution? by no means.

The right to be without a government, which seems to have been the principle of the first French revolution? certainly not; for the Parisian workmen who expelled Charles X., fought in the name of the Waterloo charter.   Well, then, why after the Parisian three days were the workpeople of the English towns so deeply agitated?   Why did the ruling class exhibit so much terror?   Why did nineteen-twentieths of the press demand, all of a sudden, an immediate and effectual reform of the House of Commons?   Why did Mr. Brougham declare that he had prepared a plan of reform in parliament; he who had not mentioned the subject for years, except to deride the radical reformers?   Why was he elected member for Yorkshire?   Why was Mr. Hunt elected for Preston, spite of the house of Stanley, in their own borough?   Why was parliament, which for years had scarcely received a petition for reform, now overwhelmed with such petitions?   Why did Wellington utter his famous eulogy of rotten boroughs?   Why did he, the popular dictator, resign in dudgeon, if not in a fright?   Why did Wellington and the conservatives make up their quarrel?   What brought the whigs, the proud, careless, lazy, and suspected whigs into office?   And why did those whigs introduce a bill of reform, which was to cut through the stem of the constitution?   A single word answers all these questions,—barricades!   The principle of the poor dupes who conquered at Paris, was attachment to a constitution, which gives all the powers of government to less than two hundred thousand persons out of thirty-two millions; but then the three days of Paris made, and made known, this very important discovery,—that there is a way by which the populace of a large town may beat the best of soldiers.   Not one gentleman took part with the populace of Paris: a general, since a minister, and still a favourite of the new king, being asked to lead them, said,—pooh! the rabble, the *canaille!*   Such was the opinion of military men, of all men, concerning the relative force of mobs and household troops.   All at once, opinion as to this matter ran into the other extreme.   In England, cannon balls became as

nothing compared with pavement stones ; strapping guards-
men looked like dwarfs, and the smallest artisan was a
giant. This new faith produced the most general and
violent agitation ever known in England, without bloodshed. The workmen of the towns used to shake hands
when they met in public, though they had parted not an
hour before, and expected to meet again during the day ;
and then, when one of their leaders did but talk of workmen at Paris, tears ran down their unwashed cheeks, and
they shook hands again, this time with an earnest grasp.
The work-people in the country, not so well informed on
foreign affairs, and more secret in their ways, appeared
gloomy and savage. All the other classes, nobility, clergy,
gentry, placeholders, stockholders, manufacturers, merchants, and tradesmen, were disturbed by one of two extreme sentiments ; either fear amounting to terror, or hope
equal to joy. Such of them as admired the constitution
turned pale when you mentioned barricades, and used to
skulk about with downcast looks, as if some great misfor-
tune had befallen them. The others, if whigs, were in high
spirits ; that is, certain of coming in ; and, if downright
enemies of the constitution, of rotten boroughs, privileges,
dear law, jobs, and monopolies ; these, I say, never met but
with sparkling eyes, to laugh and brag over the prospect.

The effects of a given power may be small or great, according to the susceptibility of the matter on which the
power acts. The discovery of barricades could not have
affected the whole English nation so deeply, or perhaps at
all, if that nation had been contented with its political institutions. The physical discovery of the Parisians led to
this great political discovery in England ; that the nation
had outgrown its laws. What followed might have been
foretold, nay, as to its main features, was foretold, by careful
observers.

The rural paupers, the serfs of England, rebelled ; and
the farmers, who down to that time had been reckoned
warm friends of the constitution, notwithstanding their distress, appeared to sympathize with the rebels. Thus about
a third of England was more or less in a state of insurrection, without any physical means of restoring order.
While fires were blazing and mobs exacting higher wages
in the country, a new king met a new parliament ; and
Wellington, the popular dictator, the wisest of statesmen,
wisely seized that opportunity to declare solemnly in favour
of the most perfect constitution ever framed by the ingenu-

ity of man. In one day all the duke's popularity was gone.
The most humane, liberal, clear-sighted of men, the greatest statesman, the benefactor of his country and mankind,
became, all in one day, observe, hard-hearted, narrow-
minded, wooden-headed, every thing worthless.   The sud-
denness of Wellington's fall in the public esteem shows the
extent to which he had deceived the nation, and they him.

While the shout of execration was at its height, the day
arrived when the king and his ministers had engaged to
dine at Guildhall with the citizens of London. Wellington
advised the king not to attend the feast. As the king was
very popular at the time; and popular, be it said in passing,
because his bearing towards the populace presented a
striking contrast with the haughty reserve of his late bro-
ther; this being the case, it was supposed by some, that
Wellington's advice to the king had been dictated by personal fear.   This charge, brought against one who probably never was afraid, is not worth refuting.   Why then
make the populace believe that the government was afraid
of them ? Because the government was afraid of the populace; not the ministers on account of their own persons, but
every member of the government on account of the constitution; terrified at the thoughts of barricades.   Would
the presence of ministers in the city have raised barricades ?
There was great risk of it, to say the least; and if barricades had been raised, who shall tell where the insurrection would have stopped ? Considering the inflamed state of
the peasantry, and of the workmen in the towns throughout
England and Scotland; considering, further, the extremely
artificial state of English society, the great number of
people who live from hand to mouth by pursuits not agricultural, the influence of confidence and credit in feeding
those people, and the crash that would have followed if any
thing had occurred to disturb seriously the ordinary course
of industry and trade ; bearing all this in mind, we shall
conclude, that Wellington acted prudently in avoiding the
city feast.   Still the breach of the king's engagement with
the citizens was treated as a great popular triumph, which
indeed it was; and Wellington, who till then had been
feared as much as hated, was now despised. I do not give
too much importance to the failure of a city feast.   In the
progress of revolutions, great events seem to hinge upon
trifles.   Some aldermen missed a dinner; but this was the
first time when the friends of the old English constitution
showed any fear of its enemies.

The dinner things were hardly removed from Guildhall, when the House of Commons objected to the new civil list, which Wellington proposed for the new king. Owing to the confusion of parties which had now taken place, about fifty conservatives voted against the duke and the constitution: *Quos Deos vult perdere prius dementat.* They would have voted for reform of parliament the next day, when Mr. Brougham, moved by the barricades of Paris, was to have brought forward a plan for mending the constitution ; but Wellington resigned, Mr. Brougham's motion fell to the ground, and the whigs came in, giving three great pledges to the nation. They promised, first, to maintain peace ; which, as there was no war, nor prospect of war, meant that they would not get up a war to divert the nation from its purpose of reform : secondly, they promised retrenchment, that is, to diminish the power which had moved the constitution ; and thirdly, a full and effectual reform of the House of Commons, meaning a great change in the constitution itself.

The people were overjoyed, but not disposed to confide implicitly in the whigs, who had often deceived the people, and who, as members of the aristocracy, were suspected of a strong attachment to the oligarchy of boroughmongers. The people, therefore, formed themselves into societies for promoting reform, and, partly by petitions, but still more by means of the press, told ministers what the nation understood by "full and effectual." Above all, they threatened openly, in so many words, that if the whigs should offer them a mock reform, they would take a revolution. At length, on the memorable 1st of March, 1831, the whig cabinet produced their bill, themselves alone being aware of its contents until it was laid before the House of Commons.

An abstract of the whig bill would not describe it so well as an account of its reception by the three great parties which then divided the country.

The conservatives, including those who had quarrelled with Wellington on account of Catholic relief, were delighted with the bill : they chuckled, and laughed, and clapped their hands. Was there ever, said they, any thing so extravagant ? The whigs must be mad. Thank God, they had gone far enough. Such a bill ! revolutionary was too good an epithet for it. So ridiculous, so preposterous a bill would not be read a first time. The whigs must resign ; they had cut their throats ; nothing could be better.

The feeling of the moderate reformers was expressed by one of the richest men in England, a whig, but leaning to utilitarian opinions.* He declared in the House of Commons, that the bill took away his breath. Perhaps he was affected, not so much by the bill itself, as by the evidence which the introduction of such a bill by the cabinet furnished, of the force of the popular will.

The decided enemies of the constitution having carefully examined the bill, said—It is a good first step; pass it, pass it !

In a week there were but two parties ; enemies of the bill or anti-reformers, and friends of the bill or reformers. The conservatives made up all their quarrels, seeking only to throw out the bill : the whigs and reformers forgot all their differences, bent only on passing the bill. But, what is more remarkable, the conservatives now called themselves reformers, and the reformers swore that they were conservatives.

The House of Commons, thinking with the conservatives that the whigs had indeed gone too far, would not pass the bill. The press, representing the nation, stormed for a general election, and the whigs dissolved parliament. In the general election, the conservatives were signally defeated. In vain did they, by pointing out that the bill would disfranchise many poor men, try to enlist the physical force on their side ; in vain did they declare for reform generally, pressing their hands on their hearts and vowing that they had never been friendly to abuses ; in vain also did they put forward images of revolution, confiscation, and bloodshed : it was all in vain ; they were beaten, wherever it was possible, by means of unions, subscriptions, the king's name, brickbats, and a single pledge,—" the bill, the whole bill, and nothing but the bill."

Parliament was already reformed. The new House of Commons would have passed the bill in a month, if the whigs had proposed such a course. In that case, probably, the lords would have wanted courage to reject the bill, and the constitution might have appeared to reform itself. But the whigs, deliberately as it seems, managed matters so that the bill was eventually carried by physical force. By encouraging opposition to the bill in the commons, by carefully promoting discussion and delay, the whigs restored the habitual insolence of the conservatives, who had been subdued by

* Mr. John Smith, the banker, of London.

the general election; and, when the bill found its weary way into the lords, everybody, the whigs alone excepted, knew that their lordships would reject it.

There was yet a way of passing the bill constitutionally; that is, by a creation of peers. Such a measure might even have revived a belief in the beautiful harmony of the constitution. But the whigs seem to have been bent on giving importance to the physical force. Though all who wished the inevitable revolution to take place without violence, implored the whigs to create peers, they pursued their wilful way; and the lords rejected the bill.

If the whigs, afraid of their own bill, imagined that its rejection by the lords would enable them to satisfy the people with a less effectual reform, they were soon undeceived. The reformers now put forward images of revolution, confiscation, and bloodshed; political unions were formed in London and the agricultural districts, where hitherto they had not been thought of; the expediency, rather than the lawfulness of refusing to pay taxes, was now openly discussed at public meetings and by the press; and the blindest might see that the people were about to take the question of reform into their own hands. The whigs, however blind, saw this, and promised that the bill should pass unaltered. No one doubted that they had made up their minds to create peers; and the fury of the people subsided.

As the rejected bill could not be brought forward again in the same session, parliament was prorogued and reassembled. This time, a week might have sufficed for passing the bill in the commons. The whigs thought fit to discuss it all over again with the conservatives; and this farce, from which the people turned in disgust, lasted near half a year. Still no peers were created; and at length suspicion began to fall upon the king, who till now had been the most popular of English monarchs.

Once more the bill was taken to the lords, who boldly declared that they would not pass it. Make peers! peers or a revolution! was now the cry all over England, Scotland, and Ireland. Some whigs hurried to Windsor and advised the king to make peers. His majesty, who, there seems no doubt, would have said, yes, if the proposal had been made six months earlier, was pleased, in his royal wisdom, to say, no. The whigs, who were never wanting in pride, resigned; and Field-marshal the Duke of Wellington became once more, in name at least, prime-minister of England.

The conservatives now thought to govern England by the sword. For ten days England was governed by newspapers and political unions. It was not an interregnum, as some have said, but a good strong government, orderly too, and, like that of the United States, a government which gave immediate effect to the public will. How the king, the lords, the new minister, and the ex-ministry settled the matter among them, has never been told; but after the political unions and newspapers had governed vigorously for ten days, the whigs got in again, and the lords, civilly, humbly, in haste and without even a wry face, passed the whole bill. In one word, the new constitution of England was obtained by physical force. The conservatives said it should be so; and so it was.

I have dwelt so long on the manner of the late change in the English constitution, because it appears more important with a view to the future than the change itself. But, though the change itself, if it were to be judged by the elections which have taken place according to the reform bill, would not appear very important; though it would appear trifling if estimated by the paltry reforms of abuses which have thus far resulted from it; still it has, to all intents and purposes, produced a new constitution, as will be seen in the long run. Some of those to whom the reform bill gives the right of voting for members of parliament, were prevented by a trick* from exercising their franchise; others were deterred from voting by the fear of offending their landlords and rich customers; these two classes together being so numerous, that fewer persons, it is believed, voted at the late election than at the last election of an unreformed parliament. Some again, and not a few, were induced by bribery or intimidation to vote for conservative candidates, while many would have voted for better candidates, if better there had been. In fact, the late general election took place when the nation, fatigued with two years of violent excitement, was in a state of exhaustion. But, though the result of that election be a House of Commons which does not appear to differ materially from the houses that were got together under the old constitution, still there can be no doubt, that a majority of

* By fixing so early a day for the payment of taxes already due, such payment being one qualification for voting, that many electors were taken by surprise, and missed the right of voting at the next general election.

its members are responsible to their constituents, or that they will be made to feel their responsibility ; whether at the next general election or sooner is not a very important question, considering the certainty almost of a general election within three or four years. But at all events, whenever the class to which the reform bill gives the right of voting for members of parliament shall choose to exert themselves, they will direct the government of England. The constitution is changed, howsoever little evidence of the change may be furnished by the composition, or the acts, of the first reformed parliament. The present, then, is worth but little attention when compared with the future. Those who, taking the narrowest view of affairs, treat the present as if there were neither a past nor a future, may be pleased or dissatisfied with things as they are ; but the prospects of the English as a nation will not be discovered by discussing present party politics. Let us, therefore, having looked back, now look forward ; steadily, without affection or fear, so as to form just opinions on a subject in which are interested, not the English alone, but also the French, the Germans, the Poles, trampled on and scattered ; every one, of whatever country, who rejoices in the progress of civilization, every friend of liberty in the world, every miserable slave if he did but know it, and all the oppressors, as they may learn too late.

The new constitution is neither an oligarchy nor a democracy. In what then is to consist the force of the government ?

An oligarchy may be maintained either by soldiers or corruption. Soldiers are out of the case in England ; for with no other force to maintain the government, hundreds of thousands would be required, while it is hardly doubtful that, ere long, those who can, when they please, direct the government, will insist on a diminution of the army. And, as to corruption, it is easy to see, first, that the jobs and monopolies which were insufficient to preserve the old constitution, would, if maintained, be entirely thrown away upon the much greater number who can now vote for members of parliament ; secondly, that the new government of the uneasy class will lose no time in cutting away jobs and monopolies. The whig ministry lately declared, that the government of England should no longer be carried on by patronage : they will be made to keep their word, sooner or later.

A democracy requires neither guards nor corruption,

being supported by the affection of the whole people.   But the new constitution excludes from legislative power a great majority of the people, the whole body, we may say, of the working classes : it must want the force which maintains a democracy.

Thus, on the most general grounds, we may conclude, that the new constitution will not last ; but let us come to particulars.

By the new constitution, instead of three, there are but two orders in the state.   Power has been taken from what was the highest class, and the mockery of power from what was the lowest class.   We must now speak only of two orders, the higher and the lower, the rulers and the governed.

Who formed this mongrel government ?   Who bestowed the power of legislation upon too many for an oligarchy, too few for a democracy ?   Was it the class who now, on paper at least, are omnipotent ?   Certainly not.   Could they have extorted the new charter, unaided by those whom it does not acknowledge ?   Certainly not.   The reform bill was carried by physical force ; and those who compose the physical force know this, are proud of it, boast of it, and will never forget it.   Did they approve of the bill ?   As a step, yes ; but merely as a step, declaring that they had rather no bill than this bill, if it were to be a final measure. Universal suffrage, was, is, and will be the object of the working classes.   Assemble a body of them, and say—Is a pauper, an ignorant, hungry, gloomy slave, qualified to choose who shall make the laws ?   No, they will answer ; but with universal suffrage the law-makers will take care that there be no paupers: universal suffrage we consider a security, the only security, for universal ease, instruction, and content.   But, good people, with universal suffrage, you, the working class, who form so great a majority, would be the only class represented in parliament ; you would make laws for the sake of your class alone, laws not good, perhaps bad, for the other classes.—They reply: That is the very point : your objection to universal suffrage is our objection to a limited suffrage : the higher class, we fear, will make laws for the sake of themselves alone, laws not good, perhaps bad, for us.   Besides, we are told continually by the classes above us, that what is good for them must be good for us : we think so ; and therefore, say we, let all vote for the good of all.   Are we ignorant ? instruct us: discontented ? mend our condition : dishonest,

you say ? give us rights and enjoyments to value. Universal suffrage, we believe, will do all this; but at any rate, we,
who know our strength, are resolved to try the experiment.

Such is the feeling of the working classes. Will the
middle or uneasy class attempt to preserve their monopoly
of power ? Not without great dishonesty ; for they owe
their charter to the working class, who won it for them on
a complete understanding, that it should be a step, and nothing but a step, in reform. The physical force, exhausted
by three years of excitement, has not yet asked for an ex-
tention of the suffrage. Until this demand shall be made,
nothing may happen to disturb the subsisting union between the middle and the working classes ; but when the
demand shall be made, if it be resisted, if the petitions of the
majority be met by counter-petitions from the select few,
then must a violent quarrel take place between the two
classes. Traitors and knaves would be the merited terms
bestowed on the minority. But minorities, when power is
in question, are deaf to the voice of reproach. If the new
constituency should have nothing to fear except bad names,
they would not, probably, compel their representatives to
extend the franchise ; but we shall readily perceive, that
the majority have a better assurance of good faith in the
minority, than the right to call them traitors and knaves.

The rulers and the governed will no longer be separated
by an intervening class. Except in political power, the
less rich of the ruling order are on a level with the less
poor of the subject order. None of the circumstances can
exist, which formerly placed the physical force at the disposal of those who made the laws. A daily and familiar
intercourse must take place between the two orders ; and
whatever the inferior order may suffer, they will attribute
to the selfishness or malice of the others. In the next place,
the property and persons of the new ruling order are at
the mercy of the new subject order. Not that the position
of the poorest class, as to the persons and property of the
other classes, is changed, but the poorest class may now
have a motive for attacking persons and property which
were always at their mercy. By the old constitution,
power was given to individual wealth; by the new one, the
aggregate of wealth will be represented. Instead of one
very rich man possessing great power, fifty persons of
moderate wealth will possess some power. Now the person and property of a great boroughmonger were not en-
dangered by any sudden anger of the poor towards him;

but a farmer, a manufacturer, a dealer of whatever kind almost, to whom the new charter gives the suffrage, must live by day and night in the midst of the excluded, and his property must at all times be subject to attacks from them. It is well known that the richer class of people at Preston would have returned the heir of the house of Stanley at the election of 1830, rather than that very ignorant and foolish demagogue Mr. Hunt, if they had not been afraid of the populace : they were afraid that their factories would be burned if they should take part against the popular candidate.   In 1830, just after the three days of Paris, the higher order at Preston had a foretaste of what the elective bodies of all such towns may expect, whenever the lower order shall be in a state of excitement.   That the voters for county members should be affected in the same way, seems probable, when one reflects that in a good part of the south of England wages have been raised and kept up by means of stack burning.

If it were to come to a trial of strength between the two parties in open warfare (which God forbid !), the result must inevitably be favourable to the great majority.   Retrenchment, which among other things means fewer soldiers, is one of the great objects of the new ruling class. Besides, the education, as some call it, of the poor, has had this good effect,—that soldiers, though taken from the most degraded class, have now some feeling for other people, as well as some political notions, among which is a suspicion that, in time, perhaps, officers may be taken from the ranks. Already the new parliament has declared, in opposition to the whig cabinet, against the flogging of soldiers.   Without flogging, degraded men cannot be made to observe military discipline ; and with the end of flogging, therefore, must come a better selection of men for soldiers.   Thus, as the moral character of the soldiers shall improve, as they shall learn to respect themselves, they will learn also to respect others ; and it will become more and more difficult to employ them in keeping down the bulk of the people.   A national guard has been talked of for the protection of the new ruling order ; but a national guard, from which the hardy poor were excluded, would be, as anti-jacobin Windham said to the armed shopkeepers forty years ago, a great depository of panic.   Moreover, there is the discovery of barricades ; on which, however, I for one set less value than most people, except as it will maintain the confidence of the poorer order in their own strength.

But a trial of strength between the two orders is highly improbable. The proceedings by which the reform bill was carried show that the government of England is liable to dictation from the physical force, whenever that force chooses to exert itself. I say England, because the liability in question depends on a state of political economy which is peculiar to England. In no country does so large a proportion of the people live from hand to mouth by pursuits not agricultural. In America, in Ireland, in any of the states of Europe, except Holland perhaps, a pretty general insurrection of the poorer class might take place, and might even last some time, without producing very serious consequences. Supposing it to produce a temporary stagnation, or even a stoppage, of credit and business, still most of the people would have food at hand, while the remainder, being few in proportion to the producers of food, might be victualled without much difficulty. But in England, where the proportion of rural population is so small, where such great masses of the people are congregated out of the way of obtaining food, save by the regular course of industry, and where, by reason of the most comprehensive combination of power and the most minute distribution of employments, the regular course of industry depends so much upon confidence and credit; there, I say, any social convulsion, if it should last but a week, must produce a series of convulsions, one more violent than the other. Stop, for but three days, the course of credit, trade, and industry which feeds the population of the great towns in England, and in three days more that population would be frantic: it is needless to dwell on the consequences. But how easily, does it appear, might such a stoppage occur, when one reflects on the sensitive nature of credit, on the misery and discontent of the poorer order, on their common object, and, above all, on their just apprehension of the means by which the new constitution was torn from the old oligarchy. During the interregnum, as it is called, of 1831, the walls of London, Manchester, Birmingham, and other great towns, were placarded in these words—"To stop the duke, go for gold." The people, by means of their savings' banks, did go for gold to the Bank of England; and so did help, at least, to stop the duke. Some of his friends, selfish madmen, who thought their own property in land secure at all events, and some tory underlings whose obscurity was a kind of protection to them, would have braved this attack upon credit; but the new ruling order, whose daily bread rests upon industry, trade, and credit, to whom the right of voting is as nothing when compared with peace and order, will never, we may believe, provoke a serious disturbance.

From all these considerations, only one conclusion can be drawn ; namely, that the new aristocracy have no existence but on paper ; that if gratitude, and a sense of honour, should not impel them to extend the suffrage, if they should be deaf to reproach and to such reasoning as is here presented to them, they must yield, nevertheless, to force or fear, sooner or later.

Let us suppose the new ruling class wise in time ; that having wrested power from an oligarchy by means of the physical force, they admit all men to an equal share in the power of making laws.   That would be a pure democracy. In a democracy, the laws are made by the greatest number. In England, the greatest number consists of labourers, poor, discontented, and ignorant.   The laws of England, then, would be made for the supposed advantage of the poor. To a very poor man, whose sole property was his labour, who by constant labour was able to earn not more than enough to support a miserable existence, whose only prospect was want in his old age and a career of wretchedness for his children ; to a man in this condition, laws, which should cause a revolution of property, would appear the best. Generous minds, full of sympathy for the miserable, and a love of equality, may be blind to this conclusion ; others, bigoted in attachment to democracy, may deny its truth, which, however, is plain to those who think as well as feel, and think without prejudice.   Even now, some disposition is shown, ay, even by the intelligent but uneasy class, to make laws which would be most unjust to the owners of some kinds of property.   I allude to the proposed depreciation of money, which, in proportion to its extent, would diminish the receipts of those who are entitled to fixed payments.   But if uneasiness put such notions into the heads of the new ruling order, what may be expected from the misery of those who would govern under the future democracy ? The question is answered by reference to arguments used in support of the plan for depreciating the value of money. " A great robbery," say the advocates of depreciation, " was committed thirteen years ago by the vile boroughmongers, who, by raising the value of money, enabled all creditors to exact from their debtors more than was due : we now propose an act of justice, by returning to the standard in which so many contracts were made, in which, above all, great part of the national debt was incurred; but not of complete justice, since this measure will not give back to its rightful owners that which has been wrongfully taken from them during thirteen years." Unquestionably, during thirteen years, many receivers of fixed payments have obtained more, and a great deal more, than they ever contracted to receive; but during the thirteen years, many new contracts have been made; and if the value of money were now restored to the old standard, the creditors under these new contracts would be cheated, just as debtors were cheated before. To repair one great robbery, therefore, another great robbery is proposed. That the robbery which has been perpetrated was the work of the "vile boroughmongers" may be true; but see to what this argument leads. "Every work of plunder performed by the vile borough-mongers is liable to be overhauled;" say you so? Then what becomes of the national debt? Was the capital, of which the interest is now paid by the nation, spent for the good of the nation? Was it not squandered, or rather cunningly laid out, for the preservation of boroughmonger-ing? Did the nation agree to replace that capital, or to pay thirty millions a year for ever? When that debt, miscalled national, was contracted, the nation had no voice in public affairs. It follows, that the nation is not bound to pay a debt which was incurred by a faction for anti-national purposes. Nay, further, if every arrangement of the boroughmongers is to be vitiated by proof of its injustice, to whom belong those great estates, which have been kept together by means of provisions out of the public purse, for daughters and younger sons? To the nation, which has paid for them over and over again, by salaries to those among whom they must otherwise have been divided. Once acknowledge the principle on which some of the uneasy class now propose to alter the value of money, and there would be no end of confiscation. But this principle, which "men of property and education," being uneasy, are not afraid to assert, would be all in all with a legislature moved by the wretched. Nor can one deny, having regard to nothing but the truth, that many of those who actually compose the poorer order in England, would gain immensely by spunging out the national debt, abolishing tythes, and converting all the great estates into national property, which should be sold piecemeal at the rate of twenty shillings per acre. The example of France is before us. At this time, indeed, the poorer order in France is very miserable ; but those who composed that order fifty years ago, the wild animals of Labruyère, were deeply indebted to confiscation ; and I have spoken here only of that portion of the English poor, who should obtain land, debt free and tythe free, for twenty shillings per acre.

But now turn to the other side of the picture. How many comfortable people must be made wretched by such a transfer of property as would make some of the wretched comfortable ! The general transfer of property from the rich to the poor, which took place in France, may have been consistent with the principle of utility, the greatest happiness of the greatest number ; but in the present social state of England, any large measure of confiscation would injure the majority. So barbarous was the state of industry in France half a century back, so many checks to production did the state of property occasion, that a general transfer of property, by removing those checks and by stimulating industry, led at once to an increase of production : property had changed hands, but the nation was richer than before. In England, on the contrary, where millions of people have, one may say, been called into existence by machinery, where capital does so much more than labour, where production has been carried so far, and depends so closely on the use of large masses of capital in combination, where the relations of industry are become so complicated and delicate ; here any legislative attack upon property would cause a decrease of production. If property were rendered insecure in England, capital, that it was possible to hoard, would be hoarded ; capital, that was not fixed, would be moved to other countries. That very skilful application of capital, that most productive application of labour, which enables less than one-third of the English people to raise food for the remainder, depends on security of property. The great steam-power of England would be next to annihilated, if property should become insecure. Thus, with respect to England, confiscation is synonymous with destruction. Make a scramble for property in England, and the best part of the thing to be scrambled for would disappear. One may imagine the result ; the scenes of contention and suffering, which must end in England's ruin ; which might make England a hunting field, or a place fit to receive convicts from America. But I pass on, with a hope that some other, having words at command, may describe the prospect as plainly as I own I see it. Who is there that does not see it, clearly or

vaguely ?   Why do we hear continually in England of apprehensions for the future, all the more serious for not being
exactly defined ?   And who, that will take the trouble to
think on this subject, but acknowledges the blackness of the
prospect ?

Still, fearful as is the prospect, great as the danger appears, there may be a way of escape.   The danger being
thoroughly understood, some means of averting it may be
discovered.   The English are not apt to despond.   In knowledge, judgment, and moral courage, they surpass all other
nations, according to my humble opinion.   But this occasion
will tax their best qualities to the uttermost.   In England,
it is no longer a speculation whether democracy be consistent with high civilization.   This is the experiment which
the English are about to try.   Who is there that does not
wish them success ?   If they should succeed, then all the
talk about the difference between old and new countries will
go for nothing, anywhere ; and, in time, the greatest hap-
.piness of all will be everywhere secured : if they should
fail, misery and vice will be deemed the natural lot of the
greatest part of mankind ; and the world, save as England
may suffer by the experiment, must go on as before.   A
single error may cause the failure of this great experiment.
It becomes, therefore, the duty of every man, who has re-
flected on the subject, to make known his view of the best
course of proceeding.

The misery and ignorance of the bulk of the English
people render them unfit to enjoy, or rather fit them to
abuse, a great extension of the suffrage.   If their circumstances were as easy as those of the working class in
America, they might be better instructed than American
workmen (whose solitary mode of life is very unfavourable
to learning), and therefore better qualified to take part in
choosing the legislature.   In that case, there would be no
objection to universal suffrage, every thing in its favour remaining as at present.

Admitting this, two practical questions arise.

First—Is it possible that arrangements should be made,
to render the English working class comfortable, satisfied,
and as wise, at least, as the working class in America?

Secondly—Is it possible that such arrangements should
be made in time ?   Or, in other words, may universal suffrage be postponed until such arrangements shall have produced the desired effect; that is, until the whole people

shall be qualified, by ease, content, and knowledge, to vote for members of parliament?

Let both of these questions be answered in the affirmative; and it will appear that democracy may be established in England without the least check to civilization, without the least injury to any, with the greatest benefit to all: decide either of these questions in the negative, and England becomes, first a field of battle, and then a waste, compared with the present.

The latter of these questions, though by much the less difficult to answer, takes precedence in the order of time. The subject class may presently demand universal suffrage; and they have the means either of enforcing their demand or of producing that convulsion to which universal suffrage may lead, if it should come too soon. Resistance, then, to the demand for universal suffrage might be the shortest and the worst way to universal suffrage. Which is the longest, and therefore the best way to the end of a journey that must, at all events, be performed either quickly or slowly? But, though delay, postponement be the object, there is not a year to lose. To hesitate about taking the long and the safe course, would be like a decision in favour of the short and dangerous one. This is why the means of postponing universal suffrage without serious disturbance, deserve to be considered before measures for rendering universal suffrage safe, if not desirable.

Admitting that a demand for universal suffrage would be irresistible if made in earnest, there appears but one way of postponing universal suffrage; namely, by preventing the demand for it. Force being out of the question, may not the bulk of the people be persuaded to abstain from demanding that, which, after a while, they might receive as a matter of course? Government, said lately a young whig nobleman when speaking of Ireland, must be feared in order to be loved. He meant, of course, in order to be obeyed; and the sentiment was not so monstrous, considering the ignorance, cowardice, and slavishness of the long oppressed people of Ireland. But the English have been "educated;" they are a brave, though not a martial race; and they are bent on moving onwards to democracy or ruin. Their government may fear them; but fear will not make them submit to their government. For the first time in Europe, the people must be guided, if at all, by persuasion and kindness. What these may effect is now the question.

The actors in this case must be a majority of the reformed House of Commons, as soon as that house shall truly represent property in the aggregate. Let us suppose the House of Commons so constituted, anxious to persuade, not force, the poorer orders to abstain from demanding universal suffrage. In that case, what would the house do? what would it leave undone? what would be its principle of action?

In that case, the representatives of the richer order would adopt this principle of action :—*Such legislation as must take place, if parliament had been chosen by universal suffrage, all the people being fit to exercise the right of voting.* Jeremy Bentham would have called it the postponement-of-universal-suffrage principle : its efficiency will be seen by noticing a few of its inevitable consequences.

1. Some radical member proposes, that buildings and other objects of curiosity, the property of the nation, should be open to the public without payment. How would the house decide?   Would they let the poor visit Westminster Abbey, St. Paul's, and the Tower? or would they, like former parliaments, vote for the " vested rights" of deans and door-keepers ?   According to the above principle, the decision would be in favour of a right which has long been withheld from the poor. If parliament had been elected by universal suffrage, all the electors being fit to choose representatives, a proposal to this effect would be adopted as soon as made. Such a measure, paltry as it might seem to " great statesmen," would go some way in persuading the poor to abstain from demanding universal suffrage.

2. Another radical observes, that the parks at the west end of London are very pleasant to the rich who live near them ; that the poor, who crowd the east end of London, would find a park in their neighbourhood very pleasant ; and that it would be easy to give them one, not an atom of enjoyment being taken from the rich. By a parliament in which all were represented, the proposal would be received with acclamations. And why not a park for the smoke-dried people of Manchester, who at present can breathe fresh air only by tramping up and down a dusty or muddy road ? Joseph Hume complains of the expense. · The abolition of a few sinecures would settle that point. If, however, public funds may not be diverted to public purposes, if no public money is to be spent for the comfort of any but the rich, then let the rich pay for universal suffrage : you would find it a dear bargain, Mr. Hume.

3. A third democratic conservative suggests, that the cost of postage for letters shall be defrayed by the government ; that the poor as well as the rich shall send and receive letters free of postage. What ! extend to all the

privilege of franking ? Yes ; and because, for one reason, you would destroy the privilege by extending it. In America, universal suffrage promises to establish universal freedom of postage ; and we are supposing the English parliament to legislate as if it had been elected by universal suffrage. But the frightful expense ! The Americans are not frightened at the expense ; but they have no great army to support ; nor would the English have to support a great army if the poorer order were gratified by such measures as this. Moreover, one might easily prove that a remission of taxes equal to the cost of this measure, would be far less advantageous to the public than this measure, however costly. But, at all events, as this measure would be approved by a parliament representing all, all being fit to be represented, so therefore would a parliament, chosen only by the richer order, approve of it, having regard to the postponement-of-universal-suffrage principle.

This principle is not new : it is eighteen hundred years old at least ; meaning, *do as you would be done by.* For proclaiming this principle, Christ was crucified, Paul striped, and Sidney beheaded. For neglecting this principle, England was punished by losing the affection of America, the French nobility by the loss of their estates, Charles Stuart and Louis Capet by the loss of their heads. Do, one might say to those who will soon direct the House of Commons, do unto the poorer class as you, being in their places, would have them, in your place, do unto you. Honestly, steadily, boldly abjuring deceit, hesitation, and fear, follow up this generous principle of legislation ; and the poorer order will wait for universal suffrage, though miserable for a time, still with patience.

Supposing the reformed House of Commons compelled to adopt this effectual method of postponing universal suffrage, yet they might be troubled in their course by a class of men, whose object seems to be mischief for mischief's sake. Troubled indeed, but not more than troubled, not checked, still less stopped. Even the mere annoyance would not last six months. By passing a few bills, such as a parliament elected by universal suffrage, content and instruction would surely pass, the reformed parliament would destroy that power to tease, to create trouble and mischief, which the feebleness and pride of a cabinet of lords has bestowed upon two classes, the ignorant demagogues and wild conservatives : harmless grumblers and broken jobbers they would be called, if, indeed, they were not utterly forgotten, after one year of genuine Christian legislation by the reformed House of Commons.

The question that remains is by far more difficult. May arrangements be made to qualify the bulk of the English people for choosing representatives in parliament ?

Volumes have been written to prove, that arrangements for that purpose could not have any permanent effect; and tons of books and pamphlets, reckoning but one copy of each, to suggest various measures for the cure of poverty and ignorance. Hitherto, those who contend that the greatest part of mankind is doomed by nature to misery and degradation, have had the best of the argument. It is not necessary on this occasion to interfere between these two parties. The question on which they dispute must be settled one day or other. Leaving it to be discussed in an English parliament, chosen by the whole people, the present object is to ascertain by what means the English poorer order may be qualified to take a part in that discussion. The present question, therefore, though more difficult than that which has been just examined, is a small practical question, when compared with that great abstract question which divides the Malthusians and their opponents : it relates only to one generation. Truly, if a way should be found to bestow comfort and knowledge upon one generation of the poorer class, that might be a step to the permanent cure of misery and vice ; but sufficient for the day is the evil thereof: the present difficulty is great enough, though trifling, it may be, when compared with the other. Let us then limit the question.

May arrangements be made to bestow comfort and knowledge on *one generation* of the English poorer class ?

Yes, without doubt, says a believer in the omnipotence of education ; increase the number of schools for the poor, and of mechancs' institutions; send teachers into the rural districts; take off the taxes on knowledge ; proceed—

Stop friend ; all this is supposed to have been done with a view to the postponement of universal suffrage.

He continues ; Then you suppose the poor taught, that their own comfort depends on themselves, that their well-being is in their own hands, that, by prudently keeping their numbers under the demand for their services, they may exact high wages,—

Stop again : All this is good, maybe necessary for the permanent well-being of the labouring class ; but the greatest imaginable prudence, though made universal to-morrow, would have no effect on wages for twenty years to come. Would you prudently get rid of children already born ? If not, you propose to teach prudence, the highest wisdom, to a miserable race, without leisure, over-worked, anxious, and discontented ; to make the cart drag the horse ; to produce a cause by means of its own effect. Prudence, wisdom is the end ; the means, high wages, leisure, peace of mind and instruction. A world of trouble has been wasted in the endeavour to instruct the wretched. You must begin at the beginning. Bestow ease on the working class, and then, indeed, you may teach them to dread the return of misery. The first step is to raise wages. "When we deliberate about the means of introducing intellectual and moral excellence into the minds of the principal portion of the people, one of the first things which we are bound to provide for is a generous and animating diet. The physical causes must go along with the moral ; and nature herself forbids that you should make a wise and virtuous people out of a starving one. Men must be happy themselves before they can rejoice in the happiness of others : they must have a certain vigour of mind before they can, in the midst of habitual suffering, resist a presented pleasure ; their own lives and means of well-being must be worth something, before they can value, so as to respect, the life or well-being of any other person. This or that individual may be an extraordinary individual, and exhibit mental excellence in the midst of wretchedness ; but a wretched and excellent people never yet has been seen on the face of the earth. Though far from fond of paradoxical expressions, we are tempted to say that a good diet is a necessary part of good education ; for in one very important sense, it is emphatically true. In the great body of the people, all education is impotent without it."*

The first step is to raise wages. But how shall wages be raised, except either by increasing the amount of employment, or by diminishing the number of labourers ? In no other way, beyond a doubt ; not by strikes at Manchester, nor by *Swing* fires in Kent ; not by spade husbandry, nor by paper money ; not by giving books to hungry paupers, half-starved weavers, and parish apprentices, nor by accumulating more capital, and wasting it on foreign loans and far off ruinous speculations ; but by increasing

* Art. Education, Supplement to the Encyclopædia Britannica, by James Mill, Esq.

the proportion which employment bears to labour. How to raise immediately the proportion which employment bears to labour, and to maintain the higher proportion for twenty years or so; this is the question on which, if I have taken a just view of the political prospects of the English, depends their existence as a wealthy and civilized nation.

Here I must refer to the note, in which I have sought to explain the coincidence in England of overflowing wealth with extensive uneasiness and wide-spread misery. In order to raise wages immediately, the field for the employment of English capital and labour must be enlarged; whereby profits, and the rewards of many services not called labour, would be raised at the same time as the wages of labour. The whole world is before you. Open new channels for the most productive employment of English capital. Let the English buy bread from every people that has bread to sell cheap. Make England, for all that is produced by steam, the work-shop of the world. If, after this, there be capital and people to spare, imitate the ancient Greeks; take a lesson from the Americans, who, as their capital and population increase, find room for both by means of colonization. You have abundance, superabundance of capital; provide profitable employment for it, and you will improve the condition of all classes at once. Instead of lending your surplus capital to foreign states, or wasting it in South American mines, whereby no additional employment is given to English labour, rather, like the Americans, invest it in colonization; so that, as it flies off, it may take with it, and employ a corresponding amount of surplus labour, if there be any. How this might be done, and how capital so invested might be recovered at pleasure, is stated elsewhere, but cannot be thoroughly understood by Englishmen till they shall learn the causes of certain peculiarities in the social condition of America. These, also, I have endeavoured to explain in some of the following notes. May the explanation assist to point out a way, by which the English shall escape from that corrupting and irritating state of political economy, which seems fit to precede the dissolution of empires!

NOTE VI.

FREE TRADE IN CORN, AS A MEANS OF ENLARGING THE FIELD OF EMPLOYMENT FOR ENGLISH CAPITAL AND LABOUR.

Subject of this note stated—Wide difference between facts in America and the English theory of rent—American theory of rent—Various kinds and degrees of competition for the use of land—Facts—Effects of a free corn trade on the several kinds of competition for the use of land—With cheap bread, the rental of England must be greater—Gradual repeal of the corn-laws hurtful, for a time, to landlords and farmers ; and not useful to any class of labourers—Sudden repeal of the corn-laws beneficial to all classes.

WITH respect to the foreign corn-trade of England, there is but one point left for examination. The risk of depending on foreigners for the staff of life, the wisdom of protecting domestic agriculture, the folly of importing corn from abroad when you can reap it on your own native soil, the injustice of allowing foreign farmers, who are lightly taxed, to compete in your own market with your own farmers, who are heavily taxed ; all these fallacies having been thoroughly exposed by English writers ; and the mischievous influence of the corn-laws in limiting the English field of production being felt, if not understood, by the new ruling order, no one doubts that the reform parliament, as soon as it shall truly represent the new class of voters, will establish a free trade in corn. But an important question remains ; whether the corn laws ought to be repealed suddenly or by degrees. Now the object of what follows is to show, and principally, by correcting an error into which English political economists have been led by their ignorance of America, that the repeal of the corn-laws, if gradual, would, for a time, be injurious to farmers and landlords, without being very useful to any class of labourers ; but if sudden, would be beneficial to all those classes, and to the landlords in particular.

That whatever is good for a portion of society must be good for all, is a general principle or rule ; and no one denies that the repeal of the English corn-laws would be good for some classes of Englishmen. On general grounds, therefore, it would follow, that a free trade in corn must be beneficial to all Englishmen. The fact may be at variance with this *prima facie* conclusion ; but if so, it forms an exception to the general rule ; and those who maintain the exception are bound to prove that it exists. Yet what has been the course pursued by the friends and enemies of the English corn-laws ? Both parties have taken for granted, and have built all their arguments on the bare assumption, that, in proportion as a free trade in corn must be beneficial to owners of capital and labour, it would be injurious to owners of land. As in stating that high wages must necessarily cause low profits, that the prosperity of the master depends on the misery of the workmen, so in this case, the English economists have taken pains to set different classes by the ears. The fifteenth edition of the celebrated *Catechism on the Corn Laws*, which contains all the common arguments for and against free trade in corn, begins thus : " For whose benefit are the corn-laws ?—*Manifestly*, of those who support them, the landlords." Those laws are, no doubt, intended for the benefit of the landlords ; but so close a reasoner as Colonel Thompson will admit, that between the intention and the fact there may be a wide difference. He concludes his very able work, as he begins it, by asserting that "the landlords are kept at the public expense." It may be so ; but where is the proof ? Take it for granted, most of the economists and landlords would answer. I venture to say, no : on the contrary, I notice the bare assertion, which you would substitute for proof, in order to show that an argument, having for object to establish that a free trade in corn would be good for the owners of land as well as for the owners of capital and labour, is not, upon the face of it, irrational.

The way in which, it is said, free trade in corn would injure the landlords, is by a diminution of their rents. The first step, therefore, in the inquiry, is to ascertain the nature of rent.

This point is already settled by the English economists. When, say they, the increase of capital and population leads to the cultivation of inferior land, people are willing to pay for the use of superior land. This payment, which is always equal to the difference between the greater and less natural productiveness of more and less fertile soils, constitutes rent. Other things, they add, enter into rent, vulgarly speaking, such as the interest which the tenant pays for the use of the landlord's capital fixed in buildings and improvements ; but, speaking philosophically, rent is a payment for leave to use land of superior natural fertility, and nothing else is rent.

According to this statement, we should have to deduct from the rental of England :—

1. The interest of hundreds of millions of capital, fixed on the land, and the property of those who own the land :—

2. All that is paid for the superior position of some land; that is, the greater vicinity to manure and a market.

3. All that is paid, over the payment for superior natural fertility, for accommodation land in the neighbourhood of towns and villages.

4. All that is paid for land used for purposes of pleasure and amusement, such as gardens and pleasure grounds, the tenants of which look, not to profit, but to gratification.

5. All that is paid for the use of land as building ground.

But it may be, that all these payments under the name of rent, amount to a great deal more than what is paid for the superior natural fertility of land. If so, rent, philosophically speaking, is but a small fraction of rent in the vulgar tongue.

The philosophical theory of rent is made to rest, by all the English economists, on a statement directly at variance with the truth ; namely, that little or no rent is ever paid in countries where the most fertile land may be obtained for a trifle in unlimited quantities. Before contradicting this statement, it will be well to show, by two examples out of hundreds, how emphatically it is made.

" So long," says Mr. Mill, " as a part only of the best land is required for cultivation, all that is uncultivated yields nothing; that is, nothing which has any value. It naturally, therefore, remains unappropriated, and any man may have it who undertakes to render it productive. During this time land, speaking correctly, yields no rent."[*]

" On the first settlement," says Mr. M'Culloch, " of any country abounding in large tracts of unappropriated land, *no rent is ever paid ;* and for this obvious reason, that no person will pay rent for what may be obtained in unlimited quantities for nothing. Thus in New Holland, where there is an ample supply of fertile and unappropriated land, *rent will not be heard of until the best lands are cultivated.*"[†] Again, " in *New Holland, Indiana, and Illinois,* and gen-

---

[*] Elements of Political Economy, sec. Rent, p. 31, 3d edit.

[†] Professor M'Culloch's Principles of Political Economy, chap. Rent, p. 433, 2d edit.

erally in all situations *in which no rent is paid,* and the best of the good lands only are cultivated."

Statements to the like effect might be quoted from every treatise on rent that has been published in England.

Now the fact is, that in the town of Sydney in New Holland, the rent of land is nearly as high as in London; that a very high rent is paid for land in Hobart's Town, Van Dieman's Land, in Montreal, in the new town of York, Upper Canada, and in every town of the United States, not excepting those which have been created within these two years; that in the immediate neighbourhood of all such towns a considerable rent is paid for garden ground and accommodation land; and that in all new settlements, whether American or Australian, *where there are but few roads,* the competition for land in the neighbourhood of a market, or of a road which leads to a market, is so great, that all such land, unless it be utterly steril, is reckoned more valuable than the most fertile land far from a market, and either yields rent accordingly, or enables its owner to take a greater produce to market, which comes to the same thing. The most ample proof of this assertion will be found in every published account of New South Wales and Upper Canada, in the published histories of most of the United States, and in every book of travels in America which notices the value of land. There have been published, in London and Edinburgh, certainly, not less than three hundred volumes, each of which contains evidence of the greatly superior value of some land in countries, where the most fertile land may be obtained in unlimited quantities for next to nothing; and showing too, that in all such cases the value of land depends, hardly at all on superior natural fertility, but almost entirely on greater vicinity to labour for raising produce, and to a market for disposing of it. There are so many witnesses to this fact, whose evidence is so much alike, that I should take from the force of their united testimony by quoting a part of it.* All good private libraries in England abound in such evidence, as Mr. Mill and Mr. M'Culloch would acknowledge after one hour's search in books relating to " new countries." If nature had provided markets in waste countries, or if mankind could fly, easily carrying great weights through the air, then, in-

---

* For another purpose, there is collected in the Appendix, No. 2, a number of facts, which establish that rent, and a high rent too, is paid in new countries, where unlimited quantities of fertile land may be obtained for a trifle.

deed, the value of land used in producing food for market would depend on superior natural fertility, and where unlimited quantities of the most fertile land might be obtained for nothing, without flying too far, no rent would be paid for the use of land in producing food for market.   Even in that case, however, rent would be paid for the use of land in various other ways, as for gardens and buildings. As it is, land speculators in Australia, Canada, and America, calculate that, because, in new settlements, the difference between different portions of land in respect to advantages of position must necessarily be very great, therefore, in a new settlement, the difference of value between different portions of land must necessarily be very great. Thus it frequently happens, that when one of the westerns tates of America, or some land-jobbing company, fixes on a spot in the wilderness as fit for a town, marks out the future streets by notches on the trees, and fixes a day for selling the district in lots by auction, hundreds of people congregate, build houses *upon wheels*, and make ready for the sale by estimating the future different values of the different lots. Captain Basil Hall describes admirably one case of this sort, in which twelve hundred people had assembled in the forest, and built seventy moveable houses, weeks before the day of sale.   The different lots of land sold at such auctions, are, generally, of pretty equal natural fertility, being equally covered by dense forests of the same kind of trees ; yet while still covered by the forest, they sell for very different prices.   And this is the case, not only with respect to town lots, but also as to lots which it is foreseen will be, though not in the future town, more or less distant from the future market.   In fact, the greatest trade in America, that of land jobbing, by which more fortunes have been made than by any other : a trade in which three out of four Americans engage at some period of their lives, either singly or in companies ; this trade, by which even a London company has lately made immense profits in Canada, which last year produced to the American government, the greatest of land-jobbers, nearly 700,000*l.* ; this trade of land-jobbing, of which it would seem that the English economists have never heard, depends principally upon the superior value which, in countries where unlimited quantities of the most fertile land may be obtained for a trifle, land derives from superior position.   The English theory of rent, therefore, whether correct or not, is made to rest upon a great misstatement of fact.

Now the American theory of rent is this. Rent consists of a yearly payment for the use of land. But much land, which might be turned to all the purposes of man, yields no rent. Land, for instance, on the south coast of New Holland,* or far west of the Mississippi, which is still·un-inhabited, yields no rent; and never will yield a rent until there shall be people desirous to use it. ·Indeed, no one would pay for the use of land, which no other person was desirous to use. Rent, therefore, arises from competition for the use of land.

Competition for the use of land is of various kinds and of various degrees.

First, touching the kinds of competition; these are various, because land is used for various purposes. In England land is used for growing corn, for breeding and fattening cattle, for producing milk, kitchen vegetables, and fruit, for the growth of timber and other raw materials of several manufactures, for the sites of warehouses, factories, houses in towns, villas, and mansions, for pleasure-grounds, parks, and game-preserves, besides an infinity of other purposes.

The degrees of competition vary with the various kinds of competition. The highest degree of competition occurs near the Exchanges of such towns as London, Liverpool and New-York. In those spots land is measured, not by the acre, but by the yard and foot; and yields, or is worth, a rent which may be called enormous, compared with the highest rent ever paid for the use of land in producing food. No competition whatever occurs in such spots as Dartmoor, for example, or the tops of mountains in Wales, where soil and climate are equally unfit for residence, for producing food, and for every other human purpose.

Such spots yield no rent; and any one might appropriate them, if the actual proprietors were not induced to maintain their titles by a vague hope of mineral discoveries, or for the vain pleasure of calling their own, though without the least advantage, so much more of the earth's surface. The lowest degree of competition occurs on these spots, which are so distant from towns and roads as to be unfit for any other purpose than the production of food, and of which the produce, owing to a bad soil or climate, or both,

---

* Though, as in the case of the sale described by Captain Hall, a London company lately offered to the British government 125,000l. for 500,000 acres of land on this desert coast. The offer was made, with a view to profit by the sale, at very enhanced prices, of land in the neighbourhood of a future market; why the offer was refused, may be seen in the Appendix, No. 3.

as well as to distance from markets and manure, is little more than sufficient to cover the expense of cultivation. This lowest degree of competition may produce a rent of some pence per acre ; while the highest degree of competition yields a rent of some thousand pounds per acre. Between these two extremes, various amounts of rent are produced by various degrees of competition.

This view of the subject will be made more clear by reference to some facts.

1. Part of Dengy Hundred in Essex consists of land reclaimed from the sea, and uniformly of the greatest natural fertility ; not merely producing large crops, but, since the soil is light as well as rich, producing them with a small outlay of capital. Farther, between this land and the metropolis there is easy water communication ; so that manure is easily obtained and the produce is easily conveyed to the best market. Yet, for this land, the average rent paid, deducting tithes, is not more than twenty-five shillings per acre ; while for land not more fertile, in some parts of Warwickshire, used only for producing food, and not nearer than the Essex farms to manure and a market, a rent of from two to three pounds per acre is obtained. That the produce of the Essex land is greater even than that of the land in Warwickshire, is shown by the higher amount paid for composition of tithes in the former case. But how are we to explain the difference of rent ? Of mere theorists the most profound would be at a loss to account for the lower value of the land in Essex : it is explained by the unhealthiness of the Essex marshes, which indisposes farmers to settle there ; so that when the lease of a farm expires, either no one bids against the old tenant, or no one bids more than the old rent. Many considerable fortunes, accordingly, have been made by farmers in that part of Essex, who retained as profit much of what they or others would have paid for rent, if the competition for farms had been as great in the thinly-peopled Essex marshes as it is in the healthy and populous county of Warwick. This circumstance, though not bearing on any of the kinds of competition mentioned above, is remarkably illustrative of the doctrine, that different kinds and degrees of competition arise from various causes.

2. All the land for some miles south, east, and west of Dunkirk (Downchurch) in France, consists naturally of downs of loose sand, blown up from a gaining sea-shore on to a deep subsoil of sand, without water, and as steril as

the most naked rock. Yet in this district the rent of land is considerably higher than in the very fertile district which, on the opposite coast of England, divides the Isle of Thanet from the rest of Kent. Why ? If rent be paid because, as Mr. Mill says, in the beginning of his chapter on rent, " land is of different degrees of fertility,", we should go on to say, because the English land is naturally steril, while the French land is naturally rich. The fact, however, is this ; at least this is the way in which the people about Dunkirk account for the high rents yielded by their naturally steril land. Time was when the district was uninhabited, and then, of course, no rent was paid. But a church having been built on the barren downs, and its patron saint, Eloi, being in great repute, pilgrims flocked thither from all parts of France and the Low Countries. By this means a town was established. In time, the inhabitants of the town constructed a port ; roads were next made from the port across the downs to the populous highlands which had once formed the sea-shore, and afterward canals in various directions ; the flatness and softness of the sandy district offering great facilities for canal-cutting. In the end, the means of communication became more abundant in this district than in any other part of France, as they are still : and the result was, that the population of the district became very great, towns and villages being built at a short distance from each other ; that by means of canals, clay and other manures were easily obtained, and being applied to the sand, rendered it more productive than the ancient highlands of chalk ; while those canals, again, afforded great facilities for taking produce to market. In this way, the cost of production in the market becoming less and less by means of art, the naturally steril downs about Dunkirk, which have never been used except for producing food, became more valuable, subject to a higher degree of competition, than the rich marsh lands between Sandwich and Reculver, on which the population is scanty, and of which every acre, in comparison with any part of the French Low Countries, is distant from market.

3. The garden grounds on the banks of the Thames, not far from London, are worth four or five, and in some cases ten times as much as alluvial land of equal natural fertility, which is either more distant from manure and a market, or which, though nearer to manure and a market, is not required to supply a demand for produce of a perishable nature. Thousands of like cases might be cited.

4. Of late years, in England, many cases have occurred in which the construction of a bridge between a town and mere farm land on the other side of the river, having enabled the inhabitants of the town to use such farm land for gardens, for the keep of cows, for turning out horses, and other purposes of utility or pleasure, has caused the rent of such land to rise, with a corresponding fall in the rent of accommodation land on the town side of the river. In these cases a bridge, which has nothing to do with natural fertility, causes a higher rent in one place, and a lower rent in another, by means of higher and lower degree of competition for the use of land.

5. Every one at all acquainted with rural affairs in England or Scotland must know of cases in which the making of a canal or a road has raised the rent of land throughout the borders of the new line of communication. In such cases, what the tenant saves by a decrease in the cost of manure, and of taking produce to market, falls to the landlord in the shape of rent; in such cases, a higher rent may be paid with the same profit as before, and is paid because a higher degree of competition has taken place.

6. But how much more striking is the increase of rent on and around some parts of the borders of new lines of communication, which are chosen for the sites of towns or villages. In these cases ground rents, garden rents, and accommodation rents, are now paid for land which before yielded rent for only the second degree, perhaps, of natural fertility; such higher rents being paid because some of the highest degrees of competition have been created where only the lowest degree existed before. The land around every English town which has much increased during the last thirty years furnishes to numbers an example of this kind with which they must be familiar; a case in which, through the increase of wealth and population, land which formerly yielded only garden and accommodation rent now yields building rent; land, which formerly yielded only a farming rent, now yields garden and accommodation rent; and land, still used for farming, is more productive with the same cost, or as productive with less cost, and is therefore worth a higher rent, in consequence of more manure and a greater demand for farm produce in the neighbourhood of such mere farming land.

7. On that part of the coast of the Mediterranean formerly subject to the Genoese republic, very little corn and no meat was ever produced: on the other side of the Appen-

nines, in Piedmont, there are districts which produce scarce any thing but corn and cattle; and part of the produce of those districts is consumed in the Genoese territory. Yet the rent of land, on the mountainous coast of the Gulf of Genoa was, a few years back, and probably still is, considerably higher than in those very fertile districts of Piedmont, from which the Genoese derive a part of their food. This difference of rent is easily explained. In Piedmont, there was no competition for the use of land, except in producing corn and meat. The soil of Genoa being unsuited to the production of corn and meat, the Genoese turned their industry into the channels of manufactures and commerce, whereby they were enabled to obtain corn and meat from foreign soils. Obtaining corn and meat with an outlay of capital much less than would have been required to raise the same produce on their own territory, they created, by the increase of wealth and population, a demand for productions, which were easily raised on their own soil, such as garden vegetables, fruit, olive oil, silk, and wine. Thus land which, if it had been used for growing corn or feeding cattle, would at best have returned a produce not more than sufficient to replace capital with profit, and for which therefore no rent could have been paid, now yielded a rent equal to the difference between the value of the produce and the cost of production. In this case, land which was steril for one purpose, became fertile for another. Then, as by means of importing corn and meat, the wealth and population of the state increased, roads were carried into narrow valleys which before had been shut against competition, and thus the land of those valleys, which before had been worth nothing, came to be valuable, and to yield rent accordingly. Lastly, with the further increase of wealth and population, owing entirely to the continued cheapness of corn and meat, there occurred an extensive demand for the use of land in many ways besides cultivation. The inhabitants of Genoa the Magnificent (magnificent, because without corn-laws) required, besides houses, warehouses, and other buildings within the city walls, country villas, pleasure gardens, and ornamented grounds. For these, the staff of life being cheap, they could well afford to pay without regard to profit. Thus much land acquired a value far exceeding the difference between the value and the cost of things raised for sale. What had occurred near the city of Genoa, took place more or less at other places on the coast, where there arose such towns as

Spezia, Noli, Voltri, and Savona, and where some land, steril for producing corn or meat, came to yield a rent for the use of it in producing other things : while some land, neither more nor less fertile for any purpose of cultivation, yielded a rent much higher than was ever paid for the most fertile land used in producing commodities for market. The original cause of all, or nearly all the rent paid in the Genoese territory, was the importation of corn and meat, which produced all the higher degrees of competition for the use of land on spots where, unless the staff of life had been imported from foreign soils, the lowest degree of competition could hardly have existed. How the Genoese would stare if Mr. Mill, explaining to them the cause of high rent in their steril country, were to begin with the first sentence of his chapter on rent: " land is of different degrees of fertility !"

From considering the above facts, it appears that rent is produced by an infinite variety of causes: each cause, however, operating by way of competition for the use of land ; and that some kinds of competition are far more powerful, produce a much higher rent than others. Let us now see what, in England, are the main circumstances that regulate the degrees of competition for the use of land.

First. Superior natural fertility.

Secondly. Superior productiveness arising from improvements, such as draining, fencing, building, &c.

Thirdly. Superior vicinity to manure, which is the same as superior natural fertility.

Fourthly. Superior vicinity to markets, which reduces, by so much, the cost of taking produce to market.

Fifthly. A demand for milk, fruit, and kitchen vegetables, which will not bear long carriage.

Sixthly. A demand for pleasure gardens, pleasure grounds, and ground for all the purposes of building.

Superior natural fertility alone produces some competition: add improvements, which are equal to greater natural fertility, but which must be called fixed capital, and a higher degree of competition takes place ; superadd vicinity to manure and to markets, when a still higher degree of competition occurs, with a still higher rent: produce a demand for accommodation land, when competition takes place in the highest degree but one : produce a demand for pleasure gardens, pleasure grounds, and building ground, when the result is the highest degree of competition and the highest rent. How, in England, a free trade in corn would affect these several degrees of competition for the use of land, and the aggregate rental of the country, is the practical question before us.

Let us suppose that if the English were free to buy corn in the cheapest markets they could anywhere find, there would no longer be any demand at all for English corn, wheat, barley, and oats. In this case, competition for the use of land in growing corn would cease altogether.

If this competition should cease altogether, bread not becoming any cheaper, the general competition for the use of land in producing food would be greatly reduced. But since the object of free trade in corn is to obtain cheap bread, we have a right to presume that, the corn-laws repealed, bread would become much cheaper. Let us suppose, taking the extreme case supposed by the landlords, when they say that a free trade in corn would be ruinous to them, that bread should be obtained at half its present price. In that case, the demand for all other kinds of food would increase with the cheapness of bread. But, even if the demand for other kinds of food were doubled, it does not follow, as a matter of course, that the new demand for the produce of land would have the same effect on competition as the demand which had ceased. Whether or not this would be the case, depends upon two proportions; first, the actual proportion between corn land and land used for growing other kinds of food; secondly, the proportion which the demand for food not corn would bear to the present demand for food not corn, if the price of bread were reduced by half. These are points which might perhaps be ascertained by a diligent government. Supposing that the new demand for food not corn, would be equal in effect to the present demand for corn and for food not corn, in that case the corn-laws might be repealed without even a momentary decrease of demand for the use of land in producing food; and, at all events, after a while, the increase of people and wealth, owing to the cheapness of the staff of life, would raise the demand for food not corn up to the present demand for all kinds of food.

How would this, either presently, or before long, affect the various degrees of competition?

1. Superior natural fertility would be as valuable as ever. Might it not become more valuable? or rather, might not much land, which has now but the fourth or third degree of fertility for the growth of corn, become of the second or first degree for the growth of other kinds of food? As

the Genoese soil is not fit for the growth of corn or meat, but is fit for the growth of wine, silk, and oil, so the soil, or rather climate of England is more fit for the growth of food not corn, than for the growth of corn.   Thus cheapness of bread extending to some land, which is inferior for its present purpose, a superior quality for new purposes, would rather augment than decrease the effect of the lowest degree of competition.   Towards the increase of this effect, also, the growth of raw materials for manufactures, such as timber and wool, instead of the growth of corn, a change which could not but ensue in many cases, if the English were to buy their corn with manufactures, would operate very considerably.

2. Capital fixed upon land, as well as, we may add here, the unfixed capital of the farmers, would be as valuable as ever.   Fifty years ago this would not have been the case; because at that time the art of producing animal food by tillage had made little progress in England; but at this time, every English farmer knows how to raise meat with the plough.   If a demand for animal food, milk, butter, cheese, and meat, should take the place of a demand for home-grown corn, some farmers, no doubt, would convert a portion of their corn land into meadow; but considering the great skill of the English in growing artificial food for cattle, and how the power of growing such food would be increased by the greater number of cattle kept, that is, the greater quantity of manure, a large proportion of the present corn lands would, it seems inevitable, be used for the growth of turnips, potatoes, beetroot, clover, tares, lucern, and such like food for cattle, which can be raised only by the same sort of capital as is used in raising corn, and which, on the score of climate, would be raised with less expense than corn.

These two are the only kinds of competition for the use of land that would be affected by cheapness of bread, so long as wealth and population had not increased.   But inevitably, if bread were cheap, wealth and population would very rapidly increase.   Whatever the effect of cheapness of bread on these two kinds of competition without an increase of wealth or population, it would manifestly be much greater after such increase.

But now we have to consider the influence of a great increase of wealth and population on the four higher degrees of competition.

Let us suppose the population and wealth of the country

to be doubled; a supposition by no means extravagant, after supposing that the staff of life had been very cheap during one generation. In this case, the extent of roads, though not doubled, would be greatly increased. On many of the new lines of roads, as well as on those which exist already, market towns would be built in spots where, at present, neither manure can be obtained nor produce sold. In the next place, a large proportion of the people called into existence by cheapness of bread, would reside in towns; so that, with double the actual population, the town population would be much more than doubled. In this way, land, which is now of second or third rate quality in respect to position, to manure, and a market, would become first rate and second rate. Thus, also, the extent of land required for producing perishable food, such as milk, fruit, and kitchen vegetables, would be more than twice as much as it is now. And, finally, the demand for pleasure gardens, pleasure grounds, and for building ground, would be more than doubled with the supposed increase of wealth and population. Whatever the increase of wealth and population year by year, all the higher degrees of competition for land would be much more rapidly extended.

Thus, while a free trade in corn might extend to some land, which is of inferior quality for the growth of corn, a superior quality for the growth of other things, not lessening the value of any capital fixed upon land, but rather increasing the power of such capital by spreading a mode of cultivation more suited to the soil and climate of England; while competition for superior natural fertility, and the use of fixed capital, might be rather increased than diminished, the influence of all the higher degrees of competition would, it seems quite plain, be extended incalculably. The aggregate rental of the country must necessarily increase to the same extent. All land-owners, indeed, would not derive equal benefit, in proportion to their present rentals, from such an extension of the higher degrees of competition. The greatest increase of wealth and population would not cause any increase of competition for land in the neighbourhood of the London exchange, where already the very highest degree of competition exists, and the very highest rent is obtained; nor, probably, would the value of any land now used as building ground be much increased by the greatest increase of wealth and population. The effect of greater wealth and population would be to extend to land, now subject to one of the lower degrees, a higher degree of competition; but already so large a portion of the surface of England is applicable to those purposes which create the higher degrees of competition, that but few landlords could miss reaping some share of the great increase of aggregate rental which, if this view of the subject be correct, must result from a free trade in corn. If so, bread cannot, one should think, be made too cheap, nor be made cheap too soon for the landlords.

But here a consideration arises, which is of great importance to the landlords. Two ways of making bread cheap are proposed; that of suddenly repealing all the laws which restrict the importation of corn ; secondly, that of substituting for the present truly whimsical laws a fixed duty on imported corn, and providing that the duty shall decrease year by year until it cease altogether. The ground of this latter suggestion is tenderness for the landlords, farmers, and farm labourers. Give them time, say some of the advocates of cheap bread ; give the agriculturists time, so that the transition from corn-growing to other kinds of production being gradual, not even a passing injury may be suffered by any of them. Now this gradual method of proceeding appears to me to be the only way in which the agriculturists may be injured by a repeal of the corn-laws ; and the only way, too, in which the other classes could fail, for a time at least, to reap much advantage from cheapness of bread.

First, as to the landlords. Let us suppose that twenty years were allowed for the reduction of bread to half its present price, and that a twentieth part of the whole reduction should take place in each of the twenty years. In that case, each year would bring a fall in the price of bread equal to one-fortieth of the present price. With so slow a decrease in the price of bread, little or no improvement could take place in the condition of the bulk of the people, because the number of labourers would increase as fast as bread became cheaper ; and thus, though every year there would be more labourers to eat bread, nay, even though all the labouring class should eat more bread, the class of labourers generally, who form the bulk of the people, would not be able to purchase more animal food. The price of bread being reduced by so slow a process as to give time for a corresponding increase of people, money wages would fall with the price of bread, and the quality of labourers' food would not be raised. In this case, the increase of demand for animal food would not be more rapid than the increase of population generally. But if, on the contrary, bread were suddenly reduced to half its present price, then, as the labouring population could not increase suddenly, the bulk of the people must be able to purchase a great deal more than twice as much animal food as they purchase now. At present, they buy very little animal food. By giving to the bulk of the people the power to buy animal food, the present demand for animal food might be immediately doubled, trebled, or even quadrupled ; and thus the transition from corn-growing to the production of other kinds of food might not have to wait upon the increase of population. If the slow process were adopted, a considerable decrease of the demand for home-grown corn might take place, before population had increased enough to increase the demand for animal food : whereas, if the sudden process of repeal were adopted, the power of the whole labouring class to buy animal food being thus suddenly and greatly increased, then the increase of demand for animal food would more or less correspond with the decrease of demand for home-grown corn. In this way, the transition from one kind to another kind of production might take place without even passing loss to the owners of land. If, then, bread is to be made cheap, the cheaper the better and the sooner the better for the landlords.

Secondly, as to the farmers. These, like the landlords, might suffer from a slow process of repeal, which should cause a decrease in the demand for home-grown corn, without a corresponding increase of demand for other things which English farmers could raise. In fact, what has just been said of the landlords ought rather to have been said of the farmers, since the landlord could suffer only through the farmer's loss. Supposing transition from corn-growing to other kinds of production inevitable, the thing which the farmers have to fear is temporary stagnation. The best way to produce a temporary stagnation of farming business seems to be, by enabling the bulk of the people to buy foreign corn without enabling them to buy English milk, butter, cheese, and meat : the only way to prevent such stagnation, by suddenly making bread very cheap, so that the demand for farm produce not corn should at once equal, if it did not exceed, the present demand for corn and other things together.

In two points of view more, the farmers appear to be interested in a sudden repeal of the corn-laws; first as capitalists, and secondly as holders of leases. " A farmer," says the author of Cheap Corn best for Farmers,* " is as much a capitalist as a shopkeeper or a manufacturer ; and the profits of farming capital must be lowered by any cause which lowers the profits of other capital.   A farmer's gain cannot be permanently greater than that of other capitalists. He has, in common with other capitalists, a very strong interest in high profits."   Of course he has ; and is not one object of free trade in corn to raise the profits of capital generally, by enlarging the English field of production ?   If, by the purchase of bread from other countries, the field of production should be so much enlarged as to raise the common rate of profit, farmers' profits could not but rise ; and the sooner, of course, this change should take place, the better for the farmer, as for the manufacturer and shopkeeper. Secondly, supposing the aggregate value of land to be raised, partly in consequence of land which was inferior for one purpose becoming superior for other purposes, and still more by the extension of all the higher degrees of competition, many leases, which now are only contracts, might become bonds for the landlord, and, for the tenant, securities worth a premium.   Supposing the demand for other things than corn to become suddenly greater than the demand for corn and other things, and supposing, further, a rapid increase of wealth and population, one can imagine landlords envious of their tenants under lease.

Thirdly, what would be the influence of cheapness of bread, obtained slowly or suddenly, on the condition of agricultural labourers ?   " Oh ! take pity on the poor labourers," say some landlords ; " if you put an end to the growth of corn in England, you will diminish employment for that unfortunate class, and so lower their wages."   This profession of tenderness for the pauper herd means : Beware of increasing the poor's-rate, which falls on us landlords. And though a good part of the poor's-rate, levied in the corn districts of England, be not borne by the landlords, all that part, namely, with which the farmers pay wages, and which must have been paid without poor-laws, still, since paupers maintained in idleness are kept by the landlords, it is true that, as agricultural labourers were thrown out of employment, the landlords would have to keep more people. But it does not follow, that the poor's-rate would increase because the number of persons to be maintained in idleness

* Mr. Henry Drummond, who founded the professorship of Political Economy at Oxford, and who, in this pamphlet, recognises the doctrine, that profits depend on the proportion between capital and the field of production.

was greater. The rate payers would have the benefit of
cheap bread, like all other classes, except the paupers,
whose money allowance would be diminished as bread became cheaper.   Thus, even supposing a great decrease of
agricultural employment, in consequence of a great decrease
in the price of bread (and one could not take place without
the other) it might be as broad for the landlords as it was
long ; not to reckon their greater means of paying the
same amount, in consequence of the greater value conferred
upon their land by extending to it higher degrees of competition.   For three reasons, however, it appears probable,
nay certain, that cheapness of bread, if it should come
suddenly, would not throw any agricultural labourers out of
employment ; in which case, the difference between cheap
bread and dear bread would be so much pure gain to the
payers of poor's-rate.   Because, first, as capital now used
in corn-growing could be easily used in producing other
kinds of food, so could corn-growing labour be easily turned
to the production of turnips, potatoes, beetroot, clover,
tares, lucern, &c., and to the management of sheep and
cattle.   Transition, then, is not so much to be feared as
stagnation; and the way to prevent stagnation is to make
the transition suddenly ; a new and perhaps a greater demand for the produce of farm labour arising at the moment
when the old demand should cease ; not waiting for the increase of population.   Because, secondly, if, which may be
doubtful, the various modes of cultivation substituted for
corn-growing should require fewer hands than are now employed in agriculture, still, all the cheap corn brought to
England must be purchased with English labour ; and this,
as it could not increase suddenly, would bear a less proportion to employment, so soon as a free trade in corn had provided profitable investments for great masses of capital now
lying idle or about to go abroad.   If any one should say
that agricultural labourers would not be fit for those occupations by which cheap corn was purchased, I would ask
him, whether the wild Irish cottiers be fit for the great
quantity of manufacturing work which they perform in
England ? and would tell him further, that during the last
war between America and England, American husbandmen found no difficulty in turning their hands to all sorts of
manufacturing employments.   Lastly, because the more
productive use of the national capital, without reckoning
any increase of it, would create a new demand for labour
in a hundred kinds of work, for which peasants are already

quite fit ; such as, merely for example, in building factories, warehouses, houses, and mansions, in making wharves, roads, canals, bridges, gardens, and pleasure grounds, in cultivating kitchen vegetables and perishable fruit, in porterage and domestic service ; which new demand could not, for some time, be supplied by a corresponding increase of people.

All these reasons for concluding, that cheapness of bread would rather increase than diminish employment for agricultural labourers, are so many reasons, likewise, why bread cannot become too cheap, nor become cheap too suddenly for the good of that miserable class. It must be acknowledged, however, that a class already so abject, would not be injured by that gradual repeal of the corn-laws which, lowering the demand for English corn without for some time raising the demand for other productions of English land, would injure the present race of farmers and landlords. In that case, some agricultural labourers who now work for pauper's allowance, would receive pauper's allowance without working for it ; and the difference would fall upon the landlords, after, in some cases, falling on tenants under lease. Cases might occur, in which the paupers would become the landlords by eating the whole rent, though without any change in their condition either for better or worse. Verily, the more one reflects on the subject, the more plain does it seem, that the lords of the soil are deeply interested in making bread very cheap as quickly as possible. But this, probably, they will never understand ; for do not they set their faces against rail-roads : blind to the certainty of profit and thoughtful only of their pheasants' tranquillity.

All the other classes, manufacturers, shipowners, merchants, dealers, professional men, clerks, and workmen of every kind, whose comfort depends on the rates of profit and wages, that is, on the proportion which these classes and their capital bear to the field of production ; these classes, though they and their capital would increase slowly with a gradual fall in the price of bread, might not obtain higher profits and wages unless the price of bread should fall more rapidly than they and their capital should increase. If the field of production were enlarged by slow degrees, capital and labour might increase at the same rate ; in which case there would be no change of proportion among the three elements of production. In that case, the wealth and population of England would increase, far more rapidly, perhaps, than since the war ; there would be more capitalists and more labourers, more factories, warehouses, ships, roads, and houses, more signs of wealth; but no improvement in the condition of either capitalists or labourers. Whereas, a sudden enlargement of the means for employing capital with profit, so great an enlargement suddenly that capital and labour should for some time bear a lower proportion to the field of production, must raise profits and wages both together. For the sake, then, of the industrious classes generally, bread cannot be made too cheap, nor be made cheap too soon.

Referring to the preceding note, all classes, and especially the new ruling order, have a deep political interest in making bread very cheap all at once. It will be impossible to qualify the bulk of the people for taking a part in the government unless their wages be raised, unless they obtain some leisure and peace of mind. Their wages will not be raised, if they should increase in number as fast as bread becomes cheaper. As respects them, the object is to make the staff of life very cheap, without a fall, if possible with a rise, of money wages : and this can be accomplished, if at all, only by a great and sudden fall in the price of bread. For the sake of all classes and on every account, therefore, it appears that, rather than get rid of restrictions on the corn-trade by a slow process, which should begin to-morrow and end twenty years hence, the English would do far better if they had sufficient patience to leave the corn laws untouched for twenty years, and then repeal them at one blow.

NOTE VII.

CLOSE RELATION BETWEEN THE FOREIGN CORN-TRADE OF ENGLAND AND THE FOREIGN TRADE OF CHINA.

Object of the English in a free corn-trade—Very cheap corn not raised except by slaves—Why so—Direct trade between English manufacturers and the producers of cheap corn, must be very limited—Indirect trade for procuring cheap corn, by means of direct trade with the Chinese Empire.

THE foreign corn-trade of England and the foreign trade of the Chinese empire appear, at first sight, to be subjects not closely related; but a very brief inquiry will show the most intimate connexion between them.

A free trade in corn would be of but little service to the English, if there were not plenty of people in the world ready to buy English manufactured goods with cheap corn. To every trade there must be two parties: he who sells must buy, and he who buys must sell. The English can produce very cheap cotton and woollen goods, and very cheap hardware; but of what service would it be to them to produce more of these cheap things, without a market in which they could be exchanged for cheap corn? It is very important, therefore, with reference to the foreign corn-trade of England, to see who in the world are the producers of the cheapest corn.

Very cheap corn is not produced anywhere, in large quantities, except by the labour of slaves, black or white, called slaves or serfs. This is a fact so well known, that as a fact one need not dwell on it; but why is it, that serfs in Poland, and slaves in America, produce cheaper corn than freemen anywhere?

More than one English economist would perhaps say, that the peculiar cheapness of slave-grown corn is owing to the cheapness of slave-labour; the wages of such labour consisting only of a bare subsistence for the labourer. But in what country, except North America and some new colonies, do the wages of free labour employed in agriculture much exceed a bare subsistence for the labourer? Perhaps, speaking generally, it might be shown, that slaves have more to subsist on than free labourers employed in agriculture, as undoubtedly farm-horses in England, being a valuable property, are better fed than English peasants. But, it might be said, the subsistence of slaves, though more in quantity, is less in cost, by reason of the cheapness of the produce of their labour on which they live. To say this, however, would be to put the effect for the cause. In the next place, considering the prime cost of slaves, a very important point, their stupidity, the cost of curing them when ill, and of maintaining them during sickness, their carelessness, and the great cost of keeping them in order, with the loss occasioned by the total escape of some of them and the cost of getting back some who escape; taking all these points into consideration, it will be seen that the labour of slaves is dearer than that of freemen, though the produce of their labour be cheaper. If labour were the only element of production, this contradiction could not occur; the labour being dear, the produce could not be cheap. But land also is an element of production. Wherever very cheap corn is produced, land is very cheap; and though in such cases the corn be raised by slaves, its cheapness seems attributable to the cheapness, not of the labour which raises it, but of the land on which it is raised. Still it will be asked, if this were the case, why should not very cheap corn be raised by free labourers on cheap land. Because, I answer, where land is very cheap and all men are free, where every one who so pleases can easily obtain a piece of land for himself, not only is labour very dear, as respects the labourer's share of the produce, but the difficulty is to obtain combined labour at any price. As the two greyhounds running together catch more hares than four running separately, so the labour of slaves, though dear compared with that of free labourers in most countries, is, being combined, much more productive, in proportion to the number of hands employed, than the divided labour of freemen wherever land is very cheap. This explains why slavery and great cheapness of land have generally existed together ; showing besides, that the cheapness of corn raised by slaves is owing, not to the cheapness of slave-labour, but to the cheapness of land ; that same cheapness of land being also the cause of slavery. I have dwelt fully on this point in a note on the origin, progress, and prospects of slavery in America.

Now the master of slaves and serfs would not be apt to produce cheap corn for the English market, if he had no prospect of being paid for it except with English manufactured goods. A Polish or Russian noble, or a slave-owner in Virginia, if he were to exchange the produce of his land directly with a Manchester manufacturer for the produce of steam-engines, would hardly know what to do with his purchase. The English will be able to obtain a great deal of very cheap corn, only by an indirect trade ; selling their manufactured goods where such things are in great request, for things which are in great request with the producers of cheap corn ; just as the Genoese buy corn and meat in Piedmont with salt-fish and hard money, which they first obtain by means of trade with North and South America. By what indirect, and perhaps very complicated traffic, cheap corn would come to England in consequence of cheap manufactured goods going from England, the English government need not inquire : that is a point which may safely be left to the traders, and any meddling with it by the government could not but be hurtful. But, whether there be in the world a sufficient demand for manufactured goods to enable the English to obtain cheap corn by some indirect trade, is a question of the greatest moment to the whole people.   Further, if there be any foreign restriction on the foreign demand for English manufactured goods, restrictions which it is in the power of the English government to remove, interference for that purpose is a proper office, a bounden duty, of government.   The nation who, but for the existence of certain restrictions on trade, would probably buy the greatest amount of English manufactured goods, are the Chinese; and it so happens that the Chinese possess a good deal of that commodity which, being in great request everywhere, would be readily exchanged for cheap corn, namely, silver.   Thus, between the question examined in the following note and that of the English foreign corn trade, there is a close and very important relation.*

NOTE VIII.

MEANS OF EXTENDING FREE TRADE TO THE WHOLE COAST OF CHINA.

Interest of the Americans in this question—Chinese restrictions on trade—The Chinese people more inclined to commerce than the English or Americans—Chinese government dislikes foreign trade on political grounds—Restrictions lead to a free trade—Description of the free trade which actually takes place in China—Obstacles to the extension of this free trade—Several modes of removing those obstacles—One mode will endanger the trade between America and China—Safest, cheapest, and best mode, commercial stations near the coast of China—To be formed, if not by Englishmen, then by Americans.

A GREAT change in the English trade with the Chinese is about to take place.   The strict monopoly of that trade by the holders of India stock will presently cease.   The English will soon be free, so far as their own government is concerned, to trade with the Chinese; but it does not follow that the Chinese will be free to trade with the English. To every trade there must be two parties; and the advantages derived from trade depend on combination of power, or concert, for the distribution of employments.   How are the English to obtain cheap silver, the produce of Chinese labour, wherewith to purchase cheap corn, the produce of

---

* See, further, Note on the Art of Colonization.

Virginian labour, if the Chinese are not permitted to buy hardware and cotton goods, the produce of English labour? The escape of the English from a certain restraint will not of itself set the Chinese free. On the contrary, there appears some reason to fear that the removal of restraints on the English may lead to greater restraints on the Chinese; and not merely as respects their trade with the English, but also in their trade with the Americans and others. And, at any rate, the trade between England and China could not be much enlarged without removing the actual restrictions on that trade, which are independent of the English, which depend either on the Chinese government or on the habits of the Chinese people. The nature of those restrictions and the means of entirely removing them form the subject of the following remarks, which are addressed to the Americans as well as to the English; seeing that both nations are concerned in the establishment of a free and secure trade with China, and that if the English will not establish such a trade, the Americans may do it for them, as will be shown presently. If I were to add, that some steps had been taken with this view by Americans, not a few of the English would be jealous of their " transatlantic brethren." Good! the sooner the two nations begin to rival each other in undertakings of this kind, the better for both of them.

Much as the English and Americans are given to trade, in that respect they are far surpassed by the people of China. " The propensity to truck, barter, and exchange," which Adam Smith describes as the original cause of wealth and civilization (it is the first cause after a surplus produce has been obtained by combination of power), is stronger and much more general in China than in any other country. Upon this point there is abundant evidence.* Yet the Chinese have made less progress in the art of navigation than any other people addicted to commerce; and their government exceeds all others, whether of past or present times, in animosity to foreign trade. Upon these main facts, the commercial disposition of the Chinese people, their ignorance of navigation, and the dislike of their government to foreign trade, must turn every speculation on the present subject.

The people of China are most desirous to trade with foreigners; but their ignorance of navigation prevents them

* For the information of Americans, some curious evidence of the industry, skill, and commercial disposition of the Chinese people is printed in the Appendix (No. 1).

from trading out of China. Their foreign trade, therefore, is necessarily conducted in China, and depends on the presence of foreign dealers and foreign ships. This point should be carefully borne in mind. Trade with the Chinese never has been, and for ages to come never will be, conducted without the presence of foreign dealers and foreign ships on the coast of China.

But the Chinese government detests or rather dreads foreigners, and lays all sorts of restrictions on their presence in China, confining them to a single port and subjecting them to many insults and injuries. If the propensity of foreigners to trade with the Chinese, and of the Chinese to trade with foreigners, were not stronger than the Chinese government, there would be no foreign trade in China. That government, however, has not much power over its own subjects. The men who compose it are not Chinese, but Tartars, who conquered China about two hundred years ago. Like the Mohammedans who conquered India, and the English who conquered and colonized Ireland, they are perfectly distinct from the subject race. The weakness of the rulers of China arises partly from their foreign origin, and partly from the great extent of their empire. Such power as they possess depends solely on the ignorance and timidity of their subjects. Hence their dread of foreigners and their apparent animosity to foreign trade. If people could buy and sell without personal intercourse, the Tartar government of China would, by all accounts, encourage foreign trade for the sake of revenue. It is not the trade which they dislike, but the traders. Nor is their dread of foreigners surprising. "The history of European commerce in the East is really nothing but the history of a continued series of usurpations; nor can any one acquainted with the subject feel surprised, that such native princes as had the means excluded those from their territories whose object was, not to maintain a fair and friendly commerce, but to extort oppressive privileges and to make conquests."* But, in addition to the fear lest foreigners should make conquests in China, the rulers of that country, being themselves foreigners and conquerors, dread lest their own subjects should be led, by intercourse with other foreigners, to think of rebellion. We have it in evidence that the mandarins of China were, like the mandarins of England, terrified at the great French revolution. Every restriction which the government of China imposes

* Edinburgh Review, No. CIV.

on the intercourse between its subjects and foreigners, its acuteness and diligence in limiting that intercourse to what is indispensable for carrying on a very limited trade, the strict enforcement of rules by which foreigners were prevented from moving beyond a narrow spot set apart for their use, and foreign women are excluded from China, the care with which on such occasions as embassies to Pekin foreigners have been guarded, watched, and led, as it were, caged, through the empire; all these, and many more practices of the same kind, may be traced to a political feeling; to a nervous horror of revolutionary principles. The emperor and his mandarins are anti-jacobins; not stout, like George III. and his boroughmongers, but very timid, being enervated by gluttony, excessive venery, and the use of opium.

But the feebleness and cowardice of the Chinese government have two opposite effects upon trade; producing numerous legal restrictions, and encouraging the people to set those restrictions at naught. Wheresoever trade is restricted there are smugglers. On the coast of China, where everybody, opportunity serving, is a trader, all the people are smugglers; not excepting the officers employed to prevent smuggling. Of the foreign trade of China but a small part is carried on according to law. Moreover, the legal trade, in which there are only seven Chinese dealers, and which is confined to a small number of commodities, is a trade by which foreigners lose. The English East India Company would have lost more than they have gained by the legal trade, if they had traded to the same extent without a monopoly of the *British* market. There will be no legal trade in China when the Company's monopoly of the British market shall cease. My authority for this statement is Mr. Marjoribanks, chief of the Company's factory at Canton. The following question and answer occur in his late examination before a committee of the House of Commons:—" *Q.* If the tendency of the trade in China is to get into the smuggling line, will not the Company, acting on different principles, and being from its circumstances unable to enter into that trade, be at a disadvantage against persons who have no scruples of that description?—*A.* If the question put to me contemplate the subversion of the Company, I think we should be all smugglers in China together, *and there would be no legal trade in China.*" Just so: when there shall not be any body exclusively privileged to sell tea in England, nobody will buy tea of the seven privileged Chinese tea dealers. The English monopoly supports the Chinese monopoly : put down the one, and down goes the other.   To some extent, every witness examined by the House of Commons helps to confirm this opinion; and none more effectually than the servants of the Company, who seem to have overlooked that an argument against their own privileges would be drawn from their admission, that the Canton monopoly depends on the monopoly in Leadenhall-street.   On other occasions the partisans of the Company have taken great pains to conceal the importance of the illegal trade; perceiving, of course, that if that illegal trade, in which they take no direct part, should appear more important than the legal trade, their monopoly of the English market and of the coast of China as an English trading station, would be considered doubly unjust and injurious to the English people. With this view they have spoken in sneering terms of the illegal trade, calling it the smuggling trade, and swearing that " respectable merchants" would not engage in it; the fact being, all the while, that a large proportion of the smuggling trade consists of the sale of opium to the Chinese ; that the importation of opium is strictly prohibited by the Chinese government, " on a moral principle," as Mr. Marjoribanks assures us ; and that the opium smuggled into China is grown by the Company in India, sold by the Company, with a full knowledge of its destination, to those who smuggle it into China, and smuggled into China by means of licenses from the Company, without which the foreign smuggler could not enter the Chinese seas.   So much for the delicacy of the most " respectable merchants" in matters of trade.   But in truth, those who conduct the illegal trade of China do not smuggle, properly speaking.   They buy and sell whatever they please, of whom and to whom they please, without let or hindrance from the government. The imperial edicts, which forbid the Chinese to quit their own country for any purpose, and which declare that no Chinese, save only the seven Hong merchants of Canton, shall deal with foreigners; these orders are all moonshine, mere sham, as were the English laws against bribing at elections.   The Chinese mandarins, like the English boroughmongers, are among the first to treat the law as a dead letter.   Thus, while legally trade is nowhere so much restricted as in China, the Chinese enjoy greater freedom of trade than any other commercial people ; as will appear by the following instructive, and, one may add, entertaining account of what is called the smuggling trade.

Extracts from Dobell's Residence in China.

" In defiance of an annual edict from the emperor, making it death to smuggle opium, the enormous quantity of nearly 4000 chests is imported every year to Macao and Whampao. * * * * * It is a business that all the inferior mandarins, and some of the higher ones, their protectors, engage in: so that opium is carried through the streets of Macao in the most barefaced manner, in the open day. Large boats, armed, having from thirty to forty men, ply between Macao and Canton when that market offers an advantageous price.

* * * * * * * *

" I have known many persons send large sums of specie by these boats to Macao, at a moderate rate, and never heard of an accident happening to them in any way. All metals are prohibited from being exported, except zinc ; there are, however, immense quantities smuggled into the English East India cotton ships, whenever they wish to buy more than the portion allowed by government."—Vol. ii. p. 148.

" The Chinese have an extensive foreign commerce carried on by their own junks to Japan, Cochin China, Siam, Tonquin, Sumatra, Java, Borneo, Macassar, and indeed to all the Indo-Chinese islands. The Chinese declare this trade is the most important of any of their external relations ;* and we may believe them when there are said to be upwards of 40,000 tons of shipping occupied with that and the salt trade. We know, also, that a Chinese junk, bound to the islands, carried a cargo of from 3 to 500,000 dollars' value in China ware. nankeens, silks, ready-made clothes, books, writing-paper, ironmongery, tea, instruments of husbandry, iron, cloth, &c. &c."—Vol. ii. p. 175.

" Nothing can be more barefaced than the manner in which smuggling is conducted in open day at Whampao."— Vol. ii. p. 132.

---

* It is wholly contrary to law.

Extracts from the Evidence delivered before the Select Committee of the House of Commons, on the Affairs of the East India Company, &c. First Report.

CHARLES MARJORIBANKS, Esq., a servant of the East India Company in their China factory for seventeen years, the greater part of that time resident in China.

" Has any change taken place in the trade within your recollection ?—Yes, very considerable changes have taken place in the foreign trade generally. One of the greatest changes which has taken place, and which, in my own opinion, will sooner or later affect the security of our trade, IS THE ENORMOUS EXTENT OF THE SMUGGLING TRADE NOW CARRIED ON IN CHINA ; among the islands in the mouth of the Canton river, to a very great extent indeed ; so much so, that if the Chinese government had the inclination, *I do not imagine they possess the means of putting it down,* at least by any marine force which they have."

" Will you be good enough to state to the committee, if you know, in what other articles, besides opium, the smuggling trade is carried on upon the coast of China ?—I conceive that at present it extends to articles, *more or less, of every description ;* not on the coast of China, but among the islands in the mouth of the Canton river."—" Articles of British manufacture ?—I am not aware of any individual instance where smuggling of articles of British manufacture has existed ; *but I know nothing to preclude it.*"

" You have stated that the smuggling trade in China has become very extensive ; has not the increase of that smuggling trade a tendency to injure the fair trade ?—I think it has a tendency to do so, in as far as articles smuggled into the country that evade duty can be sold at a profit, when articles which pay government duties cannot."—" Is not the opium trade in China, which you state to exist to the extent of 13,000,000 or 14,000,000 of dollars a year, entirely an illicit trade ?—*Entirely prohibited by the Chinese government.*"

" Has not the Chinese government, in its conduct towards foreigners, who have attempted to fix themselves in their harbours, shown itself a shrewd government, acutely understanding its own interests ?—I think that the Chinese are a highly intelligent people, remarkable for their industry and perseverance ; but I think they are oppressed with one of the most corrupt governments that ever weighed down the energies of a people."

" If it should be the case, that the American or foreign merchant has carried on a trade of this (prohibited) description with profit, when the Company have been carrying it on with loss, would not that prove that their trade has been, in this article at least, better conducted than that of the Company ?—It might not prove that it was better conducted, for it might arise from the circumstances I have stated, of some of those goods having been smuggled into China, having evaded the Chinese duties."—" If the tendency of the trade in China is to get into the smuggling line, will not the Company, acting upon different principles, and being from its circumstances unable to enter into that trade, be at a disadvantage against persons who have no scruples of that description ?—If the question put to me contemplates the subversion of the Company, *I think we should be all smugglers in China together, and there would then be no legal trade in China.*"

" Would not the temptation to smuggling be irresistible if the trade was carried on in small vessels ?—I imagine that individuals who do not much respect the laws of the country will not consent to pay duties which they can evade by acting in opposition to those laws."—" Is the smuggling carried on among the Chinese by what are called outside merchants ?—This term is applied in common to all merchants not members of the Hong ; some of them are smugglers, some mere shopmen."

JOHN FRANCIS DAVIES, Esq., a servant of the East India Company in China, who travelled for six months through the interior of the empire.

" What impression, in your opinion, would be produced upon the Chinese generally by throwing open the trade *to British merchants generally? The whole body of smugglers at Canton would rejoice.* The government would, in the first instance, view it with jealousy, as they view every change ; and when they came to lose their revenue, they would view it with hostility. They have already, in consequence of the *extraordinary amount of smuggling (not only relative to contraband articles, such as opium, but in the case of articles that pay duty)*, lost so much that they have issued edict after edict directed against those individuals and those nations who principally partake in this smuggling trade ; and it is impossible to suppose that they would go on *ad infinitum* in their endurance, or consent to the conversion of the whole trade of Canton into a smuggling intercourse."*

" Can you state the probable amount of the tonnage employed in the country trade carried on between India and China, with reference to the Company's tonnage ?—The report on the table speaks to that fact ? it is nearly equal, at all events, to that of the Company. It arises, not from there being so large a quantity of tonnage actually employed, but from the quickness of the returns, and from the comparative smallness of distance, enabling one ship to make two voyages in the year."—" Is that trade carried on without the intervention or assistance of the Company's servants at Canton at all ?—*A very large portion of it consists of smuggling trade*, and therefore must be entirely out of the Company's cognizance."

" Is there not a very considerable smuggling trade in other articles imported into China from Europe ?—I believe that a great deal has been smuggled into China."

"Have the Hong merchants themselves taken part in this smuggling trade?—Far from it ; they were sold, not to Hong merchants, but to outside shopmen."

" You were understood to state that some of the Hong merchants have been ruined by their mixing with the smuggling trade ?—Not at all ; they have been ruined *by the smuggling trade*. They pay heavy duties and exactions to the government, on account of the advantages which their situation affords them in the monopoly of the regular trade ; and, as the smuggling trade must necessarily be carried on by persons who do not pay those heavy exactions, and who in fact frequently evade the regular duties, they must necessarily be ruined by the extension of such a course of transactions."

" Have you any means of judging what proportion of the whole imports into China consists of the smuggling trade? It is impossible to say exactly how much, because the smuggling is secret, and therefore not so open to investigation : but with regard to opium, we know that the amount of the annual importation into China is upwards of 10,000,000 of dollars."

" Were you at Canton in September, 1828 ?—I was."

" Did you hear that a ship called the Merope had returned

* It is a question of power, not of inclination.

to Canton after having been a voyage as high up as to Ningpo, having made a very profitable voyage, and converted the whole of her cargo, to a very large extent, into specie?—*It must have been entirely surreptitious, if she did;* and I judge that her cargo was opium."

" Do you conceive that such a thing would be possible? I should say very improbable, until the fact spoke for itself; from surmise, I should say it was a thing that could not easily occur, but that *by smuggling* a ship might manage to introduce goods in that way."

" You have stated that the Chinese government have issued many edicts against smuggling; have those edicts been carried into force or not?—They certainly have, *to the utmost capability of the weak Chinese government.* I would say, that they have rather shown the hostility of the Chinese government to the system, than that they have been very effective in suppressing it."

" Do you consider that smuggling has been decreased by them, or the contrary?—I should say that *the weak and ill-organized government of China cannot follow up its edicts by a corresponding effectiveness; and they have probably, in a great measure, proved unavailing.*"

CHARLES MARJORIBANKS, Esq.

" Has not the smuggling trade in camlets increased?—A good many Dutch camlets have been imported by Dutch ships; and camlets have also been imported on private account."

" Are the committee to understand, that although the trade of opium is prohibited under very severe penalties, yet that the quantity imported, and the prices at which it is sold, are as regularly known as any other article which is authorized and regularly imported?—*It is made no secret of;* it is generally known by the parties who deal in it, and they communicate it to others. *The prices of opium are always given in the Canton Register, a public newspaper.*"

" Can you inform the committee how the trade of opium is carried on?—When I first went to China, the opium-trade was at Macao, from which it went to Whampoa, and is now confined to the islands at the mouth of the river. The opium smuggling-boats go alongside the ships in the open face of day, and the opium is delivered to them on their presenting what is called an opium order from the agent in Canton."

" Is this trade carried on within the view of the officers of government and the men-of-war boats of the Chinese? —Frequently within the view of the men-of-war boats."

" Are these boats stationed on the part of the Chinese authorities within reach and view of this trade?—Not regularly stationed : they frequently go and come there. *They are constantly manœuvring about, and often report to the Canton authorities that they have swept the seas of all smuggling ships.   The ships remain there just the same.*"

" Then, in point of fact, it may be said that the smuggling trade in opium is carried on with the connivance of the Chinese authorities?—With the connivance of the lower government authorities; I am not prepared to say of the higher authorities."—" Is that the case in the smuggling of other articles?—Yes, it is."

" Under what privilege is silver exported?—The Chinese laws prohibit the exportation of any metal: dollars are allowed to be exported from China, *but not bullion, but it has always been exported to a large amount.*"

" Are not the smugglers of China a very powerful body? do not they move in considerable fleets upon the shore?—Not in fleets; but their boats are very well manned and armed."—" *Do not they set the government at defiance?—Entirely, I should say, when they have sea-room.*"

" Do you suppose that the government is capable of keeping them under?—*They possess no marine force capable, in my opinion, of suppressing them.*

" Is the force of the smugglers upon the increase or upon the decrease?—*The smuggling trade of China is materially upon the increase.*"

" Are the transactions of the smuggling trade carried on with as much fidelity and regularity on the part of the Chinese as the transactions of the regular trade?—*With wonderful regularity*, considering the nature of the trade; certainly not with the same regularity as those of the legal trade."

Mr. John Aken, formerly master of the Investigator, and afterward commander of the Exmouth, trading between India and China.

" Is it not a fact, that they (the outside merchants) bring the boats alongside, and then it is thrown out of the ship into the boats?—Yes: when I sold my opium I gave an order upon the chief officer to deliver it ; but the person to whom I sold *it takes the risk entirely in taking it from the ship; he pays me for it before he gets the order."*—" What does he generally pay you with ?—In dollars *or sy-cee."**

" Do you happen to know the method by which the opium is smuggled into the country ?—They take it from alongside in smuggling boats that are well manned and armed, and there are a great many rivers, branches, and islands, and different places, and they are off directly with it, *and they put all the government boats at defiance.* I have seen that myself. I have seen four mandarin boats surrounding my ship when I had thirty chests of opium to smuggle, and I was prevented from going to sea on account of the opium, and I sold it to the people. I went down myself and saw the way that they smuggled it; they stripped the chest entirely away, and took nothing but the opium, and put it into bags; and we opened the lower-deck port, and in one moment they put the opium into the boat, and all hands were off in a moment ; we did that in a very heavy shower of rain. There was a cry out about three minutes afterward, but the boat was gone like a shot."—" Were the mandarin boats lying near ? —One was lying a-head touching the ship, another was lying at the stern, and another was lying upon the opposite side."—" They were there to prevent smuggling ?—Yes."

" *Do you obtain greater or less price for your opium in proportion to the degree of vigilance of the mandarin boats ? —No, I never knew any difference made on that account."*

" If the mandarin boats had not been there, should you have obtained a larger price ?—I do not think we should have got more ; *they always make certain of it; and it always struck me, that there was an understanding between the smugglers and the mandarin boats ; there is an apparent vigilance kept up which has no existence in my opinion. I have been told so by a number of people."*

" Might not other commodities, of small bulk, be introduced into China by the same means ?—*I should think they could, very easily."*

" Do you happen to know whether it is a practice with regard to any other commodities except opium ?—Saltpetre, which is a bulky article, is smuggled. *I used to smuggle it myself ; at least I carried it there, and it was smuggled by the people to whom I sold it.*

" Is saltpetre a prohibited article in China ?—No, you can sell it to the government if you please ; but we cannot

* Silver bullion, of which the exportation is prohibited.

sell it so well to the government. We can generally get about two dollars a pecul by smuggling it."

" Is that on account of the duty paid to government ?—I think it is."—" Have you known of any other article being smuggled ?—I think, sometimes, broad-cloth is smuggled." —" By the Americans or the English.—By the English. I once carried two bales of cloth, and it was smuggled, I know, but wherefore I cannot say, because it did not belong to me."

Second Report of Minutes of Evidence.

Mr. JOHN ARGYLE MAXWELL, who resided at Sincapore for more than six years, and who went several times to Canton.

" Do you know whether there is much smuggling in China in the articles of export?—As far as my own experience went, I found the parties who were not Hong merchants *ready to make a bargain either way*, that is, to deliver the article as a smuggled article at Lintin, or in the usual way at Whampoa."

" Have you ever known of the country ships proceeding to Chinese ports, north of Canton, and trading with the natives ?—I have heard of several of those adventures."

" Can you state what the cargoes were that they took ?— The cargoes generally consisted of opium almost altogether; in some cases they took a little saltpetre, I believe."

" Did they find any difficulty in effecting sales with the natives ?—I understood that they always effected sales ; I did not hear that there were any extraordinary difficulties."

"What were the ports they went to ?—Many of the ports have escaped my recollection, but I remember the port of Chingchoo, and Chusen, and the island of Formosa."

" Do you know where these ports were situated ?—Chingchoo is in the province of Fokien."

" What reception did you understand the natives gave those adventurers ?—I believe they gave a good reception. A Spanish gentleman, who was a supercargo in one of the expeditions, told me that he landed on Formosa, and walked several miles. I recollect his mentioning particularly that he observed the remains of European houses there, which he considered to have been the remains of those that were occupied by the former Dutch factory at Formosa."

" Do you know how long it is since that factory was removed ?—I should think more than 100 years."

" Did you understand that the sales which were effected at the northern ports were at a considerable advance above the Canton prices?—I could not understand that there was any great advance. I heard the parties mention that *they found the Chinese dealers there in possession of regular price-currents from Canton, stating the stock on hand of opium, and other circumstances connected with the market.*"

Captain ABEL COFFIN.

"Have you been at Sincapore and Siam?—I have."—" Have you found any quantity of Chinese junks there ?—At Siam a large quantity."

" What quantity have you ever seen there at one time ? —I should think eighty."

"Of what size ?—Some of them would carry 700 or 800 tons, and some others perhaps 200 or 300."—" Do these junks carry on an extensive trade with different parts of China besides Canton?—They are principally from other parts ; very few from Canton."

" Do they import teas in any considerable quantities into Siam ?—They do."

" Did you find any Chinese teas there?—A large quantity. I should have had no difficulty at any time in loading one, two, or three ships of the size that I had there."—" What quantity of tea ?—Principally black teas : Souchong and Congou of very good quality."

Extract from a Statement delivered to the Parliamentary Committee, by Mr. CRAWFURD.   Third Report.

" The Chinese junks, properly constructed, pay no measurement duty, and no kumsha or present ; duties, however, are paid upon goods exported and imported, which seem, however, to differ at the different provinces. They are highest at Amoy, and lowest in the island of Hainan. The Chinese traders of Siam informed me that they carried on the fairest and easiest trade, subject to the fewest restrictions in the ports of Ningpo and Sianghai in Chokian, and Souchon in Kiannan. Great dexterity seems everywhere to be exercised by the Chinese in evading the duties. One practice, which is very often followed, will afford a good example of this. The coasting trade of China is nearly free from all duties and other imposts. The merchant takes advantage of this, and intending in reality to proceed to Siam or Cochin China, for example, clears a junk out for the island of Hainan, *and thus avoids the payment of duties. When she returns, she will lie four or five days off and on at the mouth of the port, until a regular bargain be made with the custom-house officers for the reduction of duties. The threat held out in such cases is to proceed to another port, and thus deprive the public officers of their customary perquisites.* I was assured of the frequency of this practice by Chinese merchants of Cochin China, as well as by several commanders of junks at Sincapore. From the last named persons I had another fact of some consequence, as connected with the Chinese trade, viz. that a good many of the junks carrying on trade with foreign ports to the westward of China, often proceeded on voyages to the northward in the same season. In this manner they stated that about twenty considerable junks, besides a great many small ones, proceeded annually from Canton to Souchon, one of the capitals of Kiannan, and in wealth and commerce the rival of Canton, where they sold about 200 chests of opium at an advance of fifty per cent. beyond the Canton prices. Another place where the Canton junks, to the number of five or six, repair annually, is Chinchoo, in the province of Shanton, within the Gulf of Pechely, or Yellow Sea, and as far north as the 37th degree of latitude."

WALTER STEVENSON DAVIDSON, Esq.* a merchant, a naturalized Portuguese, chief of a large mercantile house at Macao.

" Have you any means of judging whether the trouble attending the sale of opium is less now since the ships were removed from Whampoa, and stationed themselves at Lintin, outside the river ?—I should say, that I do not believe there is much difference in the trouble, but a vast difference in the anxiety ; because, in the one case, they were liable to seizure any day, in the other case they lie in a spot where *they can defend themselves against any power that can come against them.*"

" You mean to say, that the trade in your time, while the ships lay at Whampoa, was more difficult than it is now ? —More full of anxiety ; *there was no difficulty in it : it was a very good business.*"

" Did you ever know of any other articles except opium

* Now a Banker in London.

being smuggled ?—I have heard of a great many, but I never smuggled any other articles myself in the import trade."

" With regard to the exports ?—In exports *I smuggled very largely of silver, because it was a prohibited article,* as well as opium, and so was tutenog, I believe ; and the rule which guided me was, that I would smuggle the articles which were prohibited, but not those upon which a direct duty was laid."

" What responsibility did you consider to attach to you as an agent, selling a prohibited article like opium ?—*In a pecuniary point of view I never considered it was a responsibility that could be valued, nor did I ever charge, or pretend to have a right to charge, any thing for it;* personally, of course, every man who resides in China runs a great risk ; the government, for instance, as I have stated, knew full well that a ship was at Whampoa with a quantity of opium, that she was to my consignment; and they might have imprisoned me any day, and said, till you pay 100,000 tales you shall not be released."

" Did that ever happen during your residence there ?— Never."

" Did you ever hear of its happening ?—*Never : I do not think that in the history of trade there has been an instance of it.*"

" What risk do you consider you ran in smuggling silver ?—*None whatever beyond the seizure of the silver,* with which they are always exceeding well satisfied."—" Have you known many seizures made ?—I have known some, but *very few indeed, the parties are so exceedingly expert.*"

" In your time did the Chinese undertake to put the silver on board for you ?—Yes."

" What rate did you pay them for it ?—I bought the silver of them, and they undertook to put it on board : it was delivered on board, and I paid them *sometimes before* and sometimes *after they brought me the captain's receipt for it.*"

" Then your own risk was at an end ?—Entirely, except when I chose to step out of the way and trusted them, which I have often done with all those parties, both in silver and in opium."

" Are you not aware that those Custom-house boats are moored astern and on the quarter of every vessel ?—Custom-house boats are ; but I am not aware that the boats whose duty it is to seize those parties are moored there ;

they are far too weakly manned and armed."—" Are you aware that those boats permitted the opium to be landed? *Decidedly."*—" Could they prevent it if they pleased ?— *That does not follow ; they may not be strong enough. I have known instances of the Chinese opium boats overpowering all force where it was a very large quantity, and it was worth their while killing and wounding men, but generally they do not attempt it."*—" *On such an occurrence happening, have you ever known any notice taken of it by the government ?—Never."*

Captain CHARLES HUTCHINSON, a commander in the navy, who commanded the ship called the Bombay Castle, from Liverpool to India, and remained in the latter place for five years. He went three times to Canton, three several years from Bombay, with cargoes of cotton and other Indian articles.

" Supposing the Chinese were to put a stop to the export of teas altogether, are you of opinion that the prohibition would be effectually enforced, so as to prevent its being sent to Sincapore ?—I think it is extremely probable that they would be enabled still to bring it to Sincapore, but I am not certain.

" What do you apprehend would be the effect in China of a total prohibition of the export of teas ?—It would be difficult to say. The Chinese government feel themselves to be *a very rotten sort of government ; they know that the people are ready to revolt in many of their provinces, and they would therefore be very cautious how they gave any cause of discontent to any part of their empire ;* but whether they are particularly afraid of that part of it situated near Canton, I cannot tell. There are some of the provinces where they are much more inclined to revolt and to resistance than in that, particularly the province of Chingchoo.

" You are aware that tea can be exported from other ports of China besides Canton, in Chinese junks ?—Yes, because it is brought to Sincapore from other parts."—" *Is it brought from the tea provinces ?—It is brought by canals to the coast, and then put on board the junks, who bring it to Sincapore.*

" Are the junks that come to Sincapore with tea loaded at Canton, or at ports nearer the growth of the tea ?—At ports nearer the growth of the tea, I believe ; I know they are not loaded at Canton.

" Are there any goods that are reckoned prohibited goods in China exported by the country ships?—*A large quantity in almost every ship; they chiefly consist of cassia and a coarser kind of silk, upon which the duties are too heavy to be taken in the regular way; they are therefore bargained for with the outside merchants, to be smuggled on board the ship, and it is done with as great facility as the regular trade; the mandarins being all feed and permitting it.*

" Did you ever know of an interruption to this irregular trade?—*None whatever; it is as easily carried on as the regular trade.*

" Is a *large portion* of the assorted cargoes exported from China articles prohibited or subject to such duties that they are generally smuggled?—Yes."—" And with the knowledge and connivance of the mandarians?—Certainly. There is an island near Whampoa called French Island, where those smugglers live. Goods intended to be smuggled are sent to French Island, and you receive notice the night before at what hour the cargo will be brought: the mandarins then surround the ship, and wait for the smuggling boat; when it comes alongside they send a man in a canoe to count the packages, that no more may be brought to the ship than they have received their fee for. *In fact, their whole government is one system of corruption from top to bottom.*

" Do not you think that the facilities they afford to smuggling arise from an anxious desire to extend the foreign commerce?—*Certainly, in the people; not in the government, of course.*

" In the officers of the government, do you attribute it to a desire to obtain a suitable remuneration in return for the sum of money they have given for their offices?—Certainly.

" It being notorious that all those offices are paid for?—So I have always been told.

" Could not cotton goods be smuggled to other ports?—There was a difficulty in smuggling at other ports when I was in China, but some ships with opium succeeded to a certain extent. Since I left that country, I understand that they have smuggled to a larger amount, and I suppose other goods as well as opium."—" Do you think that the smuggling could be carried on with the same ease at those other ports as at Canton?—I should think not, because at *Canton it is systematized.*"

Third Report of Minutes of Evidence.

John Stewart, Esq. a member of the committee, who went to China seven times, in the years 1800, 1803, 1804, 1805, 1806, 1807–8, and in 1817.

"Is it your opinion that the Chinese government would find it very difficult to put an end to the foreign commerce with England?—I think they could do it; but I am of opinion that if the Chinese government were to put an end to that commerce, it would produce great misery in China, and particularly at Canton, where it is carried on.

"Would the government, in your opinion, be strong enough to accomplish the putting an end to the trade?— My opinion is, that an edict of the Emperor of China might be so enforced as to put a stop to all the *regular* foreign trade carried on with China; but I DO NOT THINK THAT THE CHINESE GOVERNMENT COULD PREVENT SMUGGLING BEING CONTINUED FROM THE COAST OF CHINA, EVEN IF THEY PUT A STOP TO THE REGULAR TRADE.

"Then you do not mean to say that you think the Chinese government would have power to put a final stop to the progress of the trade?—*No! I think that a smuggling trade would be carried on on the coast of China to a very considerable extent, in spite of any act that the Chinese government might adopt."*

Robert Rickards, Esq., who resided in India twenty-four years, being on the Bombay establishment, and had during that time good opportunities of seeing what passed in the trade between India and China.

"Are you aware of the peculiarities of the Chinese government with regard to trade, and that a comparison cannot therefore be fairly made between India and China as to any expected increase?—I know that the Chinese government have imposed restrictive regulations upon the foreign trade of their own country; but I know at the same time *that these regulations are completely set at nought by the commercial spirit of the people.*

"If, therefore, English ships were prohibited going to China, I conceive that supplies of tea and other Chinese articles *might just as easily be got from Sincapore, or Java, or other ports in the Eastern Archipelago,* as they can now from China itself. These then are the grounds of my belief, that, under all circumstances, *we have the means of con-*

trolling the trade with China, even more effectually than the Chinese government itself; for when the Chinese merchants and the mass of the community find that they have an interest in carrying on certain branches of trade, they will do it, as is sufficiently manifest in their importation of opium and export of silver, *in spite of the most severe laws that can be enacted by their own government.*"

JOHN CRAWFURD, Esq., appointed parliamentary agent to the inhabitants of Calcutta. He resided in the Upper Provinces of the Bengal Presidency for five years, in Calcutta one year, in Penang three years, and in Java six years. One year he went on a mission to Siam and Cochin China. He resided in Sincapore about three years; afterward was appointed commissioner by the governor-general in the Birman empire; then went as envoy from the governor-general to the court of Ava; after which he returned to Calcutta, and eventually to Europe.

" Supposing an interruption to take place in the European trade of China, are you of opinion that a considerable quantity of tea might be brought in Chinese vessels to Sincapore or some other emporium in the Eastern Archipelago? —I conceive so. I think it was a great point, during the discussions respecting the former charter of the East India Company, to establish that fact themselves. Mr Drummond, now Lord Strathallan, gave it distinctly in evidence, that a very large quantity of tea might be imported into Europe through such a channel. The evidence is to be found upon the records of the Committee of the House of Commons, I think in 1812. It seemed, indeed, to be a settled point, especially in reference to the Philippine Islands and others. I have a short entry on this subject, taken out of a note-book that I kept at Sincapore; it is dated the 22d of August, 1825, and is the result of a conversation with the commanders of some junks. ' The tea consumed in Cochin-China is brought from Tchaotchen, on the confines of Canton and Fokien, but in the jurisdiction of the former, to Hainan, from which it comes to Saigun and other places.—It is all the produce of Fokien. Into Saigun there are annually imported about 70,000 boxes of tea, of twenty catties each, and into Hué about 10,000 boxes. It is impossible to conjecture the quantity brought into Tonquin, as a great part of it is imported by land. The price of the ordinary qualities at Tchaotchen and Canton is twenty-six dollars per pecul. The same tea would be sold at Saigun for forty dollars. My informants state that any quantity whatever of tea may be imported into Sincapore, which the market may demand, from Chaotcheou, Changlim, and other parts, either black or green. *The commanders of junks will do this in spite of any regulations to the contrary.'*"

JOHN STEWART, Esq., M.P.

" Do you think the trade could be carried on in the neighbourhood of Canton, in any of the islands?—Yes; I imagine that tea might be conveyed, and in all probability would be conveyed, to the islands on the coast of China; *it might be smuggled from thence, or it might be sent in Chinese vessels to the Islands of the Eastern Archipelago, and could be exported from thence.*

" Would it be sufficient to supply the wants of this country?—If the Chinese permitted the export of tea in their own vessels, I am decidedly of opinion that a sufficient quantity might in that way be exported from China to supply the wants of all Europe.

" Do you suppose that they would do that under such circumstances?—I think they would; the Chinese are a people of great commercial enterprise, and I think they would be disposed to send tea wherever they could find a sale for it with advantage."

Captain JOHN MACKIE.

" You have resided in India several years?—I have, for ten years."—" From what period?—From 1820 to the latter end of 1829.

" Did you command a ship in the China trade?—I commanded a Spanish vessel on the coast of China.

" What was this vessel engaged in?—In the opium trade."
—" She was sailing under Spanish colours?—She was.

" What ports of China have you visited?—I visited the port of Amoy, and all the ports between that and Canton.

" Were you entirely engaged in the opium trade?—Entirely; I carried also a little saltpetre.

" What was the name of the ship?—The St. Sebastian.

" Whom was she owned by?—Spaniards."—" Did any part of the cargo belong to British merchants?—Entirely British."—" Can you state any other ports in China that you touched at besides Amoy?—Not any other principal ports; I touched at all the ports between Amoy and Canton.

"You lay off some ports, did not you?—I lay off the port called the Cape of Good Hope, and the Island of Namo.

"At what distance is the Cape of Good Hope from Canton?—About 300 miles to the north-east.

"Did you find good shelter for your ship?—Excellent; all those harbours are as safe as the port of Canton itself.

"Was the trade you carried on authorized by the laws of China?—*I understood it was not authorized, but it was done quite openly.*

"*In the same way that the opium trade is carried on at Canton?—The very same.*

"Have you ever experienced any difficulty in carrying on the trade although not formally sanctioned by the Chinese laws?—*Never the least.*

"Who were the parties with whom your trade was carried on?—The Chinese merchants.

"Resident at any particular points?—Some of them from the city of Amoy, some from Ta-ho, and Namo, and some from inland towns.

"Have you got better prices for those articles than could be got at Canton?—Yes.

"What was the difference of the price?—About 100 dollars upon the chest of opium, or 125, and sometimes 150, or even higher.

"Is that (the port of the Cape of Good Hope) near any town?—Yes, it is within fifteen miles of a very large city, the city of Ty-ho.

"From the time of your arrival, how long were you detained before you disposed of the whole of your cargo?—From fifteen to twenty days.

"Why did you make your returns in bullion only?—I was particularly desired by the agents of the brig to take nothing else.

"Could you have had returns in the produce of the country?—*I could have had returns in any produce of the provinces, such as sugar, tea, cassia, tortoise-shell, nankeens, or any thing that could be had.*

"You would have had no difficulty in completing your cargo of these articles?—Not the least.

"In what manner is the produce of the north-eastern provinces sent to Canton?—I presume it is principally sent by sea, from the number of large junks always upon the coast.

"Have you seen tea sent by sea?—Yes; I have been on board of two junks entirely loaded with tea.

"What was the size of them?—They could not have been less than 200 tons.

"From whence did they come?—They came from Amoy, and they were bound to Canton.

"Did you board the junks?—I boarded both of them, and sent letters by them to Canton."—"Were those letters regularly received?—They were received in due course.

"Do you think you could have loaded your vessel with teas of good quality?—*I have no doubt I could of the very best quality. I have no doubt I could have had any sort of Chinese produce that I wished.*

"What species of woollens do you think you could have disposed of?—Principally long ells and fine broad-cloth; blankets and camlets also would have sold very well; *they are in ready demand all along the coast of China.*

"Were there any duties paid to the government upon those cargoes?—I never paid any duties; but I understood that upon all opium that is taken away from the ships the inferior officers of the government get about twenty dollars for every chest; the Chinese pay that themselves; the ships pay nothing.

"Did you ever pay any port-charges of any kind?— Never.

"Were you ever annoyed by any of the Chinese authorities?—No. I have been requested, as a favour, to shift my situation, as the principal officer was coming; and I have gone away and come again, in one or two days.

"Perhaps a legitimate trade was not your object?—Not at all: we were trading in prohibited articles.

"Do you imagine that the contraband trade is more profitable than the authorized trade?—*I have never been in the authorized trade, and therefore cannot state that.*

"Did any other British ships under the British flag prosecute the same trade that you did at that time?—Yes; there was an English ship, the Merope, belonging to Calcutta; the Velletta; the Eugenia; the Fanecena, and the Dhaule schooner.

"What were those vessels?—All English vessels belonging to the port of Calcutta.

"Where were they trading to?—To Formosa, and the port of Nimpo, which is considerably to the north.

"Is not that in the province of Kiangnan?—I believe it is.

" Did those ships go to Amoy ?—One of them I think did, but they did nothing; they knew that nothing could be done by the merchants; the Merope touched off Amoy, but did not go in, because she could not trade in opium.

" Had you any communication with the commanders of those vessels ?—Frequently, although we had different interests, all except the Merope.

" Was your interest the same as the Merope ?—She had an agent of ours.

" Did you understand from the commanders of those vessels, that they carried on trade as easily as you did ?— With the same facilities; although I believe I was rather more fortunate than they were, being engaged in the trade earlier.

" At the ports you have named, do you know whether the import and export duties are paid to the government ? —*I am not aware of duties; I never heard the duties mentioned.*

" Did the Americans ever engage in this trade ?—American vessels have gone to the coast, but I believe on British account.

" Did the British vessels you have named visit any ports besides those you have mentioned ?—The Merope traded to the port of Chingchoo and the Island of Formosa.

" Did the Merope go to Nimpo and the Cape of Good Hope ?—*Yes; she touched at every port on the coast.*

" Which do you conceive is the best station for carrying on the trade ?—The best station I ever found, was between the Island of Namo and the Cape of Good Hope.

" Why do you conceive that to be the better ?—Being the centre between two very large towns.

" Have you ever been off the province of Fokien ?—Yes.

" What harbour did you go into there ?—I went into one of the ports of Chingchoo.

" What was the species of cultivation you saw when you landed there ?—The only species of cultivation I have seen was rice and sugar.

" Is the trade, which you have described as being carried on when you were there, still carried on ?—It is.

" In what year was this ?—In 1823 and 1824. Afterward I lay as a depôt-ship at Lintin."—" How long were you altogether in China ?—Four years and a half.

" In what year were the British ships you have mentioned there ?—They were there in the same year as myself; and

I left some of them lying as depôt-ships at Lintin; they are lying there now as depôt-ships.

" Do you know of any ships having been there last year? —No; I do not know of any ship; there was one vessel went up in 1828 when I was there, and delivered a cargo upon the coast.

" What are the depôt-ships?—*They are ships that lie outside of the Island of Macao, to receive opium, or any other goods that are wished to be deposited on board of them.*

" *Then you have no knowledge of any lawful trade carried on there at all?—Not the least.*

" Were the others obliged to move sometimes as well as you?—*Yes; we moved as a favour to the mandarins;* the mandarins come down once or twice a year, and send a person to warn you to shift yourselves.

" You were obliged to shift your station?—We were not obliged to do this, but *it was to favour them, that they might make a report that it was all clear.*

" What number of ships do you remember there at any one time?—I have seen as many as twenty ships at one time.

" How many European ships?—I have seen 10 European ships, and a considerable number of American ships."

If this be not free trade, what is? Establish a trade in corn and Manchester goods on the same footing between England and America; in that case it would be quite needless to repeal the English corn laws and American tariff. But here we must draw a distinction of first-rate consequence. The foreign trade of China, though perfectly free in its nature, is restricted in extent. Though free from bonds, permits, and taxes, it cannot at present be extended beyond the Bocca Tigris, and even on that one spot it is not secure. Upon this distinction the whole question turns. The people of England, by paying an extravagant price for tea, have enabled twenty-four men in London and seven men at Canton to carry on a trade which is called legal, but which ought to be called the losing trade. How to increase this trade is not worth asking: the grand point is to extend, not to alter, the free trade, which the Chinese call *Smug-pigeon,* and which, though of limited extent, is perfect in its kind.

What then is it that prevents the free trade from spreading to the whole coast of China, and increasing beyond any assignable limit? The political fears of the Chinese government. Therefore, says an Englishman, send another embassy to Pekin; instruct the ambassador to swear, like Lord Amherst, that he has no commercial objects, that he is sent across the world " to manifest the regard of his Britannic majesty for his Imperial majesty, and to improve the relations of amity that so happily subsisted between their illustrious parents Kien-lung and George the Third :" but this time do not trust altogether to the ambassador's skill in the art of lying ; back him with armed ships ; order him to talk of English conquests in India ; tell him to frighten the mandarins by a display of English power, and if necessary by the use of force : this is the way to calm the political fears of the Chinese government. And to destroy it likewise, we may add. No one who is acquainted with that government can doubt, that such a mission, if given, not to a priggish lord of the bedchamber, but to a man (a man, said Bonaparte, is wanted in China), would be entirely successful; that it would open the whole coast of China to the presence of Englishmen and English ships. But this object accomplished in this way, what would be the other consequences of thus exposing the weakness of the Chinese government to its own subjects and to foreign nations? Look to it, Jonathan! John Bull would have gone to work in this way long ago, if the English Hong had not been deeply interested in preserving every bar to the extension of free trade in China. The English Hong is at end. Be alive, Jonathan! Your smug-pigeon with the China-man is in danger.

Even mere threats from the English government, though couched, as no doubt they would be, in the form of a demand for redress of grievances, would, if they had for object the particular advantage of English traders in China, be viewed with jealousy by several governments of Europe, and still more by the United States. Suppose, however, that disregarding the jealousy of other nations, the English had compelled the mandarins to establish the trade of Englishmen in China on a satisfactory basis, would not the Dutch, the Russians, the French, and above all the Americans, demand, each nation for itself, as with equal facility they all might obtain, similar concessions from the feeble mandarins? Such demands on the part of some, at least, of those nations, would, it seems hardly doubtful, be the inevitable consequence of the successful use of force or threats by the English government. Thus the weakness of the government of China would be exposed in more than one instance, to its own subjects and to other nations. Other exposures of the same kind could not but ensue. Foreigners of all nations would enter China, and further expose to the people, not the weakness only, but the iniquity also, of the government. Next, the foreigners of each nation, having obtained some footing in China, would, if we conjecture from experience, seek to obtain privileges, each party striving to gain more than its rivals, and to injure them as much as possible. Either the nature of man is not always the same, or the history of European settlements in distant countries is false, if this would not be the case. Considering also that each party of foreigners in China would be so far removed from the control of its own government as to act almost without responsibility, there is reason to expect that the rivalry among those foreign adventurers would not be confined to trade, but would extend, as soon as it had been shown that the mandarins were unable to resist aggression, to interference between the people and their masters, to the excitement of revolt and civil war, and finally to territorial acquisition. In this way, contests must arise between some of those parties of foreign adventurers; and by degrees each party would, probably, enlist its distant government in the quarrel, until, at length, the miserable government of China being dissolved, or rather dissolving, as soon as its weakness had been made conspicuous, China would become, as Hindostan has been in modern times, a theatre of war for foreign nations. What has preserved China from the fate of India? The constancy of the mandarins in rejecting, as they would have avoided contact with the plague, every proposal from foreigners for the establishment of friendly intercourse. *Timeo Danaos et dona ferentes* has been the never-failing answer of the Chinese government to offers of friendship and advantage from other governments. In vain did the Dutch ambassador Titzing, a fat man, crawl upon all fours into the imperial presence, and remaining in that posture, beat his head nine times upon the ground; in vain did the lords Macartney and Amherst exhaust the arts of their craft to wheedle the lords of China into a belief that it was for the advantage of the great emperor to be on terms of friendship with the illustrious king; in vain have been self-abasement, rich presents, flattery, coaxing, prayers, lies, and remonstrances, when employed by the governments of Europe in order to obtain such a footing in China as might have furnished pretexts for measures of another kind. The existence of the government of China has been preserved by the constancy of the mandarins in rejecting offers of foreign friendship. The utter impracticability of the Tartars is their only defence. Break through that single barrier, and they must be swept away by a flood of internal revolt and foreign pretension.

If the existing government of foreigners were destroyed, it must be succeeded by another government of foreigners; since the ignorant, timid, and slavish people of China, being incapable of governing themselves, would tacitly invite foreigners to rule them, and would find nation after nation eager to undertake the task. In the end, probably, the English, who command the sea, would govern China as they govern India; and that the people of China would, in the long run, gain incalculably by such a change, there cannot be the least doubt. But what, in the meanwhile, would become of the foreign trade of China? And what could the people of England gain by ruling the Chinese empire? Not reckoning the gratification of national pride as an advantage, they would gain nothing beyond free commercial intercourse with the Chinese people. But they might miss this, aiming at it in this way; not to mention what they might lose in the confusion arising from the jealousy of other states, and the destruction of the Chinese government.

Still, if it were possible to counteract the political fears of the mandarins otherwise than by adopting measures of compulsion under the name of diplomacy, such measures, whatever the consequences likely to result from them, might be thought expedient. But considering the immediate evils that might arise from measures of compulsion, and the jealousy with which they would be viewed by the Americans at least, such measures, however easy, however sure of ultimate success, and however just when viewed with a mercantile eye, will not be thought expedient by the English, provided it be shown that a commercial intercourse with the Chinese people, free of its nature, and without limit as to extent, may be established without delay permanently, at little cost, without making a demand or even asking a favour of the trembling mandarins, and lastly, without exciting any national jealousy. To show all this, is the object of what follows.

Sir Stamford Raffles founded the commercial station of Sincapore, in the belief that the Chinese free traders would readily find their way to that port in their own ships. He was mistaken by above twenty degrees. Near twenty years' experience has shown that the distance between Sincapore and the most commercial parts of the Chinese coast is much too great for junk navigation. But Raffles, who was a man, has pointed out the way to extend the free trade of China without diplomacy or war ; not only without further alarming the poor mandarins, but so that, with the extension of free trade, their present terrors should entirely subside. In order to give to the free trade of China its utmost possible development, the only thing wanted is a free market-place ; a place to which Chinese dealers could easily resort ; where foreign ships might lie undisturbed by wind or government, and where foreigners might live in security ; a mere market-place, convenient for Chinese dealers, and out of the control of the Chinese government.

Along the whole coast of China there exist not less than a thousand islands, some of which possess all the requisites of a trading port ; good anchorage, shelter from all winds, and plenty of fresh water. There are more habitable islands near the coast of China, than along any other coast in the world of the same extent. But now observe another peculiarity : those islands are not subject to the government of the main land. Some of them are uninhabited ; some are inhabited by a few wretched fishermen, who govern themselves ; and some by a race of pirates, who make war against the Chinese government, occasionally putting a stop to the coasting trade, murdering great numbers of Chinese, levying tribute on the continent, and at times making peace with the mandarins on very advantageous terms. Some evidence on this point appears in a note below.* The emperor of China claims dominion in England, and makes his subjects believe that he receives tribute

---

* The Lion continued thus several days working off the China shore, without gaining a mile. She then stood over for Formosa, where there was less current against her, and she made some progress ; but the turbulence of the weather was such, that she sprung both topmasts, and was obliged to return to the Ladrones, in order to be in some degree of shelter, for the purpose of being refitted, and capable of renewing her efforts to get forward. Several piratical vessels, filled with Chinese, were hovering in this neighbourhood, and had very lately taken several Chinese junks, and plundered the adjacent islands. The practice of these pirates is to make slaves of such able-bodied men as they take prisoners, to put the rest to death, and to sink the junks, and burn the houses, after taking out whatever they deem valuable."—*Staunton's Embassy to China*, vol. ii. p. 521.

" During the time the pirates infested the coasts, numbers of salt junks

from that country ; but in fact, and in right too, his power is limited by the water's edge of the Chinese coast. At sea, the pirates are his masters, and neither he nor his ancestors ever conquered the islands. Those islands, therefore, are open to be used by anybody for any purpose. If one of the Ladrones or Pirate Isles, were turned into a market-place for the traders of all nations, the English and Chinese Hongs, were they not *in extremis*, might complain that the vested rights of the pirates had been attacked ; but who else could find fault with the conversion of one of those robbers' nests to so excellent a use ?

Not the Chinese government, to whom the founders of the market-place would say :—You dread foreigners ; we keep out of your way. You forbid us to enter your ports, Canton excepted: we withdraw from Canton. You trem-

were intercepted by them, and salt rose to an extravagant price. At length the Company were obliged to negotiate with the admiral of the pirates, and paid a certain sum for every vessel he furnished with a passport.

" After a while, the captains and crews of the salt junks became leagued with the pirates, and used to convey to them, clandestinely, provisions, stores, ammunition, &c. The government detected the connivance, and laid an embargo, of a sudden, upon the returning salt junks.—The pirate admiral, finding his supplies cut off, invaded the country about the inner passage, leading to Macao, where he cut all the ripe rice, and carried it off, as well as a great number of women, whom he presented to his followers. His name was Apo-Tsy, a very formidable robber, who had an immense fleet of junks, and upwards of 20,000 men under his command. He at length became so daring, that he intercepted the boats carrying cargoes to the ships at Whampoa, and committed depredations on land within eighteen miles of Canton. The viceroy became alarmed, for he had no army to oppose him, and was forced to employ an English armed country ship to drive him out of the river. Many naval engagements took place between the Chinese warships and the pirates ; but the latter invariably obtained the victory. The Portuguese at Macao were also called upon, or rather told their offer would be accepted, to fit out ships against the pirates, and a sum of money would be granted to them by the Canton government. However, very little good resulted in the way of fighting ; but the Portuguese rendered the viceroy an essential service, in the way of negotiation, as mediators between him and the pirates. Apo-Tsy positively refused to listen to the viceroy's promise of an amnesty, should the pirates return to their allegiance, without the Macao government becoming security for the faithful performance of the contract. The Macao government, therefore, came forward, and pledged itself to the admiral, who immediately submitted with all his followers. He was made governor of the province of Fokien, and his followers were all pardoned. During the wars with the Chinese, the pirates took a fleet, commanded by a thai-tuk, or admiral, who was uncle to the present emperor. Apo-Tsy had some dislike to the Chinese admiral ; and when he took him, ordered him to be beheaded. The present emperor (Tao-Kuang) on coming to the throne, sent the governor of Fokien a polite message to say, that the laws of China required blood for blood, and he therefore sent for his head instead of his uncle's. There was no excuse to be made, and Apo-Tsy's head was conveyed to Pekin."—*Dobell*, vol. ii. p. 153.

ble lest we should sow revolutionary principles among your people by residing with them ; henceforth there shall be no intercourse between them and us, save for the purpose of exchanging goods; and that intercourse shall not take place within your dominions.   Hitherto, between you and us there have been frequent quarrels ; but now all grounds of dispute is gone ; we demand no rights, ask no favours. Well we know, that you cannot prevent your people from coming to us for trade in this our new, our own market-place ; and sure we are that if you could do so, you would not ; because if you should do so, the present arrangement, which ought to relieve you of all anxiety, must be superseded by diplomacy, which would frighten you extremely, and in the end, probably, realize your worst fears. The step that we have taken was devised expressly for your comfort ; tremble no more ; we bid you farewell for ever.

Nor could the Americans object to an English, any more than the English could object to an American trading station near the coast of China ; provided that, in either case, the market-place was free, that is, open to all nations on perfectly equal terms.   Why not so in an island used merely for trade, as well as on the main land, where, if the Chinese government permitted trade, they would, as far as they might be able, treat all the foreign traders alike?   The English exclude the Americans from Sincapore.   It so happens that Jonathan suffers little by John Bull's meanness in this affair ; Sincapore being, I repeat, more than twenty degrees too far south for its intended purpose ; but Jonathan has a right to his revenge, and may take it, over-coming evil with good, by establishing a Sincapore in the proper place, for the use of English as well as the Chinese and Americans.   Concert between two nations, whose origin, language, and real interests are one, would be better still, and would not be difficult, if the English ministers, instead of being proud, lazy, selfish lords, were, like the American ministers, active men of business, liable to be removed for neglecting the public good.

If, however, this happy change should not occur in time, there are islands enough on the coast of China for all nations to choose among, who may wish to establish a market-place for trade with the Chinese ; and for two reasons it is very desirable that more than one such trading station should be established.   Because in the first place, the more numerous such stations, the more easy would be the total suppression of piracy on the coast of China ; and secondly, because if there were but one station, nearly opposite the mouth of the Canton river, such free trade as now takes place in that river, though it would go to that new market-place, would not be extended to the northern maritime provinces, where the greatest demand for foreign goods exists and where the principal exports of China are raised. To show how much would be saved by a direct trade with the northern maritime provinces, and how extensive such a trade would probably become, some conclusive evidence is given below.*

* The Dutch ambassador and his suite, on their return from Pekin in 1796, passed through what may be considered the richest and most populous provinces of China; and Van der Braam's account of the journey abounds with information on the state of the maritime district in the neighbourhood of the great Blue River, or Yang-tse Kiang, which rises in the mountains of Thibet and traverses the Chinese provinces of Setchuen, Konquang, and Kiang-man ; and falls into the sea at no great distance from the mouth of the Hoang-Ho or Yellow River, the second river of China, and indeed of Asia. Van der Braam, one of the most phlegmatic of Dutchmen, described what he saw at the moment of seeing it, and without the least appearance of exaggeration : yet his journal, in that part of it which relates to the temperate maritime provinces, becomes a mere catalogue of villages, towns, cities, canals, aqueducts, bridges, and other signs of a dense, industrious, and wealthy population. Has the East India Company any trade with this part of China ? No direct trade whatever, and if some little indirect trade by means of internal carriage, still almost without being conscious of it. Considering that this is the heart of the Chinese Empire, that the climate requires woollen cloths, which are a staple production of England, and that the entrances of two wide rivers would afford great facilities for conducting the unauthorised trade, this, beyond all comparison, appears to be the spot where the trading disposition of the Chinese people ought to be cultivated.
" Can you," Mr. Marjoribanks is asked, " say whether the demand for English woollen manufactures in China is capable of being increased according to the increased supply ?" and he answers—" I imagine that, if our manufactures could be introduced *into the northern provinces* of the empire, the demand for them would decidedly increase."—" Are there any insuperable obstacles to the introduction of our woollens into the northern parts of China ? The ports of China being hermetically sealed against us for many years ?"—" What do you consider the impediments to a greater extension of trade ? The limits which the Chinese have set to the foreign trade ; their confining it to one remote corner of one of the southern provinces of the empire. The articles which we import into China are carried to the northern provinces through the interior of the country."
" The black tea imported by the East India Company is grown and manufactured in the province of Fokien, with the exception of about one-third of that sort called by us Bohea, which third part is produced in the north-eastern corner of the province of Canton. The green tea is all grown in the provinces of Kiang-nan, Kiang-si, and Che-kiang, but chiefly in the two former."
Mr. Davies, like Mr. Marjoribanks, a servant of the Company, and of course a friend to the monopoly, says—" the tea trade would be more beneficial, because I conceived it would be larger, if it were near to the centre of

One word touching the cost of establishing the most free, and perhaps most extensive trade in the world. The reckless jobbing of those who managed the old English constitution has, together with the uneasiness arising from low profits, led to such a passion for retrenchment, that the new English government will probably be denied funds for many a useful purpose. But, in this case, no public funds are required. The harbour dues of Sincapore (which is little more than a stopping-place for English ships) the mere harbour dues of that ill-chosen and merely English port, are sufficient to defray the expense of maintaining it. The trade of a well-chosen market-place on the coast of China, open to all nations on equal terms, must produce, from moderate harbour dues alone, more than enough to cover the cost of establishing and preserving it; supposing the work performed in the American fashion, with a view to utility, not in the old English fashion, with a view to robbing the public. Besides, referring to the preceding remarks on the causes of the value of land, to the value of land at Sincapore, Penang, and Batavia; a value produced mainly by the competition of Chinese settlers; and bearing in mind that as many Chinese as could find room would settle in a free market-place near the coast of China, it would seem that great profits might be made by an outlay of capital in the way proposed. The English are puzzled to find investments for their capital. But if their expiring Hong should for the present forbid them to lay out money in this way, why do not they lend money to the Americans? and who was it that lately negotiated a loan between English capitalists and the city of New-Orleans? it was Joshua Bates, himself an American, chief of the first commercial firm in England, deeply engaged in American trade,

the empire; that very great accession to the prices of tea which arises from the long land-carriage would be avoided, if the trade were nearer to the tea provinces.   *   *   *   *   *   *
"With all that has been done, the facilities" (of internal carriage) "are in a very inferior state to what they might be. The river which brings the tea to Canton from the frontier of the province, where it has to cross a high mountain, is a mere trout-stream for a great portion of the way; and foreigners of all descriptions have been obliged to wait for months at Canton, on account of there not being enough water in that river to float the vessels that bring the teas."
On this head, more evidence of a conclusive nature might be brought forward; but what has been given will satisfy most readers. Those who wish for further information on the subject, will find it in Van der Braam's work in the accounts of Lord Macartney's and Lord Amherst's embassies, in Captain Hall's account of Loo Choo, and in the Parliamentary Reports.

and intimately acquainted. with the trade of China. An Anglo-American company could not, indeed, make money, by extending free trade to the whole coast of China, without the sanction of some government, without a flag and a charter. Penn, who made money even by planting a colony on the desert coast of America, had a charter from his government, but beyond that piece of parchment, no assistance. The present English ministers would not grant a charter for the purpose in question, which they would dislike as a dangerous example of cheapness, without patronage, in the management of great public undertakings. They would prefer a costly embassy to Pekin. Lord Amherst's pocket-money, forming part of the great sum expended on the last embassy, was 40,000*l.* ; more than six times the yearly pay of his American majesty. The English ministers, then, would spurn at a proposal for effecting a public object with private funds ; that is, carefully, cheaply, without patronage, as they lately refused a charter to some of the best men in England, who wished to employ private funds in founding a Pennsylvania on the south coast of New Holland. But their time is nearly up ; all the usefulness that was in them having been got out of them. Meanwhile, before their successors shall be named by the new ruling order, striped bunting would do as well as the union jack ; and an Anglo-American company willing to speculate on the establishment of market-places for free teade with the Chinese, would not be rebuffed at Washington.

At Washington, New-York, Boston, Baltimore, or Philadelphia, what follows may be read with interest.

Questions submitted to Mr. Aken, with his answers.*

1. What have been your means of becoming acquainted with the foreign trade of China ?—I commanded the ship Exmouth, of 725 tons, from Calcutta, and visited China under a license from the East India Company in 1817, and spent four months in the Canton river. In the following year I again visited China in the same ship, and again spent four months in the Canton river. In 1819 I made a similar voyage. On all these occasions the whole of a mixed

* Mr. Aken resides in London. Great part of his life has been spent at sea : there are but few coasts in the world that he has not visited ; and his character as a navigator is established by the work of Captain Flinders, who appointed him master of the Investigator discovery ship.

cargo, worth as much as 60,000l., was consigned to myself; and I had the entire disposal of it, as well as the charge of reloading the ship, acting as captain and supercargo.

2. What do you conceive would be the effect on the unauthorized trade, of establishing insular commercial stations near the coast, and in the most favourable situations?—The effect would be, that the Chinese would very readily enter into all your views of trade. *Great numbers of Chinese would settle themselves in such stations, in order to conduct trade. They would enter heart and soul into the spirit of a free trade, which nothing could prevent them from establishing.* They have all kinds of craft along-shore, the junks being from 20 to 500 tons; and they would come with their vessels to the commercial stations, bringing with them Chinese products to be exchanged for European and other products. The government has no power to prevent the people from trading even in the Canton river, and could not by any means interfere with a trade carried on at a short distance from the main. My opinion of establishing such stations for trade is, that it would be most advantageous, and would cause a very great increase of the foreign trade of China ; but it would destroy the trade of the Hong merchants, and of the East India Company also, if Englishmen were not prevented from trading at the stations.

3. What in your opinion are the most proper places for such stations? on this point be so good as to furnish any information that you may think calculated to be of use.— On account of the unskilfulness of the Chinese as sailors, it would be advisable to have more than one station, in order to keep up a trade with a great extent of coast. Suppose you had several stations ; I would begin with one island, called *Pulo Condore*, in latitude about 8 deg. North, almost within sight of the coast of Cambodia ; which island was settled by the English 130 years ago ; but they were cut off by the Macassar soldiers whom they employed. I have been close to this island and all round it. It is inhabited by a few fishermen. The anchorage and shelter are good ; and I was assured by the people who came from the island to my ship, that there was plenty of good water there. The next situation would be one of the Great Ladrones, or Pirate Isles, near the mouth of the Canton river ; and the best of these islands appears to me to be Neong-kong-oa, where there is good anchorage for a great number of ships, and plenty of water. This island, on the north side of the great Lema Channel, used to be inhabited by pirates of the

most ferocious character. The Chinese government could not prevent a settlement from being formed there, nor interfere with the settlers afterward. Another place for a station, at which a great trade would soon spring up, is one of the numerous islands in the neighbourhood of Amoy, in latitude 24 deg. North. I have not visited this part of the coast; but from such charts as we have, and what I have heard from those who have sailed further north than Canton, I have not any doubt that several islands, well suited for the purpose, would be found in the neighbourhood of Amoy. The most important place for a station is still further north, near the mouths of the great rivers; but of this part of the coast I know only that it has many islands; as may be said of the whole coast of China, which is more studded with islands than any other coast in the world.

" Cette île (Formosa), quoique située vis à vis la province de Fokien, et à trente lieues de la côte, n'etait pas soumise à l'empire de la Chine, qui n'a point la passion des conquêtes, et·qui par une politique inhumaine et mal entendue, aime mieux laisser périr une partie de sa population que d'envoyer la surabondance de ses sujets dans des terres voisines. Ou trouva que Formose avait cent trente ou cent quarante lieues de tour. Ses habitans à, en juger par leurs mœurs et par leur figure, paraissaient descendus des Tartares de la partie la plus septentrionale de l'Asie. Vraisemblablement la Corée leur avait servi de chemin. Ils vivaient, la plupart, de pêche ou de chasse et allaient presque nus. Les Hollandais, après avoir pris sans obstacle toutes les lumières que la prudence exigent, jugèrent que le lieu le plus favorable pour un établissement étoit une *petite île* voisine de la grande. Ils trouvaient dans cette situation trois avantages considérables; une defense aisée, si la haine ou la jalousie cherchaient à les troubler; un port formé par les deux îles; la facilité d'avoir dans toutes les moussons *une communication sûre avec la Chine.* La nouvelle colonie se fortifiait insensiblement sans éclat, lorsqu'elle *s'éleva tout d'un coup à une prospérité qui étonna toute l'Asie.* Ce fut à la conquête de la Chine par les Tartares qu'elle dut ce bonheur inespéré : ainsi les torrens engraissent les vallons de la substance des montagnes ravagées. Plus de cent mille Chinois, qui ne voulaient pas se soumettre au vainqueur, se réfugièrent à Formose. Ils y portèrent l'activité qui leur est particulière, la culture du riz et du sucre, *et y attirérent des vaisseaux sans nombre de leur nation.*

Bientôt l'île devint le centre de toutes les liaisons que Java, Siam, les Philippines, la Chine, le Japon, et d'autres contrées voulurent former. EN PEU D'ANNÉES ELLE SE TROUVA LE PLUS GRAND MARCHÉ DE L'INDE."[*]

[*] The Abbé Raynal's Philosophical and Political History of the Establishments and Commerce of Europeans in the two Indies. Vol. i. p. 286. Paris Edition of Amable Costes & Co.

NOTE IX.

SOME SOCIAL PECULIARITIES OF THE AMERICANS.

Peculiar state of religion—Causes of superstition without bigotry or fanaticism—Inquisitiveness—Rudeness of the backwoodsmen—Bigotry in patriotism—Neglect of learning.

Most English travellers in America hurt their credit for veracity by describing instances of the most violent religious phrensy. In England, many people do not believe Mrs. Trollope's story of the "anxious benches:" I do, not doubting either, but satisfied, that throughout the less populous parts of the Union people often meet for the express purpose of working themselves into a state of superstitious madness. To overrate the crazy doings of a camp-meeting in the back woods would be impossible. Bodies writhing, arms swinging, legs dancing, eyes rolling ; groans, shouts, howls, and shrieks ; men knocking their own heads against trees, and women tearing the clothes off each other's backs ; the congregation frantic with fear of the devil, and the preacher drunk with his own gibberish ; it is all true, and of common occurrence. Captain Hall would say, it arises from the want of a spending class to set an example of decorum in public worship; or from the want of loyalty, to which he attributes so many of Jonathan's peculiarities. Mrs. Trollope would have the English believe, that superstition in America is owing to democratic government. Some, again, find a cause for it in the want of a state religion ; adopting the notion of David Hume, and supposing that "each ghostly practitioner, depending for subsistence on the liberality of individuals, continually endeavours by some novelty to excite the languid devotion of his audience, without regard to truth, morals, or decency in the doctrines inculcated ; and that thus every tenet is adopted that best suits the disorderly affections of the human frame, customers being drawn to each conventicle by new industry and address in practising on the passions and credulity of the populace." Another set of Englishmen, who, in their abstract love of democracy, cannot bear to be told that some things in America might be mended ; haters of church establishments, too, who therefore disagree with David Hume ; these, when asked to account for the excesses of love feasts and camp meetings, lay all the blame on the oppressors of those puritans who colonized New-England, concluding that the fanaticism which arose from persecution has been handed down to living Americans and spread over the Union by emigration from the New-England states. The doctrines of Mrs. Trollope and Captain Hall are not worth, the others will not bear, examination.

Hume's argument in favour of church establishment supposes the existence of a " populace," liable from their profound ignorance to be deluded by needy speculators in religion. But there is no populace in America ; and those congregations, whether under roofs or in the forest, which most resemble the inmates of a madhouse are composed of people whose knowledge goes beyond reading and writing ; shrewd, worldly-minded, calculating, industrious buyers and sellers, and what is more, politicians represented in a local parliament and in congress, who make the laws which they have to obey ; laws which, measured by the rule of utility, show more practical wisdom in the makers than the " greatest statesmen" of Europe can pretend to. On the other hand, the spirit of puritanism is extinct in America. The founders of New-England, as their hot zeal arose from persecution, so were they, always excepting the Quakers, persecutors in their turn, more cruel than the oppressors from whom they had fled ; and far more bigoted, since they persecuted as they had suffered for religion's sake, while the churchmen who had hunted them out of England were moved by a spirit altogether worldly. But that bitter, that most vindictive religious zeal, which dictated the first laws of the New-England colonies, is now unknown in America. The *odium theologicum* did not descend to the grandchildren of the puritans. Scenes have been lately acted at Exeter-Hall, in London, exhibitions of furious religious bigotry, such as it would be impossible to get up in America ; where all sects are tolerant, and not one takes half so much pains to make proselytes as several sects in

England. Of the many religions that flourish in America, one only, of course, can be true; yet is there no one sect which zealously declares all the others in the wrong. In things spiritual, as there is neither favour nor persecution from the government, so bigotry and fanaticism, in the English sense of those words, have perished. In order to describe the peculiar state of religion in America, one must use words not commonly applied to the subject.

The Americans, speaking generally, are religious by habit, but not constantly, not mixing up things spiritual with things temporal; not showing, I had almost said not feeling, religious sentiments, except when they meet for public worship. The custom of attending public worship is almost universal; and to neglect it would be considered indecent; but so completely has custom taken the place of zeal in this matter, that what form of worship a citizen prefers is perfectly indifferent to all the other citizens, like the colour of his coat. Members of the same family, even, belong to congregations of opposite tenets, without the slightest interruption of domestic peace. Moreover, avowed deists, who in England would be scouted as infidels, are as much respected as the most devout Christians, provided they belong to a sect, and congregate once a week to profess their limited faith. Lukewarmness, indifference this would be called in England, and has been called by English writers; but some other expression must be found for it, since among the most tolerant congregations in America are those which occasionally work themselves into a state of religious phrensy. Sobriety in general, with occasional fits of intoxication, seems a more correct description of spiritual matters in America. The general sobriety is explained by a total separation between religion and politics; but this does not account for the occasional drunkenness. What is the cause of that religious phrensy now and then exhibited by people, whose ordinary religious feelings are so tolerant and sober, so much the reverse of bigotry and fanaticism?

The terms of the question point to an answer which explains this curious moral phenomenon. Violent occasional excitement of the mind appears to be a physical want with those, whose ordinary condition either does not require or prevents much mental exertion. None take such delight in getting drunk with spirits as the savage whose monotonous life keeps his mental faculties in a state of torpor. Rum in America, whiskey in Ireland, gin at present in England, opium in Turkey and China, and tobacco in Spain, are substitutes for moral stimulants. But where in the wide world shall be found any considerable number of people, whose minds are not actively employed by their common pursuits, and who yet forego the use of extraordinary stimulants? Nowhere. The rule is universal, including those savages, who for want of spirits, drugs, music, shows, romances, and idols, are said to intoxicate themselves by twirling round till they fall. The kinds of mental stimulants which it seems in man's nature to require, differ with the infinite variety of men's circumstances. The spirits of a water-drinker are raised by one glass of wine, drank without company; while an habitual wine-drinker is not elated by a dozen glasses, nor by two dozen, unless there be others to drink with him. The solitary prisoner is exhilarated by obtaining a single companion, drunk, he knows not why, when he returns to society; while on him who enjoys social intercourse every day, it has no unusual effect. There would be no end of examples to show that different circumstances or states of mind produce a craving for mental stimulants very different in kind and degree; that in this case, as in so many more, what is one man's meat is another man's poison.

Now, the dispersed inhabitants of America, and in particular of those new settlements where love-feasts and camp-meetings are most common, pass a great part of their lives in solitude; not in absolute solitude, like that which, when inflicted as a punishment, produces death or insanity, but out of the way of social intercourse, each family being isolated from all the others, except on rare occasions, when they congregate in spite of distance and bad roads. The effect on the mind of this lonely and monotonous existence, can hardly be conceived by Englishmen generally, to whom the stillness of the country gives fresh and pleasant feelings. To a lone American family, there is nothing so delightful as one of those occasions when many families meet for any purpose; and when thousands meet for a religious purpose, the congregation, excited by a total change of scene, by the unusual confluence of numbers, and by the novelty of an impulse common to many, are easily intoxicated by eloquence, of which the object is to inflame their already heated imaginations. The preacher may or may not be as sincere as his audience; but in either case he is not to be blamed for their extravagance. Instead of causing the phrensy over which he presides, he only helps to gratify a desire, the desire for some violent mental excitement, which has resulted from sameness and solitude. A wandering preacher in America does not create, but only supplies, a demand for his services; visiting thinly-peopled districts, not with a view to delude the scattered inhabitants, but because he knows that they already long for his presence, that they are waiting for a dose of superstitious terror; and that if he should not help them to devil-worship, they would send for some other dealer in that, to them, intoxicating drug.

It has been remarked, that on these occasions of self-sought delirium, the women are wilder than the men. And this might have been expected; because as almost everywhere women lead a more lonely and monotonous life than men, they are more susceptible of excitement from novelty and crowds. They are so especially in the back-settlements of America, where travelling, if not dangerous, requires energy and bodily strength, not to mention how much time. In such spots, men pass weeks together without exchanging two ideas; women, months, or even years, without forming one. If the men did not attend markets, fairs, and elections, they would probably be as wild as the women at love-feasts and camp-meetings. The peculiar extravagance of the women, on such occasions, helps to account for the extravagance of both sexes; and this view of the subject is confirmed by reflecting that they who compose the wildest congregations of America, when they return home after a fit of superstitious intoxication, are as diligent as ever in their ordinary pursuits, more contented than before, and, touching religion, not less tolerant and sober, not a whit less different from English bigots and fanatics.*

* Mr. Flint, in his Geography and History of the Western States, after showing the utility of camp-meetings, writes—" Nine-tenths of the religious instruction of the country is given by people who itinerate, and who are, with very few exceptions, notwithstanding all that has been said to the contrary, men of great zeal and sanctity. These earnest men, who have little to expect from pecuniary support, and less from the prescribed reverence and influence, which can only appertain to a stated ministry, find at once that every thing depends on the cultivation of popular talents. Zeal for the great cause, mixed imperceptibly with a spice of earthly ambition, and the latent emulation and pride of our nature, and other motives which unconsciously influence, more or less, the most sincere and the most disinterested—the desire of distinction among their contemporaries and their brethren—and a reaching struggle for the fascination of popularity, goad them on to study all the means and arts of winning the people. Travelling from month to month through dark forests, with such ample time and range for deep thought, as they amble slowly on horseback through their peregrinations, the men naturally acquire a pensive and romantic turn of thought and expression, such as we think favourable to eloquence. Hence the preaching is of a

It would be a great mistake to suppose that obstacles to social intercourse are confined to the newest settlements. When the states were colonies, waste land was usually given away by their governments, often in vast tracts to persons who had no means of cultivating them, and who, therefore, either left the land in a desert state, or disposed of it to others at so very cheap a rate that individuals readily obtained more land than they could possibly cultivate. In either case, the dispersion of the people was very great; for either the desert, wanting roads, was a bar to intercourse among the people who surrounded it, or each settler fixed on it was, still by want of roads, separated from all the other settlers. But since the government of the United States has, generally, instead of giving away new land, sold it by auction to the highest bidder above a fixed minimum price, some new states, which offered peculiar attractions, have been more densely or rather less thinly peopled than some of the old colonies, and far better provided with roads, which are more easily made in proportion as they are less wanted, that is, in proportion as the people are less dispersed. Still, above two-thirds of the inhabitants of America pass the greater part of their lives in comparative loneliness; in a state which, if it could be imagined by hill squires in Wales, even they would call unbearable solitude. It is a state of existence not readily imagined by any Englishman, quite incomprehensible by those who have always lived in towns; but the Englishman, who shall conceive what it is, will be at no loss to account for many American habits and customs, besides that peculiar kind of superstition which displeases English travellers.

The officers of Captain Parry's second voyage, after being cut off from the world for more than two years, landed on one of the Shetland islands, and were invited to dine with a party of the inhabitants. At this meeting, I have been told, questions and answers formed the whole conversation; the voyagers, though craving for news, being obliged to gratify the habitual inquisitiveness of those secluded islanders. In like manner, the curiosity of Americans is not a vulgar trick, nor, as some will have it, a fruit of democratic government, but a result, natural and inevitable, of a faulty mode of colonization, in which no thought was

highly popular cast, and its first aim is to excite the feelings. Hence too, excitements, or in religious parlance, 'awakenings,' are common in all this region."—*Quoted by Stuart*, vol. ii. p. 456.

ever taken to keep a due proportion between people and land.*

The American of the backwoods has often been described to the English as grossly ignorant, dirty, unsocial, delighting in rum and tobacco, attached to nothing but his rifle, adventurous, restless, more than half-savage. Deprived of social enjoyments or excitements, he has recourse to those of savage life, and becomes (for in this respect the Americans degenerate) unfit for society. As the evils of society, misery, and vice produced by misery, are unknown in America, as they would have been quite as well avoided with a greater concentration of the people; as, indeed, the produce of American industry might have been greater if the people had been less dispersed, the semi-barbarism of American backwoodsmen is an unnecessary evil; and an evil, too, without the least countervailing advantage; but, though caused without a motive, still it has been caused by all the governments which have disposed of new land in America, from that of Queen Elizabeth, which bestowed twenty-five millions of acres upon an individual, to that of President Jackson, which sells new land at the very low price of five shillings per acre.

Americans are accused of presumption, conceit, and gross national vanity. Allowing for exceptions in the more populous parts of the Union, and especially in the great seaport towns, the people of America may, in this respect, be likened to the Tartar conquerors of China, who, being themselves barbarous, consider all but themselves barbarians. The least civilized Americans, those in a word who despise the old country, make up, like the Chinese mandarins, for want of bigotry in religion, by excessive bigotry in their patriotism. Some creoles of New South Wales visiting England, thought London a miserable place when compared with Sydney. The settlers of New South Wales and Van Dieman's Land, adjoining colonies, planted by the same people, in the same way, and nearly at the same time, cannot bear, if we may judge by their books and newspapers, any comparison between the two very similar sheep-walks, which does not represent one as greatly superior to the other, according to which set of colonists

---

* "I found them very inquisitive; far more so than any of the New-Englanders I have ever met with; but I afterward learned that these people had lately come from a remote part of the country, where, probably, there were no schools."—*Stuart*, vol. ii. p. 345.

may be addressed. Nearly all colonists, it is remarked, or at least nearly all people born in dispersed colonies, are fanatically proud of their own wild country, and love to disparage the rest of the world. This narrowness of mind, arising from ignorance, seems proper to the barbarous conquerors of China; but, in colonies planted by the most civilized nations, it is a degenerate sentiment, a step backwards from civilization to barbarism, and out of the course of nature, which seems favourable, stoppages reckoned, to the improvement of mankind. In such cases, the ignorance which promotes conceit and mean pride, is a result of dispersion; the original cause of it in America being not democracy, Captain Hall, but the low price of new land.

But the Captain Halls of England, when they contend that democracy produces neglect of learning in America, make out a case which has some show of truth. The memory of Franklin, say they, honoured in Europe, is despised in America, save by a few whose eccentricity goes to prove the rule. Subject colonies produced scholars and philosophers: the democratic Union depends on England for literature, or rather for a supply of novels, the only books suited to the American market. In all the United States, there is not an observatory; Copley and West could not live in America; Cooper and Irving publish in Europe. Among nations called civilized, the Americans are the most neglectful of fine arts, science, and philosophy; and in America the cultivation of learning has fallen off with the progress of democracy. Therefore, in America, democracy is unfavourable to the cultivation of learning.

This statement of facts is true;* and the conclusion appears true to many in England, because English travellers in the United States have carefully shut their eyes to a circumstance by which they might have accounted for most of the social peculiarities of America. Democracy, that is, political equality, which lays open to all alike every

* " Men of science, too, and of literature, not a small body in England, will find but few persons in the United States not engaged in professional business, and have not, in that country, the means of resorting to great public libraries, which they find in England indispensable for their pursuits. They find but few people *disposed to sympathize with them in the objects which interest them.* The United States do not offer a desirable asylum for persons of this description, even if they are in straitened circumstances. It will be much more for their happiness to contract their style of living in England than to make a voyage to America."—*Stuart,* vol. ii. page 427.

career of ambition, and makes usefulness the standard of merit, must surely be very favourable to the cultivation of learning; more especially when accompanied, as it is in the United States, by universal ease, which bestows leisure upon all. The Americans are the only people in the world blessed with leisure and equality. If political equality should be established in England, together with high profits and wages, who can doubt that the English would advance rapidly in every department of knowledge. Why then have the Americans degenerated in this respect? why do they set a lower value on knowledge than the colonists of Franklin's time?

" Though," says Adam Smith, " in a rude state of society there is a good deal of variety in the occupations of every individual, there is not a great deal in those of the whole society. Every man does or is capable of doing almost every thing which any other man does or is capable of doing. Every man has a considerable degree of knowledge, ingenuity, and invention, but scarce any man has a great degree. The degree, however which is commonly possessed, is generally sufficient for conducting the whole simple business of society. In a civilized state, on the contrary, though there is little variety in the occupations of the greater part of individuals, there is an almost infinite variety in those of the whole society. These varied occupations present an almost infinite variety of objects to the contemplation of those few, who, being attached to no particular occupation themselves, have leisure and inclination to examine the occupations of other people. The contemplation of so great a variety of objects necessarily exercises their minds in endless comparisons and combinations, and renders their understandings in an extraordinary degree both acute and comprehensive." But rudeness and civilization are effects as well as causes. By going further back, by substituting *dispersed* for *rude*, and *concentrated* for *civilized*, we get nearer, at least, to the truth. In the history of the world, there is no example of a society at once dispersed and highly civilized; while there are instances without end, in the history of colonization, of societies which, being civilized, became barbarous as soon as they were dispersed over an extensive territory. That division of each man's labour among several employments, which, says Adam Smith, is the immediate cause of ignorance, is an effect of dispersion; and dispersion interferes with the cultivation of knowledge in another way; that is, by obstacles to social intercourse, to the interchange of ideas, to the exercise of the mental faculties. By adding to this consideration one fact, the difficulty may be solved.

The citizens of the United States are a more dispersed society than the colonists of Franklin's time. When Jefferson wrote the declaration of independence, the vast regions west of the Alleghanies had scarcely been opened for settlement. Washington became a soldier in contests with the Indians on the western frontier of Virginia, which is now the eastern frontier of states more extensive than the dependent colonies. Even if the increase of people had been equal to the acquisition of land, still the dispersion would have been greater, because the interior settlements are, by reason of their great distance from the sea, more deficient in natural means of communication. Washington often foretold some of the evils that would result from spreading towards the west, unless the eastern and western states were connected by canals and good roads. His warning was neglected until lately, when the eastern states became alarmed at the amount of emigration to the west. In those eastern states, the dependent colonies that were, they talk now of Washington's inspiration, and are most anxious to establish means of intercourse with the western settlements : they will find it difficult to remedy their own error. The western wilderness was theirs, and liable to be treated in the way most for their advantage. They thought only of gratifying their national vanity, by extending as much as possible the surface of the Union. Not content with promoting emigration to the wilderness, when their own population was so scanty that they ought rather to have encouraged immigration from Europe, they sent to Europe for the purpose of acquiring more wilderness, and in one case actually paid hard money for an accession of mischief.* The result is, that population has spread, not merely as fast as it has increased, but faster ; that there are fewer people to the square mile than when population was about a quarter of its present amount ; and that this smaller number of people in proportion to land, besides being separated from each other by greater dis-

---

* " The acquisition by the United States in 1803, of the territories belonging to France in North America, including New Orleans, Louisiana, and the Mississippi, was a most important one. The negotiations resulted in the cession of the French territory in North America, *exceeding in extent the whole land then belonging to the United States*, for sixty millions of francs."—*Stuart*, vol. ii. p. 227.

tance, are not so well provided with the means of social intercourse. Where there are markets, there the people live together; but these are few and far between. When the Americans would probably have been without markets, and to what they are indebted for the existence of markets, is shown in the following notes.

NOTE X.

ORIGIN, PROGRESS, AND PROSPECTS OF SLAVERY IN
AMERICA.

Declamation against slavery—History of the origin and progress of slavery
in America—Cause of slavery—Prospects of slavery in the British West
Indies—In the United States—Possible means of abolishing slavery in
the United States without a servile war.

" THE existence of slavery," says Mr. Stuart,* " in its
most hideous form, in a country of absolute freedom in most
respects, is one of those *extraordinary anomalies for which
it is impossible to account.*"

The writer of the declaration of American independence
has also written—" What an incomprehensible machine is
man! who can endure toil, famine, stripes, imprisonment,
and death itself, in vindication of his own liberty, and the
next moment be deaf to all those motives whose power
supported him through his trial, and inflict on his fellow-men
a bondage, one hour of which is fraught with more misery
than ages of that which he rose in rebellion to oppose. But
we must wait with patience the workings of an overruling
Providence, and hope that that is preparing the deliverance
of these our suffering brethren. When the measure of their
tears shall be full—when their tears shall have involved
heaven itself in darkness—doubtless a God of justice will
awaken to their distress, and, by diffusing a light and liberality among their oppressors, or, at length, by his extermi-
nating thunder, manifest his attention to things of this world,
and that they are not left to the guidance of blind fatality."

" Every American," says an English writer,*—" every
American who loves his country should dedicate his whole
life, and every faculty of his soul, to efface the foul blot of
slavery from its character. If nations rank according to
their wisdom and their virtue, what right has the American,
a scourger and murderer of slaves, to compare himself with
the least and lowest of the European nations, much more

* Vol. ii. page 113.
† Edinburgh Review, No. LXI. Art. " *Travellers in America*," attributed
to Mr. (now Lord) Brougham.

with this great and humane country, where the greatest lord dare not lay a finger on the meanest peasant? What is freedom where all are not free? where the greatest of God's blessings is limited, with impious caprice, to the colour of the body? And these are the men who taunt the English with their corrupt parliament, with their buying and selling votes. Let the world judge which is the most liable to censure—we, who in the midst of rottenness, have torn the manacles off slaves all over the world, or they who, with their idle purity and useless perfection, have remained mute and careless while groans echoed and whips clanked round the very walls of their spotless congress. We wish well to America—we rejoice in her prosperity—and are delighted to resist the absurd impertinence with which the character of her people is often treated in this country. But the existence of slavery in America is an atrocious crime, with which no measures can be kept—*for which her situation affords no sort of apology*—which makes liberty itself distrusted, and the boast of it disgusting."

These passages describe the feeling of Englishmen generally, and of not a few Americans, with respect to slavery in America. But when was any great evil cured by mere declamation? and what but mere declamation is there in these passages? Like other evils, slavery in America has its causes; and until these be removed, the evil effect must continue. No Englishman, no American, as far as I know, has taken the trouble to ascertain the causes of slavery in America. Had this been done, it might perhaps appear, that *the situation of America does afford some sort of apology for the foul stain upon her character.* The causes of slavery in America will be found in a brief history of its origin and progress; and, these ascertained, the prospects of slavery may be examined with some chance of a useful result.

The first European colony in America was planted by Spaniards in the island of St. Domingo, or, as it was originally called, Hispaniola. The first Spanish colonists of St. Domingo received from the Spanish crown extensive grants of the most fertile land. The settlers carried with them an abundance of capital, and each settler obtained more good land than he could possibly cultivate. But land and capital are not the only elements of production. In order to produce wealth, the first colonists of St. Domingo wanted labourers. If some of them had laid out a portion of their capital in conveying labourers from Spain, the other settlers, who had not so expended a portion of their capital, would have been able to pay for the service of such labourers more than those could have paid who had diminished their capital by conveying labourers from Spain. Those who had not so diminished their capital, offering higher wages than those who had, would have enjoyed what the former had expended capital to procure. This does actually occur very often in modern English colonies. Thus, unless all the settlers had agreed that each should take out a number of labourers in proportion to his capital, none of them could have had any motive for laying out capital in that way. Moreover, if such an agreement had been possible, and its execution practicable, the labourers taken out by the capitalists, to a place where every one could obtain plenty of good land for a trifle, would have ceased to be labourers for hire ; they would have become independent land-owners, if not competitors with their former masters in the market of labour. This also does actually occur every day in several modern colonies. Consequently, the first Spanish settlers in St. Domingo did not obtain labourers from Spain. But, without labourers, their capital must have perished, or at least must soon have been diminished to that small amount which each individual could employ with his own hands. This has actually occurred in the last colony founded by Englishmen —the Swan River settlement—where a great mass of capital, of seeds, implements, and cattle, has perished for want of labourers to use it ; and where no settler has preserved much more capital than he can employ with his own hands. The first settlers in St. Domingo remaining without labourers, their only prospect was a solitary, wild, half-savage existence. Nay, they might have died for want. Of the colonies planted in modern times, more have perished than have prospered. Those settlers might have died of want, because their own labour, not being combined in any degree, but being cut up into fractions as numerous as the individuals, might not have produced enough to keep them alive. In the colonies of modern times, thousands of people have died from this cause, and some in the last colony founded by England. Urged by this want of labourers, the first settlers in St. Domingo persuaded the Spanish government to include in each of its grants of land *a proportionate grant of natives.* The most ancient grants of land in Hispaniola mention the number of natives which each grantee was authorized to treat as cattle. This was the origin of slavery in America.

The colonists, by means of the supply of labour thus obtained, readily acquired wealth ; for they could now employ many hands in the same work, at the same time, and for a long period of time, without intermission. Other Spaniards, inflamed by the accounts which reached Spain of the success of the first colonists, hurried to St. Domingo, and, obtaining grants of natives as well as land, prospered like those who had gone before them. In the course of a few years, the prosperity of Hispaniola excited, as that of the United States does now, the envy and admiration of Europe. But the colonists, regardless of the fable, killed the goose for its golden eggs: they destroyed the feeble natives by overworking them. The colony had hardly reached a very flourishing condition when the source of its prosperity was dried up. In this emergency, it occurred to the dejected settlers that the neighbouring islands were inhabited. To those islands some of them repaired, and seized the natives, whom they sold to the planters of St. Domingo. This was the first slave-trade carried on in America.

But the discovery of a supply of labour, which seemed inexhaustible, was not calculated to teach the colonists either caution or humanity. As they had overworked and destroyed the natives of St. Domingo, so they worked to death the slaves whom they procured from other islands. It has been said that in religious and moral England, there are men who make a practice of buying an old or diseased horse for the value of its skin, and driving it without food till it dies; the motive assigned for such barbarity being the clear profit obtained by the use of an animal, which costs nothing for keep while in use, and yet sells, when dead, for as much as it cost alive. Somewhat in like manner, the planters of St. Domingo found it more profitable to work slaves to death, and replace them, than to preserve their existence by suiting their work to their strength. This wholesale murder of stolen Indians produced a feeling of indignation in Europe. Las Casas, the Clarkson or Wilberforce of his time, founded a sect of abolitionists; a party closely resembling in many points the European and American abolitionists of the present day. They spared no pains for the attainment of their object. By exciting the best feelings of human nature, by spreading throughout Europe detailed accounts of the cruelties to which Spanish slaves were subject, by circulating tracts, by an extensive correspondence, by worming their way into courts and councils, by enlisting on their side the tender but powerful influence of women, by extraordinary watchfulness to seize every opportunity, and diligence in turning it to account, and still more by their unalterable constancy of purpose, they at length made an impression on the government of Spain. But although the king of Spain listened to the abolitionists, he was unwilling to ruin the planters : he consented to protect the Indians to the utmost extent, using modern language, that was compatible with the rights of property and the interests of slave owners : in other words, he expressed compassion for the slaves, because this was required by public opinion, but he would do nothing for them. The question was in this state when the abolitionists themselves proposed, that the planters might spare the feeble natives of America by procuring hardy negro slaves from Africa. The suggestion was adopted, and found to answer its purpose. Red slavery was abolished, and black slavery established ; and this was the beginning of a slave-trade between Africa and America.

The first English settlers in America obtained from Queen Elizabeth a grant of land to the extent of two hundred miles in every direction from the spot on which they might establish themselves. They found a country which they described as a paradise, and to which the queen, delighted with their account of it, gave the name of Virginia. Instead, however, of proceeding without delay to cultivate a very small part of the fertile territory at their disposal, they were tempted by its very extent to wander up and down upon it ; until the capital which they had taken with them being consumed, they were reduced to famine, and gladly seized an opportunity of returning to England. In the following year another settlement was made under the same grant and on the same spot ; but though on this occasion the settlers had an ample stock of seeds, implements, and cattle, with provisions for two years, every one of them perished ; by what means, indeed, can only be inferred, since the skeleton of one man was all that remained of this colony when a third body of emigrants from England reached the place of settlement. In two years this third body of emigrants had disappeared like the second. Thus, three attempts to take advantage of abundance of good land, "the sole cause," says Adam Smith, " of the prosperity of new colonies," entirely failed; attempts, too, directed by Sir Walter Raleigh, a man eminently qualified to ensure their success. Why those attempts failed may be conjectured from what happened to the first body of English settlers in America that did not perish.

The first English colony in America that did not perish was planted in Chesapeake Bay, under a grant from King

James I., who bestowed good land upon the settlers, not by the acre or the mile, but by degrees of latitu le, and without limit as to longitude. In this case a few hundred persons, amply provided with capital, and led too by men of experience and conduct, obtained more land of very great natural fertility than existed in the densely-peopled country that they had abandoned. In the course of twenty years they were joined by nearly as many thousand emigrants; yet at the end of that period the population of the colony was less than two thousand souls. This most uncommon decrease of people was occasioned by extreme misery. Of the first settlers, each was able to obtain as much good land as he desired to call his own. From this great abundance of good land, nothing being done to counteract it, there arose two evil consequences in particular. In the first place, nearly every one became independent of all the others, working by himself in solitude, and therefore dividing his labour among so many occupations that he could bestow but little of his time on the production of food, while that small portion of his labour which was so employed produced but little, because scarce any operation of agriculture is very productive unless there be employed in it several pairs of hands in combination and constantly, in the same particular work, at the same time and for a considerable period of time together. Secondly, as nearly every one took possession of a great deal more land than he could possibly cultivate, the greater part of what he possessed became, by becoming his, as a desert which surrounded him. No roads were made, because, as every settler did every thing for himself and by himself, that combination of power which is indispensable to the construction of a road was out of the case. Thus each settler was surrounded, not merely by a desert, but by a desert which was next to impassable. Further, much of the capital which had been taken out, such as cattle, seeds, and implements, perished either on the beach or in the forest, because the owners of it could not preserve that well-regulated labour without which it is impossible that capital should be increased or even preserved. As every colonist was isolated, so all wanted both the means and the motive for raising any surplus produce; and any unfavourable accident, consequently, such as a wet harvest time, or an incursion of the Indians, reduced many to want, cut off some by famine, and brought the colony to the verge of destruction. The records and traditions of Virginia leave no doubt, that the first inhabitants of that country suffered, during a long course of years, every conceivable hardship.

The colony was on the point of being abandoned, when five hundred emigrants, most of them of the labouring class, arrived from England. He who is accustomed only to what takes place in densely-peopled countries, may imagine that this influx of labourers into a society, whose only want was the want of labourers, must have produced the most happy results. But this was not the case : the evil cause existed still, and produced the same evil effect. The great plenty of land led nearly all the newly arrived emigrants to become isolated settlers ; there were more colonists for a time, but not one was in a better condition, or had a better prospect, in consequence of an increase of numbers. At length, the whole body of settlers, dispersed, and prevented from helping each other, were unable to raise enough food for their subsistence. Their bright hopes frustrated, general disappointment produced discontent, selfishness, and a reckless disregard of all social ties. The founders of Virginia were not more remarkable for their great disasters than for their atrocious crimes. They are described as resembling hungry wild beasts ; and if we must speak of them as human beings, it is not harsh to say, that they appeared to have crossed the Atlantic for the purpose of cutting each other's throats without restraint from any law.

Such was the deplorable state of this colony when a circumstance occurred, which, though accidental and apparently trifling, has proved one of the most important events in the history of America. A Dutch ship laden with slaves made its appearance in James's River. Want of provisions had induced the captain to put in there, and he was therefore ready to dispose of his living cargo for a trifle. These slaves were bought ; and this was the beginning of slavery in the United States.

The slaves were set to work, some in raising food, some in cultivating tobacco. For the first time in this colony there was combination of labour and division of employments. Tobacco, although denounced by King James as a vile and nauseous weed, was already prized in Europe ; and the soil and climate of Virginia were peculiarly suited to its growth. Those settlers, therefore, who by obtaining slaves were enabled to employ many hands constantly in one work, in preparing the ground for tobacco plants, in watering the plants, in preventing the growth of weeds, and in gathering, drying, and packing the leaves, now raised a commodity exchangeable in the markets of Europe. In this way they obtained various supplies, which they could not have obtained in any other way. In this way also they found the means of purchasing more slaves. As the number of slaves increased, the cultivation of tobacco was extended ; some roads were made, and solid houses were built. In the course of a few years the face of the colony was changed, and the tobacco-planters of Virginia became noted for their prosperity.

The frightful condition, both physical and moral, of the settlers, up to the time when they obtained slaves, was almost a bar to the emigration of women. It is supposed that the proportion of males to females, who emigrated to this colony during the first thirty years of its existence, was above twenty to one. While the colony was in a state of misery and disorganization, none of the settlers could have desired, nor could any of them have easily procured, wives to share their misfortunes. But when they had acquired the means of comfort and order, they naturally longed to be husbands and fathers. As that longing was created by the combined and constant labour of slaves, so was it gratified. The settlers offered to the captains of English ships two hundred and fifty pounds of prime tobacco for each young woman of pure health and good temper, whom the latter should bring from England, harmless, and bearing a certificate of honest manners from the clergyman of her parish. At that time, as at present, England abounded in young women, beautiful, gentle, and virtuous, but without the least prospect of happiness in marriage. The English captains, therefore, easily fulfilled their commissions, and finally conducted a very extensive commerce in tobacco and marriageable girls. From this curious traffic, which, considering the abundance of good land in Virginia, could not have taken place without slavery, sprung a large proportion of those illustrious Americans, who dared the first trial of perfect equality in government among whites.

The prosperity of Virginia led to the establishment of more colonies, as well in the islands as on the mainland, of America. With the increase of white population in America, the number of American slaves increased, in some measure by breeding, but for the most part by importation from Africa. At length the horrors of the African slave-trade raised up a new set of abolitionists. The value of slavery to the white men of America would be proved, if by nothing else, by the great and manifold obstacles which the abolitionists had to surmount before their object was even partially effected. Their purpose was to abolish slavery in America. With greater exertion and difficulty than attended the establishment of some wide-spread religions, they have accomplished no more than the abolition of a trade in slaves between Africa and a part of America.

Las Casas probably knew how slavery began in America. By his proposal to substitute black Africans for red Indians, he seems to have acknowledged the difficulty, he may even have perceived the impossibility, of combining the labour of free-men, and raising a large net produce in countries where every one may obtain more good land than he can possibly cultivate. But Las Casas had lived in America, and witnessed the opera-tion, first of abundance of good land, and next of slavery. The modern project of abolition was conceived by a youth in an English university ; and, though Clarkson visited the West Indies, it was not till his feelings had been inflamed by contem-plating from a distance the abominations of slavery. At all events, Clarkson and Wilberforce expected that the abolition of the African slave-trade would put an end to slavery in America. Never was there a greater mistake.

The American and English slave-trade with Africa was not abolished till the English in the West India islands and the Americans on the continent had procured an ample stock of slaves. Their property, neither in these nor in the progeny of these, was affected by the abolition of the trade with Africa. In order to keep up their stock of slaves, in order to increase that stock indefinitely, it was now required that, instead of re-sorting to Africa for fresh supplies, they should breed slaves at home. But in doing this they found no difficulty. Thus, slavery in America, instead of being extinguished by the abo-lition of the African trade, was placed on a surer foundation than when it depended on that traffic.

It must be acknowledged, however, that the abolition of the African trade has produced some mitigation of the evils of slavery in America. While that trade continued, it was often found more profitable to work slaves to death and replace them, than to preserve them by suiting their work to their strength. In order that they should not decrease, still more in order that they should increase, it became necessary to treat them with some consideration, with just so much consideration as a stock farmer bestows upon his cattle. So far the slaves of America owe to the abolitionists a decided improvement in their condition.

But this improvement has not extended over all British America. An important distinction must here be drawn be-tween the islands and the mainland ; a distinction the more necessary, because Englishmen generally suppose that there is

no great difference, if any, between the state of slavery in the
United States and the state of slavery in the West Indies.
The good land of the islands is of limited extent, while that of
the continent has no assignable limits. The same piece of land
will not produce sugar for many consecutive years without a
great increase of expense ; and nearly all the good land of the
islands has been exhausted by the cultivation of sugar.   Since
that land was exhausted, the growers of sugar on the continent
have had a great advantage over the same class of people in
the islands. So great has been the advantage, that assuredly,
if the produce of the continent had been let into the markets
of Europe on equal terms with the produce of the islands, the
islanders would some time ago have ceased to produce sugar.
In the British islands especially, it is obvious that the cultivation of sugar has been preserved by means of a monopoly of
the British market. But as that monopoly was required by the
exhaustion of the soil of the West Indies, so it encouraged the
further exhaustion of that soil, till the profits of sugar growing
in the West Indies were reduced to that amount which, with
the monopoly, was just sufficient to prevent sugar-growing
from being abandoned. Consequently, since the abolition of
the African slave-trade, the planters of the West Indies have
not had a strong motive for increasing the number of their
slaves. It was not the abolition of the African trade, but the
exhaustion of all the good land at their disposal which deprived them of this motive. Between those two events there
is no connexion, except parity of time. If the African slave-
trade had not been abolished, if it had continued to render unnecessary the preservation of slaves, still the greater profit of
killing and replacing slaves would not have counteracted the
loss of profit arising from the necessity of cultivating land
which every year decreased in fertility.

But with a close monopoly of the finest market in the world,
the planters of the British West Indies might for ages have
continued to grow sugar with some profit, and might have retained a motive for keeping up the number of their slaves. If
they had preserved a close monopoly of the British market,
the people of Britain would probably have made up for the
continued decrease in the fertility of insular land by continually paying a higher price for insular sugar. Though the
produce would have been less and less, the profit might have
remained the same, in consequence of the price becoming
higher and higher. But " the West India interest," as the
island planters are called, though they have long enjoyed very
great influence in the legislature of Britain, were not permitted
to flourish in this way at the expense of the British people.
During the last war, the English took from the Dutch their

continental settlements in America; and at the close of the war they determined to keep those colonies, making a compensation to the Dutch by agreeing to pay a vast sum to the Emperor of Russia, provided (such is the complication of European politics) the Belgians and the Dutch, who hated each other, and had been united at the peace, should not choose to separate.   The West India interest could easily have prevented this acquisition; but they were blind to its consequences.   It broke up their monopoly of the British market. By bringing continental sugar into competition with insular sugar, it prevented the island planters from raising the price of their sugar in proportion to the decrease in the fertility of their land.   This acquisition was a mortal blow to the West India interest.   Ever since it took place, none of them have made large profits, many of them have been ruined by the cultivation of sugar; and the total ruin of the whole of them, in so far as their West India property is concerned, seems inevitable.   These circumstances have had a peculiar effect on insular slavery.   What with the progressive exhaustion of insular land, and the opening of the British market to sugar produced on land that was not exhausted, the island planters have, for some years past, been without a motive for keeping up the number of their slaves, while they have had the strongest motive for working them to death.   The result is well known ; a decrease of population such as if pestilence and famine had done the work.

Turning to the United States, we find that the abolition of the African slave-trade has led to a striking improvement in the condition of slaves.   The increase of white population in America did not increase the proportion of free labourers to capitalists, and did not therefore diminish the value of slaves. On the contrary, as every freeman could readily obtain land of his own, with that increase of whites, of freemen, persons wanting labourers bore a greater proportion to labourers, and the demand for slaves increased accordingly.   As every one, not being a slave, could obtain for a trifle more good land than he could possibly cultivate, all capitalists felt the want of combined labour.   All those whites, consequently, who settled in the slave states became anxious to procure slaves.   The African trade being abolished, those who wanted slaves could obtain them only from those Americans who already possessed them.   This great demand for slaves, great in proportion to the increase of whites in the slave states, and to the increased demand in the other states for the produce of combined labour, led to the establishment of a new trade in America ; the trade of breeding slaves for sale.   The extent and importance of that trade may be estimated by reference to one or two facts.

The black population of the slave states has increased much more rapidly than the white population of those states ; and the slave population has increased at a somewhat greater rate than the free population of the whole Union.   There are two millions of slaves, and if we reckon the average value of a slave at 60*l.*, the capital invested in slavery is 120,000,000*l.* Taking the yearly increase of slaves in the United States to be at least 60,000, and the average value of a slave to be 60*l.*, the produce in money obtained by the breeders of slaves, *merely for breeding*, is 3,600,000*l.* per annum.*   These statements will suffice, without further explanation, to show that the abolition of the African slave trade has worked a great improvement in the condition of American slaves.

But the abolition of the African slave-trade would not have had this effect, if the original cause of slavery had not steadily continued to operate.   Considering how slavery arose, and in what way it has progressed in America, its original and permanent cause seems to be *super*abundance of land in proportion to people.   Other considerations come to the support of this view of the subject.

That superabundance of land to which the English economists, from Adam Smith downwards, attribute the prosperity of new colonies, has never led to great prosperity without some kind of slavery.   The states of New-England, in which negro slavery was never permitted, form no exception to the general rule.   Adam Smith, in his chapter on " the causes of the prosperity of new colonies," tries to establish by a pretty long argument that the wonderful prosperity of the Greek colonies was owing to " dearness of labour," to " high wages," which enabled the bulk of the people to save and to increase as rapidly as possible : whereas the unquestionable fact is, that all the work performed in those colonies, whether in agriculture or manufactures, was performed by slaves.   All work in Brazil has been performed by the labour of slaves.   In New South Wales and Van Diemen's Land, prosperous colonies, capitalists are supplied with slave-labour in the shape of convicts.   That they set the greatest value on this labour, is proved by their extreme fear lest the system of transportation should be discontinued ; although the evils which it produces are too many to be counted, and too great to be believed in England.   Finally, though the puritans and the followers of Penn, who founded the colonies of New-England, flourished with superabundance of land and without negro slaves, they did not flourish without slavery.   Though their religious sentiments prompted them to

* 200*l.* and 300*l.* are common prices for a well taught and able slave. As much as 600*l.* is sometimes given for a young man of superior skill in some lines of industry.—*See Stuart*, vol. 2, page 195.

abstain from the purchase of negroes, so severely did they, on that very account, feel the want of constant and combined labour, that they were led to carry on an extensive traffic in white men and children, who, kidnapped in Europe, were virtually sold to those fastidious colonists, and treated by them as slaves. But the number of Europeans kidnapped for the purpose of sale in those parts of America where negroes could not be sold, though considerable, in proportion to the number of settlers then wanting combined labour, was small when compared with the number of Europeans, who, first decoyed to America by the offer of a passage cost free, and the promise of high wages, were then transferred for terms of years to colonists who paid for their passage. These, under the name of *redemptioners*, were, for a long period, the principal servants of those colonies in which slavery was forbidden by law. Even so lately as within the last twenty years, and especially during the last war between England and America, which put a stop to Irish emigration, vast numbers of poor Germans were decoyed to those states which forbid slavery, and there sold for long terms of years to the highest bidder by public auction. Though white and free in name, they were really not free to become independent landowners, and therefore it was possible to employ their labour constantly and in combination. Lastly, even in those colonies which never permitted negro slavery, negroes have always been considered, what indeed there seems reason to conclude that they are by nature, an inferior order of beings. A black man never was, nor is he now, treated as a man by the white men of New-England.* There, where the most complete equality subsists among white men, and every white man is taught to respect himself as well as other white men, black men are treated as if they were horses or dogs. Thus, notwithstanding superabundance of land, black men have always found it difficult to rise above the condition of labourers for hire; and thus such blacks as either escaped, or were allowed to go free, from the slave states, to settle in the other states, provided servants for the capitalists of those other states. The large proportion of black servants in New-England has always been remarked, and it is remarkable at this moment in Philadelphia, the strong hold of Quakerism.† In

* " The freedmen of other countries have long since disappeared, having been amalgamated in the general mass. Here there can be no amalgamation. Our manumitted bondsmen have remained already to the third and fourth generation, a distinct, a degraded, and a wretched race."—*President Nott, of Union College, New-York*—quoted by Mr. Stuart.

" Few people of colour in the churches, and such of them as are there, *assemble in a corner separate from the rest of the people.*"—Stuart, vol. i. p. 196.

† " It is computed that there are in Philadelphia 10,000 free coloured people."—*Journal of Travels in the United States of North America and in Lower Canada, performed in the year* 1817, *by John Palmer.* The number of blacks in Philadelphia is very much greater than in 1817. By the last census

this way, the slavery of some states has, not very indirectly, bestowed upon other states much of the good and some of the evil that arise from slavery.

In another way, the states which forbid slavery have gained by it immensely without any corresponding evil. The states of America must be viewed as one country, in which there is a considerable distribution of employments, and in which exchanges take place of the different productions raised in different parts of the Union. " The division of labour," says Adam Smith, meaning the distribution of employments, " is limited by the extent of the market." The great fishing establishments of the non-slaveholding colonies were set up for the purpose of supplying the slaves of the West Indies, Maryland, Virginia, Georgia, and the Carolinas, who were employed in raising tobacco, rice, and sugar ; commodities exchangeable in the markets of Europe ; commodities which have never been raised on any large scale in America except by the combined labour of slaves. A great part of the commerce of the northern states, of Boston, New-York, Philadelphia, and Baltimore, has always consisted of a carrying trade for the southern states ; the one work of raising produce for the markets of Europe and conveying it thither being so divided, that the produce was raised by the southern and conveyed by the northern states ; a division of employments which depended on the labour of slaves, since, if a produce had not been raised fit for distant markets, carriers would not have been required, and since such produce could not* have been raised by labour, uncertain and scattered as free labour always is with superabundance of good

---

of the American people it appears, that in 1831, there were in the state of Pennsylvania 37,900 free coloured persons; in the state of New-York 44,869 ; and in Ohio 37,930.

" The whole establishment (on board the ' North America' steam-boat, New-York) of kitchen servants, waiters, and cooks, all people of colour, on a great scale."—*Stuart*, vol. i. p. 40.

" Nothing can be more disgraceful to the people of the United States, nor more inconsistent with their professed principles of equality, than their treatment of free people of colour. They constantly subject them to indignities of every kind, and refuse altogether to eat or drink with them."—*Stuart*, vol. i. page 507.

* " The following is Mr. Timothy Flint's account of a Louisiana plantation. ' If we could lay out of the question the intrinsic evils of the case (he had been alluding to the state of the slaves), it would be a cheering sight, that which is presented by a large Louisiana plantation—the fields are as level and regular within figures, as gardens. They sometimes contain 3 or 4000 acres in *one* field ; and I have seen from a *dozen to twenty ploughs*, all making their straight furrows through a field, a mile in depth, with a regularity which, it would be supposed, could be obtained only by a line.' This description is quite correct. The drills of the finest turnip fields in Norfolk, or even on Mr. Rennie's, of Phantassies, beautiful farm in East Lothian, are not more accurately drawn ; nor is the whole management more admirable than the lines and the cultivation of the cane on one of the great plantations of Louisiana."—*Stuart*, vol. ii. page 215.

land. At the present time, which is the great market for the surplus produce of farmers in the non-slaveholding states on the western rivers? New-Orleans. And how could that great market have existed without slavery?* Capitalists again, natives of the states which forbid slavery, reside during part of every year in the slave states, and reap large profits by dealing in rice, sugar, and cotton, exchangeable commodities, which, it must be repeated, have never been raised to any extent in America except by the labour of slaves. A New-Englander may boast that slavery was never permitted in his state, as a baker may pride himself on being less cruel than his neighbour the butcher; but the dependence of the northern on the southern states for a market for their surplus produce, for a demand for the produce of their industry in a thousand shapes, is as close as the dependence on each other of the baker and the butcher who deal together. In the division of employments which has taken place in America, the far preferable share, truly, has fallen to the northern states; but that division of employments did not precede, on the contrary it followed, combination of labour in particular works, and the surplus exchangeable produce obtained by that first improvement in the productive powers of industry. The states, therefore, which forbid slavery, having reaped the economical benefits of slavery, without incurring the chief of its moral evils, seem to be even more indebted to it than the slave states. If those who forbid slavery within their own legal jurisdiction should also resolve to have no intercourse or concern with slave-owners, to do nothing for them, and to exchange nothing with them, we should see an economical revolution in America, that would prove better than a thousand arguments the value of slavery in a country where every free man can obtain plenty of good land for a trifle.

Let us now turn for a moment to those new countries in which the people have had superabundance of good land without slavery. Not a single one of these societies has greatly prospered: many have perished entirely, and some remain in

---

* " He (Colonel Coleman) had come up the Appalachicola and Chattahooche rivers, and was now on his way to New-Orleans to buy pork and provisions for his slaves. He has only got forty slaves upon his property; but he tells me that twenty slaves are necessary for every 100 acres of sugar-cane land." —*Stuart*, vol. ii. page 155.

" One of our stopping places for wood, not far above the confluence of the Mississippi and Ohio, was at Mr. Brox's farm on the west side of the river. He has 700 acres of fine land, about 100 head of cattle, and an innumerable quantity of pigs. He says he has no difficulty in selling all the produce of his farm; he disposes of his stock *to the New-Orleans butchers*, who go all over this country to make their purchases; and there are merchants who have great depôts of grain, salted pork, and other agricultural produce, *which they scour the country to collect, and afterward carry to New-Orleans.*"—*Stuart*, vol. ii. page 302.

a deplorable condition. From these last, two striking examples may be selected.

It would be unfair to dwell here on the misery, in conjunction with superabundance of good land, which belongs to many savage nations; but an allusion to such cases is not misplaced, if made only for the purpose of explaining that the present inquiry is confined to the operation of superabundance of good land on civilized societies, among whom private property is established, who possess some knowledge of the productive arts, and who practise to some extent that division of classes and employments which, on the principle of mutual assistance, adds to the productive powers of industry. The most remarkable instance, perhaps, of such a society, having at its disposal an unlimited quantity of good land, is the Spanish colony of Buenos Ayres. The vast plain which lies between the South Atlantic and the mountains of Chili contains hardly any sterile land. Nearly the whole of it consists of the most fertile soil, which, though in a state of nature, exhibits vegetation more luxuriant than could be produced in the greater part of Europe by the most skilful cultivation. This land is naturally fit for cultivation; since throughout the pampas there are no dense forests like those which once covered Pennsylvania, nor any swamps like those which still remain on the shores of the Gulf of Mexico. On a district extending one hundred and eighty miles from the coast, nature produces the richest crops of nothing but thistles and clover, and on another district, extending four hundred and fifty miles farther to the west, nothing but a profusion of grass without a weed. The climate of the whole plain resembles that of Italy, with this difference in its favour, that it is not rendered unwholesome by malaria. This, then, was the finest situation in the world, in which to take advantage of abundance of good land. The Spaniards, who got possession of these fertile plains, emigrated from one of the civilized European states. Yet, according to the best information that can be obtained of a society now more than half-barbarous, this colony never prospered. Capital has never obtained high profits, nor labour high wages. On the contrary, the colony seems to have languished throughout its career, and though the people have increased, it has been less quickly than people now increase in some of the oldest and most densely-peopled countries of Europe. During some years, this colony has been an independent state ; but the people, dispersed over their vast and fertile plains, have almost ceased to cultivate the good land at their disposal ; they subsist principally, many of them entirely, on the flesh of wild cattle ; they have lost most of the arts of civilized life ; not a few of them are constantly in a state of deplorable misery ; and if they should continue, as it seems probable that they will, to retrograde as at present, the beautiful pampas of Buenos Ayres will soon be fit for another experiment in colonization. Slaves, black, red, or yellow, would have cultivated those plains, would have been kept together, would have been made to assist each other; would, by keeping together and assisting each other, have raised a surplus produce exchangeable in distant markets; would have kept their masters together for the sake of markets; would by combination of labour have promoted division of employments; would, cattle themselves, have preserved among their masters the arts and habits of civilized life. That slavery might have done all this, seems not more plain than that so much good would have been bought too dear if its price had been slavery.

The last colony founded by Englishmen has severely felt the want of slavery. On the west coast of New Holland there is abundance of good land, and of land too, cleared and drained by nature. Those who have left England to settle there have carried out, among them, more than enough capital to employ such of them as were of the labouring class. The capital taken out, in seeds, implements, cattle, sheep, and horses, cannot have been less, in money value, than 200,000*l.*; and the labourers must have amounted to a thousand at the very lowest. What is become of all that capital and all those labourers? The greater part of the capital has perished; some few of the labourers have died of hunger; some, falling into extreme want, have been glad to escape to Van Diemen's Land, where there are slaves; and the remainder are independent land-owners, isolated, not well supplied with even the necessaries of life, and as wild as Englishmen could become in so short a time. This colony may prosper in the course of years; but for the present it must be considered, when compared with the expectations of those who founded it, a decided failure. Why this failure with all the elements of success, a fine climate, plenty of good land, plenty of capital, and enough labourers? The explanation is easy. In this colony there never has been a class of labourers. Those who went out as labourers no sooner reached the colony than they were tempted by the superabundance of good land to become land-owners. One of the founders of the colony, Mr. Peel, who, it is said, took out a capital of 50,000*l.* and three hundred persons of the labouring class, men, women, and children, has been represented as left without a servant to make his bed or fetch him water from the river.* The writer of the first book concerning this colony states, that landing in

* My authority for this statement is a gentleman, lately in England, who went to the Swan River as Mr. Peel's agent.

Cockburn Sound with goods taken from England, he did, with some difficulty, procure workmen to place his goods under a tent; but that there, for want of workmen to remove them, they remained till they were spoiled, as the tent became rotten. In such a state of things it was impossible to preserve capital. While Mr. Peel was without servants his capital perished; but as soon as his capital had perished for want of servants, those who had been his servants insisted on his giving them employment. Having tried a life of complete independence, and felt the pains of hunger, they now wanted to become labourers again. At one time Mr. Peel was to be seen imploring his servants to remain with him, at another escaping from their fury at his not being able to give them work. The same thing happened in many cases. In each case, it was owing to the facility with which people, labourers when they reached the colony, became independent land-owners. Some of these independent land-owners died of hunger;* and at a time too when, as it happened, a large supply of food had just reached the colony from Van Diemen's Land. Why were they starved? because where they had settled was not known to the governor, or even to themselves; for, though they could say " we are here," they could not tell where any one else was: such was the dispersion of these colonists in consequence of superabundance of good land. Many of them, both capitalists and labourers, capitalists without capital and labourers without work, have removed to Van Diemen's Land; the cost of passage for the latter being defrayed by settlers in that slave-holding prosperous island. Some have wandered from the original place of settlement towards King George's Sound, in search, say they, of better land. Others, men of unusual courage and energy, remain on the banks of the Swan River, knowing well that the partial ruin of this colony is not owing to want of good land. These, one of whose chief inducements to settling in this colony was an undertaking from the English government that no convicts should be sent thither, are now begging for a supply of convict labour. They want slaves. They want labour which shall be constant and liable to combination in particular works. Having this, they would raise a net produce, and have division of employments. Not having convict labour, they will long for African slaves; and would obtain them, too, if public opinion in England did not forbid it. Without either convicts or slaves, they may have hordes of wild cattle, which supply food almost without labour; but they cannot have much more. Considering the superabundance of capital and labourers in England, the disposition of capitalists and labourers

* My authority is Mr. Peel's agent, Mr. Elmsley.

to emigrate in search of new fields of employment, the great natural advantages of this colony, and the false accounts of its prosperity now and then received in England, we should wonder that emigration to the Swan River had almost ceased, if that very fact did not show that by settling in this colony no well-informed man can expect to better his condition. But the failure of this last experiment in colonization will have one good effect, if it help to teach the English and Americans, that the original and permanent cause of slavery in America is superabundance of good land.*

The prospects of slavery in the West Indies and the United States may now be briefly considered; and, the cause of slavery being ascertained, with some chance of a useful result.

The slaves of the West Indies have just been turned into apprentices. As if on purpose that they should still be made to work like slaves, the planters' monopoly of the British market is preserved. Or, perhaps, since the negroes would not be worth a farthing apiece without the monopoly, it is preserved as an excuse for giving compensation to the planters. The monopoly being worth 2,000,000l. a year, the English buy it for 20,000,000l., let the sellers keep it, and will pay 2,000,000l. a year as before, by way of bribing the planters to make the apprentices work like slaves. This they call reformed legislation. It will probably be defeated by the apprentices; but, at all events, in however bungling or, maybe, bloody a way, slavery will soon cease throughout the British West Indies.

If means be not soon found to abolish slavery in the United States, gradually and peacefully, it seems more than probable, that, what with the rapid increase of American slaves, already more than two millions, and the emancipation of eight hundred thousand English slaves in the neighbourhood of the United States, the slaves of the continent will, at no distant day, right themselves in the midst of Jefferson's thunder. "The Americans," says Mr. Stuart, "conceive that the increasing numbers

---

* Miss Martineau, the most entertaining of writers on political economy, in order to show how a society obtains wealth, has described the supposed case of some English people settling in a waste country, living together, combining their labour and dividing their employments. It is in this way, and only in this way, no doubt, that wealth is ever obtained; but any thing like the supposed case hardly ever, perhaps never, existed. If Miss Martineau had planted her settlers in an island of such an extent in proportion to their numbers that they should *necessarily* have lived together, her story would have been perfect; but she places them in a vast wilderness of good land, in a situation which, if we are to judge by all experience, is inconsistent with the combination of labour and the division of employments.

of their slaves require more coercive laws and greater severity of treatment ; and are proceeding on this principle, every year increasing the hardships of their almost intolerable situation, and adding new fetters to those which are already too heavy for them to wear." But what will the Americans conceive when the fetters worn by eight hundred thousand English slaves shall have been broken by act of parliament, or by those slaves themselves . Greater harshness in proportion to the greater danger will doubtless be their policy. That policy, which Mr. Stuart says, " no one unconnected with America can wish may prove well-founded," is founded on experience. Experience has taught all slave-owners, that education and slavery, kindness and slavery, cannot go on together. As the slaves of the United States shall become more numerous, and as the danger of their learning that they are men shall become greater, either they must be set free, or greater pains must be taken to maintain their ignorance, torpidity, and submissiveness ; to hold them, mentally, in the state of brutes. But this policy may defeat its object, leading sooner perhaps than might otherwise have happened to a great servile war. That the slaves, once roused, would easily prove a match for their immediate masters, may not be doubtful ; but if the force of the whole Union were brought against them, ten millions of whites to two millions of blacks, they would, almost certainly, be conquered, and for a time subdued as before. In either case, there would be plenty of thunder ; in either case, the prospect is as black as possible.

Will the Americans voluntarily set free their slaves, not having any substitute for the combined and constant labour of slaves ? The answer is, that they will not, of their own accord, destroy property which they value at 120,000,000*l.*, and which is really worth that sum at market.

Is there any prospect of such a fall in the value of slaves as might render slavery not worth preserving ? Of this there is not, at present, the slightest prospect ; because the white population wanting slaves increases as fast almost in number as the slaves themselves, and faster in capital, for using which slaves are wanted ; because superabundance of good land will continue to make slaves valuable, by enabling every freeman who so pleases to become an independent land-owner.

But, considering that the Americans pay 3,600,000*l.* a year for the increase of slave-labour, that the English pay about the same sum for the maintenance of idle paupers, might not these two sums, making together 7,200,000*l.*, be so employed in conveying to America the surplus labour of England, that, before very long, free-labour should be substituted for slave-labour in

America ? Supposing the cost of passage from England to America to be 10*l.*,* the yearly expenditure of 7,200,000*l.* in this way would take from England to America 720,000 labourers every year ; about twelve times as many as the yearly increase of American slaves. In three years, the number of labourers so taken to America would be 160,000 more than *the whole number of American slaves.* In three years, then, it might be supposed, this great amount of immigration would extinguish slavery in America by the substitution of free-labour. But who would suppose this, that has observed the effects of superabundance of good land.† The 2,160,000 labourers taken to America might all of them, and would most of them, cease to be labourers for hire soon after landing in the new country ; they would become independent land-owners, competitors with American capitalists in the market of labour, and buyers of slaves. So vast an amount of immigration, therefore, instead of diminishing, would probably augment, the value of American slaves, and render the abolition of slavery in America still more difficult.

Still, as in America, the whites are ten millions and the blacks but two millions ; and as the whites increase at nearly as great a rate as the blacks ; as the twelve millions will, there can hardly be any doubt, become twenty-four millions in the course of twenty-five years or less, is there no prospect that land will rise in value, so that every freeman shall no longer be able to obtain for a trifle more good land than he can possibly cultivate ; so that the value of slaves shall fall ; so that the proprietors of slaves, being most of them proprietors of land, shall be ready to liberate their slaves, gaining on the one hand as much as they might lose on the other, or more ? Of this there is no prospect ; for three reasons. First, because, however rapidly population may increase, the quantity of land appropriated by individuals will increase at the same rate ; because, in short, the colonization of new wilderness will go on as fast as population shall increase, so that every freeman will still be able to obtain for a trifle more good land than he can possibly cultivate. Secondly, because the land east of the Alleghany Mountains has been exhausted to a considerable extent, not merely for the growth of sugar, as in the West Indies, but fairly worn out by unskilful cultivation ;‡ and thus, from this ex-

* The actual cost of a pauper's passage, with more and better food on the voyage than he obtains in England, is about 7*l.*
† See extract from Captain Basil Hall's letter to Mr. Wilmot Horton, in a note to Note I.
‡ A writer in the Edinburgh Review (Professor M'Culloch, I suspect) attributes the exhaustion and abandonment of land, in the eastern states, to a want of animal manure, in consequence of the work of cattle being performed by men. Would not farms in England soon be exhausted if English farmers had no

hausted district to new land in the western districts, emigration,
both of whites and slaves, has taken place to a great amount,
and is still going on rapidly ; so that in those exhausted districts, a fall rather than a rise in the value of land may be expected. Thirdly, because where the moral evils of slavery
exist, there whites settle for one purpose only, that of gaining
by the combined labour of slaves. But the greater part of the
whites of America are content to share from a distance the
economical advantages of slavery, without incurring its moral
evils by going to live among slaves. The new settler on the
Ohio can sell his honey, which may be raised without combined labour in that particular work, for tobacco, which may
not, without hearing the smack of a slave-driver's whip, or the

manure but what is furnished by their *working* cattle? There are many districts of Europe, such as the mountainous coasts of Spain and Italy, not to
mention great part of China, where agricultural work is almost entirely performed by men, and where, notwithstanding, land is kept in the highest state
of fertility by means of animal manure. The exhaustion of land in America is
one of the evils, over and above slavery, resulting from superabundance of good
land. The single, independent land-owner and cultivator might not be able to
live, still less to raise any surplus produce, if he were fixed on the same piece of
land. He whose labour is already divided among so many occupations, would
act a foolish part in adding to them the occupation of fetching manure, from a
great distance perhaps, and the occupation of laying manure on his land, when
for a trifle he can obtain of land very rich by nature more than he can possibly
cultivate. His labour being an isolated fraction, and being divided again among
many employments, he must depend on nature for more than half the work.
Keep him isolated, so that none shall help him nor he help any, so that he shall
be obliged to do for himself all the many things required by him ; do this, and
prevent him from moving from one piece of land to another as the natural fertility of each piece is exhausted, and the result must be poverty, like that of the
small French cultivator or Irish cottier. " We find all the farmers," says Mr.
Stuart, " perfectly aware of the importance of fallow and green crops, but generally of opinion that they *dare not* attempt that system, on account of the high
price of labour in this country in relation to the value of land ; *ne sumptus
fructum superet*, according to the sound advice of Varro. The price" [scarcity
at any price] " of labour too, is the great obstacle to all sorts of ornamental improvements, such as the formation of gardens *and keeping them up*."—Vol. i.
page 254.
    " Let the settler be well advised, and not acquire land which has been
already impoverished by cropping, and which has become foul and lost the
vegetable mould."—*Stuart*, vol i. page 254.
    " When you talk to them (the farmers) of the necessity of manuring with a
view to preserve the fertility of the soil, they almost uniformly tell you that the
expense" [meaning scarcity at whatever expense] " of labour renders it far
more expedient for them, as soon as their repeated cropping very much diminishes the quantity of the grain, to lay down their land in grass, or make a purchase of new land in the neighbourhood, or even to sell their cleared land and
proceed in quest of a new settlement, than to adopt a system of rotation of crops
assisted by manure. There is great inconvenience, according to the notions of
the British, in removing from one farm to another ; but *they make very light
work of it here*, and consider it to be merely a question of finance, *whether they
shall remain on their improved land, after having considerably exhausted its fer-
tilizing power, or acquire and remove to land of virgin soil*."—*Stuart*, vol. i. p. 258.
    " If he obtains land near his first farm *after he has worn it out*."—*Stuart*, vol. ii.
page 359.

responding cry of slaves. If the white population of America were to be doubled every five years, instead of five-and-twenty years, the population of the slave states, where slave-owners own land, would not become sufficiently dense to raise the value of land, and lower the value of slaves.

Superabundance of good land! If we have ascertained the cause of slavery in America, a little declamation on the subject may be allowed. The white Americans, speaking generally, would rejoice to get rid of slavery. They are men with the feelings of men ; they can feel compassion and fear; they do pity their miserable slaves, and they hear the not far distant thunder, which threatens to steep half the Union in blood, and to ruin the other half. A successful rebellion of the slaves would more or less affect every white man in America, by causing a total revolution in all the markets for the produce of every kind of industry; and this the Americans in general know full well. Knowing this, they must also know what is the cause of slavery. Have they ever inquired whether it is possible to remove that most evil cause? They cannot alter the proportion between people and land in America ; but the proportion between people and land *with a good title to it,* is within their control. It is not often in America that any one uses land without a title ; and this might easily be prevented altogether. The title to new land is given by the government. The government, therefore, or the people acting upon their government, are able to regulate the proportion between numbers and acres of appropriated land. In the colonies of old that proportion depended on a thousand caprices, on the whims of an English king, of his colonial minister, of the minister's clerks or parasites, on the colonial governors, their clerks and parasites; all of whom bestowed grants of land pretty much as it pleased them; but in the United States, which have adopted a system nearly uniform in the disposal of new land, the proportion between numbers and acres depends on the price per acre which Congress thinks fit to require for all new land. The actual price is about five shillings per acre ; and the sale of new land at this price yields near 700,000*l.* a year. That amount of revenue is employed for the general purposes of government. If it were employed in conducting pauper emigration from Europe, it would convey every year to the United States 80,000 persons of the labouring class; more than the yearly increase of slaves. If the price for new land were raised, so as to prevent those labourers from becoming independent land-owners until others had followed to take their place; if the fund obtained by the sale of new land should thus become greater every year, and should always be employed in fetching labour from Europe ; if by this increase in

the price of new land, and this immigration of labour, the people were less dispersed than they are, should help each other
more, should produce more with the same labour, should have
a higher rate of profit and a higher rate of wages; if, finally, a
greater proportion of people to land in the states already settled, should raise the value of land by means of all kinds of
competition, over and above competition for superior natural
fertility, then might free labour take the place of slave labour,
then might the owners of slaves and of land set free their slaves
without loss, then might slavery be abolished without injury to
any one, with the greatest benefit to all. By means of some
plan of this kind, and by no other means, does it seem possible
that slavery in America should be peacefully and happily abolished. Those Americans who would not prefer Jefferson's
thunder, may, I trust, think it worth their while to examine this
subject further in a subsequent note on the Art of Colonization.

NOTE XI.

APOLOGY FOR THE AMERICAN TARIFF.

Opinions of Englishmen respecting the tariff—Moral advantages of the tariff—
Economical advantages of the tariff—Difference of feeling between the
Southern and Northern States respecting the tariff—The tariff good, upon
the whole, for the people of America, and therefore a work becoming democratic government—When the tariff may be repealed with great advantage
to America.

THE following passage from an article in the *Times* newspaper on the late dispute between South Carolina and the
United States, describes fully the opinions which are prevalent
in England on the subject of the American tariff. " *All* political writers in this country have visited with censure the present policy of the American general government in attempting
by high protecting duties to force the establishment, or to encourage the extension of manufactures in the United States.
With the high price of labour that exists in the United States,
with their scanty supply of moneyed capital, with their unlimited
range of uncultivated or half-improved soil, it was almost *a
crime against society* to divert human industry from the fields
and the forests to iron forges and cotton factories. Nature had
pointed out the course which they ought to pursue for perhaps
half a century to come, till the plough and the spade had followed the axe of the woodcutter into their 'primeval wilder-
nesses of shade,' and till happy plantations had been formed on

the deserted domains of the Indian huntsman, from the Atlantic to the Ohio, and from the Mississippi to the Pacific. She had directed them to cling to the bosom of mother earth as to the most fertile source of wealth and the most abundant reward of labour. She had told them to remain planters, farmers, and wood-cutters—to extend society and cultivation to new regions—to practise and improve the arts of the builder, the carpenter, and the naval architect; to facilitate every means of internal communication—to promote every branch of internal trade—to encourage every variety of landed produce—but not to waste the energies of their labour, or to interrupt the course of their prosperity, by forcing at home the manufacture of articles which foreigners could supply at half the price for which they could be made in America."

Englishmen who lean to democratic opinions are, most of them, if well-informed, advocates of free trade. To these the American tariff is a very sore subject. If let alone they would say nothing about it; and as it is they do not say much. But they are not let alone. The conservatives place them in this dilemma—If, say those friends of the old commercial system, as of every thing old; if democratic government be good for a people, conducive to the benefit of all, and so forth, then protection of domestic industry is for the public good, since the American tariff was established by a democracy; not preserved, mind, but begun and brought to perfection, deliberately, carefully, and in spite of arguments to the contrary: if, on the other hand, the exclusion of foreign goods be hurtful to a people, what becomes of your government by all for the benefit of all? In this case, you cannot defend both free trade *and* democracy; which do you give up?

The question is galling to an English liberal, puzzles, and therefore irritates him. Hang the Americans with their tariff. one hears such a one complain, their stupidity is unaccountable. Another, admitting the stupidity, lays the blame on those governments of Europe which have set the Americans a bad example; as if precedent were an excuse for indulging mean and malignant passions. These terms are applicable to the grasping, selfish, and jealous spirit which dictated the commercial system of Europe; but they are quite inapplicable to those who established the American tariff; as I will now endeavour to prove, by showing that a prohibitory system is, upon the whole, useful to the people of America, and therefore a work becoming democratic government.

One motive with some supporters of the English corn-laws is a fear lest the free importation of cheap corn should cause a great increase of town population; artisans, living together, talkers, readers of newspapers, intelligent, given to politics, unmanageable, radical; "fierce democrats." If, say they, you sacrifice the agricultural to the manufacturing and commercial interests, the glory of England will pass away; meaning, if you repeal the corn-laws, the number of our stupid country paupers will perhaps be less, while the number of knowing people, living in towns, independent of us, will surely be greater. No doubt but the free importation of cheap manufactured goods would have a contrary, a precisely opposite effect in America; that is, would cause a decrease of town population and an increase of rural population. If English manufactured goods were let into the United States duty free, that portion of the capital and labour of America which is now employed in making goods of that kind, would be devoted to agriculture. Upon this point there can be no dispute. Let us further admit, that the Americans might obtain better and cheaper manufactured goods by raising corn for the English market than by making such goods themselves; just as the English might obtain better and cheaper corn with steam engines than with ploughs. If so, the Americans lose by the tariff, speaking economically; but now turn to the political side of the account.

Is it desirable that a very large proportion of the people should consist of husbandmen, such as the English term clodhoppers; earth-scratchers* they ought to be called in America? Yes, without doubt, provided this be the only way in which every member of the society may obtain plenty; but in America, profits and wages both are so high, that if an economical sacrifice for a political gain be made, it is not felt. Not being felt it is not a sacrifice; while the gain is palpable. Supposing that American industry is less productive than it might be, still it produces enough; and in order to make it produce more than enough, a great political advantage must be sacrificed; the advantage of so much town population as would have consisted of mere husbandmen if the tariff had not excluded foreign manufactured goods.† In America, whatever tends to keep people together is of inestimable advantage. Camp-meetings are very useful, as they bring people together, though

* "An English farmer," says Washington, writing to Arthur Young, "ought to have a horrid idea of the state of our agriculture, or of the nature of our soil, when he is informed that one acre with us only produces eight or ten bushels. But it must be kept in mind, that where land is cheap and labour dear [scarce], men are fonder of cultivating much than cultivating well. Much ground has been *scratched,* and none cultivated as it ought to be."

† "This gentleman told me that the first child born at Rochester (New-York State), after the settlement of the place, *eighteen years ago,* was his son. The place only contained 1,000 inhabitants, and now (1828), about 13,000. There are cotton works, power-looms, woollen factories, ELEVEN FLOUR MILLS, AND SIX OR SEVEN CHURCHES."—*Stuart,* vol. i., page 81.

but now and then. The tariff, by inducing so many people to become manufacturers, has prevented so many people from becoming backwoodsmen; has created and maintains so many towns, with roads between them; has bestowed upon all the people in and near those towns the great advantage of social intercourse; has checked emigration from old settlements to the western wilderness, fixing so much population as would otherwise have rolled on towards the Pacific. The tariff, therefore, counteracts in some degree the barbarising tendency of dispersion; and for that most useful quality is well worth some economical sacrifice, if there be any.

I say, if there be any; for the economical sacrifice is not so plain. Supposing that if there were no tariff, the manufacturers of America would employ their capital and labour in agriculture, skilfully, like the English, with sufficient combination to obtain the greatest produce with the least number of hands; in that case, capital and labour being applied with the utmost skill to the very fertile soil of America, corn of all kinds would be raised so as to be sold for a lower price than the lowest price for which corn was ever sold; and in this way the Americans would obtain from the English (the English tariff being repealed), the cheapest manufactured goods. Under that supposition the economical loss resulting from the tariff might be reckoned very great. But capital and labour would not be so applied to the soil of America. Judging, at least, from all experience, the capital and labour which were diverted from manufactures to agriculture would, *because* it was agriculture, *because land was in the case*, be divided into small separate parts, and employed in the least skilful manner, trusting for little to skill, to nature for much,* and obtaining, even with that most generous nature, but a small produce in proportion to the num-

---

* " All the unburnt new lands in the northern, middle, southern, and western states have been, and still are, uniformly valued beyond their real worth. When the tract on the Green Mountains of Massachusetts was first settled, the same luxuriant fertility was attributed to it which has since characterized Kentucky. About the same time it was ascribed to the valley of Housatonnuc in the county of Berkshire. From these tracts it was transferred to the lands in New-Hampshire and Vermont, on the western side of the Green Mountains. From these regions *the paradise has travelled* to the western part of the State of New-York, to New-Connecticut, to Upper Canada, to the countries on the Ohio, to the south-western territory, and is now making its progress over the Mississippi into the newly purchased regions of Louisiana. The accounts given of all these countries successively was extensively true; but *the conclusions which were deducted from them were in a great measure erroneous. So long as this mould remains, the produce will regularly be great, and that with very imperfect cultivation; but this mould, after a length of time, will be dissipated;* where lands are continually ploughed it is soon lost; on those which are covered with grass from the beginning, it is preserved through a considerable period. At length, however, every appearance of its efficacy, and even of its existence, vanishes." —Dr. Dwight—quoted by Stuart, vol. i., page 264.

ber of hands employed ; just as in America, capital and labour (slaves excepted) are now employed in agriculture. In this case, many who do now obtain plenty of manufactured goods, though dear, might not be able to obtain any at whatever price.

The tariff, besides, is an act of combination ; an agreement among the people for distribution of employments. Those farmers for whom the tariff, by creating towns, has created markets* near to their own farms, would, by a repeal of the tariff, lose those markets, and must convey their net produce to more distant markets, if such there were, and if the cost of such longer conveyance did not deter them from raising food for market. Either then their industry would be less product-ive, the cost of its produce at market being greater ; or they would be less industrious, like hundreds of thousands of settlers far away from a market for net produce, who loiter away one half of their time, and waste a good deal of the other half by dividing their labour among several employments. Division of employments, says Adam Smith, meaning the reverse of di-vision of labour, is limited by the extent of the market ; he might have added, and so is industry itself.† Each manufac-turer then, and each of those farmers who now live near to a town, becoming isolated cultivators, without a motive for rais-ing more than should supply their own wants, would soon be contented with a rude house, coarse food, and rough clothes as necessaries, with tobacco, rum, a rifle, and ammunition as lux-uries. This does nearly always happen to those, who impelled by a spirit of adventure settle far away from any market. In this way the American demand for manufactured goods would be less, the wants of so many people would decrease, and the sum total of things useful or agreeable to man enjoyed in Amer-ica would be less ; a loss, economically speaking, or I have yet

---

* "He (a farmer near Springfield in Illinois) has advantages, too, in point of situation, being nearer to the Galena lead mines, to which he last year sold 8,000 wooden posts at three dollars per hundred. He had been in Scot-land ; but there was no land in that country to be compared (he said), to that of his farm. Finding him so much disposed to praise, I asked him how he was off for servants. His answer was marked ; ' you have hit the nail on the head—it is difficult to get servants here, and more difficult to get good ones.' "—*Stuart,* vol. ii., page 359.

† "The power of exchanging is the *vivifying principle of industry.* It stimulates agriculturists *to adopt the best system of cultivation,* and to raise the largest crops ; because it enables them to exchange whatever portion of the produce of their lands exceeds their own consumption, for other commodities conducive to their comforts or enjoyments ; and it equally stimulates manufac-turers to improve the quantity and variety of their goods, that they may thereby be enabled to obtain a greater quantity of raw produce. A spirit of industry is thus universally diffused ; and that apathy and languor, which are character-istic of a rude state of society, entirely disappear."—*Professor M'Culloch's Edition of Smith's Wealth of Nations. Note* 19, vol. iv., page 474.

to learn the alphabet of political economy.   The loss, morally or politically speaking, need not be mentioned again.

But, an English economist may ask, why should not the Americans combine with the English for a division of employments, between the two nations, which would be equally useful to both parties ?   Because, I answer, general combination of power, which leads to general division of employments, is useless, or rather impossible, without combination of capital and labour, and division of employments in particular works.   Exchange to any great extent cannot take place unless *two* parties raise a surplus produce, unless the produce of *both* parties be great in proportion to the hands employed ; and in America particular combination of power, with particular division of employments, will not take place so long as any quantity of good land may be obtained by anybody for the low price of five shillings per acre.   Evils resulting from the very low price of waste land meet one at every turn in America.

With slaves, however, this particular combination of capital and labour is possible in America.   The whites of the southern states are able to raise cheap commodities ; much, that is, in proportion to the hands employed ; commodities which being cheap would be exchangeable in the English market.   To the whites of the southern states, therefore, the tariff is injurious, limiting their foreign market for the sale of corn, rice, tobacco, cotton, and sugar.   This accounts for their dislike of the tariff. But the northern states, wanting slaves, want besides those southern markets which slavery and the tariff combined provide for the various products of their industry, other markets, nearer to their own particular works ; a demand for the produce of much divided capital and labour, for dear commodities which would not bear the cost of conveyance to very distant markets ;* and this want of domestic markets is to some extent

* " Potatoes, turnips, ruta-baga, peas, lucern, &c., are all to be seen here (New-York state), in small quantities, but not so well managed as in well cultivated districts of Britain.   The high price [scarcity] of labour is the great obstacle to the management which those crops require.   It is *not because the farmer does not understand his business* that such crops are apparently not sufficiently attended to, but because he, in all cases, calculates whether it will not be more profitable for him to remove his establishment to a new and hitherto unimpoverished soil, than to commence and carry on an extensive system of cultivation by manuring, and fallow, or green crops.   Such a system may be adopted *in the neighbourhood of great towns,* where *many green crops are easily disposed of,* and where manure can be had in large quantities and at a cheap rate ; but it is in vain to look for its adoption generally, or to expect to see agricultural operations in their best style until the land even in the most distant states and territories be occupied, so that the farmer may no longer find it more for his interest to begin his operations anew, on land previously uncultivated, *than to manage his farm* according *to the method which will render it most productive.*" * * * * " From what I have been told, I suspect it will be found that, after the effect of the vegetable matter on the surface of the land cleared,

supplied by the tariff. The affection of the northern states for the tariff is thus fully explained. As in the southern states slavery, so in the northern states the tariff, is an expedient, a shift, for correcting the mischievous influence of dispersion.

Well then, it may be said, if the two divisions of the union have such different interests, in consequence of the difference between their respective shifts for correcting the mischievous influence of dispersion, why should they not have separate governments, a northern and a southern union ; one with, and the other without a tariff ? For several reasons. First, because the expedient of the south is useful to the north, providing extensive, though distant markets for the products of northern industry,—for the manufactures, ships, steamboats, cattle, and very many things besides, which are produced in the states that forbid slavery, which would not be produced if there were no demand for them, and for which there would be less demand if the southern states, having free trade, should buy what they required in the cheapest market they could anywhere find.* Secondly, because the special expedient of the south could not be maintained without assistance from the north ; the force of the whole union being required to preserve slavery, to keep down the slaves. If the southern states, urged by hatred of the tariff, should declare themselves independent, they would presently lose that power of raising exchangeable commodities which is the groundwork of their dislike to the tariff. Losing their slaves, they too, like the northern states, would want a tariff to counteract dispersion, to preserve some combination of capital and labour, and some division of employments ; or, at the least, to create domestic markets ; a demand for the produce of scattered capital and labour. Give and take, live and let live, is a maxim everywhere understood. In order to preserve their own special expedient, slavery, the southern states must put up with the special expedient of the northern states, which is the tariff. Upon the whole, therefore, the tariff appears useful to the people of America ; and, as the people of America govern themselves for their own good, it will not probably be repealed, though it may be altered in various ways, until the price of land shall rise considerably through the increase of people a century hence, or earlier by

is at an end, the average crops of all sorts of grain are, according to the prevailing system of management in this state, *a half, or nearly a half, less than on similar soils in Britain.*"—*Stuart,* vol. i, page 162.

* Mr. Stuart, speaking of a district in the state of Illinois, says, " There is never any want of a market. Every thing is bought by the merchants for New-Orleans or for Galena, where a vast number of workmen are congregated, who are employed in the lead mines on the north-western parts of this state." New-Orleans is a great market, because of slavery ; Galena, because of the tariff.

the will of the people, who can put what price they please upon grants in the desert. If the price of new land were such that free labour should always be obtainable for combination in farming, then, with a greater produce from capital and labour, with higher profits and higher wages, the Americans would raise cheaper corn than has ever been raised; and, no longer wanting a tariff, might drive with the manufacturers of England the greatest trade ever known in the world.

NOTE XII.

THE ART OF COLONIZATION.

Introduction—Nature and limits of the subject—The ends of colonization as respects the mother-country—The extension of markets—Relief from excessive numbers—Enlargement of the field for employing capital—Ends of colonization as respects the colony—The means of colonization—The disposal of waste land—The removal of people—Co-operation of the mother-country—The foundation of colonies—The government of colonies.

INTRODUCTION.

CONSIDERING that the world has been peopled by the removal of people from old societies to settle in new places, and that the large portion of the earth which is still a desert will probably become inhabited by the same means, but certainly by no other means; seeing, therefore, that the art of colonization is one of vast importance to mankind, it does appear strange that this subject should not have been thoroughly examined by any writer on political economy. Under the head of *Colonies* we have, indeed, many treatises; but not one, as far as I know, in which the ends and means of colonization have been fully described, or even noticed, with so much as a show of method and accuracy. Of those treatises, some are confined to a mere history of the Greek colonies; while in others, which profess to embrace the whole subject of colonial policy, not only is the subject examined superficially and carelessly, but whenever the writer appears to be in earnest, he either dwells on points which are foreign to the matter in hand, or mixes the plainest misstatements of facts with the grossest errors of reasoning. Two examples will suffice to prove this assertion.

Professor M'Culloch, in a note appended to Adam Smith's chapter on the "Foundation of Colonies," after giving a list of works on colonial policy, says, "The article *Colony*, in the

Supplement to the Encyclopædia Britannica, written by Mr.
Mill, is one of the ablest of the recent disquisitions on the subject." A most able disquisition it is truly, on several subjects,
but not on colonization. It contains the shortest and clearest
explanation ever given of the symptoms of poverty in old
countries ; some very good reasons why transportation is a
very bad mode of punishing criminals, and some very conclusive arguments against commercial restrictions and bounties ;
but of colonization, its objects and means, Mr. Mill says next
to nothing. He says, indeed, that " colonization, with a view
to the relief of the mother-country by a diminution of numbers, deserves profound regard ;" and then proceeds to recommend, as " the best means of checking the progress of population," that " the superstitions of the nursery should be dis-
carded," in order to the adoption of a physical check to the
procreation of children. Returning to colonization with a view
to relief from excessive numbers, he disposes of the whole subject in a few lines ; saying, that on two conditions, but not
otherwise, " a body of people may be advantageously removed
from one country for the purpose of colonizing another ;"
when, first, " the land which they are about to occupy should
be capable of yielding a greater return to their labour than the
land which they leave ;" and secondly, " when the expense of
removal from the mother country to the colony, which is
usually created by distance, should not be too great." This is
all. The " *Conclusion*" of Mr. Mill's essay, accounts for his
having been content with uttering a pair of mere truisms on a
subject which, he says, deserves profound regard. Here he
asserts the " tendency of colonial possessions to produce or
prolong bad government," and emphatically condemns colonization as a fruitful source of jobs, monopolies, and wars. Be it
so ; but is this the only matter of bad government ? would
there have been no wars, monopolies, or jobs, without colonies ?
is every thing bad, including the wealth of nations, which has
formed the matter of jobs, monopolies, and wars ? are we to
regret the existence of the United States because they were
not founded without some great evils ? has not colonization
been a source of much good, as well as of some harm to mankind ? may not the evils be avoided in future, more good than
ever being obtained ? is there not in the founding of new states,
as in the government of old ones, a way of proceeding better
than all the others ? If Mr. Mill had asked himself these questions before he wrote on colonies, his essay would probably
have deserved Mr. M'Culloch's admiration. In that case he
would have told us something, at least, about the United States,
which still receive from other countries, and pour forth to reclaim the wilderness, great streams of population ; about the

influence of this gradual increase of land in proportion to the increase of people, in rendering a people fit to enjoy self-government or democratic institutions ; about the increased enjoyments of Europe, arising from the discovery of new productions in her colonies; about the stimulus given to European industry and skill by the formation of new markets ; about the reasons why, since the time of the ancient Greeks, at least, colonization has not been made useful for relieving an old country from excessive numbers ; and perhaps, about the best means of reclaiming desert countries with that all-important object. As it is, his essay may be called a treatise, and a very able one, on population, punishment, monopolies, and patronage, with a few careless remarks on colonization.

Adam Smith has written at great length on Colonies, but not with much more care than Mr. Mill ; as the reader will perceive who shall take the trouble to examine the following statement of "*the Causes of the Prosperity of New Colonies.*"*

" The colony of a civilized nation which takes possession either of a waste country, or of one so thinly inhabited that the natives easily give place to the new settlers, advances more rapidly to wealth and greatness than any other human society."

This assertion does not rest on facts. Some few new colonies have advanced very rapidly in population ; but scarce any have advanced rapidly to wealth and greatness ; while, as I have had occasion to observe before, the greater number of colonies have perished, or at least have remained for a long while less prosperous and civilized than their mother-countries. Among bodies of people who take possession of a waste country, the general rule seems to be, very slow progress towards wealth and greatness, with an exception now and then. The exceptions are not very striking. The only exceptions that strike one at all are the United States, Upper Canada (for Lower Canada was never a prosperous colony), and the penal settlements of the English in Australia. An increase of population, taken by itself, proves nothing ; since in Ireland, one of the most miserable countries in Europe, people have increased of late years almost as fast as in the United States. The progress of the United States in wealth, since they became independent, has not been nearly so great as that of England during the same period. No one pretends that the settlers of Upper Canada are a wealthy people ; and their prosperity, such as it is, seems to be owing mainly to an amount of immigration, both of capital and people, from a rich old country, far greater than ever occurred before in the history of colonization. As for the

* See Professor M'Culloch's Edition of *the Wealth of Nations*, vol. ii., page 460.

penal settlements of the English in Australia, they are societies altogether unnatural ; having been founded, and being maintained by the government of England with the produce of taxes paid by the people of England. Some persons, not convicts, are established there. These the English government supplies with slaves free of prime cost. The convict labourers, being forced to work in combination, raise more produce than they consume. But of what use would be surplus produce without a market in which to dispose of it ? Such a market the English government provides for the farmers of New South Wales, by maintaining a civil and military establishment, which costs 300,000*l.* a year. The local government buys the surplus produce of the settlers, either with bills drawn on the English treasury, or with specie sent from the English mint. With these bills and this money the settlers obtain various articles of comfort and luxury ; manufactured goods from England, wine from Spain and France, sugar from the Isle of France, tobacco from Brazil, spices from the Indian archipelago, and tea from China. The government first supplies the settlers with labour, and then buys, with exchangeable commodities, the surplus produce of that labour. In this way a great trade has been maintained ;* great, that is, in proportion to the people who were there to conduct it. That trade could not but be very profitable so long as the demand of the government exceeded the supply of the colony ; and this excess of demand over supply continued until lately. The high profits of that trade, and the high wages also, which every free labourer who chose to take part in it could obtain, have induced the colonists to keep together ; while the management of that trade called for a division of employments, such as I believe never occurred before in any colony so lately established. The unnatural causes of the prosperity of this colony show, in a striking manner, that new colonies in general are not apt to be prosperous. The only *new* colonies that have been remarkably prosperous are those of the ancient Greeks. Here follows Adam Smith's statement of the cause of their prosperity.

" The colonists carry out with them a knowledge of agriculture and other useful arts, superior to what can grow up of its

* When the English colonial minister boasts in parliament of the revenue raised by duties of customs in New-South Wales, he seems to forget that the trade on which those duties are levied is nothing but a certain mode of expenditure by the English government. He might as well boast of having got a revenue by taxes on the stone and wood used in building the palace at Pimlico. A portion of the money which the English pay for keeping convicts at New-South Wales, is made to pass, and not by a very indirect process, through the hands of the custom-house officers at Sydney : whereupon the English colonial minister, who has all the patronage attendant on that distant and most costly jail, exclaims,—Here's a flourishing colony for you !

own accord in the course of many centuries among savage and barbarous nations. They carry out with them too the habit of subordination, some notion of the regular government which takes place in their own country, of the system of laws which support it, and of a regular administration of justice; and they naturally establish something of the same kind in the new settlement. But among savage and barbarous nations, the natural progress of law and government is still slower than the natural progress of arts after law and government have been so far established as is necessary for their protection. *Every colonist gets more land than he can possibly cultivate.* He has no rent, and scarce any taxes to pay. No landlord shares with him in its produce, and the share of the sovereign is commonly but a trifle. He has every motive to render as great as possible a produce which is thus to be almost entirely his own. But his land is commonly so extensive, that with all his own industry, and with all the industry of other people whom he can get to employ, he can seldom make it produce the tenth part of what it is capable of producing. He is eager, therefore, to collect labourers from all quarters, and to reward them with the most liberal wages. Those liberal wages, joined to *the plenty and cheapness of land*, soon make those labourers leave him, in order to become landlords themselves, and to reward, with equal liberality other labourers, who soon leave them for the same reason that they left their first master. The liberal reward of labour encourages marriage. The children, during the tender years of infancy, are well taken care of; and when they are grown up, the value of their labour greatly overpays their maintenance. When arrived at maturity, *the high price of labour and the low price of land* enable them to establish themselves in the same manner as their fathers did before them. In other countries, rent and profit eat up wages, and the two superior orders of people oppress the inferior one. But in new colonies, the interest of the two superior orders obliges them to treat the inferior one with more generosity and humanity; at least *where that inferior one is not in a state of slavery.* Waste lands of the greatest natural fertility are to *be had for a trifle.* The increase of revenue which the proprietor, who is also the undertaker, expects from their improvement, constitutes his profit; which in these circumstances is commonly very great. But this great profit cannot be made without employing the labour of other people in clearing and cultivating the land; and the disproportion between the great extent of the land and the small number of people, which commonly takes place in new colonies, makes it difficult for him to get this labour. He does not therefore dispute about wages, but is willing to employ labour at any price. The *high wages of labour* encourage population.   The *cheapness and plenty* of good land encourage improvement, and enable the proprietor to pay those high wages.   In those wages consists almost the whole price of the land : and though they are high considered as the wages of labour, they are low considered as the price of what is so very valuable.   What encourages the progress of population and improvement encourages that of real wealth and greatness.   The progress of many of the Greek colonies towards wealth and greatness, seems *accordingly* to have been very rapid.   In the course of a century or two, several of them appear to have rivalled, and even to have surpassed their mother cities.   Syracuse and Agrigentum in Sicily, Tarentum and Locri in Italy, Ephesus and Miletus in Lesser Asia, appear, by all accounts, to have been at least equal to any of the cities of ancient Greece."

This passage contains a curious mixture of truth and error. It is the error that concerns us here.   With respect to the colonies of Greece, there is not a word of truth in the whole passage.   The remarkable prosperity of those colonies is attributed to superabundance or extreme cheapness of land, and to dearness of labour, or high wages.   But the emigrants from Greece did not, most certainly, obtain great tracts of land over which to spread at will.   There is no instance of their having advanced far from the seashore.   Wherever they landed they had to displace warlike tribes, who, abandoning the coast after a struggle, continued to watch the intruders, and to confine them within very narrow limits ; within a short stripe of land. The first occupation of a Greek colony seems to have been to build a fortress, into which the whole body of colonists might retire when attacked.   Some of those strong places became very soon great towns ; but the quantity of land required to feed the inhabitants of one great town, formed, in most cases, the whole territory of a Greek colony from the beginning to the end of its career.   Abundance and consequent cheapness of land, therefore, was not a cause of the prosperity of the Greek colonies.   In the next place, dearness of labour, or high wages, are terms which emigrants from Greece would not have understood even.   In no Greek colony did any one ever sell his labour ; or any one pay wages, high or low ; for all the works of those societies, the cultivation of their small territory, the building of their houses, the making of their tools, clothes, furniture, roads, carriages, and ships, and also the exchanges which took place either within a colony, or between a colony and other states ; all these works, so far as respects labour, were performed exclusively by slaves.

The account, therefore, which the father of the English economists has given of the causes of the prosperity of those colonies whose prosperity is the most remarkable, is obviously, nay, grossly incorrect. From these two examples of careless writing about colonies, by the first and the last distinguished Englishmen who have professed to examine the subject, it may be inferred that the subject has never been carefully examined. They are noticed by way of apology for conducting this inquiry with a degree of method, care, and fullness, which would have been pedantic or impertinent if such a course had ever been pursued before.

NATURE AND LIMITS OF THE SUBJECT.

The word colony is used to express very different ideas. A conquered nation, among whom the victors do not settle, even a mere factory for trade, has commonly been termed a colony ; as, for example, the English factories in India, and the actual dominion of the English in that country. Mere stations, also, for military or trading purposes, such as Malta or Heligoland, go by the name of colonies. In like manner the penal settlements, or distant jails of the English, are superintended by their colonial ministers, and were called colonies even when their whole population consisted of prisoners and keepers. Two societies more different than the people of India ruled by the servants of a London trading company, and the convicts of New South Wales, before Englishmen not criminals began to settle there, could not well be imagined. But the difference between the ideas often expressed by the term colony is matched by the caprice with which that term is used. The settlements of the Greeks in Sicily and Asia Minor, independent states from the beginning, have always been termed colonies : the English settlements in America were termed colonies, though in local matters they governed themselves from the beginning, so long as England monopolized their foreign trade and managed their external relations ; but from the time when England attempted to interfere with their domestic government, and happily lost both the monopoly of their foreign trade and the management of their foreign relations, they have not been reckoned as colonies. According to the loose way in which this term has been used, it is not dependence that constitutes a colony ; nor is it the continual immigration of people from distant places, since in this respect the United States surpass all other countries. In order to express the idea of a society which continually receives bodies of people from distant places, and sends out bodies of people to settle permanently in new places, no distinctive term has yet been used. This, however, is the idea which will be expressed whenever the term colony is used here ; the idea of a society at once immigrating and emigrating, such as the United States of America and the English settlements in Canada, South Africa, and Australia.

For the existence of a colony two things are indispensable ; first, waste land, that is, land not yet the property of individuals, but liable to become so through the intervention of government ; and secondly, the migration of people ; the removal of people to settle in a new place. Further, it will be seen at once, that this migration must be of two kinds ; first, the removal of people from an old to a new country ; secondly, the removal of people from a settled part to a waste part of the colony. Colonization, then, signifies the removal of people from an old to a new country, and the settlement of people on the waste land of the new country. As in this there is more to be done than to be learned, this is an art rather than a science. In every art the means to be employed ought to be regulated strictly by the ends in view. The first point, therefore, in this inquiry, is the ends of colonization.

Two very different societies may have a common interest in colonization, though with objects widely different in some respects. The English, for example, may have a deep interest in removing people to America for the sake of relief from excessive numbers ; while the Americans, cursed with slavery, might gain incalculably by receiving numbers of people from England. The ends of colonization, therefore, may be divided into two classes ; those which belong to the old country and those which belong to the colony. Each class of objects will be best ascertained by being examined separately.

THE ENDS OF COLONIZATION AS RESPECTS THE MOTHER-COUNTRY.

It may be questioned whether, in modern times at least, any old state has founded or extended a colony with any definite object whatever. The states of ancient Greece are supposed by Mr. Mill to have sent forth bodies of emigrants deliberately, with a view to relief from excessive numbers ; and he has shown in a very clear and forcible manner, that the rulers of those states had a strong motive for seeking that relief in that way, while no such motive was likely to occur to the rulers of modern Europe.* The rulers of modern Europe, however, have had

---

* " A curious phenomenon here presents itself. A redundancy of population in the states of ancient Greece made itself visible even to vulgar eyes. A redundancy of population in modern Europe never makes itself visible to any but the most enlightened eyes. Ask an ordinary man, ask almost any man, if the population of this country be too great ; if the population of any country in Europe is, or ever was too great : so far, he will tell you, is it from being too

a motive of affection for colonies. " Sancho Panza," says Mr. Mill, " had a scheme for deriving advantage from the government of an island. He would sell the people for slaves, and put the money into his pocket. The Few, in some coun-

great, that good policy would consist in making it, if possible, still greater; and he might quote in his own support the authority of almost all governments, who are commonly at pains to prevent the emigration of their people, and to give encouragement to marriage.

The explanation of the phenomenon is easy; but it is also of the highest importance. When the supply of food is too small for the population, the deficiency operates, in modern Europe, in a manner different from that in which it operated in ancient Greece. In modern Europe the greatest portion of the food is bought by the great body of the people. What the great body of the people have to give for it is nothing but labour. When the quantity of food is not sufficient for all, and when some are in danger of not getting any, each man is induced, in order to secure a portion to himself, to give better terms for it than any other man; that is, more labour. In other words, that part of the population who have nothing to give for food but labour, take less wages. This is the primary effect, clear, immediate, certain. It is only requisite further to trace the secondary or derivative effects.

When we say, that in the case in which the supply of food has become too small for the population, the great body of the people take less wages, that is, less food, for their labour; we mean that they take less than is necessary for their comfortable subsistence; because they would only have what is necessary for comfortable subsistence in the case in which the supply of food is not too small for the whole.

The effect, then, of a disproportion between the food and the population is, not to feed to the full measure that portion of the population which it is sufficient to feed, and to leave the redundant portion destitute; it is to take, according to a certain rate, a portion of his due quantity from each individual of that great class who have nothing to give for it but ordinary labour.

What this state of things imports is most easily seen. The great class, who have nothing to give for food but ordinary labour, are the great body of the people. When every individual in the great body of the people has less than the due quantity of food, less than would fall to his share if the quantity of food were not too small for the population, the state of the great body of the people is the state of sordid, painful, and degraded poverty. They are wretchedly fed, wretchedly clothed, have wretched houses, and neither time nor means to keep their houses or their persons free from disgusting impurity. Those of them who, either from bodily infirmities, have less than the ordinary quantity of labour to bestow, or, from the state of their families, need a greater than the ordinary quantity of food, are condemned to starve; either wholly, if they have not enough to keep them alive; or partially, if they have enough to yield them a lingering, diseased, and after all, a shortened existence.

What the ignorant and vulgar spectator sees in all this, is not a redundant population: it is only a poor population. He sees nobody without food who has enough to give for it. To his eye, therefore, it is not food which is wanting, but that which is to be given for it. When events succeed in this train, and are viewed with those eyes, there never can appear to be a redundancy of population.

Events succeeded in a different train in the states of ancient Greece, and rendered a redundancy of population somewhat more visible, even to vulgar and ignorant eyes.

In ancient Greece the greatest portion of the food was not bought by the great body of the people; the state of whom, wretched or comfortable, legislation has never yet been wise enough much to regard. All manual labour, or, at least, the far greater portion of it, was performed, not by free labourers serving for wages, but by slaves, who were the property of the great men. The de-tries, find in colonies a thing which is very dear to them; they find, the one part of them, the precious matter with which to influence; the other, the precious matter with which *to be* influenced;—the one, the precious matter with which to make political dependents; the other, the precious matter with which they are made political dependents;—the one, the precious mat-

ficiency of food, therefore, was not distributed in the shape of general poverty and wretchedness over the great body of the population by reduction of wages; a case which affects with very slight sensations those who regard themselves as in no degree liable to fall into that miserable situation. It was felt, first of all by the great men, in the greater cost of maintaining their slaves. And what is felt as disagreeable by the great men is sure never to continue long without an effort, either wise or foolish, for the removal of it. This law of human nature was not less faithfully observed in the states of ancient Greece, for their being called republics. Called republics, they in reality were aristocracies; and aristocracies of a very bad description. They were aristocracies in which the people were cheated with an idea of power, merely because they were able, at certain distant intervals, when violently excited, to overpower the aristocracy in some one particular point; but they were aristocracies in which there was not one efficient security to prevent the interests of the many from being sacrificed to the interests of the few; they were aristocracies, accordingly, in which the interests of the many were habitually sacrificed to the interests of the few; meaning by the many, not the slaves merely, but the great body of the free citizens. This was the case in all the states of Greece, and not least in Athens. This is not seen in reading the French and English histories of Greece. It is not seen in reading Mitford, who has written a history of Greece for no other purpose but that of showing that the interests of the many always *ought* to be sacrificed to the interests of the few; and of abusing the people of Greece, because every now and then, the many in those countries showed that they were by no means patient under the habitual sacrifice of their interests to the interests of the few. But it is very distinctly seen, among other occasions, in reading the Greek orators, in reading Demosthenes, for example, in reading the Oration against Midias, the Oration on Leptines, and others; in which the license of the rich and powerful, and their means of oppressing the body of the people, are shown to have been excessive, and to have been exercised with a shameless atrocity, which the gentleness and modesty of the manners of modern Europe, even in the most aristocratically despotic countries, wholly preclude.

In Greece, then, any thing which so intimately affected the great men, as a growing cost of maintaining their slaves, would not long remain without serious attempts to find a remedy.

It was not, however, in this way alone that a redundant population showed itself in Greece. As not many of the free citizens maintained themselves by manual labour, they had but two resources more,—the land and profits of stock. Those who lived on profits of stock, did so, commonly, by employing slaves in some of the known arts and manufactures, and of course were affected by the growing cost of maintaining their slaves. Those who lived on the produce of a certain portion of the land, could not but exhibit, very distinctly, the redundancy of their numbers, when, by the multiplication of families, portions came to be so far subdivided, that what belonged to each individual was insufficient for his maintenance.

In this manner, then, it is very distinctly seen why, to vulgar eyes, there never appears, in modern Europe, to be any redundancy of population, any demand for relieving the country by carrying away a portion of the people; and why, in ancient Greece, that redundancy made itself to be very sensibly perceived; and created, at various times, a perfectly efficient demand for removing to distant places a considerable portion of the people —*Article Colony, in the Supplement to the Encyclopædia Britannica.*

ter by which they augment their power; the other, the precious matter by which they augment their riches. Both portions of the ruling Few, therefore, find their account in the possession of colonies. There is not one of the colonies but what augments the number of places. There are governorships, and judgeships, and a long train of *et ceteras ;* and, above all, there is not one of them but what requires an additional number of troops and an additional portion of navy. In every additional portion of army and navy, besides the glory of the thing, there are generalships, and colonelships, and captainships, and lieutenantships; and in the equipping and supplying of additional portions of army and navy, there are always gains which may be thrown in the way of a friend. All this is enough to account for a very considerable quantity of affection maintained towards colonies." For the affection of the rulers this is enough, but not for that of the nations. The nations of modern Europe have had a very different motive of affection for colonies ; a sense of the benefits derived from the discovery of new productions and the creation of new markets. Those Englishmen, for instance, who, during the last century and a half have shouted, " Ships, Colonies, and Commerce !" were good political economists. If they did not know scientifically, that all improvements in the productive powers of industry, that industry itself is limited by the extent of the market, still they felt that every new colony, or every enlargement of an old one, increased by so much the means of exchanging the produce of English labour, and by so much increased the wealth of England. Who that produces does not feel, though he may be unable to account for it, the advantage of having some other ready to deal with him for the surplus produce of his labour ? A desire for new markets has, indeed, scarcely ever been the deliberate motive for establishing a colony ; nor perhaps did any government ever establish a colony deliberately for the sake of patronage. But, colonies having been established, sometimes by the adventurous spirit of individuals, sometimes by religious persecution, the governments and nations of modern Europe had strong motives of affection towards them; the governments, for the sake of patronage; the nations, for the sake of markets. Hence the anxiety of the governments of modern Europe to retain dominion over their colonies, and their attacks upon each other's colonies: hence too, the Colonial System, as it is called ; the system of trading monopolies, which took its rise in a mistaken desire in each nation to monopolize as much as possible of that trade between Europe and her colonies, which would have been more valuable to all the nations if it had been perfectly free. Let us distinguish between the existence and the dominion of a colony ; between the existence and the monopoly of a colonial market. " There is no necessity," says Mr. Bentham, " for governing or possessing any island in order that we may sell merchandise there." But in order to sell merchandise in a colony it is necessary that the colony should exist. If Mr. Bentham had drawn this distinction, if he had separated the question of dominion from the question of existence, he would not have been led, by dwelling on the evils of colonial monopoly, to undervalue the benefits of colonial trade. His disciple, Mr. Mill, likewise, if he had drawn this distinction, would not have deprecated colonies because they have been made improperly a ground for jobs, monopolies, and wars: he might have condemned the wars, monopolies, and jobs, of which colonies have been the matter; but perceiving that the real source of those evils was not the colonies, but the badness of the European governments, he would probably have seen also, along with Adam Smith, the " natural advantages" which Europe has derived from her colonies, in spite of the tricks which those governments have played with them. The uses and abuses of colonization are very different things. While some philosophers have condemned colonization on account of its abuses, the nations of Europe, even when they promoted the abuses, had, one cannot say a knowledge, but a deep sense of the usefulness. That such " unscientific knowledge," to use terms employed by Bentham, should have been attended with very " unartificial practice," is just what might have been expected.

The objects of an old society in promoting colonization seem to be three; first, the extension of the market for disposing of their own surplus produce; secondly, relief from excessive numbers; thirdly, an enlargement of the field for employing capital. Referring, however, to a previous Note on the coincidence of overflowing national wealth with the uneasiness and misery of individuals, it will be seen, presently, that these three objects may come under one head; namely, an enlargement of the field for employing capital and labour. But first, each object must be considered separately.

I. *The extension of markets.*

Why does any man ever produce of any thing more than he can himself consume ? Solely because he expects that some other man will take from him that portion of the produce of his labour which he does not want, giving him in exchange something which he wants. From the power of exchanging comes every improvement in the application of labour, and every atom of the produce of labour, beyond that rude work and that small produce which supply the wants of savages. It is not because an English washerwoman cannot sit down to breakfast without tea and sugar, that the world has been circumnavigated ; but it is because the world has been circumnavigated that an English washerwoman requires tea and sugar for breakfast. According to the power of exchanging are the desires of individuals and societies. But every increase of desires, or wants, has a tendency to supply the means of gratification. The savage hunter, enabled to exchange his furs for beads, is stimulated to greater energy and skill. The sole ground on which it is supposed that the blacks of the West Indies will work for wages as soon as they shall be set free, is their love of finery. They will produce sugar, it is said, in order to buy trinkets and fine clothes. And who ever worked hard, when was an improvement made in any useful art, save through the impulse of a passion for some kind of finery ; for some gratification, not absolutely necessary, to be obtained by means of exchange ? As with individuals, so with nations. In England, the greatest improvements have taken place continually, ever since colonization has continually produced new desires among the English, and new markets wherein to purchase the objects of desire. With the growth of sugar and tobacco in America, came the more skilful growth of corn in England. Because, in England, sugar was drank and tobacco smoked, corn was raised with less labour, by fewer hands ; and more Englishmen existed to eat bread, as well as to drink sugar and smoke tobacco. The removal of Englishmen to America, and their industry in raising new productions not fit for the support of life, led, in England, to more production for the support of life. Because things not necessary had been produced, more necessaries were produced.* If the French

* " Rich subjects make a rich nation. As the former increase, so will the means of filling the coffers of the latter. Let contemporary nations lay it to their account that England is more powerful than ever she was, notwithstanding her debt and taxes. This knowledge should form an element in their foreign policy. Let them assure themselves that instead of declining she is advancing ; that her population increases fast ; that she is constantly seeking new fields of enterprise in other parts of the globe, and adding to the improvements that already cover her island at home, new ones that promise to go far beyond them in magnitude : in fine, that instead of being worn out, as at a distance is sometimes supposed, she is going a-head with the buoyant and vigorous effort of youth. * * * Britain still exists all over the world in her colonies. These alone give her the means of advancing her industry and opulence for ages to come. They are portions of her territory more valuable than if joined to her island. The sense of distance is destroyed by her command of ships ; while that very distance serves as the feeder of her commerce and marine. Situated on every continent, lying in every latitude, these, her out dominions, make her the centre of a trade already vast and perpetually augmenting,—a home trade and a foreign trade,—for it yields the riches of both as she controls it at her will. They take off her redundant population, *yet make her more populous* ; and are destined, under the policy already commenced towards them, and which

should know how to colonize North Africa, they may overtake the English in the skilful application of domestic capital and labour; but if they do this, it will be through the impulse arising from new markets, in which to sell the surplus produce of their industry. It thus appears, that the removal of people from an old society to a new place, may be of the greatest use to that old society, even when the people removed occupy themselves in raising objects of mere luxury, and when the mother-country has yet many steps to make in the career of wealth and civilization.

But now comes the more interesting case of a society, which, stimulated by the extension of its markets, has cultivated all that part of its territory which is fit for cultivation; a society in which the utmost skill in the application of capital and labour to agriculture is counteracted by the necessity of cultivating inferior land; a society, consequently, in which food is dear, and in which there exist the strongest motives for importing food from other countries by means of manufactures and exchange; a society, in short, which requires new markets in which to purchase the staff of life. This is pre-eminently the case of England. Imagine a country in which the quantity of air for breathing were limited, and were not more than sufficient to keep alive the actual number of its inhabitants; while of that actual number the larger portion by much obtained less than enough air; was half suffocated for want of air; in a state between life and death. Conceive further, that in this country an inexhaustible supply of food might be obtained without labour, as air is everywhere obtained. Now suppose that this society should be able to obtain air from other countries by means of manufactures and exchange. If this ability were allowed its free exercise, the population of that country would go on increasing continually, all the people being at ease, so long as the ability should last. But if the rulers of this country, having a property in the atmosphere, should forbid the people to get air from other countries, the bulk of that people must remain half suffocated, notwithstanding their natural ability to obtain plenty of the means of life. Substituting bread for air, this is the case of England with her stifling corn-laws. The English corn-laws will be repealed. As the present inquiry relates to a country like England, but without corn-laws, we may, for the sake of more ready illustration, speak of England as if her corn-laws were repealed. When that shall happen, the English will hunt over the world in search of cheap

in time she will more extensively pursue, to expand her empire, commercial, manufacturing, and maritime, to dimensions to which it would not be easy to fix limits."—*A Residence at the Court of London; by the Hon. Mr. Rush, Env. Ex. and Min. Plen. from the United States to England.*

corn. But where will they find any? Not in countries situated like England; not in any country where land is dear. They will find cheap corn only in countries where land is cheap; in countries where the proportion which land bears to people is so great as, first, to render unnecessary the cultivation of inferior land, and secondly, to encourage a large proportion of the people to occupy themselves with the growth of corn. But is not this the description of a colony, according to the sense in which the term colony is here used? a country having room for more people, with more room at hand for the greatest increase of people. Poland is such a country; as was England when the bulk of Englishmen were serfs. But there are three reasons why such a country as England was then, is not the most fit to provide cheap corn for such a country as England is now: first, because in the then barbarous and despotic state of the English government, no dependence could have been placed on English industry for a regular supply of corn: secondly, because in the then barbarous condition of the English people, capital and labour were not applied to the growth of corn with that skill which renders the produce great in proportion to the hands employed: thirdly, because the savage ancestors of the English would not have cared to buy such objects as those, with which alone the English of this day could buy foreign corn. The market would have been very insecure; the corn brought to it not very cheap; and of that corn, whether cheap or dear, but a small quantity would have been brought to market. This is precisely the case of Poland, where the market is liable to be shut up by the whim of a tyrant; where the produce of agricultural capital and labour, though, by means of slavery, greater than it would be if the capital and labour were cut up into fractions as numerous as the cultivators, is much less than it would be if the same number of Poles should cultivate the same land with English skill; and where the demand for English goods is by no means equal to the supply that could be afforded, nor likely to become so. Whereas in a colony planted by Englishmen, civilized and well-governed, the highest skill in the application of capital and labour to the growth of corn, might conspire, with great cheapness of land, to the raising of cheaper corn than has ever yet been raised; while so cheap a market for the purchase of corn would not only be as secure as any distant market ever was, but might be extended continually with the progress of colonization. Why such very cheap corn has not been raised in any English colony, is a different question, slightly noticed before;* and the means of raising very cheap corn in a colony, without slavery, will be care-

* See Note VII.

fully examined among the means of colonization. Here my object has been to show, that for such a country as England, a chief end of colonization is to obtain secure markets for the purchase of cheap corn ; a steady supply of bread, liable to be increased with an increasing demand.

The trade which the English should conduct for obtaining cheap bread from their colonies might be of two kinds ; direct and indirect. Supposing that very cheap corn were raised in Canada, the English might buy such corn with the manufactured goods of Leeds, Manchester, and Birmingham ; this would be a direct trade. But it might very well happen, that the Canadians should be able to raise, not more corn than the English should be able to buy, but more than they should be able to buy *with manufactured goods*. In other words, the demand of the Canadians for English goods might be much less than the demand of the English for Canadian corn. But the Canadians would require many things, besides English goods, which are not producible in Canada : they would require tea and silver, for instance. The English, then, might first buy tea and silver of the Chinese with manufactured goods, and then buy corn of the Canadians with tea and silver. But the demand, again, of the Chinese for English goods might not be sufficient to supply in this way the demand of the English for Canadian corn. For one thing, however, the demand of the Chinese is very urgent, and would be without limit ; for food in every shape ; for the means of life. Here, then, is the groundwork of the most extensive commerce that ever existed in the world. Supposing that cheap food were raised in the English colonies of Australia, which, though far from England, are near to China, the English might buy such food with manufactured goods ; with that food buy tea and silver of the Chinese ; and with that tea and silver buy cheap corn of the Canadians. In this case, combination of capital and labour for division of employments among four different nations, would be of the greatest service to all of them ; to the Australian colonists, the Chinese, the Canadian colonists, and the English. A great number of cases like this might be reasonably supposed. From this case, which, though supposed, is very likely to occur, it will be seen that a colony, at the antipodes even of its mother country, might help to supply that mother country with cheap corn ; and by means of the cheapness of land which is an attribute of colonies. Both by a direct and an indirect trade, colonies might, according to their number and extent, enlarge the field for employing capital and labour in the mother country, at home, without reference to the emigration of people or the removal of capital into distant fields of employment. The warmest imagination could hardly exaggerate the benefits which a country like England might derive from such enlargements of her domestic field of production; could hardly reckon at too much the new demand for labour at home, in building, machinery, and manufactures; for the produce of domestic agriculture, corn alone excepted; for ships; for the use of mercantile capital; and for all kinds of services not usually called labour.

But, it may be said, a country like England, having no corn-laws, might obtain all these benefits without colonies. "The possession of colonies," Sir Henry Parnell would say, "affords no advantages which could not be obtained by commercial intercourse with independent states."* Here, again, the question of dominion is mixed up with the question of existence. Independent states! which are the independent states that could produce very cheap corn for the English market? The United States: truly; but the United States are as much colonies as were the never dependent colonies of Greece. Canada, on the other hand, being dependent, is neither more nor less fit than the United States to produce cheap corn for the English market. Let us banish altogether, for the present, the idea of monopoly or dominion. Of him who has done this, I would ask, What country, in which land is cheap, is most fit, on other accounts, to provide the English with cheap corn? Not Poland; because there property is insecure, industry unskilful, and the people barbarous: not Buenos Ayres, where land is cheaper than in any other country, being obtainable in unlimited quantities for nothing, of the richest quality, already cleared and drained by nature; not Buenos Ayres, because the people of this colony are barbarously unskilful, and have no desire for English goods; not Ceylon, because, though that country be improperly called an English colony, its inhabitants are not anxious to obtain English goods: none of these, but the United States, Canada, and the English settlements in South Africa and Australia; because, in all of those countries, corn might be raised on cheap land, with English skill, by people anxious to buy English goods. If the English should buy cheap corn of the Canadians with Chinese tea and silver, it might be by means of selling English goods to the growers of cheap food in Australia. If cheap corn were brought to England, whether by the most straight and simple, or by the most round-about and complicated traffic, the original purchase-money of such corn must be manufactured goods, the produce of capital and labour employed in England; and it could be nothing else. Whence it follows, inevitably, that the number or extent of the markets, in which the English

---

* Financial Reform, page 251, 3d. edit.

might buy very cheap corn, must depend upon the number or extent of countries raising cheap corn and requiring English goods.   An English colony, whether dependent like Canada, or independent like the United States, might do both: it might both raise the corn and want the manufactured goods.   We may conclude then, that with a view to the greatest market for buying cheap corn, a people like the English would plant or extend colonies; nations of Englishmen born, and their descendants; using the English language; preserving English skill and English tastes; and, therefore, both able and willing to purchase English goods with cheap corn.

II. *Relief from excessive numbers.*

In modern times, no old country has ever obtained relief from excessive numbers by means of colonization.   In no case has the number of emigrants been sufficient to diminish, even for a year, the ruinous competition of labourers for employment; much less to produce any lasting improvement in the condition of the bulk of the people.   More than once, however, this has been the object, or has been called the object, of an old state in promoting colonization.   Twice since their late war with the French, the English have sent out bodies of people to colonies under the rule of the English government, for the declared purpose of checking pauperism at home : first to the Dutch colony of South Africa, and next to the English colony of Upper Canada.   On neither of these occasions was the object attained even in the slightest degree.   Both these attempts were called experiments.   This year, the English government is making, to use the expression of Lord Goderich,* another " experiment" of the same kind, by providing the funds wherewith to convey to South Africa a number of destitute children ; the prodigious number of twenty.   Considering that the population of England is fourteen millions, this experiment may be justly called child's play.   The previous experiment in South Africa, and the outlay of 60,000*l.* in taking English paupers to Upper Canada, at the suggestion of Mr. (now Sir Robert) Wilmot Horton and the Emigration Committees of the House of Commons, were hardly less preposterous, if we are to believe that any benefit to the labouring class at home was seriously expected from them.   To call experiments measures so futile, so obviously inadequate to the end in view, is an abuse of language, and one calculated to be mischievous; since, if these childish attempts had really been experiments,

* In a letter addressed to a society for the relief of orphan and destitute children.

the signal failure of them would have been a fact, tending to establish that colonization, with a view to relief from excessive numbers, must necessarily fail of its object.

Two classes of men in England, classes of the most opposite turn of mind, have decided against colonization with this view, and on grounds equally unreasonable : first, those unreasoning men who would determine questions in political economy by quoting Scripture ; secondly, men who possess in a high degree the faculty of reason, but who, having made a religion for themselves, are often under the influence of a kind of bigotry ; I mean those political economists who worship capital. Speak of emigration to one of the former class, and he will exclaim, " Dwell in the land, and verily ye shall be fed ;" to one of the latter, and he will say,—The question deserves profound regard ; but as employment for labour is in proportion to capital, as emigration would cost money and diminish capital, therefore it would diminish employment for labour, and do more harm than good.

Whether right or wrong in their dislike of emigration, those who swear by David, and those who worship capital, are equally contradicted by facts. The people do dwell in the land, but verily they are not fed. Though no labour be employed save by capital, still millions upon millions of capital are accumulated, not to employ domestic labour, but, for want of employment *for capital*, either to lie idle, or to be wasted in distant and ruinous speculations. The quotation from Scripture may be disposed of by another : " Increase and multiply, and *replenish the earth, and subdue it*." But those who object to emigration on the score of its expense deserve, on account of their reputation and authority, that their argument should be carefully examined.

The argument is stated as follows by Mr. Mill. " It has been often enough, and clearly enough explained, that it is capital which gives employment to labour : we may, therefore, take it as a postulate. A certain quantity of capital, then, is necessary to give employment to the population, which any removal for the sake of colonization may leave behind. But *if*, to afford the expense of that removal, so much is taken from the capital of the country that the remainder is not sufficient for the employment of the remaining population, there is, in that case, a redundancy of population, and all the evils which it brings. For the well-being of the remaining population, a certain quantity of food is required, and a certain quantity of all those other things which minister to human happiness. But to raise this quantity of other things, a certain quantity of capital is indispensably necessary, *If* that quantity of capital is not supplied, the food and other things cannot be obtained."*

Though the argument stated thus hypothetically, thus guarded by *ifs*, amounts to the statement of a mere truism, still the "postulate" which runs through the argument is an assumption, that emigration *would* take away too much capital; so much as to leave too little for the remaining people. Mr. Bentham assumes this without any *ifs*. "Colonization," he says,† "requires an immediate expense, an actual loss of wealth, for a future profit, for a contingent gain. The capital which is carried away for the improvement of the land in the colonies, had it been employed in the mother country, would have added to its increasing wealth, as well as to its population, and to the means of its defence, while, as to the produce of the colonies, only a small part ever reaches the mother country. If colonization is a folly when employed as a means of enrichment, it is at least an agreeable folly."

Now upon what rests this assumption? It rests upon two other assumptions, one of which is true, the other false; first, that no labour is employed save by capital; secondly, that all capital employs labour. If it were true that every increase of capital necessarily gave employment to more labour; if it were true, as Professor M'Culloch has said,‡ that "there is plainly only one way of effectually improving the condition of the great majority of the community or of the labouring class, and that is *by increasing the ratio of capital to population*," then it might be assumed that colonization would, on account of its expense, do more harm than good. But it is not true that all capital employs labour. To say so is to say that which a thousand facts prove to be untrue. Capital frequently increases without providing any more employment for labour. That this does actually happen in England, I have endeavoured to show elsewhere.§ It follows, that capital, for which there is no employment at home, might be spent on emigration without diminishing employment for labour to the slightest extent. I use the word *spent* instead of *invested*, in order to save the trouble of explaining at length, that if capital so employed were utterly lost, that loss of capital need not diminish employment for labour. No one pretends that employment for English labour was diminished, to the extent of a single pair of hands, by the loans which the English lately made to the republics, so called, of South America, to the Spanish Cortes, to Don Miguel, or Don Pedro; or by the late waste of English capital in pre-

* Article *Colony*. Supplement to the Encyclopædia Britannica.
† Rationale of Reward, b. iv. chap. 14.
‡ Introductory Discourse, in his edition of the Wealth of Nations.
§ Note IV.

tending to work mines in South America, or in glutting distant markets with English goods, sold for less than the cost of production; or by the waste of English capital in founding the Swan River settlement. Still less has employment for English labour been diminished by late investments of English capital, in foreign countries, which yield some return; such as loans to the emperors of Austria and Russia, to the kings of Prussia, Naples, the Low Countries, and France; purchases lately made in the securities of foreign governments, amounting at one time in the French funds alone to near 40,000,000*l.*; investments of English capital in the iron and cotton works of France, the Low Countries, and Germany; and finally, loans to the North American States. If all the capital removed from England in all these ways during the last seventeen years, amounting to some hundreds of millions, had been lost in conducting emigration, employment for labour in England would not have been less than it is at present.

A recent fact illustrates this view of the subject still more forcibly. During the last year (1832), it is supposed, about 125,000 people, men, women, and children, emigrated from Britain to the United States, Canada, and Australia. Of these a considerable number carried property with them, varying in amount from 5000*l.* to a few pounds over the cost of passage. The passage of the whole of them must have cost, at the lowest estimate of 5*l.* for each person, not less than 625,000*l.* Supposing that they took with them a capital of 5*l.* each, upon the average, which seems a very low estimate, emigration from Britain carried off during the last year a capital of 1,250,000*l.* Does any one pretend that this abstraction of capital has diminished, to the extent of a single pair of hands, the amount of employment for labour in Britain? Might we not rather expect, if England had no corn-laws, that these 125,000 emigrants, employing their capital and labour in a wide and rich field, would create a new demand for the produce of capital and labour employed in Britain? Let these questions be answered carefully, and it will appear that much of the capital of such a country as England may be used in promoting emigration, without diminishing, to say the least, the amount of employment for domestic labour. Whether capital might be so used with profit to the owners of it, whether, by such a use of capital, effectual relief from excessive numbers might be obtained, are questions which belong rather to the means than to the ends of colonization. Here, my sole object is to show how groundless is the objection to emigration on the score of its expense; how futile is that *a priori* reasoning, by which some conclude, that the cost of emigration would necessarily diminish, according to its amount, the amount of employment for labour at home.   I have dwelt so long on this objection, not with a view to recommend emigration by means of an outlay of English capital (for I shall endeavour to show hereafter that it would be greatly for the advantage of colonies to provide a fund for the immigration of labour), but in order to remove a prejudice against colonization, on the ground of the mischievous loss of capital which it might occasion to the mother country ; a prejudice which stops him who entertains it on the very threshold of this subject.*

Supposing that, whether by means of English capital about, at all events, to fly off to foreign countries, or by means of a fund raised in the colonies, such an amount of labour should emigrate from England as considerably to diminish the proportion which, in England, labour bears to employment ; then would the wages of labour be higher, then would the state of the bulk of the people be improved, then would relief be obtained from excessive numbers.   This great end of colonization has never been so much as seriously contemplated by the ruling class in England.   On the contrary, taught by certain economists to believe, that profits rise when wages fall, and fall when wages rise, that the prosperity of the capitalist is consistent only with the misery of the labourer, the late ruling

---

* This prejudice was once entertained by Mr. Bentham.   It depended upon a *non sequitur* which had got possession of his mind.   In the fourth book of the Rationale of Reward, M. Dumont has a chapter entitled " Bentham and Adam Smith," where he draws a comparison between the views of political economy, taken by the English and Scotch philosophers.   "Mr. Bentham," he says, " has simplified his subject, by referring every thing to one principle ; namely, *the limitation of production and trade by the limitation of capital ;* a principle which brings all his reasonings into a very small circle, and which serves to unite into one bundle those observations which cannot be so easily grasped when they are disunited."   This one principle is stated as follows in the first paragraph of Bentham's *Manual of Political Economy.*   " No kind of productive labour of any importance can be carried on without capital.   From hence it follows, that the quantity of labour, applicable to any object, is limited by the quantity of capital which can be employed in it."   Doubtless ; but then the principle is, " the limitation of production and trade by the limitation of capital" *for which there is employment.*   The words which I have added, in italics, make all the difference.   It does not follow that, because labour is employed by capital, capital always finds a field in which to employ labour.   This is the *non sequitur* always taken for granted by Bentham, Ricardo, Mill, M'Culloch, and others.   Adam Smith, on the contrary, saw that there were limits to the employment of capital, and therefore limits, besides the limit of capital, to the employment of labour ; the limits, namely, of the field of production, and of the market in which to dispose of surplus produce.   During the summer of 1831, Mr. Bentham's attention was called to this subject.   At first he urged the objection to colonization which has been here examined, but finally abandoned it.   Then, immediately, notwithstanding his great age and bodily infirmities, he proceeded to study the whole subject of colonization, and even to write upon it at some length.   His written remarks upon the subject, now in my possession, show that he lived to consider colonization, not " an agreeable folly," but a work of the greatest utility.   I am proud to add, that the form of the present treatise was suggested by one of the wisest and best of mankind.

class in England would have set their faces against any project of colonization which had seemed fit to raise wages. Late events have produced some change of feeling on this subject; and coming events, probably, will soon produce a greater change. "What," says Mr. Mill, " is felt as disagreeable by the *great men*, is sure never to continue long without an effort, either wise or foolish, for the removal of it." The new ruling class of England, those whom late events have made the great men of England, are placed in a situation which may render excess of numbers highly disagreeable to them. They may be glad to pay high wages for the security of their property ; to prevent the devastation of England through commotions arising from discontent in the bulk of the people. Even before the late change, while the fears of the great men were urging them to bring about that change, while fires were blazing and mobs exacting higher wages in the south of England, a dread of the political evils likely to come from excessive numbers, induced the English government to form a Board of Emigration, with the avowed purpose of improving the condition of the labouring class, by removing some of them to the colonies. A more foolish, or rather futile, effort by great men to remove what they felt as disagreeable, was, perhaps, never made ; but the effort, feeble and puerile though it were, tends to point out that for a country, situated like England, in which the ruling and the subject orders are no longer separated by a middle class, and in which the subject order, composing the bulk of the people, are in a state of gloomy discontent arising from excessive numbers ; that for such a country, one chief end of colonization is to prevent tumults, to keep the peace, to maintain order, to uphold confidence in the security of property, to hinder interruptions of the regular course of industry and trade, to avert the terrible evils which, in a country like England, could not but follow any serious political convulsion.

For England, another end of colonization, by means of relief from excessive numbers, would be relief from that portion of the poor's-rate which maintains workmen in total or partial idleness ; an object in which the ruling order have an obvious interest.

For England again, a very useful end of colonization would be to turn the tide of Irish emigration from England to her colonies ; not to mention that the owners of land in Ireland, most of them being foreigners by religion, might thus be taken out of the dilemma in which they are now placed ; that of a choice between legally giving up a great part of their rental to the hungry people, and yielding to the people's violence the land which was taken by violence from their fathers.

Finally, comprised in relief from excessive numbers is the

relief to many classes, not called labourers or capitalists, from that excessive competition for employment which renders them uneasy and dissatisfied. Of the 125,000 persons who quitted England last year to settle in colonies, not a few were professional men; surgeons, clergymen, lawyers, architects, engineers, surveyors, teachers, and clerks: some few of them were governesses. It will be seen, when we shall come to the means of colonization, that, if colonies were properly managed, they would furnish, according to the continual progress in their number or extent, a continually increasing demand for the services of all those classes.

III. *Enlargement of the field for employing capital.*

This end of colonization is distinct from that enlargement of the field for employing capital, which would come by the creation of extensive markets for the purchase of cheap corn with the produce of domestic industry. It may be best explained by reference to some facts. Since England began to colonize, how many Englishmen have quitted their country with small fortunes, and returned with large ones, made by means of high profits in the colonies! In the West India islands alone, millions upon millions of English capital have been employed with very great profit; millions upon millions, which, we may be sure, would not have been removed to the West Indies if they could have been invested at home with equal profit. An existing London Company has more than doubled its capital in a few years, besides paying a handsome dividend to the shareholders, by the purchase and sale of waste land in Upper Canada. In 1829, the Dutch firm of Crommelin, of Amsterdam, advanced 1,500,000 dollars to some colonists in America, for the purpose of making a canal. This money is securely invested, and yields a higher interest or profit than it would have done had it remained in Holland; a country in which, as in England, capital appears to increase faster than the field of production. The loan lately made by the London house of Baring Brothers, to the State of Louisiana, is a secure and profitable investment of English capital in the improvement of a colony. While I write, the firm of Thomas Wilson and Co. is negotiating in London a loan of 3,500,000 dollars to the State of Alabama. One condition of this loan, evidently devised to tempt the capitalists of London, is, that the lenders shall not be paid off for thirty years. Examples without end might be adduced of profitable investments made by the people of old states in new colonies; and made, too, without any permanent abstraction of capital from the old country. That great masses of English capital have been wasted in colonies is also true. Of such a case, the absurd proceedings of the London *Australian Agricultural Company*, and the capital wasted in founding the Swan River settlement, are good examples. But those sums were as well wasted in that way, as if they had been lent to Don Miguel or Don Pedro. To say that because English capital has been wasted in colonies, no more capital ought to be invested in that way, would be like saying, that because Waterloo bridge yields no profit to those who built it, no more bridges ought to be built. How English capital might be securely invested in colonies without loss, with certain profit; what would be the most secure and profitable mode of investing English capital in colonies; these are questions which belong to the next division of this subject. Here it is sufficient to have shown, by the above examples, that colonies may open a rich and wide field for employing that capital of a mother country, for which there is no very profitable employment at home.

All these ends of colonization, the extension of markets, relief in several ways from excessive numbers, and new investments for capital, may now be brought under one head; namely, a progressive enlargement, partly domestic, and partly colonial, of the field for employing capital and labour. The vast importance of this object, to a country situated like England, is more fully explained in some of the foregoing notes.

THE ENDS OF COLONIZATION, AS RESPECTS THE COLONY.

The United States are still colonies, according to the sense in which the word is used here. They receive people from old states, and send out a much greater number of people to settle in new places. For promoting the immigration of capital and people, the motive of these states seems to be precisely opposite to that of an old country in promoting the emigration of capital and people. The old country wants an enlargement of its field for employing capital and labour: the colonies want more capital and labour for cultivating an unlimited field. By pouring capital and labour into England, you would augment the competition and uneasiness of capitalists, as well as the competition and misery of labourers: by pouring capital and labour into America, you would increase the wealth and greatness of that great colony. By pouring labour only into England, you would not increase the capital of that country, because the increase of labour would not find employment; but, as labour creates capital before capital employs labour, and as, in America, there is capital enough for the employment of more labour and room for the employment of more capital, therefore, by pouring labour only into America, you would provide more capital for the employment of still more labour. It follows, that colonies situated like the United States, colonies, that is, which already possess more capital than labour, have a greater interest in obtaining labour than in obtaining capital from old countries : just as a country situated like England has a greater interest in procuring relief from excessive numbers, than from the competition of capital with capital. As the main object of an old country in promoting emigration is to send forth continually all that portion of the constantly increasing labouring class for which there is not employment with good wages, so the main object of a colony in promoting the immigration of people is to obtain as much labour as can find employment with good wages. A like difference of objects occurs with respect to new markets, and especially to those in which corn should be bought or sold. The object of the colony is to buy manufactured goods with raw produce and corn ; that of the old country to buy raw produce and corn with manufactured goods : the object of the colony is to obtain more labour, wherewith to raise the means of buying manufactured goods ; that of the old country to obtain cheap corn wherewith to support more labourers at home. But, though two persons in different places cannot meet without proceeding in opposite directions ; though, if they intend to meet, the object of one is to go in one direction, and the object of the other to go in an opposite direction ; still they have a common object, that of meeting. Just so in colonization, though the immediate object of an old state be to send out people, and that of a colony to receive people, though the colony want to sell, and the old country want to buy, the means of life ; still they have a common object, that of increasing the number and enjoyments of mankind. Their common object is to give full play to the principle of population, so long as any habitable part of the colony remains uninhabited.

This community of interest becomes still more plain, when we reflect on the object of a colony in removing people from the settled to the waste parts of the colony. Here the immediate object of the colony is the very same as that of the mother country ; an enlargement of the general field of production in proportion to the general increase of capital and labour. The object of the old country is, that room should be made for more people ; that of the colony to make room for more people. These truisms are repeated, because it will be useful to bear them in mind when we shall come to the means of colonization ; and because, hitherto, those who have had the means of colonization at their disposal would seem never to have heard of these mere truisms.

With a view also to saving time when we shall come to the

means of colonization, it will be well to notice here, in a more particular way, some of the special objects of a colony in promoting the immigration of people.

I have attempted to prove elsewhere, that want of free labour is the cause of slavery in America; not the dearness of labour, but the want of free labour at any price. Why do the settlers in New South Wales, having capital, dread above all things that the English government should cease to pour into that colony a stream of population utterly depraved and irreclaimable? The criminal code of England is more bloody than that of any other country which has a code of laws; but in New South Wales, the proportion of public executions to public executions in England is, I believe, allowing for the difference of numbers, in the ratio of 325 to 1. This is partly accounted for when we reflect, that, of the convicts sent to New South Wales, nine out of ten are men, brought to that pass, most of them, by the violence of their passions; nine men to one woman; men accustomed to unbridled indulgence and reckless of all social ties. The result need not be described. Nor is it difficult to account for the attachment of the English government to this system of reformation. If English convicts were punished by imprisonment at home, though the English aristocracy would have to bestow upon their dependents more places, such as that of jailer or turnkey, they would· miss the disposal of a number of places such as gentlemen will accept. The governor of New South Wales is a jailer; but, being called Your Excellency, and paid accordingly, he is thankful for his place; as thankful as any one ever is for a place which he has obtained by electioneering services. But how are we to account for the attachment of the richer colonists to this horrid system of transportation? By their want of free labour; by their anxiety to keep that slave-labour, without which each of them could use no more capital than his own hands could employ. They say, and with perfect truth, that if the supply of convicts were stopped the colony would be ruined. Assuredly the colony would be ruined, unless the richer settlers should find the means of obtaining either free labour, or that kind of slave-labour which they have in America.

But even with the convict system, there is a deficiency of labour. In Van Dieman's Land it is common to see one, two, or three thousand sheep all in one flock, the old and the young, the strong and the weak, all mixed together. While feeding, the strongest of a flock, so mixed, always take the van, the weakest always bringing up the rear. Thus a great number of the lambs, or weaker sheep, are starved to death; and of course, the profits of the owner of the flock are by so much dimin-

ished. Why is this loss incurred? for want of more shepherds ; of more labour. If there were in Van Dieman's Land
shepherds enough to manage all the flocks in the best way, the
increase of produce would give higher wages to the greater
number of labourers, besides augmenting the profits of the
flock owners. The soil and climate of New South Wales
appear admirably suited to the growth of tobacco, olive oil,
silk, and wine. A London company has spent near 300,000l.
with an intention, declared by its prospectus, of growing all
these things in New South Wales. Why has it not grown any
of these things? Because for the growth of any of these
things constant and combined labour is required; an element
of production wanting in New South Wales. Convict labour,
though constant when compared with such labour as is got by
the occasional immigration of free workmen, is very inconstant
when compared with the labour of negro slaves. The convict
works only so long as his term of punishment lasts, and for one
master only so long as the governor pleases, or the secretary of
the governor, or the superintendent of convicts, or some member of the colonial council ; any one of whom may suddenly,
and without rhyme or reason, deprive a settler of his convict
servants. While slave labour may be combined in quantities
proportioned to the capitalist's means of buying slaves, convict
labour can never be combined in large quantities ; because, as
the government bestows this labour, if any one settler should
obtain more than his due share of convicts, all the others would
complain of gross partiality ; and because the proportion of
convicts to settlers is so small, that without gross partiality no
one settler can have more than a few pairs of convict hands.
Favoured settlers, those who find favour with the governor and
his officers, do often obtain more than a fair share of convicts ;
but, as the favour of governors is uncertain, no motive is furnished, even in these cases of gross partiality, for the commencement of works which require the constant employment of
many hands, at the same time, in the same place, and for a
period of consecutive years. How, says Mr. Blaxland, a great
land proprietor of New South Wales ; how should our settlers
undertake to plant vineyards, when years must pass before any
wine could be got ; years during which much labour must be
employed in tending the vines ; when, for gathering the grapes
and turning them into wine, much more labour would be required ; and when, in this colony, the supply of labour is
always not only small, but uncertain?* This is why the
Australian agricultural company has not raised any exchange-

* I quote from recollection of a paper printed by Mr. Wilmot Horton, containing Minutes of a Conversation between himself and Mr. Blaxland.

able produce; save wool, which, in a country like New South Wales, naturally clear and dry, may be raised with very little labour: this is why the greater part of the 300,000*l.* spent by that company has been utterly wasted; is gone to nothing.

Why has so much of the capital perished that was taken to the Swan River? for want of labour wherewith to preserve it. Why do the few settlers that remain in that colony wish for a supply of convict labour? because they have no free labour.

In Canada, as in the United States, there is a want of free labour for works which require the combination of many hands and division of employments. The canals which the English government has lately formed in Canada could not have been finished, or perhaps begun, without a supply of labour from Ireland. The great Lake Erie canal, a work of which the public advantage, and the profit to the undertakers, was made manifest upon paper long before the work was begun, could not perhaps have been begun, most certainly could not have been finished, without a great supply of Irish labour. Capital from Amsterdam and London, and labour from Ireland, have lately been of infinite service to the United States. Theirs is the most favourable case. In all the more favourable cases, the difficulty is for masters to get servants. In the less favourable cases, such as Buenos Ayres and the Swan River, the difficulty would be for servants to find masters. In the worst cases want of labour leads to want of capital, and condemns the people to a state of poverty and barbarism: in the best cases the people would be more wealthy, would produce and enjoy more, if they were more numerous in proportion to capital. All the more favourable cases are maintained by some expedient, which more or less counteracts the want of labour; in the United States by slavery and the immigration of people; in New South Wales and Van Dieman's land by the convict system; in Canada by a constant immigration of labour by sea, greater than ever took place before in the history of colonization. If the means by which the United States, Canada, and New South Wales obtain labour, should be taken away, no others being supplied, then must those colonies soon fall into the miserable state of other colonies which have never had any means of obtaining labour. In a word, from whatever point of view we look at this subject, it appears that the great want of colonies is labour, the original purchase-money of all things.

THE MEANS OF COLONIZATION.

The elements of colonization, it is quite obvious, are waste land and the removal of people. If there were no waste land, no people would remove; if no people would remove, waste land must remain in a desert state. Waste land is cultivated by the removal of people, and people are removed by means of the motive to removal furnished by the existence of waste land. Capital for the removal of people, and for the settlement of people on waste land, being included in the ideas of removal and settlement ; the means of colonization, it follows inevitably, will resolve themselves into the disposal of waste land for the removal of people. A notice of some facts will illustrate this proposition.

The moving power for founding the first English colony in America that did not perish, was a grant by James I., to the *London Company,* of five degrees of waste land in Virginia. The power of the king to dispose of waste land induced the company to form the project of founding a colony : the power thus obtained by the company to dispose of waste land, enabled them to find people willing to emigrate, and capital for their removal and settlement. Just so, in the case of the last colony founded by England, those who founded the colony were induced to remove by receiving grants of waste land from the English government. Mr. Peel's motive for removing to the Swan River with a capital of 50,000*l.* and some hundred people, was a grant of 500,000 acres of waste land ; and the motive with which those people accompanied him was the hope of high wages for cultivating waste land, or the prospect of obtaining waste land of their own. So also, last year, when an English company offered Lord Goderich 125,000*l.* for 500,000 acres of land at Spencer's Gulf, on the south coast of Australia, intending to lay out 375,000*l.* more in planting a colony on that desert spot, the motive of those projectors was to obtain waste land. Of the 125,000 people who are supposed to have emigrated from Britain last year to settle in the United States, Canada, and Australia, the greater number were induced to remove by the prospect of obtaining waste land, and the remainder by a prospect of benefits to result to them from the disposal of waste land in the countries where they should settle. The greatest emigration of people that ever took place in the world occurs from the eastern states to the outside of the western states of America ; and here the sole object in removing is either to obtain waste land, or to reap benefits in some other shape from the late disposal of waste land. It seems needless to multiply such examples.

The disposal of waste land for the removal of people might be considered in two different points of view ; first, as that element of colonization is liable to be used by an old state ; and secondly, as it is liable to be used by a colony. Both these ways of examining the subject would lead to the same conclusion. For instance, we should determine the best mode of treating waste land, either by ascertaining how the United States might best dispose of waste land for the removal of people, or how the English, with the same object, might best dispose of waste land in Canada or Australia. But considering that the removal of people is a secondary means of colonization, depending on the disposal of waste land; seeing that it is waste land which draws people from the settled to the waste parts of the colony, and so makes room for the arrival of people from an old country, and that this prime mover, or point of attraction, exists in the colony, it will be found much more convenient to look at the means of colonization from a colonial position. If this course had been pursued before, the English would not have been as ignorant as they are of the political economy of new countries. Their economists, in treating of colonies, have worked with no other tools than those which they were accustomed to use in explaining the phenomena of an old country; have reasoned from principles, that were true in the old country, to facts that never existed in the colony. They remind one of an Englishman who, having been used to the luxury of music, carried a grand upright piano to the Swan River, and then, finding nobody to make a cupboard for him, was fain to gut the musical instrument, and use it for holding his crockery; or of that English colonial minister, who, knowing that in Europe the seas are salt, sent water-butts from England for the use of the English fleet on a fresh water sea in America. By looking at this subject from a colonial position, we shall proceed from facts to conclusions. Whatever course it would be best for the United States to pursue for drawing people from England to America, would be the best course that the English could pursue for sending people to Canada or Australia. Having ascertained what this best course is it will be easy to apply to our conclusions the foundation of colonies; and to show how an old state might best co-operate with a colony for giving to the means of colonization their greatest possible effect.

1. *The disposal of waste land.*

It is not because land is uncultivated, nor even because it is uninhabited, that it forms an element of colonization. The greater part of Prince Edward's Island, in the Gulf of St. Lawrence, though neither cultivated nor inhabited, still, being the private property of two English lords,* is not liable to be used for the removal of people: nor, indeed, is any land, to which no government can give a title of possession; since the

* Melville and Westmoreland.

motive for removing to waste land is the prospect of obtaining
a property in the land.   Considering how much land in America, South Africa, and Australia, is open to be used by individuals without a title to the possession of it, it would be surprising that so few people should ever have used land without
a title, if we did not reflect, also, on the influence of that " charm
of property," which, says M. Dumont, " is the spur of youth
and pillow of old age."   Those Americans who, under the
name of *squatters*, use land without a title, are exceptions to
the general rule.   Their motives for acting differently from
people in general will be noticed hereafter.   But while, speaking generally, people will not use land without a title, they will
obtain a title to land without using their property, or to more
land than they can possibly use.   The English company which
founded Virginia would have preferred a grant of all America
to a grant of five degrees.   Lower Canada is not the only
English colony in which English lords have obtained great
tracts of land, without using, or even intending to use, their
property.   An Englishman, calling himself the Earl of Stir-
ling, lately took much pains to make out a property in all the
land of Upper Canada.   The clergy of the political church in
Upper Canada have obtained a property in vast tracts of land
which they cannot use.   General Lafayette lately accepted
from the United States 300,000 acres of waste land which he
cannot or will not use.   In 1824, *the Australian Agricultural
Company* and the *Van Dieman's Land Company*, both of London, obtained, the one, 1,000,000, the other, 500,000 acres of
waste land, when it was impossible they should turn a fourth
part of those great tracts to any useful purpose.   The first immigrants to the Swan River obtained more land than a thousand times as many people could have cultivated.   In all these
cases and in a countless number more, so much of the chief
element of the primary means of colonization was annihilated.
Nay, further, in most of them, the destruction was extended for
a time to land that was not granted ; as, for instance, at the
Swan River, where a broad stripe of the coast, not being used,
being almost without inhabitants, and quite without roads, became, when it became the property of individuals, a bar to the
disposal of land more in the interior ; land which, if the coast
were inhabited and easily passable, might be disposed of for the
removal of people.   For the same reason, General Lafayette
has been requested to sell his grant to people who will use it ;
because, that is, being at once desert and private property, it
is a bar to the progress of settlement in all directions towards
its centre.   This again is the case with the lands of the clergy
in Canada ; and with a still more absurd kind of property
created in that colony ; namely, tracts of land " reserved" by

the crown in the midst of land which has become the property of individuals. In this last case the government behaves worse than the dog in the manger, who only prevented others from using that which he could not use himself. Besides doing this, the government of Canada injures all the people who surround its reserves of land, by interposing deserts among them : it is as if the dog had bitten the cattle, besides hindering them from eating the hay. As flour is an element of bread, so is waste land an element of colonization ; but as flour, which has been turned into pie-crust, will not make bread, so neither is waste land, which has become private property, an element of colonization. It is the disposal of waste land in a certain way, which is the primary means of colonization ; and when the land has been disposed of in another way, the power to dispose of it in the right way no longer exists. Land, to be an element of colonization, must not only be waste, but it must be public property, liable to be converted into private property for the end in view. In the art of colonization, therefore, the first rule is of a negative kind : it is, that governments, having power over waste land, and seeking to promote the removal of people, should never throw away any of that power ; should never dispose of waste land except for the object in view, for the removal of people, for the greatest progress of colonization.

This rule has never been strictly observed by any colonizing government : it has been grossly neglected by all such governments, excepting only the United States, which, since they became entirely independent, have been more cautious than any other colonizing government ever was about the disposal of waste land. One or two examples of this neglect, and this caution, will assist us in determining in what way a government ought to dispose of waste land with a view to colonization.

The most striking instance of the neglect of this rule has occurred in the Dutch colony of South Africa. Here, we are informed by Mr. Barrow, in the account of his travels through that colony, the colonial government, having absolute control over all the land in that country, disposed of that land in the following way. They first declared that any one desirous to obtain land should be at liberty to do so on one condition; namely, that of taking a hundred times, at least, more land than he could possibly cultivate. The whole district to be granted was marked out in circles, the diameter of each circle being some miles ; and any one who undertook to live in the centre of one of those circles obtained a title to all the land within the circle. What became of the land between the circles is not stated ; but all these interstices must necessarily have been so many "crown reserves." The object of this system was to separate those who should become proprietors ; to separate them all from each other, by a distance equal to the diameter of the circles; and the motive for this object was fear lest, if the colonists were not so separated, they might, as union is force, be strong enough to think of self-government. This object was fully accomplished, and the colony was effectually ruined. All the land so granted, though scarcely inhabited, still less cultivated, ceased, by this manner of disposing of it, to be an element of colonization. That such a disposal of the land had no tendency to promote the removal of people, save only that of the few persons thus scattered over the colony, becomes plain when we reflect, that there can be but one motive for emigrating to a place where all the land has become private property, namely, the hope of obtaining high wages; and that a few scattered settlers were necessarily prevented, even by their dispersion, from accumulating capital wherewith to pay high wages to immigrant labourers. If they had not obtained some slaves, that is, some combination of labour in the particular works of their farms, they would, being so scattered, and prevented from combining their own labour, have degenerated into the state of those savage descendants of Spaniards, who inhabit the plains of Buenos Ayres. As it was, a more ignorant and brutal race of men than the boors or farmers of South Africa never, perhaps, existed. The poverty and barbarism of that country, the unfitness of the greater part of it for the work of colonization, are owing, not as has been supposed, for the want of a better reason, to the badness of its soil and climate (for these very much resemble those of Spain), but to the neglect, by its early governments, of the first rule in the art of colonization.*

* " The white population at present (1828), is estimated at about 70,000. In 1806, it was not more than 27,000. From a variety of causes, some permanent, others accidental, *they have been scattered over a larger space than was consistent with mutual aid and support.* This retarded the progressive division of labour, and exposed the solitary settler to many dangers and privations, which did not operate beneficially on his habits of industry. Instead of trying how much produce of every kind they could raise, they were rather led to consider on how little they could subsist. The limits of the settlement being, perhaps, too rapidly extended, rendered defence, rather than cultivation, the chief object of public attention. It is not meant that the settlers should have been crowded together. The nature of the colony rendered that impossible. But for some time no moderation was observed in this respect; and a *great waste* of capital, and *misapplication of labour and strength,* were the consequence. The increase of population, provided the boundaries be now fixed and adhered to, will gradually correct this evil, and bring *both labour and a market more and more within the reach of the farmer.* If these views of the colony be near the truth, it will be worth considering whether, when new settlers are to be provided for, it would not be better to select locations for them in detail, as near the villages, and Cape Town, as these can be found, than to set them down in masses by themselves on the outskirts of the colony, or beyond its peopled limits. In such situations they are not merely useless, but a burthen to the community for many years— requiring new and expensive establishments for their protection, besides *wast-*

If the first Dutch governor of New-York had been able, he would probably have been willing enough to ruin that colony by planting each of the first settlers in the centre of a circle nine or twelve miles round ; but here, fortunately, the warlike temper of the natives, and the extreme denseness of the forests, made it impossible to execute such a contrivance for ruining the colony. Though, in this case, the first settlers were allowed to appropriate much more land than they could possibly use, still they were allowed to settle whereabouts they pleased. In fear of the natives, and checked by the density of the forests, they settled not very far from each other, and were thus enabled to hold some intercourse with each other, to assist each other in some degree, to accumulate some capital, to preserve in some degree the arts and civilization of their mother country. In this case, circumstances independent of the government created a sort of rule for the disposal of waste land. This case is not, therefore, an example of attention in a government to the first rule in the art of colonization : it is mentioned by way of contrast with the preceding case ; a contrast the more remarkable, since the miserable colony of South Africa and the prosperous colony of New-York were founded by the same industrious, skilful, and thrifty nation.

Two examples of some caution on the part of colonial governments in disposing of waste land may now be cited, in contrast with examples of reckless profusion.

1. Up to the year 1822, thirty-four years after the first settlement in New South Wales, and when the prosperity of the free settlers in that colony was a subject of great admiration in England, the quantity of waste land disposed of by the government was 381,466 acres ; less than the one grant obtained by Mr. Peel before he left England for the Swan River. Shortly afterward, Lord Bathurst, the English colonial minister, living in London, and knowing as much about New South Wales as about Japan or the moon, disposed of a million of

ing their own money in fruitless undertakings, begun from mere ignorance of the resources of the country. There appears to be *abundance* of unappropriated land, or at least of unoccupied, or at all events, of uncultivated land, *in most of the settled districts,* on which many thousands of industrious people might be placed, most advantageously to the old inhabitants, and with much surer prospect of providing for themselves and their families all the necessaries of life, than *in the remote places to which the stream of emigration is too often directed.* It is true, the best places in those districts have fallen to the lot of the first settlers. But locations of the second, third, or *fourth* quality, as regards soil, &c. near a good road or a town, may exceed in value, *a thousand-fold,* those of the *first* description, which possess no such advantages."—Extract from the *South African Commercial Advertiser* ; a Journal conducted by an Englishman of great intelligence and ability ; a political economist too, who, until he *saw* a new country, would have commenced an explanation of the English theory of rent, saying with Mr. Mill—" Land is of different degrees of fertility."

acres in a single grant. In one day, then, twice as much land
was granted as had been granted in thirty-four years. Up to
1822, all the land in New South Wales, except less than
400,000 acres, was liable to be disposed of as a means of
colonization. In 1828, when the population of the colony was
little more than in 1822, the number of acres rendered not
liable to be disposed of for the removal of people was nearly
3,000,000. That the greater part of this land was not used by
any one, appears from an official return, which states that only
a forty-first part of it, or 71,523 acres, was cultivated. Allowing for the very slight interference with nature, which is
termed cultivation in New South Wales, and for the turn of
colonial governments to exaggerate the prosperity of the people
ruled by them, we may perhaps conclude that not so much as
a forty-first part of these 3,000,000 acres was used beneficially.
If so, in 1828, more than forty parts out of forty-one, of the
land granted by the government of New South Wales, had
been disposed of so as to render them no longer an element of
colonization, without rendering them useful to any other purpose. The profusion of the government after 1822, arose
from the publication of Mr. Wentworth's book on New South
Wales. Mr. Wentworth informed people in England, that
land in New South Wales was worth something ; that of the
400,000 acres then granted, thousands of acres, being near to
a market, yielded rent ; that an estate in New South Wales
was a good thing to have, especially if it could be got for
nothing. All at once, the colonial office in London was be-
sieged by applicants wanting land in New South Wales.
What way so easy of gratifying a friend of government,
or the friends and relatives of the friends and members of
government ? Immense grants, accordingly, were made ;
some, indeed, to people who emigrated, but some to lords and
members of parliament who never thought of emigrating. In
this way the colony would have been ruined, but for the peculiar circumstances before alluded to, which supply the colonists
with labour, keep them together, and provide them with a
market.

2. Between the modes of granting land on the Canadian and
American sides of the line, which divides Upper Canada from
the State of New-York, there has existed until lately a very
remarkable contrast. On the Canadian side, crown and clergy
"reserves ;" unconditional grants of vast tracts to any one who
could find favour with the English minister or colonial governor ; grants of smaller tracts, but still without conditions, to
disbanded soldiers, military pensioners, and pauper immigrants ; in a word, the greatest profusion : on the American
side, a system, nearly fixed and uniform, one general and un-

varying rule, with few exceptions, for the granting of land ; an act of congress, which decrees that no waste land shall be disposed of except by a special grant of Congress, or upon payment by the grantee to the government of a dollar and a quarter per acre. The special grants by Congress are few and far between ; while the price put upon all other waste land operates as a check, almost as a bar, to the appropriation of land by persons not able, or not willing, to use their property. Mr. Stuart, after describing various marks of industry and growing wealth on the American side of the line, says : " We crossed the river * * * * * The country we passed through (on the Canadian side) was greatly over-cropped, with little appearance of industry or exertion to reclaim it. Whenever the stage stopped to water the horses, the doors were crowded with children, offering apples and plums for sale ; and we saw, for the first time on this side of the Atlantic, several beggars."* The following account of the difference between the American and Canadian sides of the line, in point of industry and wealth, is given by Mr. Pickering ; a careful observer, with strong prejudices against the Americans. " I am once again under the jurisdiction of the British government and laws, and therefore feel myself no longer an alien. Though the Americans, in general, are civil and friendly, still an Englishman, himself a stranger among them, is annoyed and disgusted by their vaunts of prowess in the late puny war, and superiority over all other nations ; and they assume it as a self-evident fact, that the Americans surpass all others in virtue, wisdom, valour, liberty, government, and every other excellence. Yet, much as the Americans deserve ridicule for this foible, still I admire the energy and enterprise everywhere exhibited, and regret the apathy of the British government with regard to the improvement of this province. A single glance down the banks of the Niagara tells on which side the most efficient government has resided. On the United States side, large towns springing up : the numerous shipping, with piers to protect them in harbour ; coaches rattling along the road ; and trade evidenced by wagons, carts, horses, and people on foot, in various directions. On the Canadian side, although in the immediate vicinity, an *older settlement*, and apparently *better land*, there are only two or three stores, a tavern or two, a natural harbour with-

* " I never observed land more in want of manure than this part of Canada (near Montreal), originally of indifferent soil, and now totally worn out by over-cropping, and in the most wretched state of agriculture. Yet the manure in a great stable-yard, belonging to the hotel where we lodged, is thrown into the river ; and obviously little use is made of it anywhere."—*Stuart*, vol. i. p. 163.

out piers, but few vessels, and two temporary landing-places."*

To what is owing this striking difference between the prosperity of two sets of people, cultivating the same soil, under the same climate, with the same degree of knowledge, and divided only by an imaginary line? What has caused the second immigration into the State of New-York, of a large proportion of the poorer emigrants from Britain to Upper Canada? These questions will be answered presently. Meanwhile, enough has been stated to show, that there must be some one way better than all the others of treating waste land for the removal of people, for the greatest progress of colonization; and that every disposal of waste land in any way but the best way diminishes by so much the power of a colonizing state to proceed in the best way.

What is the best way in which to dispose of waste land with a view to colonization? It may be supposed, that in some one colony, at least, for some short time, this best way of proceeding has been adopted, if only by accident. On the contrary, as far as I can learn, in no one colony of modern times, has any uniform system been adopted even for a week: while in nearly all colonies several ways of proceeding, the most different and often contradictory, have been pursued either within a short period or at the same time.

The nearest approach to a uniform system is that of the United States; the sale of waste land by public auction, at a fixed upset price, except as to special grants by congress. The exceptions, however, are so important as to defeat the rule. Among these exceptions are the grant of 300,000 acres to General Lafayette; grants to the amount of 6,528,000 acres to disbanded soldiers,† and enormous grants for the support of schools and colleges, as well as to the undertakers of public works, such as roads and canals. All these grants so far resemble the crown and clergy reserves of Upper Canada, that they have diminished, according to their extent, the field of colonization, and injured the settlers round about those special grants. For neither the French general, nor the disbanded soldiers, nor the schools and colleges, nor the undertakers of canals, attempted to cultivate the land which they so obtained for nothing. But General Lafayette may sell his land for less than the minimum price per acre required by Congress from all buyers of waste land. This the disbanded soldiers have actu-

* Emigrant's Guide to Canada, 1830.
† " The great Military Bounty tract, reserved by Congress for distribution among the soldiers of the late war, commences in the neighbourhood of Lower Alton. It comprehends the north-west corner of the State—about 170 miles long and 60 miles broad."—*Stuart*, vol. ii p. 3 6.

ally done :* thus counteractiag whatever may have been the object of Congress in adopting that price. In several ways, therefore, the special grants by Congress are, not merely in exception, but in downright contradiction, to the general way of proceeding.

As soon as the French settlement in Lower Canada, which was established by private adventurers, became of sufficient importance to deserve the attention of the mother country, the court of Versailles proceeded to grant all the land within reach of emigrants, and much that was beyond their reach, to certain courtiers or creatures of courtiers. Each of these grantees obtained an immense tract, on two conditions; first, that neither he nor his descendants should ever part with the property; secondly, that he should grant leases, on condition of receiving services like those required from the holders of land under the worst feudal system of Europe. In this case, court favour, than which nothing is much more irregular, was the means of obtaining property in land ; or, if we are to consider the second condition attached to these *seigneuries* as leaving them open to use by settlers, then the means of obtaining land were as irregular and whimsical as the feudal services required from tenants.   Upon the whole, however, it will seem that the establishment of these absurd lordships in the wilderness was, after the Dutch plan in South Africa, the best way to ruin the colony, by means of the restrictions thereby imposed on the useful appropriation of waste land.   In the French colony of Louisiana, on the contrary, "lands," says the Abbé Raynal, "were granted indiscriminately to every person who applied for them, and in the manner in which he desired them." Here, then, instead of a system, land was disposed of according to the irregular fancies of individuals. This might be called a rule for the disposal of waste land, if it were not clear that every gratification of an individual fancy, as to the extent and situation of grants, was calculated to prevent the gratification of other individual fancies. The historian of French Louisiana, one of the many colonies that has perished, goes on to say—"Had it not been for this original error, Louisiana would not have languished for so long a time ; immense deserts would not have separated the colonists from each other. Being brought near to a common centre, they would have assisted each other, and would have enjoyed all the advantages of a well regulated

---

* " Most of those lands have been sold by the soldiers to other individuals, and are now owned in great quantities by gentlemen in the eastern States.   *   *   * They have been sold by the soldiers for about 50 dollars for a quarter section, containing 160 acres."   Letter from Mr. Duncan, of Vandalia.—*Stuart,* vol ii. p. 396.

This is at the rate of 31¼ cents per acre ; while the upset price of land sold by Congress is 125 cents per acre.

society. Instead of a few hordes of savages, we should have seen a rising colony, which might in time have become a powerful nation, and procured infinite advantages to France."

In Upper Canada, land has been granted, *at the same time,* to favourites of the colonial court, for nothing ; to others, for bribes paid to colonial officers :* to some, on condition of paying a quit-rent to the government, which quit-rent was exacted in some cases and not in others ; to some, for nothing, because they were American royalists ; to others, for so much money per acre, paid openly to the government, and disposed of in various jobs of which the note below gives an example ; to the political clergy for nothing, as we have seen before ; and even to the grantor, to the crown itself, in the preposterous shape of crown reserves. In this colony too, while all these ways of granting land were pursued at once, during the very period of this irregularity in granting land, grants were refused with equal irregularity ; because the applicant had offended the governor ; because he asked for land in a favourable situation reserved by the governor, in his excellency's mind, I mean, for some relative or dependent ; because he wanted land, in a situation which his excellency, in his wisdom, thought not fit for settlement, and, in his power, resolved should continue desert ; because this spot was intended for the site of a town, and that for some military purpose ; because this district had not been surveyed, or this was, in the governor's opinion, too thickly peopled ; or that required more people, and was, on that day, the only spot in which a grant would be made. Such are not all, but only a few, of the very different and often contradictory grounds on which, at one and the same time, waste land was granted and withheld in this colony down to last year.

In New South Wales and Van Dieman's Land, colonies not fifty years old, land has been granted and refused on all sorts

---

* " Will you inform the committee of the sums that have been paid by the Canada Company, and their appropriation ?   *   *   *   *   Thirdly, 2,566*l.*, as *an annual compensation,* for the period of seven years, to those officers of the land-granting department in Upper Canada, who, by the adoption of the new regulations for granting lands, are *deprived of their emoluments.*" See evidence of the Right Honourable R. Wilmot Horton, M. P. and under-secretary of state for the colonies, delivered before a select committee of the House of Commons, on the civil government of Canada, 1828. The report of this committee, which fills a thick folio volume, is crowded with examples of jobbing in the disposal of waste land.

" The surveyors receive their compensation in land, and generally *secure the most valuable portions.* When I was in Canada, they would sell their best lots for one dollar per acre ; while 13*l.* 10*s.*, the fee on one hundred acres, amount to more than half a dollar per acre. I never met with any one person, among all those with whom I conversed on the subject, who did not agree, that, if a settler had but a very little money, it would be much more to his advantage to buy land than to receive it from the government."—*Letters from North America, by Adam Hodgson.* Vol. ii. p. 47.

of different and contradictory grounds ; granted by favour, for money, for public services, real or pretended, to English lords and members of parliament, because they were lords and members of parliament ; to the political clergy, to schools, and other institutions ; granted unconditionally and with conditions ; conditions fulfilled in some cases, but much oftener neglected ; granted on account of the applicant's wealth, that is, because he was able to invest capital on the land, and on account of his poverty, that is, on the score of charity : refused according to every whim of every successive governor, always a sailor or a soldier, as fit to manage a great work of public economy as Adam Smith was fit to navigate a ship or command a regiment. To save the reader's time, in order that he may be able to imagine the excessive irregularity with which land has been granted *and* withheld in these colonies, I shall state two facts, out of hundreds, which tend to establish that here, as to the disposal of new land, the government has been regular in nothing but irregularity.

1. About four years ago, General Darling being governor of New South Wales, the colonial office in London used to distribute a " regulation," by which it was declared that any person in England wishing to settle in New South Wales, would obtain, on reaching the colony, a grant of land extensive in proportion to the capital that he was prepared to invest on it. On the faith of this regulation, people used to emigrate with their capital. One of them, with the regulation in his hand, waits upon the governor, and begs for a grant of land still at the disposal of government, in the county of Cumberland ; as near, that is, to the town of Sydney as the previous disposal of waste land would allow. Has he brought a letter of recommendation to the governor, or the treasurer, or the secretary, or some member of council ? If yes, if the letter come from a powerful man or woman in England, the grant is made out. If no, then says the governor or his deputy—we wish to promote settlements in Wellington Valley, two hundred miles from Sydney, on the western side of the Blue Mountains. Take a grant there, or do without a grant : in other words, go back to England or bury yourself and utterly waste your capital in a distant wilderness. What, it may be asked, could be the governor's motive for this cruel injustice ? a desire to spread his dominion, to make the colony appear wide upon the map, to be able to boast of new settlements far apart (this is the merit), far apart from each other ! Some of the evils of this ignorant desire are well described in the following extract from a letter addressed, in 1832, by General Clausel to Marshal Soult. " Tout devenait facile, si on eût suivi le système de colonization que j'avais établi. N'ayant plus à m'occuper de

Constantine et d'Oran, j'aurais porté tous mes soins, toute mon attention, sur la ville d'Alger et les environs. Notre établissement sur ce point, aisément surveillé, eût pris, peu à peu, et sans exiger presque aucun frais, une extension suffisante. A mesure que des colons Européens seraient arrivés, on aurait gagné du terrain ; et lorsque les besoins de la colonie l'eussent exigé, on aurait pris une partie suffisante du territoire d'Oran et de Constantine. Vouloir *colonizer en même temps la régence toute entière*, vouloir mettre des garnisons sur tous les points, avoir la prétention de tout retenir dès aujourd'hui sous notre domination immediate, tout cela me paraît être un projet chimerique : en faire même l'essai serait de compromettre le succès de notre établissement en Afrique, et entrainer l'état, en pure perte, dans des dépenses ruineuses."

2. During the rule of this same governor of New South Wales, it was proposed to make a road between Sydney and Hunter's River, a spot where some settlements had been formed, but between which and Sydney there was no communication except by the sea and Hunter's River. This road was to pass through a district, the whole of which, though of course nearer to Sydney than the settlements on Hunter's River, remained in the hands of government. Now, before the government began to make the road, two or three applications were made for grants of land in this district ; small grants of less than a hundred acres each ; modest applications, considering that the applicants were persons of high official rank in the colony, and near connexions of the governor to boot. The applications were successful, of course. Somehow or other, the new road took the direction of these grants ; over or by the side of which, therefore, all travellers by land, between Sydney and Hunter's River, necessarily passed. On each of these grants a house was built ; a house, which, being licensed (for they have a licensing system in New South Wales) became an inn. These inns, then, were the only places on the line of road at which travellers could stop for rest and refreshment. Of course, such a monopoly caused the prices of rest and refreshment to be very high ; gave very high profits to the inn-keepers. Other persons, desirous to share in these high profits, now applied for grants of land on the line of road. No, said the governor, or one of these inn-keepers, you may have land on Hunter's River or in Wellington Valley ; but along this line of road no more land will be granted at present. Thus the power of the governor to grant or withhold waste land was used in this case with the effect, and one can hardly doubt for the purpose, of turning two or three of his excellency's favourites into highwaymen ; of enabling them to rob all travellers between Sydney and Hunter's River ; to rob them of somewhat less than the

difference between the cost of going round by sea and the cost of travelling on a straight road open to the competition of inn-keepers. It would not be easy to find, even in Ireland, a match for this job; but many to match it have taken place in New South Wales. My authority for this statement is Mr. Potter Macqueen, late member of parliament for Bedfordshire; himself the proprietor of a large tract of land in New South Wales, and, as such, an instance of the shameful irregularity with which new land has been disposed of in that colony.

For granting land at the Swan River settlement, regulations made by Sir George Murray and Mr. Horace Twiss, the chief and under-secretaries of state for the colonies, were published in England; but not till after Sir George Murray had granted 500,000 acres to the cousin of his colleague, Sir Robert Peel. This grant to Mr. Peel was obtained by means of a letter, which has been published, from Sir Robert to Sir George. Some member of the House of Commons having said that this transaction was a job, Sir Robert Peel defended it; and Mr. (now Lord) Brougham, the author of a book on colonial policy, rising after the right honourable baronet, declared, that for the first time the right honourable baronet had made an " unneces-sary speech;" so complete, or so unnecessary was the vindi-cation of his conduct. The grant, however, to Sir Robert's cousin, of more land than had been granted in New South Wales during thirty-four years, and the outcry that was raised against it, compelled the government to give land to other people in the same way; that is, with the most reckless pro-fusion. Thus the only advantage obtained by Mr. Peel over other settlers was his being allowed to mark out his grant upon the map in England, and to choose what he considered the very best situation. But this, though it has proved of no advantage to Mr. Peel, was very injurious to all the other settlers; because, as he had selected his grant round about the port or landing-place, so great an extent of land in the very best situation became private property as to render all the other situations very bad in comparison. If Mr. Peel had been compelled to make roads through his grant, or had obtained only such an extent of land as might easily have had roads made through it by the government, the case would have been different. As it was, his property became as a desert between the port or landing-place and the land beyond that property. Beyond that desert, however, it was declared, that all the world should be entitled to unlimited grants, on either one of two conditions, as the grantee should prefer; either an outlay of 1s. 6d. per acre in conveying labourers to the settlement, or the investment of capital on the land at the rate of 1s. 6d. per acre. The second of these conditions was flatly at variance with the first. The object of the first condition was to promote the emigration of labourers in proportion to the land granted ; but as those who had obtained land on the second condition wanted labourers, and, not having spent capital on the immigration of labourers, were able to offer higher wages than those who had, the labourers brought out by one set of capitalists were taken from them by another set ; and thus it came to happen that no one had a motive for obtaining land on the first condition. One of the conditions made the other a nullity : just as, elsewhere, the profusion of one governor and the caution of his successor, or the profusion of one and the caution of his predecessor, or the profusion and caution of the same governor either at different times, or with respect to different parts of the same colony at the same time, have had opposite tendencies ; have tended to increase, and, as the people were increasing, to decrease the proportion between the inhabitants of a colony and the land open to cultivation.

All these cases pretty well establish, that in no modern colony has the best way, or indeed any one way, of treating waste land been pursued systematically : to these cases it would be easy to add *several hundreds* of different and often contradictory modes, in which the governments of modern Europe have disposed of the chief element of colonization.

What is the best mode in which to dispose of waste land with a view to colonization ? In order to ascertain this, we must first determine what is, or ought to be, the immediate object of a colonizing government in exerting its power over waste land. The accomplishment of that immediate object would be a way to ultimate ends.

Why should any government exert power over waste land either by giving or withholding ? Why not let individuals judge for themselves as to the situation and extent of new land that each individual should like to call his own ? This course has been recommended by some English economists ;* on the ground that individuals are the best judges of what is for their own interest, and that all unnecessary interference of government with the affairs of individuals is sure to do more harm than good. But in this case, the government must necessarily interfere to some extent ; that is, it must establish or confirm a title to the land of which individuals had taken possession. Or, perhaps, those English economists, who deprecate the interference of government in the disposal of waste land, would have each settler on new land to be a " squatter ;" a settler without any title, liable to be ousted by any other man who was stronger, and who, being the best judge of his own interest,

* Especially by Mr. Mill ; in a letter to Mr. Wilmot Horton, not printed, but industriously circulated by the latter.

should think it worth while to oust the first occupier. Passing by so absurd a conclusion from the principle of non-interference, let us now suppose the case, in which a colonizing government should confine its interference to securing a property in that land of which individuals had taken possession. In this case, all the land to which it was possible that government should afterward give a title would immediately be taken possession of by a few individuals; good judges of their own interest, consulting their own advantage. But what, in this case, would become of all the other individuals who, in pursuit of their own advantage, might be desirous to obtain some waste land? This question settles the point. For the good of all, the interference of government is not less necessary to prevent a few individuals from seizing all the waste land of a colony than it is necessary to prevent robberies. As it is for the good of all that no one should be allowed to take any other one's property, so it is for the good of all that no individual should be allowed to injure other individuals by taking more than the right quantity of waste land. In the former case, government enforces a compact among all the members of a society; an agreement that any one who takes the property of another shall be punished: so, in the latter case, the interference of government with respect to waste land is nothing but the enforcement of a compact among all who are interested in the disposal of waste land; an agreement that none shall be allowed to injure the others, that the greatest good of all shall be consulted. This point settled, what, for the greatest good of all, is the immediate object of a colonizing government in exerting its power over waste land? Its ultimate object being the greatest progress of colonization, its immediate object is, that there should exist in the colony those circumstances which are best calculated to attract capital and labour, but especially labour, from an old country. The advantage of the immigrants, though one of the ends, is also an essential means of colonization. For the greatest advantage of immigrants to a colony, it is necessary that the colonial profits of capital, and wages of labour, should be as high as possible. High profits, then, and especially high wages, are the immediate object of a colonizing government in exerting its power over waste land.

In order to create and maintain a very high rate of wages in the colony, it is necessary, first, that the colonists should have an ample field of production; ample, that is, in proportion to capital and labour; such an extent of land as to render unnecessary the cultivation of inferior soils, and as to permit a large proportion of the people to be engaged in agriculture; a field, large from the beginning, and continually enlarged with the increase of capital and people. But, in the second place, it is quite as necessary that the field of production should never be too large ; should never be so large as to encourage hurtful dispersion ; as to promote that cutting up of capital and labour into small fractions, which, in the greater number of modern colonies, has led to poverty and barbarism, or speedy ruin. For securing the first condition of high profits and wages, the power of the government over waste land must be exerted actively, in bestowing upon individuals titles to the possession of land : for the second object, that power must be exerted negatively, in refusing titles to waste land. The action of the two exertions of power together may be compared to that of an elastic belt, which, though always tight, will always yield to pressure from within.

But as the belt which should press more in one place than in another, or should be more tight at one time than at another, would be defective, so would any system for granting and refusing waste land be defective which should not be both uniform and lasting.

It is easy to grant land, and easy to refuse applications for grants: the difficulty is to draw a line between the active and negative exertions of power, so as to render the proportion which land bears to people neither too small nor too great for the highest profits and wages.

With a view, not deliberate, certainly, but rather instinctive, to maintaining a due proportion between people and land, three methods of proceeding have been adopted by several colonial governments : first, that of attaching conditions to grants of land ; secondly, that of imposing a tax on the land granted, and in case the tax was not paid, seizing and selling the land for arrears of taxes ; thirdly, that of requiring payment in money for waste land before the grant was made out.

In the first mode of proceeding, the grantee obtained his land on such conditions, for example, as that of cultivating it, or that of paying a quit-rent ; and in either case the grant was liable to be recalled provided the condition was not observed. But grants of land have scarcely ever been recalled because the land had not been cultivated, or the quit-rent had not been paid. Why such conditions have nearly always been a dead letter is plain enough ; because the term " cultivation" is so general and vague that no tribunal could decide whether or not that condition had been fulfilled ; while all the holders of land obtained on that condition, including frequently the members of the only tribunal to which the question could be submitted, have made common cause to prevent the question from being raised :*

---

* The grants at the Swan River were declared liable to be forfeited unless they should be "*cultivated* to the satisfaction of the governor ;" a gentleman

because, as to quit-rents, all who obtained land on condition of paying them, including the favorites of governments, and frequently the officers of government themselves, have made common cause to prevent the recall of grants for non-payment of quit-rent. Thus, while such conditions were sure to be neglected, the certainty of being able to disregard them led so many people to acquire more property than they could possibly use, that the grantees would not have been able, supposing them willing, to have observed the conditions; would not have been able to cultivate so much more land than there were labourers to employ, or to have paid quit-rent for so much land which yielded nothing. Judging from these cases, and from very many more in which conditions have been attached to grants without an attempt to enforce them, it seems impossible to devise any after-condition, in the nature of a promise, which would hinder people from taking more land than they ought to take ; which would render the belt always tight, while always sufficiently elastic.

Secondly. Though by imposing a tax on granted land which remains in a desert state, and selling the land for arrears of taxes, some check would be put to the misappropriation of new land, still this plan is open to the same objections as the one just examined : the execution of the plan would be difficult or next to impossible : it is but another mode of attaching to grants the after-condition of cultivation. In some of the United States, truly, this plan has been successfully pursued with respect to deserts of private property, which had become private property before the plan of taxing and seizing was adopted. But why was this plan devised? Not to prevent, but to cure, the evils of deserts interposed among the settlers. Act upon this plan with respect to all desert land now private property,

deserving, on many accounts, very great respect; but, nevertheless, a naval captain, whose knowledge of " cultivation" must necessarily be small, and who, besides, owns in the colony a hundred, perhaps a thousand times as much land as it is possible that he should cultivate. Is it to be expected that he will declare his own land to be forfeited for want of cultivation?

Mr. Ellice, now war-minister of England, was asked by the committee of the House of Commons on the civil government of Canada, whether escheats of land had taken place under the 6th of George IV., which empowered the government to seize and sell lands, as to which certain conditions had not been performed. He answered, " None, that I am aware of." But then, he had just before informed the committee, that " grants had been most inconsiderately and wantonly made, in large masses, to people connected with government, to the great detriment of the country and the great nuisance of the inhabitants around ;" that land had been so granted " in large masses, since it was the fashion for every *councillor or officer connected with the government*, to get a grant of from 5000 to 20,000 acres ;" that many of " those grantees were absentees ; and some governors of the colony." The evidence of Mr. Ellice before this committee, and especially that part of it which relates to the disposal of waste land, is full of instruction for colonizing governments.

still what is to be done with the land so seized, or recovered, by the government? Is it to be granted again in such a way as to call for a second seizure, and a third grant of the same lots of land? This plan may be good for the cure of an evil, but is plainly quite insufficient to prevent the evil. It has been successful, as a cure in some of the United States, only because, since the evil arose which it was intended to cure, another plan had been adopted to prevent the evil as to all new grants.

But, thirdly, it is obvious that a government may put any degree of restraint on the acquisition of waste land, by means of conditions to be performed before the grant is bestowed; by making the grant itself conditional on some previous act by the grantee. Of this nature was a part of the plan for granting land at the Swan River; that part by which he, who had paid for the conveyance of labourers to the colony, was entitled to waste land in proportion to his outlay. Not less strictly of this nature, though somewhat more obviously, is the plan now pursued by the United States; that of requiring payment in money for new grants. This appears to be the most sure and most simple way to prevent the improper acquisition of waste land. For, though many expedients might be suggested for rendering the grant conditional on the performance of some act by the grantee, such as withholding the title until the land was cultivated, still in all of these ways of proceeding much room would be left for favour, for disputes, and evasions, as well as for miscalculation on the part of the grantee; not to mention that, if time were required for the performance of the condition of title, all new land must pass through a state of uncertainty as to its ownership; being used in some way by individuals with a view to gaining a title, and yet not the property of individuals, but liable to be resumed by the government in case the condition of a title were not thoroughly performed. The great merit of the system pursued by the United States consists in its simplicity, and the certainty of its operation.

Still the object of the government, or rather of the community, would be missed, if the payment required for waste land were not so high as to deter individuals from taking more land than, for the benefit of the whole society, they ought to take. If the price were so low that great tracts should be attainable by paying a trifle of money, individuals, speculating vaguely on some distant benefit to arise from the increase of population, would acquire great tracts without being willing, or even able, to use them; would interpose great deserts among the settlers; would produce an extreme degree of dispersion, reducing the power of capital and labour to the minimum, and rendering out of the case both high profits and high wages. Thus, at the Swan River, though some grantees paid money for their land, when they paid for the passage of emigrant labourers, still as the rate of payment was two hundred acres for each labourer, or 1s. 6d. per acre, they were not prevented from taking a great deal more land than they could use. In this case, the object of requiring money for land would not have been attained, even if the system had been uniform; if none had been allowed to acquire land save by paying money for it. So, in the United States, where, for want of combinable free-labour, slavery is, one may say, a necessity; where restrictions on foreign trade and bounties on home manufactures are, not in opposition to, but in strict agreement with, the first principles of political economy, being, after slavery, the chief means by which the people are kept together, and induced to keep each other; where, notwithstanding these expedients for promoting combination of power, it is a general practice to exhaust the fertility of land, trusting to nature for nearly all, and to skill for hardly any thing; where, though not half of the appropriated land be cultivated, the people are moving on, leaving great gaps of desert behind them, in search of more land to be treated in the same way; there, it seems evident, the price put upon waste land is too low for the object in view. And this conclusion is supported by particular facts. In the newest settlements, universally, we find much land, which is become private property without being used in any way; not even cleared of the forest; taken out of the control of the public, and yet of no service to any individual; while all such land interposes so much desert, or so many deserts, among the settlers, increasing the distance by which they are separated, interfering with the construction of roads, and operating as a check to social intercourse, to concert, to exchange, and to the skilful use of capital and labour.

On the other hand, it is equally plain that too high a price might be required for waste land. If it be for the good of all that no waste land should be granted without being used beneficially, it is equally for the good of all that none should be withheld from individuals able and willing to use it in the best way. In order to make the belt elastic as well as tight, in order that the field of production should increase gradually along with the increase of capital and labour, it would be necessary to require for new land a price not more than sufficient to prevent the improper acquisition of land; it would be necessary to make the price so low, that the acquisition and use of new land should be one of the most productive employments of capital. To make the price so high, that the acquisition and use of new land should not be one of the most productive employments of capital, would be equal to a decree that no more land should be used in any way; would encompass the settled parts of the colony, not with an elastic belt, but with " a wall of brass;" would, as soon as capital and labour had reached an excessive proportion to land, cause low profits and low wages; would prevent the immigration of people; would inevitably defeat the objects of colonization: just as if all the land of a colony were granted suddenly to a few persons neither able nor willing to use it, but willing and able to prevent others from using it.   The golden mean, a term often misapplied to some degree between right and very wrong, really signifies the right degree and nothing else : for this case, in which contrary powers are to be exerted, the power of granting and the power of withholding, the golden mean is all in all.   Some remarks will be offered presently on the class of facts which a colonizing people would take as their guide for ascertaining the best price of new land.

Meanwhile, we have to dispose of two questions hardly less important than the question of price.

First, supposing the best price ascertained, the beneficial operation of it might be checked, nay, altogether prevented in two different ways; either by opposing obstacles to the acquisition of land at that price, or by granting land on other terms. Thus, in New South Wales, where the English government has been persuaded to adopt the plan of selling new land instead of giving it away,* the governor's caprice still determines

---

* Ever since May, 1829, the Colonial Department in London has been urged, in various ways, to adopt the American plan of selling waste land, instead of jobbing it according to the English plan. For a long while, this suggestion was either fiercely opposed or treated with ridicule, by persons connected with the colonial office, and especially by Mr. Wilmot Horton and Mr. Hay, one of them lately, and the other still under-secretary of state for the colonies. This suggestion having been pressed upon the government by a society established for the purpose of promoting systematic colonization, Mr. Wilmot Horton, jealous, it would seem, of any interference with a subject, part of which had employed his thoughts for some years, became a member of the society, and then broke it up by getting into the chair at a public meeting, and zealously condemning the objects of those with whom he had professed to unite himself. But, at the same time, he greatly promoted the objects of the society by attacking their views, and thus causing those views to be examined. As an example of the assistance which he thus gave to the dispersed members of the society, I may mention, that he persuaded Colonel Torrens to join him in conducting a written controvervy with two of those gentlemen, and that, in the end, Colonel Torrens became one of the warmest advocates of the measure to which he had objected when it was first submitted to him. Not the least impression, however, was made upon the government while the Duke of Wellington's administration lasted. But, soon after the change of ministry which followed the three days of Paris, soon after Lord Howick succeeded Mr. Horace Twiss as under-secretary for the colonies, the measure suggested by the Colonization Society was, in part, adopted by the government. Defective as is that part of a measure; defective because incomplete ; still it cannot fail to be of great service to the colonies. Whatever the people of Canada and of the English settlements in Australia may gain by the check which has thus been put upon official job-

whereabouts land shall be surveyed and granted. Though any one may wait upon the governor with the new regulations in

bing in the disposal of waste land, they owe, not very remotely, to the workmen of Paris or M. de Polignac. For this great improvement they are more immediately obliged to Lord Howick; to the leading members of the Colonization Society, Mr. John Sterling, Mr. Hutt, now M.P. for Hull, and Mr. Charles Tennant, then M.P. for St. Alban's; and more especially to Mr. Robert Gouger, the secretary of the society, whose efforts to procure the adoption of its whole plan have been unceasing for several years. The successful issue of Mr. Gouger's long contest with the judgments of ignorance, the insults of pride, and the delays of idleness, should be a lesson of encouragement to the advocates of useful projects. Here follows the most correct list that I have been able to obtain of the members of the Colonization Society.

Woronzow Greig, Esq.	Sir Francis Burdett, Bart.
W. S. O'Brien, Esq. M.P.	Clayton Brown, Esq.
R. H. Innes, Esq.	T. Kavanagh, Esq. M.P.
John Hutt, Esq.	James Talbot, Esq.
I. H. Thomas, Esq.	Charles Tennant, Esq.
I. W. Buckle, Esq.	Lucius O'Brien, Esq. M.P.
John Sterling, Esq.	John Mill, Esq.
Edward King, Esq.	G. S. Tucker, Esq.
Robert Scott, Esq. (of New South Wales).	Col. Torrens.
	J. E. Bicheno, Esq.
Howard Elphinstone, Esq.	R. Trench, Esq.
Saml. Humphreys, Esq.	William Hutt, Esq.
Charles Buller, Esq.	Rev. G. V. Sampson.
C. Holte Bracebridge, Esq.	Lawrence Marshall, Esq.
John Young, Esq.	Right Hon. R. W. Horton.
E. Barnard, Esq.	John Gore, Esq.
Sir J. C. Hobhouse, Bart. M.P.	Arthur Gregory, Esq.
John Gibson, Esq.	Richard Heathfield, Esq.
Sir Philip Sidney.	Erskine Humphreys, Esq.
Hyde Villiers, Esq.	T. Potter Macqueen, Esq. M.P.
John Buckle, Esq.	Colonel Talbot, M.P.

Hon. Secretary, Robert Gouger, Esq.

The views of the society were first published in a supplement to the Spectator newspaper, and afterward reprinted in a pamphlet, entitled A Statement of the Principles and Objects of a proposed National Society for the Cure and Prevention of Pauperism by means of Systematic Colonization. Ridgway, 1830. Those views have been further explained in the following publications.

Sketch of a Proposal for colonizing Australasia; printed and circulated, but not sold, in 1829.

A Letter to the Right Honourable Sir George Murray on Systematic Colonization, by Charles Tennant, Esq. M.P. Ridgway, 1830. This pamphlet contains a Report of the Society, and a Controversy between Mr. Hutt and Mr. Sterling on one side, and Mr. Wilmot Horton and Col. Torrens on the other.

Letters forming Part of a Correspondence with Nassau William Senior, Esq., concerning Systematic Colonization, &c., by Charles Tennant, Esq. M.P. Ridgway, 1831.

A Letter from Sydney, the principal town of Australasia, edited by Robert Gouger. Joseph Cross, Holborn, 1829. Reprinted from the Morning Chronicle newspaper.

Eleven Letters in the Spectator newspaper, signed P. 1830 and 1831.

A Lecture on Colonization, delivered before the Literary Association, at the London Tavern, on December 5, 1831: by R. Davies Hanson, Esq. Ridgway and Sons. 1832.

Proposal to His Majesty's Government for founding a Colony on the South Coast of Australia. Printed and circulated, but not sold, in 1831.

his hand, saying,—I want so many acres in such a spot: take my money,—the governor may reply, No; that spot is reserved: you must choose elsewhere. Nay, until the governor have declared a spot open for settlement, until it please him to *offer* land for sale, no one can now obtain new land anywhere on any terms. Here, then, is the restriction of price, without liberty subject to that restriction. If the price fixed on land had been the right one, sufficient, that is, for the purpose of restraint, all further restraint could not but have been hurtful; could not but have interfered with the due operation of the proper price. From this example we may gather, what indeed no fact was required to establish, so obvious is the conclusion; that, along with the best price for waste land, there ought to be the most perfect liberty of appropriation at that price. This is secured in the United States by very simple regulations.

But this secured, what if there should be exceptions to the system? what if some portions of new land should be granted on some other condition than purchase, or for less money than the general price, or for nothing? The result is plain; the object sought by the best price would be defeated in proportion to the extent of exceptional grants. If land were given, as in the United States, to schools and colleges, deserts would still be interposed among the settlers; and either this would happen, or waste land would be sold for less than the price generally required by government, if new land were given for nothing by way of reward for public services. Every special grant, besides, made for nothing, or for less than the general price, would be an act of gross injustice towards those who had paid the general price: unless, indeed, the government should proclaim, before taking money from any one, that it intended to grant land for nothing in special cases. Such a declaration, however, by the government, though it would be a fair warning to individuals, and would thus prevent any injustice, could not but greatly interfere with the sale of land at the best price; for it would amount to saying, Beware, land buyers, of paying to us, the government, more than will suffice to buy land from individuals on whom we mean to bestow grants for nothing. Whereas, if the plan of selling at a fixed price were the only one, if the system were uniform, the due opera-

Plan of a Company to be established for founding a Colony in Southern Australia. Ridgway and Sons. 1831.

Article in the Literary Gazette. 1831.

Emigration and Colonization. A Speech delivered at a general meeting of the National Colonization Society in June, 1830, by William Hutt, Esq. M.P. Wilson, Royal Exchange, 1832.

Emigration for the Relief of Parishes, practically considered, by Robert Gouger. Ridgway and Sons, Piccadilly; and Effingham Wilson, Royal Exchange. 1833.

tion of the best price would be perfectly secured ; no deserts
would be interposed among the settlers ; no one would sell
land for less than the government price ; every buyer would
make his calculations accordingly ; and no one would suffer the
least injustice.

Still, notwithstanding the force of all these reasons in favour
of a uniform system, a colonial government would always be
strongly tempted to make exceptional grants ; a bad colonial
government, by the wish to favour individuals, by all the motives which anywhere lead to government jobs ; a good colonial
government, by finding this the easiest way to reward public
services and to provide for public education. In both cases,
the temptation to go wrong would become very powerful indeed after the plan of selling had been acted on for some time ;
after it had given to waste land outside of the settled districts,
or still within them, a greater value than waste land ever possessed before. Suppose the people so far kept together, so far
in a condition to help each other, that their industry was more
productive than colonial industry has ever been ; in that case
all their land would be subject to some of those advantages,
over and above superior natural fertility, for which rent is paid ;
and all the land adjoining the settled districts would be in a
state to become very soon, with the increase of wealth and
people, subject to the higher degrees of competition. Presents, therefore, of new land would now be worth more than
such presents have ever been worth : the temptation to make
such presents would be greater in proportion to their greater
value ; while that greater value of the thing desired would whet
the ingenuity of parasites and jobbers, in devising new pretexts
for an improper use of the power of government. In the case
of a good colonial government, even in the case of a government strictly representing all the colonists, the temptation to go
wrong would become stronger with an increase in the value of
new land : it would be more easy than it ever has been to reward public services and provide for public education by means
of gifts of new land. And why not, some would ask, do in the
easiest way that which ought to be done ? The question may
be answered by another. Since the easiest way to prevent a
criminal from committing more crimes is to hang him, why
not hang all criminals ? why not do in the easiest way that
which ought to be done ? Because more harm would come to
society by making the law hateful, than would be prevented by
preventing criminals from committing more crimes ; because
that very easy mode of hindering some from committing crimes
would encourage others to commit crimes, by rendering conviction, or even detection impossible in ninety-nine cases out of
a hundred. Just so, in colonization, by providing for so great

a good as public education in the easiest way, that is, by exceptional grants of land, more harm than good would be done
to society.   But if, as may easily happen, this should be denied
by those who are not familiar with the evils resulting to colonies from a profuse exercise by the government of its power
over waste land, I would remind these, that the choice does not
lie between knowledge and ignorance, but between two modes
of securing education : just as in jurisprudence, the choice is,
not between the prevention and non-prevention of crimes by
persons already criminal, but between two modes of prevention, the easiest mode, hanging, and a troublesome mode, the
reformation or confinement of the criminals.   If all the waste
land, without exception, were sold at the right price, then might
public education be provided for out of the money paid for
land ; or, the people being richer, because kept more together,
by means of contributions from the public in the shape of
taxes.   A moderate land tax, for example, would take from
each proprietor of land less than would be bestowed upon him
by a uniform system of selling new land at the best price. If,
on the contrary, the great good of public education were
sought by means of exceptional grants, a door would be left
open for other exceptions.   Those, for example, who think a
political church very good, would demand exceptional grants
for that purpose ; if real public services were rewarded by exceptional grants, such grants might be made for pretended public services.   Once allow, by admitting a single exception, that
the facility of doing good in this way is a sufficient reason for
taking this way to do good, and pretexts would never be wanting for doing harm in so easy a way ; harm of two sorts, that
which *might* arise from giving land for improper purposes, and
that which *must* arise from counteracting the desired effect of
requiring the proper price for every addition of territory.

The importance of complete uniformity in any system for
treating the chief element of colonization is so great, that I am
tempted, at the risk of tiring the reader, to illustrate my view
of the subject by a supposed case, which will be readily understood, even by those who have never witnessed the mischievous
effects on a colony of irregularity in granting and withholding
new land.

Suppose that the English government had found a mass of
pure gold in Middlesex, close to the surface of the ground, and
weighing some thousands of millions of pounds ; and further,
that it was an object of great moment to the people of England to keep up the present value of gold, neither more nor
less.   In that case, how would the government, supposing it
bent on the advantage of the people, use its power over this
rich mine ?   Here would be a very easy way of paying off the

national debt; but if this were done in this way, more evil
would come to the people than if their debt had been doubled.
Supposing, as we do, that the object was to preserve the actual
value of gold, then would the government supply the people
with enough gold to make up for the wear and tear of the currency, and to maintain, if the people and their money transactions were increasing, the actual proportion between the demand and supply of gold. But in order to issue gold enough,
without issuing too much, some rule must be adopted; would
it ever, in any case, be departed from? Clearly not; because
a general plan with exceptions would be, not a rule, but several
plans working at the same time, and perhaps in opposite directions. The rule, to be worth any thing for its object, must be
complete: that is, whatever the mode of issuing gold adopted
by way of rule, it must be strictly observed, or it would be no
rule at all. In such a case, there would not be wanting people
to ask for gold, as a reward for public services, real or pretended, as a support for religion, as a fund for charity, or for
public education. Our object, each set of applicants would
say, is so very, very important, and the facility of accomplishing
it in this way is so very, very great, that we are entitled to an
exception from the general rule. But to all of these applicants
a good government would answer: obtain gold according to
the rule; in no other way will we issue a single ounce, seeing
that our first duty in this matter is to maintain the value of
money by strictly observing the rule. But now suppose this
case with a careless or corrupt government. Here, if any rule
were adopted in appearance, the exceptions would be so many
as to make the rule a nullity. If the members of this careless
or corrupt government had sense enough to perceive, that extreme profusion in the issue of gold must soon render the
mine worthless, they would, for their own sake, issue gold with
some caution, but still with shameful injustice, favouring some
at the expense of others, granting at one time and refusing at
another, causing violent fluctuations in the value of money, and
in time ruining every one of their richer subjects, one after
the other. If the government were very ignorant as well as
careless and corrupt, it would be tempted, by the facility of
doing favours and complying with urgent requests, to issue so
much gold, that the mine would soon be worth nothing, and
there would be an end of the mischief. Colonizing governments being, nearly all of them, careless and corrupt, have,
most of them, had sense enough to perceive, that there was a
degree of profusion in granting waste land which would render
worthless their power over this element of wealth. Not so
the government which founded the Swan River colony.
There the profusion has been so great that waste land is not

worth the trouble of accepting it :* the rich mine of gold is worth nothing. But, allowing for some caution in colonial governments, the evils which it is in their power to inflict on their subjects, by the capricious exercise of their power over waste land, are greater than those which would be inflicted on the English by a very ignorant government, having power over an immense quantity of gold. It is the very caution of those colonizing governments, for their own ends, which preserves their power to do mischief. How much mischief they have done, and may yet do, by retaining power over waste land, and exerting that power capriciously, may be conceived, even by the inhabitant of an old country, who will reflect on this supposed case of a very rich gold mine at the disposal of a careless and corrupt government, and who will further bear in mind how much the value of land, of capital, and of labour, depend upon the proportion between land and people.

The last condition of a good rule for the disposal of waste land is permanency. One rule at one time, and another rule at another time, would be nearly as bad as no rule at all. The Swan River settlement has not existed five years ; but already three quite different plans have been adopted in that colony for the disposal of new land. In the description of the first plan issued by the English government, it was stated, in so many words, that another plan, which was not described, would be adopted in a year or two : another plan was adopted within less than two years after the first expedition sailed ; and then, with the change of ministry in England, came a third plan ; all within three years. The first and the last plan were as different as possible. According to the first plan, any one might obtain an unlimited quantity of land for nothing ; according to the last, no one could obtain new land except by paying five shillings, at least, per acre. Until 1831, grants were obtainable for nothing in Van Dieman's Land, New South Wales, and Canada : this year, no land will be granted except to purchasers : next year the plan of gratuitous grants may be revived. The last change of system in the English colonies was brought about, not by an act of the legislature, but simply by means of letters from the English colonial minister to the colonial governors, saying in effect :—This is the way in which you will dispose of waste land until I change my mind, or you hear from my successor. Here, says an anonymous paper issued from Downing-street on the first of March, 1831 ; here is " a

---

* Last year, a hundred thousand acres of picked land, near the Swan River, was offered for sale at the rate of less than a farthing per acre ; but no buyer could be found. At the same time, waste land was sold by the government in New South Wales and Van Dieman's Land at prices varying from five to twenty shillings per acre.

summary of the rules which it has been *thought fit to substitute* for those dated the 20th of July, 1830." Here, says another anonymous publication from Downing-street, dated January 20, 1831, is " a summary of the rules which it has been *thought fit* to lay down for regulating the sales of land in New South Wales and Van Dieman's Land." Who thought fit ? thought fit to make such very important changes in the political economy of these colonies ? The English colonial minister : but his successor may *think fit* to change back again to the old plan, or to adopt some entirely new plan ; and whatever an ignorant, lazy English lord shall please to call " a summary of rules," to that must the colonists submit without appeal. Allow that the last change is good for the colonists ; that the plan now followed is far better than the irregular and corrupt practices for which it has been substituted ; still, what security have the buyers of land, according to the new plan, against being cheated of their purchase-money by the revival of old practices ? The new plan is hateful to the colonial governments, from whom it takes their most valuable privilege ; the privilege of jobbing in the disposal of waste land. It is hateful, likewise, to those in England, who belong to what has been called " the red tape school of politics," or " the Peel and Dawson crew."* At present, the home minister might give his cousin a letter of introduction to the colonial minister, without getting for that cousin 500,000 acres of waste land. The new plan, which was suggested to the government by a society in London, came upon the colonial governments by surprise. Had they been consulted about it, they would probably, assisted by a strong party in the colonial office at home, have induced Lord Goderich to abstain from writing those letters by which the new plan has been set on foot. As it is, human nature will be at fault, if they do not exert themselves to get the old practices revived ; and they will be zealously backed by cunning allies in Downing-street. The successor of Lord Goderich, a traveller in America, is not likely to revive the old English jobbing plan or practices ; but he may, if it please him, by a stroke of his pen ; as may his successor. Whatever dependence, then, the colonists may place on the American knowledge, the industry, and maybe the pride of Mr. Stanley, they have no security, worth the name, for the continuance of the present system. That the new plan, that any plan should work well, while so liable to be changed or overturned, is quite impossible. They manage these things better in America. There, the disposal of waste land is a separate department of government. The

* See that clever organ of the political church, and of the tory party in England, the *Standard* newspaper.

general plan of selling has been established by congress : when the price has been altered, it was congress that decided on the change : congress alone can make exceptional grants.   The system is upheld by the united legislature of all the states, and is administered by persons chosen for their fitness, responsible to the people, and compelled, not only to publish an account of all their proceedings, but to proceed, step by step, in the face of the public.   Here, then, are the best securities against change ; an act of the legislature with constant publicity.   The result is, that in America, every buyer of waste land knows what he is about, makes his calculations on sure grounds : and that the government obtains, by the sale of waste land, 3,000,000 dollars a year.   If the congress of America were to raise the price of waste land up to that point, which would prevent any hurtful dispersion of the people, without causing any hurtful density of population, and should also cease to make exceptional grants, then would their rule for the disposal of waste land be quite perfect ; of the right measure, uniform and lasting ; operating like a belt, tight but elastic, all round and at all times.   This is the mode of proceeding suggested by the English *Colonization Society*.

In any colony where this perfect rule for treating the chief element of colonization should be adopted, colonization would proceed, not as everywhere hitherto, more or less, by the scattering of people over a wilderness, and placing them for ages in a state between civilization and barbarism, but by the extension to new places of all that is good in an old society ; by the removal to new places of people, civilized, and experienced in all the arts of production ; willing and able to assist each other ; excited to the most skilful application of capital and labour by ready markets for disposing of surplus produce ; producing, by means of the most skilful industry in the richest field, more than colonial industry has ever produced ; obtaining the highest profits of capital and the highest wages of labour ; offering the strongest attraction for the immigration of capital and people ; increasing rapidly ; enjoying the advantages of an old society without its evils ; without any call for slavery, or restrictions on foreign trade ; an old society in every thing save the uneasiness of capitalists and the misery of the bulk of the people. Colonization, as hitherto conducted, may be likened to the building of a bridge ; a work, no part of which is complete until the whole be completed : according to the method here proposed, colonization would be like the making of a tunnel ; a work, in the progress of which each step must be complete before another step can be taken.

Two objections to this system remain to be noticed.

1. It has been said : If the price of new land were high

enough to prevent any one from legally acquiring more land than, for the good of the whole society, he ought to acquire, people would use land without a title; the beneficial compact among the colonists, implied by a uniform and fixed rule for the disposal of new land, would not be observed by all the people: some would become *squatters*, that is, settlers on new land without a title. The answer to this objection places the merits of the system in a strong point of view.

It is a remarkable fact, that in the history of American colonization, there is but one instance of a person having settled *totally* out of the reach of markets; the case of the celebrated Daniel Boon, who is known, for what? for his eccentricity. Invariably, then, it may be said, when people use land without a title, they keep within reach of some market in which to obtain, by the sale of what their own labour produces, something which their own labour will not produce. They do not intend to cut themselves off from all social intercourse; they use land so near to the settled districts that it is liable to be taken from them as colonization advances. In many cases, *squatting* has been encouraged by a regulation, which awarded to the holder of land without a title, when the land should be taken from him, compensation for the improvements which he had made upon the land. But, in every case, the *squatter* expects that his land will be taken from him: nay, in most cases, he intends to abandon it as soon as he has exhausted its natural fertility. The object of the *squatter*, then, is merely to get a few crops from a virgin soil, and then to remove for the purpose of exhausting another spot of virgin soil. But this, Americans know, and Mr. Stuart informs the English, is a general practice in America; not only with squatters, but with those who have paid for land. Why this practice? Because, as I have explained before,* of the minute division of labour in America; because labour, so minutely divided, would not, perhaps, even support the isolated labourer, unless the unproductiveness of his labour were counteracted by the great productiveness of a virgin soil. It is the extreme cheapness of new land which causes this minute division of labour. At all events, calculates the *squatter*, I must work by myself: if I must work by myself, I must, in order to live, use and exhaust a virgin soil: where's the use of paying for land when one's only object is to destroy its fertility? Here is the *squatter's* motive for using land without a title. If the price of new land were such as to keep the people together, so that they might combine their labour, it would be for the interest of every one to remain where he could be assisted and give assistance: the motive of the *squatter* would entirely cease. As it is, no one goes beyond the reach of markets: in that case,

* See Note X.

we have a right to presume, no one would go out of the way of all the great advantages which belong to combination of labour. It appears, therefore, that, by putting a sufficient price upon new land, *squatting*, instead of being encouraged, would be prevented. This will be still more clear, when we shall see with what great rapidity colonization would advance; how very soon a *squatter*, if there were one, not going out of the reach of markets, would be overtaken by society, provided the purchase-money of all new land were employed in accelerating the progress of colonization.

2. The second objection is, that into a colony, where new land was not obtainable except by purchase, neither capitalists nor labourers would be disposed to immigrate; but that, on the contrary, from such a colony both classes would be disposed to emigrate to other colonies not far off, where new land was obtainable for nothing.

We cannot decide this point by reference to facts; because in no colony has that price ever been required for new land which, together with perfect liberty of appropriation, would ensure the greatest productiveness of industry, or, in other words, the highest profits and wages. But there are some facts which tend to show, that the attractive power of a colony would be increased by putting a sufficient price upon all new land. Why have so many English and Irish labourers, who had emigrated to Canada, removed from Canada to the United States? from a colony where land was cheaper to one where it was dearer. The only rational answer is, because employment was more regular, with higher wages, where the people were in some degree kept together than where they were carefully dispersed. Why is not the Swan River colony, where, under a fine climate, land is so very cheap; why is not this a favourite colony with English emigrants, both capitalists and labourers? Why have so many people, both labourers and capitalists, emigrated from the Swan River to colonies where land was dearer? Why does it happen, when a large tract of new land is bought by an American company, and resold by them in lots with great profit, that to this spot people flock, both capitalists and labourers, and here congregate for the advantages which come from mutual assistance. In this last case, as to a great tract of country, the company take the place of government, and will not part with any land except at a higher price than that which they have paid to the government. In all these cases, people are attracted from a worse to a better proportion between land and people; from lower to higher profits and wages. That it should be so, is consistent with the principles of human nature and political economy. True it is, that people now and then go from a better to a worse proportion between land and people; as when citizens of the United States emigrate to Canada: but these are exceptions to the general rule; just as those who ruin their fortunes and destroy their health by excessive debauchery, do that which is contrary to their own interest, and therefore contrary to a law of political economy and human nature. The case of those capitalists who emigrate from an old country, led on by the hope of acquiring wealth, by obtaining for little or nothing immense tracts of wilderness, arises from profound ignorance. If this case support the objection under review, then, when a child is poisoned by mistaking night-shade berries for red currants, it goes to prove that children have no sentiment of self-preservation. These men act like the colonial minister of England, who sent butts for holding fresh water to ships that were floating on a fresh water sea. Judging of a desert country by what they see in one thickly peopled, they dream of domains and millions till they awake, having lost their all. But the people of a colony, in which there existed the advantages of a proper degree of concentration, could not be ignorant of those advantages; and the existence, for the first time, of those great advantages would surely become known both in other colonies and in the mother country. Such a colony, then, would be highly attractive: how much more attractive, both to capitalists and labourers, than colonies have ever been, will be seen in the following section of this treatise; where it is explained, that if all the purchase-money of waste land were properly disposed of, capitalists in the colony would always be supplied with labour, and every labourer reaching the colony might surely become not only a land-owner, but, something more grateful to one of his class, a master of other labourers. The first colony in which labour was plentiful, though dear, and in which labourers might be sure to become masters as well as land-owners; the first colony in which there was the good without the evil of an old society, would probably attract people, both capitalists and labourers, from colonies in which, along with the good, there was all the evil of a new society.

II. *The removal of the people.*

In a colony where new land was supplied in proportion to the wants of a people increasing rapidly in wealth and numbers; where the produce of industry was so great as to give high profits and high wages, where, consequently, all should possess the means of removal, and where, moreover, the land newly become the property of individuals should increase very rapidly in value, by very soon becoming subject to the higher kinds of competition which produce rent; in such a colony, there would be motives in plenty for the removal of people from the settled to the waste parts of the colony. Colonization would go on of itself, through the increase of people, by births in the colony. But more quickly than in proportion to such increase, colonization could not go on, unless means were found to remove people from some old country. For the immigration of people from an old country, the inducement, we have seen already, would be high profits, and especially high wages. Those who would come in search of high profits may be supposed to possess the means of coming. But those who would most desire to come in search of high wages, are the poorest of the poor in old countries; so poor as to be unable to move from one to another part of their own country; people who live from hand to mouth, never having any property save their own thews and sinews. This, however, is the class of people whose immigration into a colony it would be most useful to promote; a class who, as labourers should become capitalists and land-owners, would fill their place in the market of labour; becoming themselves, in time, capitalists and land-owners, and having their place filled, in turn, by immigrants of the same class. These, however strong their inducement to emigration, cannot move without assistance. If they are to move at all, the cost of their passage must be defrayed, or at least advanced, by somebody. It might be greatly for the advantage of the old country to defray the cost of their passage; but here we are considering only the means which a colony possesses of promoting immigration without the aid of an old country. The question then is,—How may a colony advantageously pay for the immigration of labour? that is, build a bridge, as it were, toll free, for the passage of poor labourers from an old country to the colony?

Reflecting on the urgent want of labour that occurs in all colonies which prosper, we may be sure, that great pains have been taken by people in colonies to devise some means of obtaining a regular supply of labour from old countries. The supplies of labour obtained by kidnapping in the old English colonies of America, by the late immigration of poor Germans into the United States; poor Germans who, ignorant of the laws and of the language of America, were liable to be held in a state of bondage; and by the transportation system in New South Wales and Van Dieman's Land; all these supplies of labour depended on a kind of slavery. Every scheme of the sort, that did not establish a kind of slavery, has failed the moment it was tried. On the principle of the *redemptioner* system, that of payment by a capitalist for the poor immigrant's passage, re-payment being obtained by the immigrant's labour, many schemes have been tried, and have failed, in Canada,

New South Wales, Van Dieman's Land, and South Africa ; not to mention the Swan River. And yet nothing can be more plain than that the capitalists of a colony and the labourers of an old country would find it for their mutual advantage to act on this principle. About the advance by the capitalist there is no sort of difficulty ; so much greater would be to him the value of the poor immigrant's labour for a few years, even at high wages, than the cost of the immigrant's passage. Nor is there any difficulty in finding poor labourers willing, nay eager, to engage with colonial capitalists for a certain term of service in the colony. The difficulty lies in this ; that without some kind of slavery, the capitalist has no security for repayment of his outlay ; that the labourer, as soon as he reaches the colony, laughs at his engagement ; that what the capitalist brings to the colony in the shape of labour, ceases to be labour the moment it reaches the colony ; or, at all events, is never labour over which he who paid for it has any control. During the last fifteen years, some thousands of poor labourers, to speak within compass, have been conveyed from England to English colonies at the expense of colonial capitalists, and under engagement to work for those who had paid for their passage. " There is no instance on record," says Mr. M'Arthur, the greatest capitalist of New South Wales, " where settlers have been able to prevent their *indented servants*, hired in England, from becoming dissatisfied, and then leaving them after their arrival." At the Swan River, the first settlers had hardly landed before the governor was required to punish *indented labourers* for refusing to work for those who had brought them from England. In Canada, universally, labouring servants taken from England and Ireland by capitalists, under engagement to repay with labour the cost of their passage, have quitted those to whom they were bound, to work for others, who, not having laid out money in that way, could afford to pay higher wages than those who had. If it had been possible to enforce such contracts, what Canadian would have written : " Place us on an equal footing with New South Wales, by giving us a share in those benefits which must, more or less, accrue from convict labour ?"* In vain have severe laws been passed to enforce the observance of such contracts by the labourer, and to prevent such immigrants from being employed except by those who had paid for their immigration. It has been all so thoroughly in vain, that the difficulty, not to say impossibility, of conducting immigration in this way, seems to be established.

* Suggestions on the propriety of re-introducing British Convict Labour into British North America. By a Canadian, 1824.

To meet this difficulty, an ingenious writer in the *Quarterly Review** has proposed to create a colonial fund for the immigration of labour, by means of a tax on wages. Thus the poor labourer brought to the colony would repay the cost of his passage by a deduction from his wages; and the fund so raised would be employed in bringing more labourers, who, in their turn, would repay the cost of their passage, and provide a fund for the immigration of other labourers. The principle of this suggestion is excellent; but is the execution of it more practicable than the enforcement of contracts for service, which are based on the same principle? Unless the price of new land were raised up to the golden mean, there would be scarce any hired labour to tax; scarce any wages from which to make a deduction. But supposing the poor immigrants should, during a certain period, work for high wages, how is the tax-gatherer to distinguish workmen, whose passage had been paid for them, from those who had paid for their own passage, or from those born in the colony? If very severe laws have failed to hold immigrant labourers to their engagements, what law could be devised that would induce them to remain subject to a deduction from their wages? In a word, the scheme appears to be impracticable.

This scheme may have been suggested to its author by the proposal of the *Colonization Society*.† Their proposal was, That, no waste land being disposed of by the government except by public sale at a fixed upset price, all the purchase-money should be employed in bringing poor labourers to the colony. As labourers brought to the colony in this way would in time, ninety-nine out of a hundred of them, purchase land with savings from their wages; and as this deduction from their wages would be employed to bring more labourers, who in their turn would save money and buy land, the proposal of the society may be said to be founded on the same principle as the suggestion of the *Quarterly Review*: namely, the repayment by the immigrant's labour of the cost of his passage. But over that suggestion the proposal of the society has some great advantages, which will become manifest as we examine the plan more closely.

1. This plan would be very easily carried into effect. The experience of the United States shows, that it is very easy to raise a fund by the sale of waste land. Not to reckon how much larger the fund raised in that way by the United States would

---

* Presumed to be Mr. Powlett Scrope.

† The number of the *Quarterly Review*, in which this scheme was proposed, appeared not long after the publication of *A Letter from Sydney*; in which the impossibility of holding apprenticed labourers to their engagements was explained at length.

be, if the price of new land were brought up to the golden mean, and if no exceptional grants were made, the Americans do actually raise by the sale of waste land near 700,000l. a year. What could be more easy than for the United States to spend this income in fetching labour to America? We have only to suppose that congress should choose to do this, and we suppose the plan of the English *Colonization Society* carried into effect without any sort of difficulty.*

2. Pursuing this case, for the sake of more ready illustration, the disposal of this fund in this way would bring to the United States in the first year (reckoning the cost of each immigrant's passage to be 7l.) 100,000 labourers. But as the income which the United States obtain by the sale of waste land has been steadily increasing for years, along with the increase of people by births and immigration, so would that fund increase much more rapidly, if each year's income were employed in bringing to the United States people who must otherwise have remained at home. The added labour of 100,000 persons in one year would provide the means of purchasing land to meet the wants of a population so growing in numbers; would provide a fund for the next year's immigration, corresponding with the additional demand for labour arising from the increase of capital, and of land the property of individuals. According to the extent of land sold, would be the increase of demand for labour wherewith to cultivate the new land; and according to the extent of land sold, would be the amount of the fund for

* The most simple method of laying out the Immigration fund would, probably, be the formation of a Board of Immigration, instructed to make open contracts with ship-owners for the passage of labourers from Europe to America; to the amount in each year of the immigration fund obtained in the previous year; and at a certain rate for each labourer landed *in good health* at the port named in the contract. When the English government first sent convicts to New South Wales, they used to contract with ship-owners for the passage of convicts, at the rate of so much per head for the number *embarked*. As the captain was to feed the convicts during their voyage, it was for his interest that they should be sickly, or that they should die. Under these contracts, accordingly, half, and sometimes two-thirds, of the inmates of a convict ship used to die during the voyage. The punishment of transportation was, in at least half the cases, the punishment of death. It was not till this murderous system had been pursued for some years, that the English government discovered the faulty nature of those contracts. At present, the rate of mortality on board convict ships is said to be lower than the rate of mortality among the English nobility. How was this change brought about? Simply by contracting, instead of for the number embarked, for the number *landed in the colony*. As the captain or ship-owner is now paid only for those who reach their destination, it is greatly for his interest to keep all the passengers in good health. Contracts under which the ship-owner was paid only for those who were landed in good health, the state of each passenger's health being ascertained by medical officers in the colony, would be a better security for the well-being of the immigrants during their passage, than all those minute enactments which the English parliament has made for the regulation of emigrant ships.

procuring fresh labour.   Supposing a fund for immigration to be got up in some other way than by the sale of new land ; as, for example, by a tax in the old country, or by a tax on wages in the colony, there would be no measure for suiting the supply of labour to the demand.   Too much immigrant labour might be introduced at one time, and too little at another.   If the supply were not in some way regulated by the demand, all kinds of evils would ensue.   Unless the supply were regular, unless those who should become land-owners were replaced immediately by new comers, the same obstacles would exist that exist now, to the commencement of works which require the constant employment of many hands ; and thus, when a great supply of labourers should arrive, employment for them might be wanting.   Gluts of labour, arising from uncertain immigration, do frequently happen in Canada and the State of New-York.   The cause of these gluts is explained by Mr. Tennant in a letter to Mr. Senior.   He says—" I have conversed upon this point with capitalists both of Quebec and New-York ; and I have often heard them explain the circumstance in this way.   ' Notwithstanding' (say they) ' our having capital wherewith to employ labour, we have found such immigrations of labour a great evil ; because we felt that it would be impossible to *retain* such labour if we had hired it.   Our capital was ready for many operations which require a considerable period of time for their completion ; but we could not begin such operations with labour which, we knew, would soon leave us.   If we had been sure of retaining the labour of such emigrants, we should have been glad to have engaged it at once, and for a high price : and we should have engaged it, even though we had been sure it would leave us, *provided we had been sure of a fresh supply whenever we might need it.*' From these and other facts," says Mr. Tennant, " it may be safely inferred, that the cause of the gluts of labour in Canada and New-York might be removed by rendering the supply constant and regular ; thus permitting a much greater supply in the course of ten years, without distress, than has ever yet taken place in a similar period with distress."   Now, by the plan of the *Colonization Society*, the supply of labour *must* be constant and regular : because, first, as no labourer would be able to procure land until he had worked for money, all immigrant labourers, working for a time for wages and in combination, would produce capital for the employment of more labourers ; secondly, because every labourer who left off working for wages and became a land-owner, would, by purchasing land, provide a fund for bringing fresh labour to the colony.

Still, it may be said, this rule for avoiding at all times any glut of labour would be obtained, even if the fund for immigration were raised by the old country, provided no land were granted save upon payment of the proper price ; because, in that case, all labourers would be employed for a time in creating capital for the employment of more labourers, and thus the demand for fresh labour in any given year would always be equal to the supply of immigrant labour in the previous year. Agreed ; but here there would be no rule for a sufficient supply of labour : the evil of too great a supply would be avoided, but not the evil of too small a supply ; because nothing would show plainly to what extent the demand for labour had increased. Nothing, at least, would show this half so distinctly as the amount of land sold. We might, indeed, regulate the supply of labour by the amount of land sold, even if the labour were brought by a fund raised out of the colony: that is, the old country might spend, on the emigration of labour to the colony in one year, a sum precisely equal to the sum raised in the previous year by the sale of colonial land. But the object of so measuring one fund by the other would be secured, as a matter of course, if the whole fund obtained by the sales of land were spent in procuring labour. One of the greatest merits of this plan, therefore, seems to consist in its self-regulating action.

3. We have seen already, that it would be greatly for the advantage of a colony to put one price upon all new land without exception, if merely with a view to the increase of the first element of wealth, land, in due proportion to the increase of the other elements, capital and labour ; that by requiring this price, as a rule for the supply of new land, the colonists, being sufficiently kept together, would raise more produce, would get higher profits and wages, would have more physical enjoyments, to say nothing of their escape from the moral evils of great dispersion ; and that, consequently, it would be well to put the best price upon all new land, even though the money so raised should not be employed in any useful way. Under the supposition of the money being wasted, the buyer of land would pay for justice and uniformity in the disposal of land, and for a free choice as to the situation and extent of his grant ; he would pay also for the assurance that no other could obtain land by favour, without payment, for the certainty of not being undersold by land-owners who had obtained their property for nothing ; he would pay for all the advantages of that *system*, of which his individual payment was a part. But if the money were not wasted, he would pay, besides, though paying no more, for whatever useful purpose the money might serve. If the money were spent in procuring labour, he would pay, not merely for his title to the land bought, but also for justice and uniformity in the disposal of new land, for a free choice, for the

value conferred upon all land by a due concentration of the people, for a system which must hinder ruinous fluctuations in the value of land; and further, he would pay for labour wherewith to cultivate his land; for markets in which to sell the produce of that labour; for population, which must render the whole of his land subject to one or more of those higher kinds of competition which lead to the payment of rent.   Nominally, he would receive for his outlay—land, or the title to hold and sell land: in reality, he would obtain the land for nothing; paying for a great number of other things, without any of which his land might be worthless; along with all of which, it must, no sooner than it was bought, be worth more than he had paid for it.   This paradox may be explained away in a moment. Mr. Peel required to invest 1s. 6d. per acre on his grant of 500,000 acres, appeared to pay 37,500l. for that tract of land. But he made the investment, which was to secure his title, in taking labourers to the settlement.   Whether the government had bestowed the land on the condition that the grantee should spend 37,000l. in conveying labourers to the settlement, or had sold the grant for 37,000l., spending the money in that way, would have been perfectly indifferent: in either case, the grantee would have paid, not for land, but for labour; he would have received the land for nothing, but subject to the condition of buying so much labour wherewith to cultivate it. The average cost of clearing waste land in Canada and the northern parts of the United States, is about 4l. per acre.   No land, it is plain, ought to be granted to remain uncleared. Now, suppose that the government should require 4l. per acre for such land, using the money to clear the land: in this case, for what would the grantee pay? not for the land, but for having it cleared.   So in the case before us, the grantee would pay for the means of cultivating his land, and for the value which that disposal of his purchase-money must bestow upon his land, rather than for the land itself.

4. It follows that, in justice to all the buyers of land, in order that the supply of labour should correspond exactly with the quantity of land granted, in order to give to all of the grantees the greatest return for their purchase-money, it would be necessary to employ the whole of the fund, obtained by sales of land, in fetching labour to the colony.   If any part of that fund were employed in any other way, neither would there be a rule for suiting the supply of labour to the demand, nor would the purchasers of land receive as much as possible for their money. The necessity, in order to make the system perfect, of avoiding any exceptional disposal of this money, is as clear as the necessity of refusing exceptional grants for the sake of a good rule by which to grant and withhold land.   This will be still more

clear when we shall look at the circumstances which would guide the government in fixing on the best price for land ; a consideration reserved till now, for the reason that will appear in the next paragraph.

5. According to the value of the thing purchased, ought to be the purchase-money. The land bought would be more, much more valuable, if the purchase-money were employed in adding to the colonial population, than if it were used for any other purpose whatever. By how much more valuable we cannot determine exactly ; but this is quite plain, that for land, of which all the purchase-money was devoted to the increase of colonial population, a higher price might properly be required than for land, of which the purchase-money was wasted, or was used in any way less calculated, than the use of it as an immigration fund, to increase the value of land. Thus, in America, those who last year paid 700,000*l.* for new land, might, with greater advantage to themselves, have paid twice the amount, or 1,400,000*l.* for the same extent of land, if the larger sum had been employed in adding 200,000 souls to the population of the United States. Thus the *Canada Company,* which has paid, or engaged to pay, to the English government 304,000*l.* for waste land in Upper Canada, might have paid twice as much for the same land with greater profit, if all their purchase-money had been employed in adding to the population of the colony ;* and if no land had been granted to other people save for money, and all the money so obtained had been employed in the same way. Let us suppose that by this employment of the purchase-money of new land, the cost of clearing land were reduced from 4*l.* to 2*l.* per acre, without any fall of wages, merely from the greater facility of employing many hands in combination. In this case, which would be better for the American settler, to pay 4*l.* 5*s.* per acre for his land when cleared, that is 5*s.* for the title and 4*l.* for the clearing; or to pay 2*l.* 10*s.* for the land when cleared, that is 10*s.* instead of 5*s.* for the title, and 2*l.* instead of 4*l.* for the clearing ? Like illustrations of the advantage which the buyer would derive from paying more, if his purchase-money were used in the way proposed, will occur to every one. This, then, is a most important consideration, with a view to determining the best price for new land. Some others appear scarcely less important.

To clear the land of wood, a certain amount of labour per acre is required. The purchase-money of the land, then,

---

* The money hitherto paid by this Company has been disposed of in various jobs ; for some account of which, see the evidence of Mr. Wilmot Horton, who helped to dispose of the money, before the committee of the House of Commons on the Civil Government of Canada.

ought to be sufficient to provide such an addition to the labouring population as would enable the proprietor to clear his land
without causing a deficiency of labour in any other part of the
colony: it ought to be sufficient to provide a fresh supply of
labour, corresponding with the new demand which the acquisition of so much new land had produced.

If the waste land were already clear of wood, and naturally
in a state fit for cultivation, as throughout the plains of Buenos
Ayres, the prairies of North America, and a great part of Australia, the cost of clearing would be saved : the land would be
worth more, by the cost of clearing, than land which required to
be cleared. The produce of any given amount of capital and
labour on the clear land would be greater, or would be got sooner
than the produce of the same amount of capital and labour employed on thickly-wooded land. It would appear, therefore,
that for land clear by nature, a higher price might properly be
required than for thickly-wooded land ; a price higher by the
cost of clearing. On the same ground, we shall conclude that a
higher price might be required for land naturally rich than for
land naturally poor : and if all the land in each colony were of
the same quality, this consideration might be a guide towards
ascertaining the best price for each colony. But the land of all
countries is more or less of different qualities; and yet it is
hard to learn with any precision, concerning waste land, which
parts will prove, on being cultivated, more or less fertile. If
this distinction could be made with precision, then might there
be two or more prices for land in the same colony, without
any departure from the rule of uniformity ; just as gold of different degrees of fineness might, under one standard, be made
to pass for different values. But, unable to make this distinction, how would the government require for each different portion of land its proper price? how avoid requiring too little for
the rich land, or too much for the poor land? The following
is one way, suggested by the practice of the United States, by
which, it appears to me, this object might be accomplished.
Take the richer land as the guide ; ascertain what would be
the best price if all the land were of the same quality as the
richer portions ; and let this be the lowest upset price at which
any land should be sold. Then open the land to buyers. The
first buyers in any district would neglect the poorer land, would
select the richer lots; which, being put up to auction at the
minimum price, would fetch whatever competition should determine. Very soon, however, if the upset price of these
richer lots had been high enough, the poorer lots, which had
been neglected, would acquire, from circumstances of position,
from the neighbourhood of roads and markets, from competition for the use of land on other accounts than on account of

superior natural fertility, a value equal to that of the richer lots when they belonged to the desert. By then, buyers would apply for those poorer lots at the minimum price; and they would be put up to auction, fetching the upset price, or whatever competition might determine.

In all cases there would be, though a general, still an unerring guide, by which to avoid requiring too high a price; namely, the rates of profit and wages in the colony. If these should be falling, and it should be seen that the fall arose from the competition of capital with capital, and of labourers with labourers, then might the government see that the price required was too high. If, on the contrary, it were seen that the fall arose from the less productiveness of capital and labour, in consequence of less skill in the application of capital and labour, in consequence of the weakness arising from greater dispersion, then it would be plain that the price of new land was not high enough. The most ignorant government could hardly fail to distinguish between these two mischievous alterations in the proportion among the elements of production; between these two opposite causes of a fall in the rates of profits and wages.

Though it appear difficult to say which would be worse, so excessively high a price as should inflict on the colony the evils of an old country, or so excessively low a price as, along with perfect liberty of appropriation at that very low price, would scatter the people so as to render them poor and barbarous; although there be little room to choose between these two ways of stopping colonization, still on one ground it would appear better to make the upset price too low rather than too high. If it were made too high, it could not be reduced without injustice to those who had paid the highest price; but if it were too low, it might be raised, not only without injustice to previous buyers, but with great advantage to them. If the price were too high, and were gradually lowered down to the golden mean, there would be mischievous fluctuations in the value of land: if the price, being too low, were gradually raised up to the golden mean, there would be a constant increase, but no fluctuation, in the value of land. An important rule, therefore, for getting at the best price, is to begin with a price obviously too low; taking care, however, that it be not so low as to defeat all the objects with which any price is required.*

* The English government makes five shillings per acre the upset price of waste land in New South Wales and Van Dieman's Land. With perfect liberty of appropriation at this price, it may be doubted whether the new plan, instead of checking, will not rather promote the appropriation of more land than is good for the whole society. In those colonies, the caution of the local governments in the disposal of new land, if that may be termed caution which had

6. When the fund for removing people is provided by the mother-country, the difference between the cost of a short and a long passage naturally directs the stream of emigration to the colonies which are nearest; but if an immigration fund were provided by the sale of colonial land at the proper price, colonies at a great distance from their mother-country would be as well supplied with labour as those which were less distant. In that case, the only effect of the difference between the cost of a short and a long passage, would be a difference, not in the manner, but in the rapidity, of colonization. For instance, supposing the cost of passage from England to Canada to be 7*l*., and from England to Australia to be 17*l*., and that the price of new land in both colonies were 1*l*. per acre, the sale of 100 acres in Canada would provide for the passage of 14 immigrants, while the sale of 100 acres in Australia would provide for the passage of all but 6 immigrants. A different proportion, then, between land and people, would exist in these two colonies. But if the price of 1*l*. per acre, with 7*l*. for the cost of passage, should give the right proportion between land and people, then it would be clear that, with 17*l*. for the cost of passage, 1*l*. per acre was too low a price for new land. In order that there should be, in the two colonies, one proportion between land and people, it would be necessary either to reduce the price of new land in Canada, so that for each 100 acres sold there should be only 6 immigrants, or to raise the price of new land in Australia, so that there should be 14 immigrants for each 100 acres sold. We are to presume, that in both cases the price of land would be such as to maintain a due proportion between land and people. If so, though the price of land would be higher in the more distant colony, that colony would be as well supplied with labour as the nearer colony, as well supplied, that is, in proportion to the demand for labour; colonization would go on as well as in the nearer colony; and the only difference would be, as the result of greater distance and greater cost of passage, that the waste land of the distant colony would not be bought and cultivated quite so rapidly as that of the nearer colony.

This difference, however, would not be inevitable in all cases. Cases might happen, in which colonization should proceed as rapidly in the more distant colony as in the nearer one. This would happen if, the land of the two colonies being of equal

a corrupt object; the exertion of their power in withholding new land, so that they might exert their power in granting new land with advantage to their favourites, has operated as a restriction on the appropriation of new land. This restriction is removed by the plan of selling at a fixed price to all who apply; and, though this plan will put an end to injustice, it will, if the price be too low, cause a worse, instead of a better, proportion between land and people.

natural fertility, that of the nearer colony were thickly wooded, and that of the more distant colony were already fit for cultivation ; as is actually the case with respect to Canada and Australia. If waste land were sold at the proper price in both colonies, a higher price being required for the land which, being clear of timber, was more valuable, then what the more distant colony should save, in consequence of her land being clear by nature, would go to swell her immigration fund. The difference might be so great as that the more distant colony should have a greater immigration fund, and a stronger power of attraction, than the nearer colony.

7. Another part of the proposal of the *Colonization Society* remains to be examined. Supposing the money obtained by the sale of land to be spent on immigration, this fund ought, clearly, to be spent in the most economical way ; in the way by which the good to be obtained by that outlay should be as great as possible. If the object were to procure, at the least cost, the greatest amount of labour for immediate employment, it would appear, at first sight, that the immigrants brought to the colony ought to be, all of them, males in the prime of life. But it is only at first sight that this can appear ; because on reflection it will be seen, that two men having to perform each for himself all the offices that women usually perform for men ; to cook his own victuals, to mend his own clothes, to make his own bed, to play the woman's part at home as well as the man's part in the field or workshop ; it will be seen, I say, that two men, each of whom should be obliged so to divide his labour between household cares and the work of production, would produce less than one man giving the whole of his time, attention, and labour, to the work of production. If the two men should combine their labour and divide their employments, one occupying himself solely with household cares for both, and the other solely with earning wages for both, then might the produce of their united labour be as great as that of one married man ; but in no case could it be more. In new colonies, men have often made this unnatural arrangement ; because all modern colonies, at least, have been founded by a number of men greatly exceeding the number of women who accompanied them. We need not stop to look at the moral evils of this excess of males. Economically speaking, it seems quite plain, the poor immigrants brought to a colony by the purchase-money of waste land, ought to be men and women in equal numbers ; and if married, so much the better.

If they were old people their labour would be of little value to the colony ; not only because it would soon be at an end ; but also because they would be weak, and because they would not readily turn their hands to new employments, to employments very often quite different from those in which they had worked from their childhood to old age. In order that the poor immigrants brought to a colony should be as valuable as possible, they ought to be young people, whose powers of labour would last as long as possible, and who would readily turn their hands to new kinds of work.

But would there be any objection to a mixture of children? To this there would be four objections. First, if the children were the offspring of grown-up immigrants, it would follow that the latter were not of the best age ; that if old enough to have children, they were too old to come under the description of the *most* valuable labourers. Secondly, children are less fit than old people, even, to undergo the confinement and other troubles of a long sea voyage.* Thirdly, when children first reach a colony, they necessarily incumber somebody. Fourthly, they cannot for some time be of any use as labourers: they cannot produce capital wherewith to attract and employ other labourers. To whatever extent, then, the colonial fund should be employed in bringing children, instead of grown-up people, the value received by the colony for its outlay would be less than need be. By bringing none but young grown-up persons, the maximum of value would be obtained for any given outlay.

But this is not all. The greatest quantity of labour would be obtained more easily than a less quantity. The natural time of marriage is a time of change, when two persons, just united for life, must, nearly always, seek a new home. The natural time of marriage too is one, when the mind is most disposed to hope, to ambition, to undertakings which require decision and energy of purpose. Marriage produces greater anxiety for the future, and a very strong desire to be better off in the world for the

---

* To be convinced of this, let any one visit a ship full of emigrants, in the Thames or the Mersey, bound to Canada. He will find those who are parents troubled and anxious, fearful of accidents to their children, restless, starting at every noise ; if paupers, glad to see their little ones stuffing themselves with the ship's rations, dainties to them, poor little wretches, who have plenty to eat for the first time in their lives ; if paupers, looking back without affection, and with hope to the future, but, being parents, with apprehension lest in the distant and unknown land of promise, the children should suffer more than they have endured at home. He will see the children, if paupers, delighted at meal times, smiling with greasy lips, their eyes sparkling over the butcher's meat, but, at other times, sick of the confinement, tired of having nothing to do, wanting a play-place, always in the way, driven from pillar to post, fretful, quarrelsome, thoroughly unhappy, and exposed to serious accidents. Those emigrants, on the contrary, who are neither parents nor children, young men and women without any incumbrance ; these he will find quite at their ease, enjoying the luxury of idleness, pleased with the novelty of their situation, in a state of pleasurable excitement, building castles in the air, glorying in the prospect of independence, thanking God that they are still without children, and if he knows how to make them speak out, delighted to talk of the new country, in which, as they have heard, children, instead of being a burthen, are the greatest of blessings.

sake of expected offspring. Of what class are composed those numerous streams of emigrants, which flow continually from the eastern to the outside of the western states of America, by channels longer and rougher than the sea-way from England to the eastern states? Not of single men, nor of old people, nor of middle-aged parents dragging children along with them, but, for the most part, of young couples, just married, seeking a new home, fondly assisting and encouraging each other, strong in health and spirits; not driven from their birth-place by fear of want, but attracted to a new place by the love of independence, by a sentiment of ambition, and most of all, perhaps, by anxiety for the welfare of children to come. This, then, is the class of people that would be most easily attracted to a colony by high wages and still better prospects. Others would be willing to come if, the old country co-operating with the colony, all in the old country were well informed of the advantages of emigration: but these would be the most willing; these would be, not merely willing, but anxious to come.

Of these, however, there might not exist in an old country a sufficient number to meet the colonial demand for labour. For example, if the United States should propose to lay out 1,400,000l. a year in bringing young couples from Ireland, this would produce a demand for 100,000 young Irish couples; but in Ireland there are not so many as 100,000 couples of the same age. There are not, perhaps, in Ireland, more than 60,000 grown up young couples who were born in the same year. As the constant emigration of all, or maybe of half the couples, who every year reach the age of puberty, must very soon depopulate any country, we may be sure that a portion only of this class would ever be disposed to emigrate. Whenever a number sufficient to meet the colonial demand for labour should not be disposed to emigrate, it would be right to offer a passage cost free to couples older by one, two, or three years, but always giving a preference to those who had most lately reached the age of puberty. Indeed, as to those of the best possible age, we can only say that it would be right to give them a preference.

Supposing all the people brought to the colony with the purchase-money of waste land to be young men and women, in equal numbers, let us see what the effect would be on the colonial population. At the end of twenty years after the foundation of Virginia, the number of colonists was about 1800; though, during the twenty years, near 20,000 persons had reached the settlement. This rapid decrease of population was, as I have endeavoured to show elsewhere,* owing

* See Note X

chiefly to the misery of the colonists; but it was partly owing, also, to this; that of the 20,000 immigrants a very small proportion only consisted of females. So that, even if the colony had prospered from the beginning, the number of colonists would probably have been less at the end of twenty years than the number of immigrants during that period. The settlement of New South Wales has so far prospered from the beginning, that no one has ever found it difficult to maintain a family: yet the population of the colony is nothing like as great as the number of immigrants. But why? simply because, of those persons, by far the greater number were men, and that, of the women, who composed the smaller number, many were past the age of child-bearing. Had those persons consisted of men and women in equal proportions, but of a middle age, the population of the colony might not have been much greater than it is: but if they had consisted entirely of young couples, who had just reached the age of puberty, the population of the colony would have advanced with surprising rapidity. Reckoning the number of immigrants in each year at 2,000, there seem to be grounds for believing* that, if all these had been young couples just arrived at the age of puberty, the population of the colony would by this time have amounted to nearly 500,000, instead of its actual amount, less than 50,000; that the progress of population and, we may add, of colonization, would have been ten times as great as it has been, with the same outlay for bringing people to the colony. At present, too, the proportion of young people in New South Wales is rather under than over the usual rate; whereas, in the supposed case, the proportion of young people would have been very much greater than it has ever been in any human society. According, of course, to this great proportion of young people would have been the prospect of future increase. If all the people who have removed from Europe to America had been young couples, just arrived at the age of puberty, slavery in North America must long since have died a natural death: no part of North America, no part of South America,† perhaps, would have been open for colonization. Considering what must, almost inevitably, have happened in this case, it seems hard to overrate the advantages within reach of the United

---

* Among these grounds are the very healthy climate of New South Wales, and the great fecundity of women in that country. Mr. Cunningham states that in the settlement of Bathurst Plains, a new colony, west of the Blue Mountains, only one natural death occurred in twelve years.

† As it is, there are some reasons for expecting that South America, where the greatest pains have been taken to disperse the people, and render them as barbarous as the Indians, will be colonized over again by emigrants from the north, who, kept together by the density of the natural forest, have preserved the power of civilization.

States, by means of colonizing their waste territory in the way proposed.

In any colony, the immediate effect of selecting young couples for immigration would be to diminish very much the ordinary cost of adding to the population of the colony. The passage of young couples would not cost more than that of any other class, or of all classes mixed ; but, along with the young couples, the colony would obtain, at the ordinary cost, the greatest possible germ of future increase. The settlers in New South Wales who, in the course of a few years, have made that colony to swarm with sheep, did not import lambs or old sheep; still less did they import a large proportion of rams. They have imported altogether a very small number of sheep, compared with the vast number now in the colony. Their object was the production in the colony of the greatest number of sheep by the importation of the least number, or, in other words, at the least cost ; and this object they accomplished by selecting for importation those animals, which, on account of their sex and age, were fit to produce the greatest number of young in the shortest time. If a like selection were made of the persons to be brought to a colony with the purchase-money of waste land, the land bought, it is evident, would become as valuable as it could ever become, much more quickly than if the immigrants should be a mixture of persons of all ages. In the former case, not only would the immigrants be, all of them, of the most valuable class as labourers, but they would be of a class fit to produce the most rapid increase of people in the colony ; to create, as soon as possible, in places now desert, a demand for food, for the raw materials of manufactures, for accommodation land, and for building-ground. The buyer of new land, therefore, would have his purchase-money laid out for him in the way best of all calculated to be of service to him. It would be well to consider this, in seeking to determine the proper price for new land, of which the purchase-money was to be thus laid out for the greatest advantage of the purchaser.

It must be seen, further, that if the immigration fund were laid out in this way, the progressive increase of that fund, by means of the increase of people wanting land, would be much more rapid than if the immigrants brought to the colony were of all ages mixed. By adopting this mode of immigration, all the means of colonization would be used with their greatest possible effect.*

---

* By the importunity of some members of the Colonization Society, the English government was induced to adopt this principle of colonization. While their board of emigration was sitting in Downing-street, a mere name for want of funds, they were persuaded to devote the money obtained by the sale of waste land in New South Wales and Van Dieman's Land to the sending of poor

The moral advantages of such a selection of immigrants would not be few. Each female would have a special protector from the moment of her departure from home. No man would have any excuse for dissolute habits. All the evils, which have so often sprung from a disproportion between the sexes, would be avoided. Every pair of immigrants would have the strongest motives for industry, steadiness, and thrift. In a colony thus peopled, there would scarcely ever be any single men or single women: nearly the whole population would consist of married men and women, boys, and girls, and children. For many years, the proportion of children to grown-up people would be greater than was ever known since Shem, Ham, and Japhet were surrounded by their little ones. The colony would be an immense nursery, and, all being at ease without being scattered, would offer the finest opportunity that ever occurred, to see what may be done for society by universal education. That must be a narrow breast in which the last consideration does not raise some generous emotion.

This is the way in which the *Colonization Society* proposed

females to those colonies. It was high time to do something towards correcting the disproportion between the sexes which exists in those colonies. Several ship loads of poor females have, in this way, been provided with a passage to the penal settlements. But with what result? The number of female immigrants is not, by any means, sufficient to cause an equal proportion between the sexes. So long as the proportion shall remain unequal, all females, not protected by a higher station, must be subject to a kind of persecution which one need not describe. It is enough to say, that the government, sending so few, has sent a certain number of women from England to become prostitutes in Australia. While the government was sending these women, it sent, side-by-side with these women, though not in the same ships, a greater number of men; as if determined to miss the object with which the women were sent. At first, the colonial office declared in print, that the passage of the women was to be paid for with the money obtained by selling waste land. This was acknowledging a new and important principle. Whether alarmed at finding themselves connected with something new and important, something not common-place, something out of the routine of office; or whether they discovered that the fund to be obtained by selling waste land would be very handy for their own private purposes; with what motive I know not; but by a new regulation of the colonial office, it is declared that the cost of sending women to the penal settlements will be defrayed out of the *colonial revenue*. Thus the fund obtained by the sale of waste land has been carried to the governor's account; and the principle of using that fund for bringing labour to the colony has been abandoned. Mr. Wilmot Horton used to contend, that whatever "the crown" might obtain by the sale of waste land was the property of "the crown;" and that touching the disposal of it, no one had any business to inquire, any more than about the disposal of secret service money voted by parliament. The change has taken place since Lord Howick, who in parliament thought fit to acknowledge the services of the Colonization Society, gave up the "Australian department" of the colonial office to his colleague Mr. Hay; once the colleague of Mr. Horton, and always, if I am not greatly mistaken, one of that party whom the Standard newspaper calls "the Peel and Dawson crew." If Mr. Hay be the author of this change, his motives for bringing it about may, perhaps, be discovered in a correspondence printed in the Appendix, No. 3.

that the purchase-money of waste land should be employed. The sum of the measures suggested by them, having regard to the objects and means of the colonies alone, is : The sale of *all* waste land by public auction at a fixed upset price, with the most perfect liberty of appropriation at that price : and the employment of *the whole* of the fund so obtained in bringing people to the colony ; a preference being always given to young couples who have just reached the age of puberty. How the mother country, the country, that is, from which the immigrants should come, might usefully co-operate with the colony, remains to be considered.

CO-OPERATION OF THE MOTHER COUNTRY.

The subject has been thus divided for two reasons ; first, because, as observed already, it was more convenient to take a colonial view of means which exist in the colony ; secondly, in order to show clearly, without any long explanation, that under a good system of colonization, by whatever government administered, people would be drawn to the colony, not driven from the mother country. By examining the subject in this way, any one may see distinctly that the advantage of those who shall remove from the mother country is a necessary condition of emigration ; that emigration to any considerable extent could not take place without benefit to the emigrants. This, however, is not the general impression in England. A different impression has been made on the English vulgar, high and low. Never having heard of emigration, save, according to Mr. Wilmot Horton's views, as a means of relief from the pressure of the poor's-rate, they have supposed that, whether or not the object was attained, the poor emigrants must be driven away for the good of those who should remain behind, instead of being drawn away for their own good. This impression, which renders the word emigration distasteful to the English, seems to have been caused by three circumstances in particular.

First. By various attempts to raise in the mother country a fund for pauper emigration, not the good of the emigrants, but that of the subscribers to the fund, was made prominent. Thus, when the government advanced 60,000*l.* for sending some poor people to Canada, it was supposed that the government wished to get rid of those people, not for their sake, but for the sake of those to whom the people were a burthen. So also, when Lord Howick brought a bill into parliament for enabling parishes to raise an emigration fund by mortgaging their poor's-rate, the advantage, not of the paupers, but of the rate-payers, was supposed to be his object. If the money employed in the first case had been provided under the name of a grant to Upper Canada, for supplying that colony with labour, the English government would have appeared to consult, not its own advantage, but that of the colony ; and the advantage of the poor emigrants, the certainty of their obtaining high wages, would have been set in a prominent light : the low and high vulgar would have seen that labour was wanted in the colony: and thus it would have appeared, not that the emigrants were driven from home, but that they were invited to another place. As it was, the simple truth, that when, in the natural progress of colonization, people quit their birth-place, they must necessarily be invited by the prospect of advantage to themselves ; this evident truth was kept out of view ; and in its room an impression was made that the poor emigrants might suffer by their removal.

Secondly. Under the experiments in pauper emigration made by the English government, poor emigrants *have* suffered by their removal. To say nothing of what happened to the poor people whom the English government sent to South Africa, the poor people whom they sent to Canada suffered great privations and hardships. They consisted of families, men, women, and swarms of children ; and, what is more important, instead of being allowed to proceed in a natural course, that is, to remain in the settled parts of the colony, working for wages, getting assistance when required from their employers and neighbours, and learning by degrees how to settle in the forest; instead of this, they were planted at once beyond the settled parts of the colony, in the midst of the forest, far apart from each other, without experience, assistance, or advice ; and even without houses in which to shelter their families. Those English paupers, becoming suddenly colonial landlords, not hardened to the climate, placed on new land where ague generally prevails, not accustomed to use the hatchet, which is the first tool used by a settler ; thus placed, like fish out of water, they suffered from heat, cold, and wet, from sickness, from wounds, and finally from a sentiment of despair. Not a few of the children died. The misery which these poor people suffered, though great pains were taken to conceal it by the author of the experiment, became known in England ; and thus a well-founded prejudice was created against emigration ; well-founded, that is, as against this sort of emigration.* But along with a dislike to this sort of emigration, there arose, as might have been expected, a dislike to all emigration.

* The absurdity of Mr. Wilmot Horton's scheme for *locating* English paupers in the forests of Canada was exposed by the *Colonization Society ;* and in the emigration bill which Lord Howick soon afterward brought in parliament, the natural mode of pauper emigration was adopted ; that of allowing poor labourers to be attracted by the high wages of the colony.

Thirdly. The English government goes out of its way to strengthen in the common people their natural sense of the evils of emigration. As it is painful to quit for ever the country of one's birth and one's affections, so is emigration necessarily attended with some evil; but this evil, it is plain, will never be incurred voluntarily, that is, if there be no sort of interference by government, without so much good as turns the scale in favour of emigration. The balance of the account must necessarily be in favour of the voluntary emigrant. But what says the English government? While Lord Howick was vainly begging the House of Commons to pass his emigration bill, imploring them to mend the condition of the peasantry in the south of England, to prevent another insurrection of that class by enabling some of them to remove to the colonies; at this very time, the judges at Winchester, and elsewhere, addressed language to the following effect to peasants convicted of rioting for better wages:—Unhappy men! your crime is enormous, and your punishment must be great. The sentence of the law is, that you be transported beyond seas for the term of your natural lives. You are going to a far country, to a country so far off, that neither will you ever hear of those whom you love best, nor will they ever hear of you. Though the law does not permit me to pass on some of you the sentence of transportation for life, still I can assure such of you, that you will never be able to return. You may have heard, from wicked men like yourselves, that it is a fine country; and you may expect to do well there. But oh, unhappy prisoners! you will suffer all the pain of being for ever banished from the country of your birth and your affections. May God, in his mercy, give you fortitude to bear so dreadful a punishment, which, however, is no more than your atrocious crime deserves.—Hereupon, some of the prisoners, single men, who had, indeed, heard that New South Wales is a very fine country, and that they could hardly fail to do well there; these put their tongues into their cheeks, and set the judge at defiance. But the wives and children of the others shed tears, shrieked, or fainted; and all through those rural districts there was weeping and lamentation. These are the districts in which, especially, it was intended that Lord Howick's bill should be of use; districts in which, among the class who were to be persuaded to emigrate, a strong impression had been made, that emigration is the greatest punishment next to death. Are we, then, to be surprised that the English generally should look upon every attempt by their government to promote emigration as an attempt to hurt the emigrants? So long as criminals shall be punished by transportation, there must necessarily exist in England a strong prejudice against any interference by the government for promoting emigration.

But why should the government of an old country ever undertake to promote emigration from that country, when all the ends, which an old country seeks in colonization, may be reached by promoting immigration to her colonies? Whether the colony be dependent or independent, all that the government of the mother country has to do at home for promoting colonization, is to take care that the poorer class at home be well informed of the advantages of going to a colony; taking care also that the necessary evil of going from home be not made to appear greater than it is, through forcing people to emigrate by way of punishment. It would be very easy, indeed, supposing either that there was co-operation between the old country and the colony, or that both were under the same government, to keep the poorer class in the old country well informed of the advantages of going to a colony. The great emigration from England which took place last year was caused mainly by the publication of letters from poor emigrants to their friends in England.* But in order that such letters should be published, it is necessary that they should be written and received. Why not, in order to promote the receipt of such letters among the poorer class in the mother country, allow poor emigrants, during some years after their arrival in the colony, to send letters by the post, but free of postage, to the friends whom they had left behind; just as, in many countries, soldiers are allowed this privilege? To such an arrangement there appears no obstacle that might not be got over with very little trouble.† In this way, not only would the necessary evil of going to a colony be diminished; that is, the emigrants would depart with the pleasant assurance of being able to communicate with their friends at home; but the poorer class in the mother country would always hear the truth as to the prospects of emigrants; and not only the truth, but truth in which they would not suspect any falsehood. The statements as to the high wages obtainable in the English colonies, lately published by a board of emigration sitting in Downing-street, though perfectly true, have not been received with implicit faith by the harassed and therefore suspicious class to

* Thousands, probably, were induced to emigrate by reading one publication of this sort; a collection of letters from poor emigrants, printed and circulated by one of the best friends of the English poor, and we may add of the rich, Mr. Poulett Scrope.

† An officer at the colonial port might give to each poor immigrant a certificate, which should authorise post-masters throughout the colony to frank letters for the mother-country that were brought to a post-office by the bearer of the certificate.

whom they were addressed; nor would any statements made by the government ever obtain so much credit as letters from the emigrants themselves. In this way, moreover, the attractive power of the colony would be made apparent to the high vulgar of the mother country; and those preachers would be silenced whose text is, " Dwell in the land, and verily ye shall be fed."

With respect to the mother country, two points remain to be examined; first, the effect of the proposed selection of emigrants in producing relief from excessive numbers; secondly, the means by which the overflowing capital of an old country might find secure and profitable employment through this system of colonization.

First—If it be true that 125,000 persons emigrated from Great Britain and Ireland last year, still this abstraction of people has not caused the least perceptible relief from excessive numbers. That great body of emigrants consisted of a mixture of all classes; masters and servants, old and young. The poorest class was composed, in great measure of families, men, women, and children, for whom a passage was provided by their parishes, with a view to get rid of them. By the removal of the children, nothing was taken from the present market of English labour; nor indeed by the removal of any but workmen. Of these last, the number removed were too small for any effect on wages. The only effect of their removal was to make room for others quite ready to take their place. But if this great body of emigrants had consisted entirely of workmen and their wives, it seems probable that considerable relief would have been obtained from excessive numbers; that more room would have been made than could have been immediately filled by other workmen. The conscription in France, during the late war, did not, perhaps, carry off so many workmen, year by year, in proportion to the then population of France, as the proportion which 60,000 bears to 24,000,000: yet it certainly had the effect of keeping the supply of labour so much within the demand, that the condition of the labouring class in France was, during the war, very comfortable compared with what it has been since the peace. One of the causes of Napoleon's great popularity was the easy state of the labouring class in France during his reign: one of the causes of the late revolution in France was the uneasy state of the working class who effected that revolution: and the miserable state of that class, in the greater part of France at this time leaves but small hope that the revolution which they effected will be of any service to them. In France, the working people now say, commonly:—Oh! if we could get back Napoleon, we should soon be better off. Without knowing it, they want so much war as should again cause the fields to be tilled by women. If, for every young man carried off by Napoleon's wars, a young woman also had been carried off, though the immediate effect on the state of the working class would have been the same, the conscription would have had a more lasting effect on the condition of the working class. Millions, perhaps, who have been born in France since 1814, would not have been born there; and this, though many would have lived, who have been born to die since 1814, if not of hunger, of disease produced by all sorts of privations, still the good effect of the conscription might have lasted till now. These considerations will direct us to a right estimate of the influence, which a proper selection of emigrants would have on the population of a country like England.

It has been reckoned,* that in England the number of marriages which take place in a year is in the proportion of 1 to about 134 souls. Assuming this calculation to be right, and the population of England to be 14,000,000, the yearly number of marriages in England is $104,477\frac{46}{67}$. Whatever would be the effect on population of preventing all the marriages, would be the effect of removing all who were about to marry. The removal, therefore, of about 209,000 persons every year for a few years would very soon depopulate England. But this effect would occur through the removal of a much smaller number. It would occur by the yearly removal of all who in each year should reach the age of puberty. How many persons in England every year reach the age of puberty has never been calculated. But it is reckoned, that the yearly births are, to the whole population, in the proportion of 1 to about 31. Taking the yearly births, then, to be $451,612\frac{28}{31}$, or, for round numbers, 450,000, and assuming that not above one-third of these, or 150,000, reach the age of puberty, it appears, that England might soon be depopulated by the yearly abstraction, for some years, of a number of persons not much greater than the number who did actually emigrate last year. Supposing the emigration of each of these persons to cost 7l., the cost of entirely depopulating England would be a yearly outlay, for some years, of 1,050,000l.; very little more by the year than a seventh part of the English poor's-rate; not much more than the supposed cost of emigration from Great Britain and Ireland during the last year. But there is a way by which, with a still smaller yearly outlay, England might be depopulated: by taking away every year a number of young couples sufficient to reduce the whole number in after years; so that the number of young couples would, in time, be reduced to one. Sup-

* See Professor M'Culloch's Note on *Population*, in his edition of the Wealth of Nations, which is full of valuable information on this subject.

posing that this might be effected, though not so quickly as if all were removed, by removing every year *half* of the young couples who had in that year reached the age of puberty, then might England be depopulated by the yearly removal for some years of 75,000 persons, at a yearly cost of 525,000*l.* The question, however, is, not how might England be depopulated, but what is the smallest proportion of young couples, whose yearly removal would prevent any hurtful increase of the population of a country like England; would put the bulk of the people at ease; enabling all to marry when nature should prompt them to marriage; preventing the death of many through want; and giving full effect to the principle of population.

Still this question is not of much, perhaps it is not of **any,** practical importance. By the proposed selection of emigrants, all that could be done would be done, towards procuring relief from excessive numbers; and in no event could too many people be removed; because, when relief from excessive numbers was obtained, emigration would stop, until the prospect of misery from excessive numbers should again render the evil of quitting home less than that of remaining at home.

By the proposed selection of emigrants, moreover, as the greatest quantity of relief from excessive numbers would be comprised in the removal of the least number of people, the maximum of good from emigration would be obtained, not only with the minimum of cost, but, what is far more important, with the minimum of painful feelings. All that old people and young children suffer more than other people from a long voyage would be avoided. Those only would remove, who were already on the move to a new home : those only, to whom, on account of their youth and animal spirits, separation from birthplace would be least painful; those only, who had just formed the dearest connexion, and one not to be severed, but to be made happy by their removal. And this, the least degree of painful feeling, would be suffered by the smallest possible number of people.

To make this selection, no interference would be required from the government of an old country. Supposing the attractive power of the colony applied to the immigration of young couples, then ship-owners and others, who had contracted with the colonial government for bringing young couples to the colony, would make known in the mother country that they were ready to convey to the colony, free of cost, persons of that description, but not of any other description. Suppose that a young single man should apply for a passage; he would be told that for the passage of a single man there was no fund, but that there was a fund for the passage of a married man and his wife; that whenever he should please to return with a young wife, they might both go to the colony cost free. Can it be doubtful that he would soon return with a young wife ? The experiment has been thus far tried ; that when, last year, the *South Australian Land Company* received applications for a passage to New Holland, from young single men out of work, and answered, "Yes, if you get married, and for your wife also," the common reply was, "So much the better ;" with a snap of the fingers, a laugh, or swimming eyes, that spoke more than the words.* In order that this selection should be made without any difficulty, all that would be required from the government of an old country is, that it should be so good as to do nothing ; that it should have sense enough to abstain from meddling with the attractive power of the colony.

Secondly—There are two ways in which this system of colonization seems calculated to give secure and profitable employment to the overflowing capital of a mother country.

In the first place, it is clear that, to whatever extent this system was pursued, the colonies would be more extensive ; that under this system, they would be extended as rapidly as possible ; and that as every new colony, or increase of an old one, would be the extension of an old society to a new place ; as the colonists would produce more with the same number of hands than colonists have ever produced, and would retain the habits and wants of their mother country ; so would this mode of colonization very rapidly increase the markets in which the mother country might buy raw produce and cheap corn with manufactured goods. One end of colonization being to enlarge the field for employing capital and labour within the mother country, that great object would be obtained most easily and most quickly by these means of colonization.

But, in the next place, in order that this most useful process should begin as soon as possible, colonies already established might require some assistance, not from the government, but from the capitalists of the mother country. Suppose that the Americans, having resolved to dispose of their fund, obtained by the sale of waste land, in bringing labour to the United States, should, with a view to the extinction of slavery, with a view to obtaining immediately a sufficient supply of free labour, be willing to anticipate that fund ? to borrow money on that security ? Could a better security for overflowing English capital be readily imagined ? In this way, capital which is now lying idle in England, or is about to fly off, taking no labour with it, would fly off, indeed, but only for a time, and would take with it, or draw after it, a correspond-

* Whoever persuaded Lord Goderich to depart from his engagement with this company, little knows how much bitter disappointment he occasioned. But what are the hopes of paupers to secretaries of state ?

ing amount of surplus labour. We have only to suppose, farther, that in Canada, South Africa, and Australia, the American plan of selling land had been adopted with improvements; we have only to suppose, in short, that the legislature of England had attended to this subject, and we suppose the opening of three more great fields for the secure and profitable employment of English capital in the work of colonization.

The enlargement of the field, however, need not stop here. While a portion of the capital of the mother country was employed in anticipation of the sales of waste land, other portions would be employed in the purchase of waste land. Immense capitals, belonging to people in the eastern states of America, are constantly employed in the purchase of new land on the western frontier, and invariably, I believe, with profit to the capitalists. The profit of such purchases would be much more certain, and would be obtained much sooner in a colony where no new land was obtainable save by purchase, and where all the purchase-money of new land was employed in bringing selected labourers to the colony. How great and rapid might be the profit of such undertakings, may be partly conceived from the success of the *Canada Company*, of whose proceedings a brief summary appears below.* This company bought land of the government, without any assurance that land would not be given for nothing to other people; and the money which they have paid to the government has been wasted; all of it in some way, most of it in shameful jobs. Nearly all the great and successful purchases of waste land in the United States are conducted by companies residing in the eastern towns. This kind of investment seems peculiarly suited to companies. The whole operation consists of paying and receiving money; paying a small sum, waiting, and then receiving a large sum. The time for waiting would be very short, if all the money paid were employed in adding to the colonial population, according to a fixed rule, and so that the greatest amount of population was added at the least cost. It would be difficult for companies to make any serious blunder: scarce any thing would be left to the neglect of agents; for there would be scarce any thing to do: and, lastly, a company, by the employment of a large capital, might take so much land in one lot or block as

* Nominal capital, 1,000,000*l.*
Capital actually invested, 151,555*l.*
Dividend of 4 per cent. per annum, regularly paid.
Assets of the company (December, 1832): 1st. Bills given by purchasers of their land, bearing interest at 6 per cent., with payment by instalments effectually secured, 113,025*l.* 2d. Land paid for by the company, but not yet sold, including the town lots of Guelph and Goderich, 460,000 acres, estimated at 15*s*, per acre, or 345,000*l.* 3d. Land remaining to be paid for, 1,658,000 acres, at the rate of 2*s.* 10*d.* per acre, estimated to sell for 15*s.* per acre, or 1,243,500*l.*

would ensure the formation of a town on their property : not by them, but by others for their good.   Becoming the proprietors of a large extent of land, there would necessarily occur upon some parts of their property those kinds of competition for the use of land, over and above competition for land of superior natural fertility, which lead to the payment of rent : every sale by them would add to the value of land adjoining that which had been sold ; and the whole business of selling might be conducted by one or two agents of common intelligence.   To show how great and how sure would be the profit of such investments, under the proposed system of colonization, I have collected a number of facts which establish that, even now, *wherever people congregrate*, new land invariably rises in value soon after it becomes private property.*   All surplus capital invested in this way would, of course, take off with it a corresponding amount of surplus labour.   Every investment of this kind would tend, in proportion to its amount, to diminish in the mother country the competition of capital with capital, and of labour with labour.

How this system of colonization would tend to enlarge the field of employment for those classes, who are not called either capitalists or labourers, is very evident.   As all the emigrant labourers would retain the habits and wants of their mother country, so would they, having plenty in the colony, create a demand for the services of those classes whose only property is their knowledge ; and the progressive increase of this demand would keep pace, exactly, with the very rapid progress of colonization.   Colonies that were brisk markets for the sale of goods manufactured in the mother country, must necessarily afford employment to persons, having the common run of knowledge, or superior knowledge, who should emigrate from the mother country.   Touching this point, it is only necessary to repeat, that a colony, founded or extended in the way proposed, would be the extension of an old society to a new place, with all the good, but without the evils, which belong especially to old countries.

This exposition of the views of the *Colonization Society* may be properly concluded by a quotation from their own statement of their principles and objects.

" To conclude : We have purposely abstained from dwelling on the improvement which this system of colonization might effect in the moral condition of the poorer classes in Britain, or on the wonderful rapidity with which, by calling millions and hundreds of millions into existence, it might people the desert regions of the globe.   Such speculations, however

---

* See Appendix, No. 2.

grateful, are unsuited to the present occasion. We have confined ourselves to statements and arguments which may be submitted to the test of rational inquiry. Any man, inquiring with a single desire to find the truth, may readily convince himself whether or not the proposed selection of emigrants would prevent all undesirable increase of people in the mother country, and, at the same time, cause the greatest possible increase of people in the colonies ; whether or not the proposed concentration of the colonists would tend to their wealth and civilization ; would furnish the greatest amount of employment for labour, and the greatest fund for conveying labour to the market. These are questions in the science of public economy which must be speedily decided. If they should be decided in the affirmative, it must inevitably follow, that the measure in question, being well administered, would save the greater part of the poor's-rate of England, and prevent, in Ireland, the greater evil of pauperism without poor laws ; that it would occasion a great and constant increase of the demand for British manufactures ; that it would extinguish slavery in South Africa, by the substitution of free labour ; and that it would enable the more extensive British colonies to defray the entire cost of their own government and protection. Moreover, if the principles of the suggested measure be sound, the measure may be adopted, not only upon any scale, that is, by degrees, so as to render its adoption perfectly easy,—but also without harm to any, and with benefit to all ; without the least injury to a single person, and with definable and manifest advantages to the poor, both those who should remove and those who should remain ; to the landlords, farmers, manufacturers, merchants, and ship-owners of Britain ; to the colonists of every class, but more especially to the land-owners and merchants ; and finally, to both the domestic and colonial governments. We beg the reader to observe that these conclusions are stated hypothetically. The accuracy of the conclusions depends on the truth of the principles, which it is our wish rather to submit for examination than to assert with confidence. But if those conclusions should turn out to be founded on reason and truth, it will be acknowledged, that objects more important were never sought by more simple means."

THE FOUNDATION OF COLONIES.

After so full a notice of the other parts of the subject, this part of it may be disposed of in few words.

If the purchase of waste land in a colony already established were a profitable mode of employing capital, so would be the purchase of the first grant in a new colony. Nay, as the first purchasers of land in a new colony would naturally select the spot on which the first town, or the capital of the colony, the seat of government, and the centre of trade, was likely to be formed, their land must necessarily, if the colony prospered at all, soon become extremely valuable. Their purchase-money would provide the colony with labour of the most valuable kind, and in due proportion to the land granted. Here, there would be no motive for anticipating by a loan the sales of waste land; because, in this case, there would never be any hurtful disproportion between land and people. The certainty of obtaining labour in the new colony would be the strongest inducement to the emigration of capitalists, ambitious to take part in laying the foundation of an empire. Thus would all the elements of wealth be brought together, with no further trouble to the government of the mother country than what should be required for establishing in the colony a fixed and uniform system in the disposal of waste land. It was the hope of being able to persuade the English government to establish such a system for the south coast of Australia, that lately induced a body of Englishmen* to project the foundation of a colony in that desert part of the world. A body of capitalists, sure of a rapid increase in the value of land, if all land were sold and all the purchase-money employed in procuring labour, was ready to buy a part of that wilderness; another body of capitalists, depending on a constant supply of labour, was ready to embark for that desert; the most numerous, wealthy, and estimable body of Englishmen that ever proposed to found a colony : and labourers in abundance were anxious to accompany them, expecting to have their passage paid for with the purchase-money of the desert land. In order to carry this project into effect, nothing more was required than some engagement from the English government, that the proposed system for the disposal of waste land should be firmly established in the intended colony; some law, or something like a law, to prevent a colonial governor, and the clerks in Downing-street,

---

* See in the Appendix (No. 3), a list of the Provisional Committee of the South Australian Land Company, with the signatures to a Memorial addressed to Viscount Goderich.

from meddling with the disposal of waste land in this colony. The best security for this object would have been an act of parliament; but those who intended to found the colony required no more than a charter from the king; a something to bind the compact into which those individuals were desirous to enter. This piece of parchment was applied for, promised, and ultimately refused; on what grounds applied for, how promised, and how cruelly refused, may be seen by a correspondence between the government and those who intended to found the colony. Part of this correspondence is printed in the Appendix. To those who are curious about the motives which may induce the government of an old country to *prevent* the foundation of colonies, as well as to those who would ascertain the motives with which, under a good system of colonization, individuals would found colonies, scarcely assisted by their government, the correspondence in question will prove highly instructive.

The old English colonies in America, now the eastern States of the Union, were not founded by any government. They were founded by individuals, not even aided by any government, save as the compact, into which each of those bodies of individuals entered, was bound by a charter from the crown of England. At that time, it had not been discovered that the disposal of waste land in a colony may furnish matter for favour and jobs: at that time, probably, a charter to prevent favour and jobbing in the disposal of waste land would not have been refused by the government of England. But, at that time, also, none of the great advantages of a fixed and uniform system in the disposal of waste land were understood by any one. The evils of profusion and irregularity have been made apparent by the good resulting from some degree of caution and regularity. What is a new state formed in the western deserts of America, if it be not a new colony? Yet how marked is the contrast between the immediate prosperity of one of those new colonies, and the early misery of one of those which were planted on the eastern coast of America! To whatever extent we may suppose that the prosperity of the newest colonies arises from caution and regularity in the disposal of waste land, so far shall we attribute the early misery of the oldest colonies to profusion and irregularity. If some degree of caution and regularity in the disposal of waste land ensure the immediate prosperity of a new colony, it seems clear, that the prosperity of a new colony would be much greater, and much more rapid, under the proposed system of selling all new land and converting all the purchase-money into the most productive labour. An old country, then, by applying this system to desert countries at her disposal, may create stronger motives than ever yet existed for the foundation of colonies by bodies of individuals.   This subject well deserves the attention of the English, who have more desert land at their disposal than any other nation, not excepting the North Americans, and who, more than any other nation, require that their field of production should be enlarged.*

THE GOVERNMENT OF COLONIES.

The advocate of systematic colonization, addressing the corrupt government of an old country, and actuated by that short-sighted policy which attends only to immediate objects, and has no faith in the power of truth, would say : Proceed in such a way that your colonies may be richer than colonies have ever been, more taxable, better worth governing.   But the corrupt government of an old country would not be cajoled by this sort of language : it would see, what must be plain to every one, that, if colonies were so many extensions of an old society, they would never submit to be governed from a distance.   Truly, if the colonists were kept together by a good system for the disposal of waste land, they would be richer than colonists have ever been, better able to pay taxes, better worth keeping in subjection : but, so likewise, would they be more intelligent, and, as union is force, very much stronger. The scattered, poor, and ignorant inhabitants of South Africa could not but submit patiently to the oppression, the sportive injustice, and fantastic cruelty of an English lord, sent across the world to do with them as he pleased.   They were incapable of governing themselves, and therefore quite unable to resist a foreign tyrant.   With the capacity for self-government comes the power to exercise it.   A people entirely fit to manage themselves will never long submit to be managed by others, much less to be managed by an authority residing at a great distance from them.   "Government from a distance," says Bentham, " is often mischievous to the people submitted to it. Government is almost always, as respects them, in a state either of jealousy or indifference.   They are either neglected or pil-

---

* Mr. Stuart, one of the soberest and most moderate of writers, supposes that the United States will obtain, by the sale of waste land, even under the present defective system, " *some thousand millions of dollars.*"   The national debt of England amounts to between *three* and *four* thousand millions of dollars. With Canada, South Africa, Eastern, Western, and Southern Australia, New Zealand (a country admirably fit for colonization), part of the north-west coast of America, Ceylon (which in many respects is quite fit for colonization), Madagascar perhaps, some desert islands in the Pacific, and great tracts of desert land in India under a fine climate ; with all these fields of colonization open to them, the English, surely, might so enlarge their field of production as to laugh at their national debt.

laged ; they are made places of banishment for the vilest part of society, or places to be pillaged by minions and favourites, whom it is desirable suddenly to enrich. The sovereign at two thousand leagues' distance from his subjects can be acquainted neither with their wants, their interests, their manners, nor their character. The most legitimate and weighty complaints, weakened by reason of distance, stripped of every thing that might excite sensibility, of every thing which might soften or subdue the pride of power, are delivered, without defence, into the cabinet of the prince, to the most insidious interpretations, to the most unfaithful representations. The colonists are still too happy if their demand of justice is not construed into a crime, and if their most moderate remonstrances are not punished as acts of rebellion. In a word, little is cared for their affection, nothing is feared from their resentment, and their despair is contemned."* But why is their anger despised? Because it is not dangerous ; because they are helpless; because they are, what is called, new societies. Let colonies be old societies in new places, and they will have the power to choose between self-government and government from a distance. That they would choose to govern themselves cannot be doubted by any one who is at all acquainted with the evils of being governed from a distance.

Bentham well describes how difficult it is for subject colonies to obtain any redress of grievances ; but he says little of the grievances of which such colonies must necessarily have to complain. If one were ill, it would be a hard case when the physician resided thousands of miles off, and months must elapse before one could hear from him by return of post ; but the degree of hardship would greatly depend on the nature of the disease. It is not very easy for people, who have never been governed from a distance, to understand the nature of the evils which are thus inflicted on dependent colonies. Every government must be supported by some kind of force. The distant government seldom maintains in the colony an armed force sufficient to preserve its authority. Some other means, then, must be adopted to make the colonists obey laws which are enacted by persons at a distance, knowing little of the colony and caring less for it ; laws too, administered by strangers, not fixed in the colony, nor in any degree responsible to the subject people. The way in which this object is commonly attained, is by dividing the colonists ; by getting up hostile factions among them ; by allowing some of them to share with the strangers in all kinds of jobs and monopolies. In order that the strangers may pillage the colony, some of the colonists are

* Rationale of Reward, b. iv. chap. 14.

allowed to pillage it.   In all the more extensive colonies which are governed from Downing-street, London, there is a strong party of colonists attached to the government, and among the worst enemies of the colonial people.   The machinery whereby misgovernment thus supports itself, is generally a council in the colony, composed partly of strangers, partly of colonists, all named by the governor ; by which mockery of a legislative assembly, the people of the mother country, when by chance they think of the colonies, are led to suppose that the colonies are pretty well governed ; while, in truth, the governor's council is a most efficient means of misgovernment, since it enables his excellency to perform, or to authorize, acts of oppression, which he would never have dared to do, or authorize, on his own single responsibility.   If a governor of New South Wales should ever be called to account for acts of cruel oppression in that colony, those acts would be defended on the ground that they were approved by the council, an assembly consisting partly of settlers, having an interest in common with the whole body of colonists.   That would be the defence ; whereas the truth is, that the colonial members of the governor's council in New South Wales have been deeply interested in that misgovernment of which they shared the profits, in the shape of contracts, undue supplies of convict labour, and immense grants of land.   In Upper Canada, says Mr. Ellice,* "it was the fashion for every *counsellor* to get a grant of from 5,000 to 20,000 acres, to the great detriment of the country and the great nuisance of the inhabitants around."   This is only a sample of the numerous ways in which some of the inhabitants of subject colonies are bribed to lend their assistance in hurting the other inhabitants ; to lend their names to the strangers, so that the acts of those strangers may be glossed over with the semblance of being approved by the colonists ; to lend their voices, and in case of need, their arms, to the strangers, so that to the force of the strangers there may be added that of a strong colonial faction.   Hence more pillage than would have satisfied the strangers ; hence the most bitter feuds among the colonists themselves ; hence, more or less, the peculiar evils which Ireland has suffered by being governed from a distance through the instrumentality of a strong domestic faction.   The evil of having to obey laws made at a distance would be great, but less than the evils inflicted in order to procure obedience to laws so made.   The government of colonies from a distance involves both kinds of evil.

So much evil would never long be borne by a colony which had been founded, or which was extended in the way here proposed.   The colony being fit, would be able to govern itself.

* Now English minister at war.

It must be confessed, therefore, that the ruling class of an old country, looking only to immediate and selfish ends, has an interest in preventing systematic colonization : a double interest ; first, as for every colony fit to govern itself there would be less room for colonies liable to be governed from a distance ; secondly, as the example of systematic colonization and colonial self-government in one place, might lead to the systematic extension, and then to the self-government of colonies, which were founded, and have hitherto been extended, without any regard to the ends and means of colonization.   Here, perhaps, we may discover why, last year, the English government prevented the foundation of a colony which, in local matters, was to have governed itself as soon as the population should amount to 50,000 souls.

In this respect, the English have reason to be proud of the wisdom of their ancestors.   All the early colonies of the English were allowed to govern themselves from the beginning ; with this single exception, that the mother country reserved to herself a monopoly of the foreign trade of the colony.   In every case, the colonial laws were made by an assembly of colonists, elected by the colonists ; and in some cases those laws were executed by officers, including the governor, who were appointed by the colonists.   The charters, in a word, under which bodies of Englishmen planted colonies in America, laid the foundation of democracy in that part of the world.   At that time, the English ruling class had not discovered how to profit by the exercise of dominion over distant colonies.   No sooner, however, did the English take possession of colonies, which had been founded by other nations without any provision for local self-government, than the aristocracy of England found out the advantage of holding colonies in subjection.   This advantage became still more clear when the English government had made a settlement in New Holland ; had established a jail there ; a society, which, of course, could not be allowed to govern itself.

As to that colony, the system of transportation is a good excuse for withholding from the free settlers the advantage of self-government, and will be maintained on that account, as well as on account of its great expense, until the new ruling class of England shall please to exert their authority.   Well-informed as the English aristocracy now are of the many advantages to themselves attendant on holding colonies in subjection, they will always be ready with excuses for not reverting to the system of colonial self-government.   They seek to deny, that the system of governing colonies from Downing-street is a modern innovation.*

* See Correspondence in Appendix, No. 3.

Those English colonies which govern themselves in local matters, are distinguished by the name of *chartered colonies,* while the others are called *crown colonies.* The crown colonies, such as New South Wales, Van Dieman's Land, and South Africa, being governed in local matters from Downing-street, London, and affording a vast deal of patronage to the noblemen and gentlemen who live in that street, are most sincerely preferred by the English government. But, notwithstanding this partial affection for crown colonies, it is a fact, I believe, that never, till last year, did the English government refuse to bestow a charter of incorporation and local self-government upon individuals ready to found a colony at their own expense: it is a fact, also, that the only colony founded by Englishmen without such a charter is the miserable Swan River settlement, the last colony founded by Englishmen.

The chartered colonies of England, governing themselves from the beginning, in local matters, have usually defrayed the whole cost of their local government: the cost, on the contrary, of governing the crown colonies has generally fallen upon England. Here are two reasons against crown colonies: first, the expense which they occasion to the country whose rulers hold them in subjection; secondly, the absence of any motive in the government of the colony for letting the colonists be rich enough to bear taxation.

The difference between the cost of governing crown and chartered colonies is very much in favour of the latter. "All the different civil establishments in North America," says Adam Smith, " exclusive of Maryland and North Carolina, of which no exact account has been got, did not, before the commencement of the present disturbances, cost the inhabitants above 64,000*l.* a year ; an ever-memorable example at how small an expense three millions of people may not only be governed, but well governed." The yearly cost of governing fifty thousand people in New South Wales was lately about 234,000*l.*, the salaries of officers alone being 53,468*l.* ; an ever-memorable example at how great an expense a colony may be, not only governed, but very ill governed.* The crown colony of

* Specimen of the salaries in New South Wales.

Governor - - - - - - - -	4,200*l.*
Colonial Treasurer - - - - - -	1,000
Colonial Secretary and Registrar - - - - -	2,000
His compensation for loss of pension - - - -	750
Naval Officer - - - - - - - -	2,585
Chief Justice - - - - - - - -	2,000
Assistant Judge - - - - - - -	1,500
Ditto - - - - - - - - -	1,500
Attorney-general - - - - - - -	1,400
Sheriff and Provost Marshal - - - - -	1,000
Archdeacon - - - - - - - -	2,000
Surveyor-general - - - - - - -	1,000

the Swan River, with about fifteen hundred inhabitants, already costs England near 7000*l.* a year : the local government of the chartered colony, which it was proposed to found at Spencer's Gulf, was to have cost, not England, but the inhabitants, 5000*l.* a year, and no more, until the population should reach 50,000 souls. Chartered colonies, those which conduct and pay for their own local government, are sure to be very moderate in their public expenses ; while the expense of governing colonies from a distance is sure to be as great as the people of the ruling country, who find the money, will allow. The cheapness of local self-government is sure to present a striking contrast with the dearness of government from a distance ; a contrast painful to those who profit by governing colonies from a distance.

Of two other reasons in favour of local self-government, one is obvious ; the other requires some explanation. First, a body of colonists, who should manage their own affairs, in their own way, for their own advantage, would be sure to manage better than any foreign government, whether on the spot or at a distance ; the local government, unless very ill constituted, would have the deepest interest in the prosperity of the colony. But, secondly, the form and substance of the local government would very much depend upon the character of the first settlers. *Magna virûm mater !* exclaims Adam Smith, when he gives to England the credit of having furnished the men fit to establish empires in America. But would those superior men have quitted England for that purpose, without a prospect of self-government ? would such a man as William Penn have crossed the Atlantic, knowing that, when in America, he should be subject to a minister like Horace Twiss,* residing in England ? The greater number, it is true, of the founders of the United States fled from persecution ; but some of them did not ; and all of them may be supposed to have been moved, in part, by a sentiment of ambition. The founders of a colony, which is to be governed by the colonists, are sure to enjoy a greater degree of consideration and importance among their companions, than they could reasonably have hoped to attain in the old society. By the mere act of removing, they become legislators and statesmen ; the legislators and statesmen of a new country too, created, as it were, by themselves. In the charters, under which the old English colonies in America were planted, we find recited the names of the men who pro-

* This gentleman, Americans ought to be told, is an English barrister, practising in the courts of chancery and bankruptcy. The Duke of Wellington made him under-secretary of state for the colonies : he was concerned in the foundation of the Swan River settlement ; and spoke, first, against the reform bill in the House of Commons.

jected and accomplished those great undertakings. It was thus, that men of a superior order were induced to run the risk of failure in those enterprises ; men who, by their energy, judgment, patience, and resolution, were especially qualified to make those enterprises succeed.   As a colony fit to manage its own affairs would not submit to have them managed from a distance, so a colony allowed to manage its own affairs would attract men fit to manage them.   In the Swan River colony, which was founded by a minister, scarce any provision has been made for good government: in the plan of an intended colony at Spencer's Gulf, a plan formed by individuals, provision was carefully made for legislation, for the administration of justice, for the support of religion,* for the education of all classes, and for the defence of the colony.   This difference is explained by the difference between a crown colony and a chartered one.   In the latter case, the charter of incorporation and self-government attracted to the undertaking men of a superior order ; men knowing what they were about, having definite objects and a clear conception of the means for accomplishing them.   Would such men have gone to a crown colony ?   The answer is, that they would *not ;* for, when Lord Goderich wanted these men to go to the Swan River, they answered, that nothing would induce them to settle " in a colony where there is no security for the inestimable advantage of local self-government."

But, though it should be allowed, that new colonies founded by charter of incorporation, and local self-government, would put the mother country to no expense for their internal government, still an objection to new colonies, which rests on the necessity of protecting them from foreign violence, remains untouched.   That necessity would certainly exist in every case where the colony was unable to defend itself.   But colonies which governed themselves, have commonly been able to defend themselves.   The colonies of Greece were able, not

---

* The provision for the support of religion, suggested by persons of a very religious turn of mind, who intended to settle in the colony, was an article in the proposed charter, which declared that in this colony there should be no political church.   This provision led a number of dissenters to join the body of intended colonists.   The dissenters began to raise a subscription among themselves and their friends for building a church, in which their mode of worship was to be followed ; when the members of the Church of England, who intended to emigrate, immediately began to raise a subscription for establishing their mode of worship in the colony.   The present bishop of London, be it said to his honour, having been consulted about the Church of England subscription, found no fault with the provision against a political church, but engaged to assist the intended settlers of his persuasion in raising money for a church of their own.   Of course, however, both these incipient subscriptions fell to the ground, when Lord Goderich refused to grant the charter which his lordship had promised a year before.   See Correspondence in Appendix, No. 3.

only to defend themselves, but to assist their parent states in resisting foreign violence. The chartered colonies of North America were able to defend themselves against their mother country, when she had the folly to attack their local independence. Dependence teaches colonies to lean upon their mother country: independence from the beginning teaches them to provide for self-defence; not to mention that a colony which manages its own affairs has more, infinitely more, to defend than a colony whose affairs are shamefully managed from a distance. Thus, while at the Swan River no provision whatever has been made for self-defence, it was proposed by those who intended to found a colony at Spencer's Gulf, that the whole body of settlers should be formed into a militia; and as the sum of 125,000l. offered to the government for the first grant of land would have conveyed to the settlement about 4000 young couples, this colony would have had from the beginning an armed force of 4000 men; a greater force, perhaps, than was ever maintained by any mother country in any new colony. In that case, too, not only would colonization have proceeded with unexampled rapidity, but the colonists, instead of being enfeebled by dispersion, would always have been strong in proportion to their numbers. Accustomed to the use of arms, choosing their own leaders, defending the work of their own hands, which is the foreign government that would have thought it worth while to attack them? A subject colony may not be harmed, may be benefited, by a change of masters. Subject colonies accordingly have, over and over again, submitted to foreigners; but when did a colony, that flourished at all, and was independent from the beginning, yield up the main cause of its prosperity, its precious independence? Judging from past facts, we may conclude, that if the art of colonization were skilfully pursued, if colonies were independent, and were founded, or extended, so as to be, not new societies, but old societies in new places, the defence of them from foreign violence would not require any outlay by the mother country. Nay more, says Adam Smith, "they might be disposed to favour their mother country in *war* as well as in trade; and, instead of turbulent and factious subjects, to become her most faithful, affectionate, and generous allies; with the same parental affection on the one side, and the same filial respect on the other, which used to subsist between the colonies of ancient Greece and the mother city from which they descended."

Passing by the exploded notion, that an old country is interested in preserving a monopoly of the trade with her colonies, we have still to inquire whether it be advantageous to colonies to enjoy privileges in the market of their mother country.

Supposing that the monopoly of the English sugar-market, enjoyed by the planters of the West Indies, takes out of the pockets of the English, and puts into the pockets of the planters, 2,000,000*l*. a year, this would seem to be a case in which colonists gain by the sort of monopoly in question. In like manner, the Canadians appear to gain what the English lose, by the Canadian monopoly of the English timber trade. Nay, in the former case, the very existence of the colonists seems to depend on their monopoly of the English sugar-market; for every one allows that, if the English were permitted to buy sugar in the cheapest market they could anywhere find, there would soon be an end to the growth of sugar in the West Indies. But has not this monopoly, on which the existence of the colonists now depends, been the cause of that unnatural state of things, under which the monopoly is of such vast importance to the colonists? If the West Indians had never possessed any privilege in the market of England, it seems probable that, warned by the decrease of their profits, arising from the exhaustion of their land, they would have diverted their capital from the growth of sugar to some other employment : they might even, from the moment when sugar grown on virgin soils came into competition with their sugar, have seen that it was for their advantage to set free their slaves, so as to convert these human cattle into competitors for the use of land. One must say, perhaps; because it is doubtful whether slaves, very numerous in proportion to their masters of a different colour, can ever be set free without a period of anarchy. But, however this may be, what have the West Indies become with the monopoly? They have become, with and by means of the monopoly, societies so monstrously unnatural as to depend for their very existence on the patience of a distant people, who do not love them, in submitting to pay 2,000,000*l*. to keep their heads above water. In like manner, though we should acknowledge that the Canadians gain what the English lose by the difference between the price or quality of Canadian timber and Baltic timber in the English market, still the Canadian monopoly produces in Canada an unnatural state of things; artificially turning to the lumber trade more capital than would naturally be employed in it, and exposing the Canadians to be ruined by so proper an act on the part of the English government as that of letting the English people buy timber of whom they please. If colonies gain for a time by monopolizing some trade in the market of their mother country, their condition is unnatural and dangerous in proportion to their gains. Such a monopoly, if its continuance depended altogether on the colonists themselves, might perhaps be defended, as the American tariff may be defended, on the score of its tendency to promote combination of labour and division of employments among the colonists; but the continuance of such a monopoly must always depend upon the good pleasure of the mother country. For every colony, therefore, such monopolies are bad ; and bad just in proportion as they seem good. For colonies founded or extended so that the colonists should combine labour and divide employments, not only among themselves, but with the people of their mother country ; for colonies that should naturally raise exchangeable commodities, such monopolies or privileges would not even appear to be good. In the intended colony at Spencer's Gulf, accordingly, it was proposed that trade, both of import and export, should be entirely free. Port Lincoln was to have been a port without a custom-house. Is this why Lord Goderich, the eloquent advocate of free-trade, willed that it should remain without ships ?

For it must be confessed, that colonial monopolies of trade in the mother country are of very great use, indeed, for holding dependent colonies in subjection. A dependent colony, brought into an unnatural and dangerous state by such a monopoly, dares not to offend the rulers of its mother country. The colonists of South Africa with their wine monopoly, of Canada with their timber monopoly, and of the West Indies with their sugar monopoly, are far more subservient to Downing-street, than they would be if the people of England were free to buy wine, timber, and sugar in the cheapest markets they could anywhere find. In this way, the people of England pay magnificently to enable their rulers to profit in another way by the dependence of colonies. It would be much cheaper for the people of England, and quite as profitable to the English aristocracy, if, the colonies being left to themselves, a sum equal to the actual cost of holding and misgoverning them were placed at the disposal of the English cabinet, under the honest name of *a fund for Corruption.* Thus would all the cost of the monopolies be entirely saved, without any decrease of ministerial patronage. But then, it may be said, the corruption would be too plain to be borne. Doubtless ; and here is seen one " public inconvenience"* that might have arisen from the establishment of a colonial port without a custom-house ; the inconvenience of an example, which, if generally followed, would have taken from the English aristocracy one of their chief instruments for holding, harassing, and depressing colonial possessions.

* See Correspondence in the Appendix, No. 3

APPENDIX.

No. I.

SIR GEORGE STAUNTON, in his account of Lord Macartney's embassy, thus describes the Chinese emigrants at Batavia.

" Great numbers of Chinese come constantly to Batavia with exactly the same views that attract the natives of Holland to it—the desire of accumulating wealth in a foreign land. Both generally belonged to the humbler classes of life, and were bred in similar habits of industry in their own country : but the different circumstances that attend them after their arrival in Batavia put an end to any further resemblance between them. The Chinese have, there, no way of getting forward but by a continuance of their former exertions in a place where they are more liberally rewarded, and by a strict economy in the preservation of their gains. They have no chance of advancing by favour ; nor are public offices open to their ambition : but they apply to every industrious occupation, and obtain whatever care and labour can accomplish. They become, in town, retailers, clerks, and agents : in the country they are farmers, and the principal cultivators of the sugar-cane. They do, at length, acquire fortunes, which they value by the time and labour required to earn them. So gradual an acquisition makes no change in their disposition or mode of life. Their industry is not diminished, nor their health impaired.

*　*　*　*　*　*　*　*

" The Chinese are said to be now as numerous as ever again in and about Batavia ; for however imminent the danger to which the Dutch allege that they are exposed by the intended former insurrection of this people, and however cruel and unjustifiable the Chinese consider the conduct of the Dutch towards them at that time, the occasion they have for each other has brought them again together ; and it is acknowledged by the latter that the settlement could scarcely exist without the industry and ingenuity of the former."

In Mr. BARROW's Voyage to Cochin China the following passages occur :—

" The next description of inhabitants of Batavia, who in number and opulence exceeds the former, is the Chinese. These people, as appears by their records, first obtained a settlement in Java about the year 1412. As intruders, but not conquerors, it is probable that they have at all times been subject to harsh and oppressive treatment; but the restrictions and extortions under which they at present (1793) labour seem as unnecessary and impolitic as they are unjust. That they should consent to the Mahomedans, Malays, and Javanese exercising their devotions in the same temple, which they built at their own expense, and consecrated to the god of their own worship, is by no means an unfavourable feature in their character; but on the part of the Dutch, who enforce the measure, it is one of the greatest insults that could well be offered. The Chinese hospital or infirmary, which was erected by voluntary contributions from their own community, and is supported by legacies arising from theatrical exhibitions and fireworks, and by a small tax on marriages, funerals, and the celebration of public festivals, is equally open for the benefit and reception of those who have not contributed towards the establishment, and who do not belong to the society. Into this admirable institution are indiscriminately admitted the infirm and the aged, the friendless and the indigent, of all nations. Towards the support of those institutions, the temple and the infirmary, their contributions are voluntary; but exclusive of these, their industry is severely taxed by the Dutch government. Every religious festival and public ceremony, every popular amusement, as well as every branch of individual industry, are subject to taxation. They are even obliged to pay for a license to wear their hair in a long plaited tail, according to the custom of their country; for permission to bring their greens to market, and to sell their produce and manufactures in the streets. *Yet to the industry and exertions of those people are the Dutch wholly indebted for the means of existing with any tolerable degree of comfort in Batavia.* Every species of vegetable for the table is raised by them in all seasons of the year, and *at times when the most indefatigable attention and labour are required.* They are masons, carpenters, blacksmiths, painters, upholsterers, tailors, and shoemakers. They are employed in the arts of *distilling, sugar-refining, pottery, lime-burning, and every other trade and profession that is indispensably necessary for making the state of civilized society tolerably comfortable.* They are, moreover, the contractors for supplying the various demands of the civil, military, and marine establishments in the settlement; they are the collectors of the rates, the customs, and the taxes; and, in short, are *the monopolizers of the interior commerce of the island; and, with the Malays, carry on the principal part of the coasting trade.*

" The influence which would naturally follow from the management of concerns so important and so extensive could not long be regarded by a weak and luxurious government without jealousy. Those arts which the Europeans have usually followed with success in establishing themselves in foreign countries, and which the Dutch have not been backward in carefully studying and effectually carrying into practice, with regard to the natives of Java, could not be applied with the least hope of success to the Chinese settlers. These people had no sovereign to dethrone, by opposing to him the claims of a usurper ; nor did the separate interests of any petty chief allow them, by exciting jealousy, to put in execution the old adage of *divide et impera*,—divide and command. With as little hope of success could the masters of the island venture to seduce an industrious and abstemious people from their temperate habits by the temptation of foreign luxuries ; and their general disposition to sobriety held out no encouragement for the importation of spirituous liquors and intoxicating drugs. For, though the Chinese who are in circumstances to afford it make use of opium to excess, yet this is a luxury in which the common people of this nation rarely think of indulging. The Dutch, therefore, who are weak in point of numbers, had recourse to a more decisive and speedy measure for getting rid of a redundancy of population, which had begun to create suspicion and alarm : they put them to the sword.

*　　　*　　　*　　　*　　　*　　　*

" This extraordinary affair took place on the 9th of October ; the whole of the 10th was a day of plunder ; and on the 11th they began to remove out of the streets the dead bodies, the interment of which occupied them eight days. The number said to have perished, according to the Dutch account, amounts to more than twelve thousand souls. Having thus completed one of the most inhuman and apparently causeless transactions that ever disgraced a civilized people, they had the audacity to proclaim a public thanksgiving to the God of Mercy for their happy deliverance from the hands of the heathen. While the Dutch, in their public records, endeavour to justify this atrocious act on the plea of necessity, they make the following memorable observation :—' It is remarkable that this people, notwithstanding their great numbers, offered not the least resistance, but suffered themselves to be led like sheep to the slaughter !' For my own part, when I reflect on the timid character of the Chinese, their want of confidence in each other, and their strong aversion to the shedding of human blood : and when I compare their situation in Batavia to that of the Hottentot in the colony of the Cape of Good Hope, where every little irregularity is magnified into a plot against the government, I cannot forbear giving a decided opinion that these people were innocently murdered. The consequences to the Dutch proved much more serious than at first they seemed to have been aware of. The terrified Chinese, who escaped the massacre, fled into the interior of the island ; a scarcity of rice and every kind of vegetables, succeeded ; and the apprehensions of a famine induced them to offer terms to the fugitives, and to entreat their return."

Sir Stamford Raffles, in his History of Java, writes as follows :

" Besides the natives, whose number, circumstances, and character I have slightly mentioned, there is in Java a rapidly-increasing race of foreigners, who have emigrated from the different surrounding countries. The most numerous and important class of these is the Chinese, who already (1815) do not fall short of a hundred thousand ; and who, with a system of free trade, and free cultivation, would soon accumulate tenfold, by natural increase within the island and gradual accessions of new settlers from home. They reside principally in the great capitals of Batavia, Semárang, and Surabáya, but they are to be found in all the smaller capitals, and scattered over most parts of the country. A great proportion of them are descended from families who have been many generations on the island ;—additions are gradually making to their numbers. They arrive at Batavia from China to the amount of a thousand or more annually, in Chinese junks, carrying three, four, and five hundred each, without money or resources ; but by dint of their industry soon acquire comparative opulence. There are no women in Java who come directly from China, but as the Chinese often marry the daughters of their countrymen by Javan women, there results a numerous mixed race which is often scarcely distinguishable from the native Chinese."

Mr. FINLAYSON, in his account of the mission to Siam Hué, in 1822, speaks as follows of the Chinese emigrants at Penang and Sincapore.

" We had not proceeded far (at Penang) before a more interesting and gratifying scene was expanded to our observation. Industry, active, useful, manly, and independent, seemed here to have found a congenial soil and fostering care. The indolent air of the Asiatic was thrown aside. Every one laboured to produce some useful object, and every countenance teeming with animation, seemed, as it were, directed to a set task. With the air, they had lost even the slender frame of the Asiatic ; and the limbs, and muscularity, and symmetry were those of another and more energetic race. These were Chinese, a people highly valuable as settlers, by reason of their industrious and regular habits, who had established on this spot the mechanical arts, on a scale which might even vie with that of the European artists, but which we look for in vain in any other part of India. It was a pleasing and gratifying spectacle—so much are we in India accustomed to the opposite—to see a numerous, very muscular, and apparently hardy race of people, labouring with a degree of energy and acuteness, which gave to their physical character a peculiar stamp, and placed them in a highly favourable point of view, when compared with the habits of the nation around them. Their manner of using their instruments, so different from the puerile style of Indian artists, had in it much of the dexterity of the Europeans : while their condition bespoke them a flourishing and wealthy tribe. All the principal shops, all important and useful employments, and *almost all the commerce of the island*, were in their hands. Under the patronage of the British government they soon acquire riches ; they meet with entire protection of property and person, and are cherished by the government, which, in return, derives benefits from their industry, and from the commercial and profitable speculations in which they usually engage.

  *   *   *   *   *   *   *

" The neatness, the industry, and the ingenuity displayed in plantations of this sort (at Sincapore) afford a very gratifying spectacle, and attest the great progress wh'ch the Chinese nation has made in agricultural science. The Chinese may be considered as the sole cultivators of the soil.

* * * * * * *

"The most prominent feature in the character of the Chinese emigrant, is industry: the best and highest endowment which he has attained. He is mechanically uniform and steady in the pursuit of what he conceives to be his immediate and personal interest, in the prosecution of which he exerts a degree of ingenuity and of bodily labour and exertion, which leave all the Asiatics at a distance. He labours with a strong arm, and is capable of great and continued exertion. He is not satisfied to bestow the quantity of labour necessary for the mere gratification of his immediate wants. Profusion and indulgence claim a share of the produce of his toils. Next in the catalogue of his virtues may be reckoned general sobriety, honesty, a quiet, orderly conduct, obedience to the laws of the country in which he resides; and, as is affirmed, a strong and unalterable sense of the important duties which parental affection inculcates.

* * * * * * *

"It must be confessed, however, that the Chinese are, in a political point of view at least, by far the most useful class of people to be found in the Indian seas or Archipelago. Their robust frames, their industrious habits, and their moderate conduct place them beyond competition. They furnish the best artizans, the most useful labourers, and the most extensive traders. Their commercial speculations are often extensive, and often of the most adventurous nature."

Mr. DOBELL, who resided in China for several years, and whose lately-published account of that country abounds with valuable information, says—

" The reader must excuse this digression on the subject of the Chinese foreign commerce, as many have asserted China to be a country wholly agricultural and manufacturing, while real experience proves the contrary. After giving this imperfect account of it, which might have been extended to a volume, and given more in detail, no one will, I think, believe that the Chinese are locked up at home. It may, indeed, be safely asserted, that they are one of the most commercial nations of the globe."*

The above descriptions of the Chinese people are confirmed by several witnesses before the select committee on the affairs of the East India Company ; from whose evidence the following statements are extracted.

Captain CHARLES HUTOHINSON, a commander in the navy, who commanded the Bombay Castle, from Liverpool, and went to India ; and remained there five years.

* Residence in China, vol. ii. page 159.

" As you were three times at Canton engaged in those transactions of commerce, what should you say, from your opportunities of observing the character and habits of the people of China, as to their disposition with respect to intercourse with other countries and carrying on trade generally ?—They have a very great avidity to trade with everybody they are permitted to trade with.　The merchants of China are extremely eager to trade with every one that comes into the country ; more so than any people I have seen.

" Do you mean to say that they are a speculative, trading, enterprising country ?—Very much so ; beyond any other I have seen.

" Should you think it is a just distinction, speaking of the Chinese nation, to say that the people are speculative, and much disposed to foreign trade, although the government is professedly adverse to communication with foreigners ?—Yes, certainly ; the government may be said to be so far adverse to trade, that it is jealous of you, knowing what you have done in India, and it is apprehensive of your intrusion ; but so long as they may be secure that nothing else would be attempted, they are as desirous of carrying on the trade as the people themselves.

" Did you happen to hear whether the British manufacturers found their way into the interior of China, or whether they were confined to districts adjacent to Canton ?—They find their way into the interior, so far as the carriage of them will allow without rendering them too dear.　They are very desirous of obtaining them, I understand, in all parts of China, particularly in many northern districts, where they require the woollens for warm clothing.

" Do you think that if there were an open trade, the Chinese would consume British cotton manufactures to any great extent ?—The Chinese admitting them only at one port, of course the consumption could not be extended so far as if they were admitted at other ports, but as far as they could be carried with advantage, the Chinese would be glad to buy them and use them."

Mr. CHARLES EVERETT, a commission merchant, who was engaged for eleven years, since the year 1818, in purchasing goods for the China market, on account of American merchants.

" Have you any doubt, from the experience you have had, that if the existing restrictions were removed, the trade to China in British manufactures might be materially increased ?—I have no doubt the trade might be increased to a considerable extent by proper management, if the restrictions were removed."

JOSHUA BATES, ESQ., an American ; agent for an American house connected with the East India trade ; then partner of the firm of J. Bates and John Baring, and lastly, partner of the house of Baring, Brothers and Co.; both of which houses had the management of the business of an American house particularly connected with the China trade.

" You have expressed an opinion, that in the event of the China trade being thrown open, it would probably centre in this country ;

would that arise from cheaper purchases of tea, or from cheaper supplies in this country, or from cheaper shipping being engaged, or from what other cause?—There would be a great export of manufactures to those regions, and of course something would be wanted for returns. They would bring back teas, and every description of produce they could find in those countries ; and not only would they bring back such, but perhaps increase them by the very act of carrying manufactures, as many of the inhabitants of those countries, who have hitherto not laboured at all, seeing such beautiful things brought out from this country, would be desirous of possessing them, and proceed to labour to get something to buy them with ; and this course of trade would bring, perhaps, more tea here than is wanted ; and the price being reduced, it would either be bought for smuggling into the continent, or for exporting to those places to which it would go legally.

" Do you consider the trade in China susceptible of any great increased stimulus ?—I see nothing to prevent it increasing very much."

Mr. JOHN DEANS, a resident in the Eastern Archipelago for twenty years.

" What is their (the Chinese people) character as traders, speaking generally ?—They are keen, enterprising traders, extremely expert in their dealings, and understand the nature of the trade of those countries in which they are settled, perhaps better than any other people.

" Have they information that enables them to carry on their commercial transactions with advantage ?—They seem to have very accurate information, and receive it very quickly too.

" What is their character as merchants, with reference to the punctuality of their dealings and the mode of transacting business ?—Those who have obtained a high reputation are extremely tenacious of it, and they are very punctual in all their dealings.

" Do they appear to possess more or less of the characteristics which are requisite for the business of a merchant than the natives of other oriental countries ?—I do not think they are exceeded by the natives of any country as a commercial people.

" Do you include European countries ?—I do.

" Is it difficult to transact business with them ?—Not the least ; —I have never had any difficulty with the Chinese.

" Have you, in point of fact, transacted much business with them ? —I have, very extensive business.

" Will you state what that business was ?—I imported largely British manufactures to Java, and the medium of communication with the natives was generally through the Chinese, who purchased from me in whole cases or bales, and retailed to natives, giving me their simple notes of hand for payment, and being always punctual in meeting those demands.

" Have you any reason to form an opinion whether the taste for European manufactures which exists among the Chinese inhabitants of Java, is peculiar to them, or whether it extends also to the inhabitants of the empire itself?—I cannot exactly state this ; the settlers are Chinese ; their habits are the same in the Archipelago as in their native country, I believe, and they readily adopt our manufactures in preference to their own, when those are cheaper and better. When I first went to Java, in 1811, they were almost exclusively clothed in Chinese manufactures, and I witnessed a revolution, which almost clothed them in European manufactures, during the time I was there.

" Have you reason to know in what light the European imports into China are considered by the Chinese people, or whether they could easily be dispensed with by them ?—I know that the imports to China are of far more importance to that empire than perhaps the tea is to this country, great as it is considered.

" Can you state to the committee any instance of the discovery of a new article, or the extension of the production of an old one, which has added to the value of the imports into China ?—I can state one, perhaps not of great importance, but it would show that there are many others with respect to which the same thing might be done. The large glasses or rummers which are used in their houses for burning a light before their gods, opposite their front door ; I noticed them on one occasion as being made of imperfect China-glass. I asked the Chinese if they would have any objection to British manufacture, if the same patterns were preserved, and they gave me patterns of them, which I brought home, and had manufactured at Birmingham. I took them out, and had them sold for a considerable price, and they have since continued to be supplied from different places to a great extent.

Mr. John Argyle Maxwell.

" Supposing the trade in tea to be thrown open, do you conceive that tea might be imported into Sincapore of a quality fit for the European market, and in sufficient quantity ?—I have no ground for speaking positively on that subject : but several of the Chinese there have frequently offered to contract with me for the supply of black teas from Fokien.

Robert Rickards, Esq.

" Have you had any communication or information enabling you to form an opinion of the anxiety of the Chinese to extend their trade ?—I believe that the Chinese are a perfectly commercial people. Wherever the Chinese have been established in Sincapore, in Java, in Borneo, and in the other eastern islands where they are settled in great numbers, they are found to be the principal traders, and the most industrious people in the country. I therefore take the Chinese, generally speaking, to be a perfectly commercial people, and exceedingly anxious to extend their commercial dealings, in spite of any restrictive regulations that may be imposed upon them by the Chinese government.

" Have you had any specific examples brought to your notice of the desire on the part of the Chinese, in other ports than Canton, to open a communication with English merchants?—Yes. I have in my possession an extract of a letter from a European merchant who had visited China, to his friend and correspondent in Calcutta. It is dated Canton, 19th September, 1823; and the extract is as follows:

" ' The Manilla people only are allowed liberty to trade with Amoy, which would have been granted to us could we have waited. A mandarin followed us *seven miles from the port of Amoy, to entreat our return,* which however our plans would not admit of. We experienced civil treatment, even from mandarins of rank, and the complaisance of the inhabitants generally formed an agreeable contrast to the haughty demeanour of the lowest here (Canton). The single circumstance of foreigners not being denied women (as they are most rigidly here, Canton) speaks volumes. No foreigner is allowed to remain after the departure of his ship. As far as we could learn, no charge similar to measurement-duty is levied on foreign ships. The government revenue is derived from an export-duty, which the foreigner pays on his export cargo; but this duty appears to be not fixed: and I suspect the injudiciousness of the mandarins in increasing it beyond bounds, is the cause of the discontinuance of the trade by the Manilla people. It is probable that, with a view to bring it back, the mandarins would now be more reasonable. They seem to say, that the Hong merchants of Amoy are pretty much in the bankrupt situation of those here (Canton). They inquired much the most for the articles from the eastern isles imported in their junks; and also for rice, *for which they rely mainly on Formosa;* but we could form no idea of the price to be obtained for them. The prices of the European articles we saw in the shops were not so much above the Canton rates as was to be expected. I am very keen for an adventure to Amoy, for the purpose of opening new channels for opium in that quarter, the chief mart of its consumption; but it is too weighty a concern for us to undertake singly; and I have contented myself with writing to Manilla for information, and with sounding our friends there on the subject. As you have already adventured in a Chinese bottom, you will, I hope, give a lift to our plans also. The foreign trade in junks is not contraband in China, since the accession of the present family (about 1660). It is *connived at by the government, and is, I believe, even licensed at Amoy.* I do not see why a junk could not load goods at Amoy or elsewhere, as if for a foreign port (Manilla, Batavia, &c.), and afterward trans-ship them to a foreign vessel waiting in the neighbourhood.' "

John Crawfurd, Esq.

" From your intercourse with those Chinese, do you conceive them to be an intelligent, active, and commercial people?—Eminently so. They are a very industrious people in every way; they are a business-like people; their manners more resemble Europeans in that part of their character than they do those of Asiatic nations.

" In industry and intelligence do you conceive them to be superior to other Asiatic nations ?—For all useful and practical purposes I think they are. There are perhaps a few points in which they are inferior to one or two other Asiatic nations, but those points are of very little moment."

John Stewart, Esq. a Member of the Committee.

" Will you state what opinion you have formed of them as a commercial people, or an anti-commercial people ?—From the intercourse I have had with the Chinese at Canton, I certainly consider them a people of very great commercial enterprise, although I believe the policy of the Chinese is against extending the foreign commerce of the country."

Captain John Mackie.

" Are you of opinion that the Chinese in the places you visited are anxious for the extension of commerce ?—I should conceive that they were, because *I have always found the Chinese inclined to buy any thing that was at all useful, of any description.*

" You conceive them to be any thing but an anti-commercial people ?—I should consider them to be quite otherwise."

John Francis Davies, Esq.

" The Chinese, if left by their rulers to themselves, would perhaps be the most industrious people in the world."

Mr. Crawfurd's Statement.

(Extracted from the Third Report of the Select Committee on the Affairs of the East India Company.)

" Have you prepared a statement for the information of the committee upon the subject of the Chinese emigrations ?—I have.

" Will you have the goodness to read it ?"

(The witness then read the same, as follows :)

" A view of the Emigrations of the Chinese to the various countries adjacent to China.

" The emigrations of the Chinese take place from the same provinces which conduct the foreign trade ; viz. Canton, Fokien, Chekien, and Kiannan. Emigrations from the two latter, however, are not frequent, and seem to be confined to Tonquin and the Philippine Islands. The emigrants direct their course to every country in the neighbourhood of China where there is any probability of finding employment and protection ; in some countries, however, they are excluded or restrained, from political motives, and in others, distance or want of room affords them no encouragement to settle. Like the European nations, they are excluded altogether from settling in Japan, on political grounds ; the government of Cochin China also affords them no great encouragement, from the same reason, and the Dutch and Spanish governments of Java and the Philippines have always looked upon them with a considerable share of suspicion.

Distance, but above all, the existence of a dense and comparatively industrious population, excludes them from the British dominions in Hindostan, where we find only a few shoemakers and other artisans, and these confined to Calcutta, Madras, and Bombay. A few, I understand, have lately proceeded to the Mauritius.

" Every emigrant who leaves China does so with the intention of returning to it, although comparatively few are able to accomplish this object. The expense of emigration to the countries to which the Chinese usually resort, amounts to but a mere trifle. The passage-money in a Chinese junk from Canton to Sincapore is but six Spanish dollars ; and from Fokien but nine. Even these slender sums, however, are commonly paid from the fruits of the emigrant's labour on his arrival, and are seldom paid in advance. The emigrants, I think, are invariably of the labouring classes, and their whole equipment for the voyage in ordinary cases consists of little else than the coat on their backs, a bundle of old clothes, and a dirty mat and pillow to sleep on. They no sooner land than their condition is prodigiously improved ; they meet their countrymen, and probably their friends or relatives ; they find immediate employment in a congenial climate, and in countries where the wages of labour are perhaps three times as high as in China, and the necessaries of life perhaps by one-half cheaper.

" The Chinese are not only intellectually, but physically superior to the nations and tribes among whom they settle. A Chinese is at least two inches taller than a Siamese, and by three inches taller than a Cochin Chinese, a Malay, or a Javanese ; and his frame is proportionably strong and well built. Their superiority in personal skill, dexterity, and ingenuity is still greater. All this is evinced in a very satisfactory manner, by the simple criterion of the comparative rates of wages of the different classes of inhabitants or sojourners at any given place where they all meet. At Sincapore, for example, the wages of ordinary labour for the different classes of labourers are as follow : A Chinese, eight dollars a month ; a native of the Coromandel coast, six dollars ; and a Malay, four ; making the work of the Chinese by one-third better than that of the first, and by 100 per cent. better than that of the second. When skill and dexterity are implied, the difference is of course wider ; a Chinese house-carpenter will earn twelve dollars a month, while an Indian will earn no more than seven ; and a Malayan thatcher or wood-cutter, for among this class there are no carpenters, but five.

" The different classes of Chinese settlers not only live apart, and keep distinct from the settlers of other nations, but also from each other. There is a very wide difference between the character, habits, and manners of the Chinese settlers, according to the parts of China from which they proceed. The natives of Fokien have a claim to a higher tone of character than any of the rest. Among the emigrants from the province of Canton there are three classes ; viz. those from the town of Canton and its neighbourhood ; the natives of Macao and other islands in the river ; and the natives of some mountainous districts of the same province. The first of these, besides being addicted to mercantile pursuits, are the best artisans, and are much disposed to enter into mining speculations. It is they who are chiefly engaged in working the silver mines of Tonquin, the gold mines of Borneo, and the Malay peninsula, and the tin mines of the latter country and of Banca. The Chinese of Macao and the other islands are held in very little repute among the rest of their countrymen; but the third class, who are numerous, are the lowest in rank. Their most frequent employment is that of fishermen and mariners; and it is from among their ranks that the European shipping, when in want, have occasionally received hands to assist in their navigation. Of all the Chinese these are the most noisy and unruly. There is still another class of Chinese, the settlers in the Birman dominions, who differ very remarkably from all that I have just enumerated. With the exception of a small number of emigrants from the province of Canton, who find their way to Ava by sea, they are all from the province of Yunan, and in point of industry and intelligence seemed, as far as I could judge, much superior to the colonists from Canton and Fokien. From all these again, the mixed races are to be distinguished by their superior knowledge of the language, manners, and customs of the countries in which they reside, and by some inferiority in industry and enterprise. It is from this class that European merchants are supplied with brokers, money-counters, &c. and they are seldom to be seen in the condition of day-labourers or artisans. The Chinese settlers, of whatever class, engage with much eagerness in agricultural employments, seldom, however, when they can avoid it, as mere day-labourers. They conduct almost exclusively the cultivation and manufacture of the catechu or terra-japonica in the Straits of Malacca, the pepper cultivation of Siam, and the culture of the cane and manufacture of sugar in Java, Siam, and the Philippines. Differing materially from each other in manners, habits, and almost always in language or dialect, and entertaining towards each other provincial prejudices and antipathies; broils and quarrels, sometimes even attended with bloodshed, frequently break out among them. These are occasionally subjects of embarrassment in the European settlements, the authorities of which have never, I am persuaded, any thing to apprehend from their combination or resistance; and I may add, that of all the Asiatic settlers in our eastern settlements, the Chinese are most obedient to the laws, and notwithstanding the superior amount of their property, and even of their numbers, afford the least employment to the courts of justice.

"The Chinese population settled in the various countries adjacent to China, may be roughly estimated as follows:—

The Philippine islands - - -	15,000
Borneo - - - - - -	120,000
Java - - - - - -	45,000
The Dutch settlement of Rhio, Straits of	
Malacca - - - - -	18,000
Singapore - - - - -	6,200

Malacca	-	-	-	-	-	2,000
Penang	-	-	-	-	-	8,500
Malayan Peninsula	-	-	-	-	40,000
Siam	-	-	-	-	-	440,000
Cochin China	-	-	-	-	14,000
Tonquin	-	-	-	-	-	25,000
	Total	-	-	-	734,700

" The population mentioned here is of a peculiar description, con-sisting, for the most part, of adult males, and of very few women or children, a circumstance easily explained. The laws of China, which prohibit emigration in general, *are a dead letter*, as far as the men are concerned, but it is imperative with respect to women and children, or perhaps, more strictly, *the manners and feelings of the people themselves* prevent the latter from quitting the country. I have never seen or heard of a female among the emigrants, and never saw a Chinese woman, except at Hué, the capital of Cochin China, where two or three were pointed out to me as objects of curiosity, who had been kidnapped and brought there when children. The emigrants however, without scruple, form connexions with the females of the country, and the descendants of these repeatedly intermarrying with Chinese, are in time not to be distinguished from the genuine Chinese either in features or complexion. In all the countries where the Chinese have been established, there exists a considerable creole population of this description, such as Java, Siam, Cochin China, and the Philippines. But in countries where they have been only recently established, the disproportion of the sex is immense. Thus, out of the 6,200 Chinese inhabitants of Sincapore, the number of females is about 360, and even of these the greater part are Chinese only by name. The extent of the annual emigrations from China may be judged from the fact, that the number which arrived at Sin-capore in 1825 amounted to above 3,500 ; and in 1826, to upwards of 5,500. The annual number of emigrants which arrived in Siam, was rated to me, when I was in that country, at 7,000. A single junk has been known to bring 1,200 passengers ; indeed, I have my-self seen one bring 900 to Sincapore. The number who return to China is considerable, but very small indeed in comparison to the arrivals. Even of these the greater number come back again; and I have known men of property, who have visited China, and returned with titles."

No. II.

PROOFS OF THE RAPIDITY WITH WHICH WASTE LAND RISES IN
VALUE, WHEREVER PEOPLE CONGREGATE, IN NEW COLONIES.

Mr. Stuart.

" The population of Troy has increased from 3,000 in 1810, to
12,000 in 1830. Property is very valuable. A tenement 65 feet
by 25 feet, was pointed out to me as having been lately sold for
4,000 dollars."

" Mr. Sloat has lately sold 200 acres of wood-land (near New-
burg on the Hudson), which he bought from the state in 1801 for
50 cents the acre, at an immense advance."

" Colonel Colman gives a very favourable account of Florida,
where the soil is good by the river side. He himself has purchased
900 acres on the banks of the Apalachicola, all of excellent land,
for which he paid 9,000 dollars."

(On the Mississippi about 300 miles from New Orleans) " we
had excellent buttermilk at one of our *stopping places* for wood,
occupied by a tenant, who pays 4 dollars an acre of yearly rent for
a few acres of ground."

" In many places on the banks of the Ohio, a great deal of fine
alluvial land, which, I was informed, sold for 10 or 12 dollars per
acre."

" Large fortunes have been made (at Rochester, which in 1818
contained 1,000 inhabitants, and in 1828, 13,000) by the purchase
and sale of building lots."

"A million of acres, which are rapidly increasing in value."

" The appropriation of land for schools, many of which have
become very valuable."

" Real property of all kinds at New-York brings great prices.
The *site* of a house, at the corner of two central streets, 29 feet in
one street and 130 in the other, was lately sold for 38,100
dollars."

" To those who would purchase land *with a view to profit*, I would
rather recommend the banks of the Hudson, within 30 or 50 miles
of New York, where the farmers have succeeded in establishing
steamboats, to carry their produce *daily to the city*."

" It may, however, be worth while to mention, that plenty of improved land is to be had in the neighbourhood of Cincinnati, varying in price *according to its distance from the town*."

" In fact, the extent of country which the United States have
acquired since the treaty of 1783, far exceeds three hundred millions
of acres in the very heart of their territory, besides the boundless
regions to the north and north-west. A great proportion of this prodigious extent of land remains with the general government, and

must in the course of years produce to the United States *some thousand millions of dollars.*"*

THE REVEREND J. FIDLER,

Author of Observations on the United States and Canada.

" The value of land in Canada is increasing regularly and rapidly. For instance, Younge-street was settled thirty-seven years ago. At that time land on it was given to any one who applied. A few years after land was worth from fifty to one hundred dollars. A lot of about two hundred acres is now worth from 1,000l. to 2,000l. on many parts of Younge-street. In the beautiful township of Oro, *lately settled;* land a short time ago was one dollar per acre : it is now worth from four to five, and increases in value from half a dollar to a dollar every year. On the Huron tract, it is now selling at from one to two dollars. Emigration is setting in that way ; and the probable consequence will be that land there, in two or three years, will be double that sum. Land has generally been found to double itself every three or four years."

" In the towns of Kingston, Brockville, &c. land is almost as high as in many parts of England ; while at a small distance from these towns it can be purchased, usually good, at two or three dollars. In York-town, an acre is sometimes worth 1,000l. or 1,200l. A little remove from this, uncleared land is worth six or eight dollars ; and a few miles further off, not perhaps above two dollars. If railroads be formed, plans of which have been laid before the legislature, and acts passed to legalize them, the land now selling at two dollars would soon be worth 10l.

Communicated by MR. CATTERMOLE, *of York, Upper Canada, and published in an Account of the South Australian Land Company.*

" When the town of York was founded, much of the contiguous land was given away to favourites, who expected that the increase of population by natural means, and by immigration, would give it value. They have not been disappointed. A person named Elmsley possessed some of this land, and when King's College was founded, the site (about five acres) was purchased by government of Mr. Elmsley for 1,200l. Fifteen years previously, this land would not have sold for two dollars per acre."

" Mr. John Masson, a tinman, living in King-street, York, took in 1830, a lease for 21 years, of a piece of land in York, measuring 23 feet in front by 80 feet deep, at a ground rent of 17l. 10s. currency, per annum ; and on 40 feet being added to the depth, the ground rent was raised to 22l. per annum. Fifteen years before, this land would not have sold for more than three or four dollars per acre."

" Mr. Francis Collins, editor of the Canadian Freeman, purchased by public auction in July, 1831, a quarter of an acre of waste land in York for 600l. currency."

* Say one thousand millions of pounds sterling ; or more, by a fourth, than the English national debt.

" Mr. M'Cullum sold in July, 1831, a village lot, situated on Dundas-street, nineteen miles from York, at the rate of 300*l.* per acre of currency."

" In the last seventeen years, the land within fourteen miles of the Erie canal has risen from twenty-five cents (quarter of a dollar) to sixteen dollars."

MR. PICKERING (late of Fenny Stratford),

Author of the Emigrant's Guide to Canada, 1830.

"Been to ask the price of land to rent (near Baltimore, U. S.). One lot of fifty acres, only half cleared, four miles from town, eighteen shillings per acre per annum : another of rich meadow land, several miles off, near the river, I was asked twelve dollars or 2*l.* 14*s.* per acre rent."

" Building lots of land (in York), within the last year or two, have risen in value very fast, on account of the seat of government being decided to remain here for some years to come."

" Niagara to Queen's-town, and indeed round the head of the lake to Dundas, Ancaster, and Hamilton, a fine country, genial air, healthy, well watered and settled, land is from thirty shillings to 4*l.* 16*s.* per acre."

" Farms sell here (on the banks of the Detroit river) from forty-five shillings to 3*l.* 10*s.* per acre : a house and some buildings included."

MR. WENTWORTH (of New South Wales),

Author of an Account of Australasia. 1823.

" The price of land, it is almost needless to observe, is entirely regulated by its situation and quality.   In the towns, it is as various as in the country ; nor is there any place in which the variation in value is so great as in the town of Sydney itself.   There it ranges from 50*l.* an acre to 1,000*l.*"

"With respect to the value of what is termed forest land, when in a state of nature, and not possessing any advantageous locality, it may generally be taken thus : In the county of Cumberland" (the county in which Sydney is placed), "fifteen shillings per acre ; in the county of Camden, including the district of Illawarra, or Five Islands" (farther from market), " ten shillings per acre ; on the banks of the Coal River" (still farther from market), " five shillings per acre : in parts more remote, two shillings and sixpence per acre."

" In the course of thirty years, the tract of land in question (the banks of the Hawkesbury), taking the unimproved land as our criterion, has evidently risen to this enormous price from having been of no value whatever ; or, in other words, each acre of land has increased in value, during the interval which has elapsed since the foundation of the colony, at the rate of three shillings and 2½*d.* per annum ; and that too, under the most impolitic and oppressive system (of government) to which any colony perhaps was ever subjected."

Mr. Boucher (of New South Wales),

Communicated to Mr. Robert Gouger.

"In the year 1831, Mr. Wentworth sold near two acres of land, situated in the main street, and near the king's wharf custom-house, Sydney, for 7,800*l.*, the whole of which, ten years previously, might have been bought for 350*l.*"

"In 1828, Mr. Unwins bought six acres of land on the Surrey Hills, about one mile from Sydney, for 650*l.* ; and in 1830 the same land was resold for 1,800*l.*"

"In 1829, Mr. Bettington purchased a piece of land situated at Cockle Bay, Sydney, comprising a frontage of about one hundred and fifty feet, and a depth of about two hundred feet, adapted for a wharf, &c. for 609*l.* This land in 1831 would have realized, exclusive of the buildings, about 2,000*l.*"

"In 1830, Mr. Simeon Lord received from the local government 6,000*l.* as an arbitration award for about two acres of land situated near Government House, Sydney. He would gladly have sold it ten years previously for 250*l.* or 300*l.*"

"Early in 1828, Madame Rens bought at auction a piece of ground in the main street of Sydney, on the site of the old Orphan School, comprising a frontage of one hundred and fifty feet, and depth of eighty feet, for 1,200*l.* ; and in 1829 sold *half* of the same plot to Mr. Horton James for 1,800*l.*"

"In the latter end of 1827, Messrs. Cooper and Levey purchased from Captain Piper, for 25,000*l.* the estate of Point Piper, situated four miles from Sydney town. This estate consisted of five hundred acres of land, having an extensive frontage to part of Sydney harbour, with a large house, pleasure-grounds, &c. It would now readily fetch 150,000*l.*, if divided into allotments of two or three acres each (for villas), and sold by auction at a moderate credit."

"Building allotments in Sydney town, in a fair situation, comprising a frontage of sixty feet and a depth of eighty feet, could be readily purchased in 1825 for from 70*l.* to 150*l.* In 1830 they usually brought at auction from 600*l.* to 1,500*l.*, according to their situation."

"On the Paramatta road, at from two to five miles from Sydney, land, having a frontage to the road, could be purchased in 1825 for 5*l.* to 12*l.* per acre: it now fetches from 30*l.* to 150*l.* per acre."

"On the South Head Road, at from one to three miles from Sydney, similar land could have been bought for 3*l.* to 10*l.* per acre: it now fetches from 30*l.* to 100*l.* per acre."

"In the township of Maitland, Hunter's River (seventy miles from Sydney), uncleared land could be readily purchased for 1 . or 2 . per acre in 1825: it is now worth from 5*l.* to 100*l.* per acre, according to situation."

"Land having a frontage to the main road, in Maitland, and not far from the court-house, is now sold for building on at from 30*l.* to 150*l.* per acre, which in 1825 would not have produced from 3*l.* to 5*l.* per acre."

" In 1827, Mr. John Smith purchased a small farm of sixty acres from Mr. Allen, situated near the town of Maitland, Hunter's River, for 250*l.* This farm has a frontage to the main road of about ten acres ; and these ten acres would now sell for 1,200*l.*, or 120*l.* each."

From MR. CURR's *Account of Van Dieman's Land.* 1824.

" The value of *uncultivated* land in the colony varies much according to situation and quality. Until of late, grants of land were sold and exchanged very currently, *without being* actually located by the settler (buyer) : and the price varies from ten to twenty shillings per acre."

" The rent of houses in Hobart's-town is very high. A cottage, consisting of four to six rooms, lets for 60*l.*, 70*l.* and 80*l.* per annum : a house of two floors, containing eight or ten rooms, for 120*l.* to 150*l.* per annum : and if in an advantageous situation, 200*l.* will be given for it."

" Farms are very frequently rented in Van Dieman's Land."

" Other persons are induced to make unequal exchanges : giving their uncultivated lands *for smaller farms in more populous situations.*"

CAPTAIN SUTHERLAND,
Communicated to the South Australian Land Company.

" Captain Sutherland, twelve years ago, received from Governor Macquarie a grant of one thousand acres, within four miles of Launceston, in Van Dieman's Land. He has expended upon it no money whatever in roads, buildings, or other improvements. Being obliged, however, to stock it, he expended 200*l.* in horned cattle and sheep, and put them upon it. It is now worth 2*l.* per acre ; the value being given by the increase of population in the neighbourhood."

" Captain Barclay received at the same time with Captain Sutherland a free grant of four thousand acres of land, about seven miles from Launceston. He has expended in building and improvements about 4,000*l.* ; and he has let it on lease for ten years at 1000*l.* a year."

Practical Notes made during a Tour in Canada in 1831, *by* ADAM FERGUSSON, *of Woodhill.*

" Much has been said of the rapid advances which the Upper Province is making, and of the rising value of property there. I was told of a case which occurred about thirty years ago, where a lieutenant in the army, being 50*l.* in arrear to a Montreal merchant, insisted, along with his promissory note, on handing over a lot of land assigned to him somewhere in the *then* Western wilderness, a security which the poor merchant regarded as much upon a par with the subaltern's note, who was about to leave Canada to join his regiment. The allotment consisted of one thousand two hundred and fifty acres upon the Lake Ontario, of which *seven hundred* were sold last year for *seven hundred pounds*, and *five hnndred and fifty* acres of the best quality reserved.   Such are the changes which time effects, without the aid of any other agent, and such cases, I was assured, are by no means rare." Page 69.

" Emigrants, unable or unwilling to purchase, will have little diffi‑ culty in providing themselves with a farm to rent, either for money or on shares, which means half the clear produce as rent.   I was told by a gentleman of a friend of his, who was very comfort‑ ably settled in this way near York, upon a farm of two hundred acres.   Eighty acres are cleared, the remainder in wood pasture. He pays only 25*l.* of rent, and clears 200*l.* per annum, besides keep‑ ing his family.

" To show how land is advancing in value, this farm, a few years ago, might have been purchased for 200*l.*, but is of course worth a great deal more now." Page 275.

" In the afternoon we reached Brandtford, a pretty considerable village, belonging to the Indians, a tract of land in this quarter having been reserved for their behalf.   It is managed by government, who account for rents and sales to the chiefs.   There had been a sale of village lots this day, and for the first time I saw the Indians assem‑ bled in any numbers.   The lots sold for 25*l.*, one-fourth of an acre, which is an immense price in Canada, and argues an expectation of Brandtford continuing to prosper." Page 286.

" The first farm which I visited was in the immediate vicinity of Albany, forming part of the princely estate of Mr. Van Rensselaer. It contained six hundred acres of fine mellow loam along the banks of the river, divided into fields by rail-fences, which cost here 4*s.* 6*d.* for sixteen feet, including boards, nails, and work ; four rails and about five feet high.

" The farm was let some years ago at two thousand dollars, or 450*l.*, which, in America, seems to be a very high rent ; but it must be recollected that its situation is particularly favourable from its close contact with the thriving city of Albany." Page 293.

In the year 1817, Mr. Robert Gourlay* circulated through Canada a number of queries, for the purpose of ascertaining facts relative to the state of that colony, among which the following question was submitted.—" THE PRICE OF WILD LAND AT THE FIRST SETTLEMENT OF THE TOWNSHIP ; ITS PROGRESSIVE RISE AND PRESENT PRICE ; ALSO OF LAND SO FAR CLEARED ; STATING CIRCUMSTANCES AS TO BUILDINGS, PROPORTION CLEARED, OR PECULIARITY, IF ANY, OF LOCAL SITUATION ; REFERRING IN EVERY INSTANCE TO ACTUAL SALES ?"

This question was answered by committees formed from among the resident owners in various townships.   The answers follow :—

* See Gourlay's Historical Account of Upper Canada, vol. i., **page 269,** et seq.

TOWNSHIP OF SANDWICH, IN THE WESTERN DISTRICT,

Settlement commenced in 1750, *and contains at present* (1817) *about*
1,000 *souls.*

" The price of wild land about twenty years ago was 1*s*. 3*d*. to
2*s*. 6*d*. per acre, and its progressive rise about 2*s*. 6*d*. for every five
years.   The present price of land is from 10*s*. to 15*s*., except in
particular situations, such as lie on the strait.   No lands have
been recently sold in the township ; the settlement has long been at
a *stand*.   Improved farms on the border of the strait, with a common farm-house, barn, and out-houses, orchard, and about fifty acres
within fence, would rate from 2*l*. 10*s*. to 6*l*. 5*s*. per acre, and more,
according to the situation and value of the improvements."

TOWNSHIP OF WALDEN, IN THE WESTERN DISTRICT,

Settlement commenced in 1784 ; *present population* 675 *persons.*

" At first settlement the price of land was from 1*s*. to 3*s*. per
acre ; the present price is 25*s*. per acre ; some land, partly cleared,
has been lately sold at 40*s*. per acre.

TOWNSHIP OF RALEIGH, WESTERN DISTRICT,

Settlement commenced in 1792 ; *present population* 273 *persons.*

" At the commencement of the settlement, lots of two hundred
acres, situated on the banks of the Thames, were sold at 25*l*.   In
1804 they sold for 131*l*. 5*s*.   The same lands are now selling for
250*l*. without improvements.   Back lands of the best quality may
be fairly estimated at one-third of these prices.

TOWNSHIPS OF DOVER, EAST AND WEST CHATHAM, CAMDEN, OXFORD, HOWARD, AND HARWICH, ON THE RIVER THAMES.

Settlement commenced in 1794 ;. *inhabited houses* 133.

" Some farms in good local situations, with tolerable buildings
and orchards thereon, well cultivated, containing two hundred acres
of land, sold for 690*l*.   The average price of lands from the first
settlement of these townships, was from 2*s*. 6*d*. to 20*s*. per acre."

TOWNSHIPS OF DORCHESTER, DELAWARE, AND WESTMINSTER, ON THE RIVER THAMES.

" The flats on the Thames have always sold high, and are now
worth 3*l*. per acre."

TOWNSHIP OF OXFORD, IN THE LONDON DISTRICT.

" A two hundred acre lot, with thirty acres cultivated land, a log
house and frame barn thirty by forty feet, is worth 500*l*."

TOWNSHIP OF WINDHAM, IN THE LONDON DISTRICT.

" At our first settlement, wild land sold for 5*s*. per acre ; at present the wild land in the unsettled parts of the township will sell for 10s. per acre; but there is wild land in the settlement that cannot be bought for 1l. 5s. per acre; and some improved farms are held at 3l. 15s. per acre, where there is not above sixty acres improved; but there have been actual sales of farms from 1l. 5s. to 3l. per acre, according to the improvement made in them."

TOWNSHIP OF CHARLOTTEVILLE, IN THE LONDON DISTRICT.

" About the first settlement of the township, land sold for 5s. per acre, but will now average about 1l. A farm of two hundred acres of land, with a log-house and barn, with fifty acres cleared and fenced, and a small orchard of bearing trees, might be purchased for about 700l. and occasionally less."

TOWNSHIP OF NORWICH, IN THE LONDON DISTRICT.

A few families arrived in 1808, *but very little progress was made till* 1811.

" About 6s. 3d. was at our commencement the price of land, and has progressively risen in value to 13s. per acre; one sale lately made of an improvement, one hundred acres, thirty-five cleared, frame barn, log-house, good fence, price 375l."

TOWNSHIPS OF WEST FLAMBORO, AND BEVERLY, GORE DISTRICT.

" Wild lands, at first settling, sold for 10l. two hundred acres; and now sell from 10s. to 1l. 10s. and 2l. per acre. Cleared land sells from 2l. to 12l. 10s. per acre, according to its situation and advantages."

TOWNSHIP OF ANCASTER, IN THE GORE DISTRICT.

" Wild lands at the first settling of this township sold at 6l. 5s. per lot of two hundred acres; now sell from 12s. 6d. to 1l. 10s. and 5l. per acre. Cleared lands sell from 2l. 10s. to 12l. 10s. per acre, according to its situation and advantages.

TOWNSHIP OF BARTON, IN THE GORE DISTRICT.

" In 1792, land sold at 1s. 3d. per acre; in 1800, 5s.; in 1806, 15s.; in 1810, 1l. 10s.; in 1817, about 2l. 10s. On an average about 5l. per acre, for an improved farm of two hundred acres, with small farms, or log-house and barn, and other out-houses. Improved farms have sold from 6l. 5s. to 7l. 10s. per acre."

TOWNSHIP OF SALTFLEET IN THE GORE DISTRICT.

" The price of new land in this township, at the first settlement thereof, rated so low as to make it no object with many. A lot of one hundred acres might be purchased for 5l. to 6l. 5s., and large quantities were actually bought and sold at these prices: it has gradually rose from that time to the year 1812, since which time it seems stationary for want of purchasers. But the average price of wild land may be rated at 1*l*. 5*s*. per acre. A farm of about three hundred acres of land, one third cleared, and a comfortable house and good barn, with a bearing orchard of one or two hundred apple trees, the whole premises being in good repair, may be purchased from 1,000*l*. to 1,500*l*. according to situation. A farm nearly answering to this description was actually sold for the highest sum here mentioned."

TOWNSHIP OF HUMBERSTON, NIAGARA DISTRICT.

"At the first settlement, when much land was held on location tickets, lots of two hundred acres could be bought for twenty dollars. The price has gradually increased, and of late years sales have been effected at 2½ dollars per acre."

TOWNSHIP OF WILLOUGHBY, IN THE NIAGARA DISTRICT,

Surveyed and laid out by order of government in 1787.

"A farm of two hundred acres, one half under cultivation, with tolerable farm buildings and orchard, now sells for 625*l*. to 700*l*. Farms, however, upon the Niagara or Chippewa rivers, will sell much higher, according to their situation."

TOWNSHIP OF GRANTHAM, IN THE NIAGARA DISTRICT.

"Farms of two hundred acres, situate on the most public roads, of a good quality, comfortable house, good barn, orchard, &c. from one hundred to one hundred and fifty acres improved, will sell for 6*l*. to 7*l*. 10*s*. per acre. Farms of one hundred acres, small house and barn, sixty acres improved, will sell from 5*l*. to 6*l*. per acre. Lands in the village of St. Catharine (the only one in township), in 1809-10 and 11, sold for 6*l*. 5*s*. per acre, now sell from 30*l*. to 200*l*. for building lots."

TOWNSHIP OF PELHAM, NIAGARA DISTRICT.

"When the settlement of this township commenced, wild land was selling at 6*l*. 10*s*. for one hundred acres; in the year 1800, at 10*s*. per acre; the present price is 40*s*. per acre."

TOWNSHIP OF CROWLAND, NIAGARA DISTRICT.

"A farm of one hundred acres, nearly contiguous to mills, with about forty acres cleared, and very neat buildings, was sold for 312*l*. 10*s*."

TOWNSHIP OF HALDIMAN, NEWCASTLE DISTRICT,

Settlement commenced in 1797.

"At the first settlement of the township, lands were worth 5*s*.

per acre; at the present time, in good situations, 15s. and in ordinary situations, 10s. per acre."

TOWNSHIP OF KINGSTON, MIDLAND DISTRICT,

Settlement commenced in 1783; *population, including the town of Kingston,* 2,850.

" Few or no actual purchases of land were made by the original settlers, as their situation entitled them to grants from government. . . . . . Farms of two hundred acres, with perhaps sixty or eighty acres cleared, with a house and barn, and within a range of ten miles of the town, may be worth from 2l. to 5l. per acre."

" At the first settlement, many persons sold their two hundred acre lots for the value of a few shillings; twelve years ago, land a few miles from Kingston sold for 2s. 6d. per acre; and lately, in the same situations, from 30s. to 40s.; but the fire-wood alone will soon be worth as much as that per acre."

TOWNSHIP OF EARNEST TOWN, INCLUDING AMHERST ISLAND, MIDLAND DISTRICT.

" At the first settlement the value of wild lands was merely nominal. They have progressively risen, and their present price may be computed at 1l. 5s. per acre. The average price of one hundred acres of land, one half improved, with tolerable buildings thereon, may be valued at 3l. per acre."

TOWNSHIP OF ADOLPHUS TOWN, MIDLAND DISTRICT.

" At the first settlement of this township, land could be purchased at 1s. per acre. It rose gradually to 5s., 10s., 15s., 20s., &c. At this moment there is no land in the township could be procured for less than 4l. per acre, and it is believed few would sell at that price."

TOWNSHIP OF SOPHIASBERG, MIDLAND DISTRICT.

" At the first settlement, land was about 1s. per acre; there is little wild land for sale here; best sales made from three to five dollars per acre."

TOWNSHIP OF LANSDOWN, JOHNSTOWN DISTRICT,

Settlement commenced in 1788.

" Price of wild land, at the first settlement, it was sold at 5l. for two hundred acres, and has gradually risen in value to one dollar per acre, at a distance from the settlement; but on the road or river it may be valued at three dollars per acre, and that without any improvement; in the centre of the town, from three to six dollars per acre."

TOWNSHIP OF CHARLOTTENBURGH, EASTERN DISTRICT,

Settlement commenced in 1784.

" The price of wild land, for the first period, say six years of the settlement, was from 1s. to 5s. per acre ; and at present, is from 20s. to 30s. the acre. A lot of two hundred acres, with thirty acres cleared, under good cultivation, with a farm-house and barn with sheds, &c. is worth from 500l. to 600l.

Travels in America in the years 1794, 1795, and 1796, by the Duke of Rochefoucault Liancourt.

Vol. 1. p. 6. Land in this neighbourhood (Philadelphia) is worth eighty dollars per acre ; six years ago it was only worth forty-two.

Vol. 1. p. 77. General Haud bought five years ago the estate on which he resides, two miles from the town, for twenty-five dollars per acre ; and has lately refused one hundred dollars, which were offered him. The price of land has risen in the same proportion throughout America, as land in the cultivated parts.

Vol. 1. p. 98. The price of ground-shares in the town of Harrisburg (founded eight years before) is from one hundred and fifty to two hundred dollars per acre, the land in the surrounding country is from thirty-two to forty-eight dollars per acre.

Vol. 1. p. 195. The inhabitants only settled here (Painted-post, State of New-York) four years ago. The soil is good, especially near the town, where from fifteen to eighteen dollars is the price for an acre.

Vol. 1. p. 261. Metcalf, three years ago, purchased his estate for 1s. per acre : of the thousand acres he then bought, he has already sold five hundred and upwards, at from one to three dollars per acre, and some have fetched twenty-five dollars. The profits which are made by speculations in land, all over America, and especially in this neighbourhood (Gennessee), are great beyond calculation.

Vol. 2. p. 10. W. Shorten bought his estate here (Oswego) three years ago, at 3d. per acre, and can now sell it for 12s.: only ten acres are cleared.

Vol. 2. p. 39. The land here (Schuylerton), which in 1785 cost a few pence per acre, and three years ago not more than five dollars, is now sold, not merely in the vicinity of the town, but also fifteen miles beyond it, for nineteen or twenty dollars per acre.

Vol. 3. p. 242. The settlement of the country between Harper's Ferry aud Coosooky Mountains is just beginning. Land fetches from seven to eight dollars the acre.

Vol. 4. p. 161. Belvidere consists of about twenty houses, but the number of inhabitants is annually increasing, and the neighbourhood is populous. The lands in the neighbourhood are sold at from forty to forty-eight dollars the acre. The town lots, which are a quarter of an acre, being at present from one hundred to one hundred and twenty-five dollars

No. III.

PART* OF A CORRESPONDENCE BETWEEN THE ENGLISH GOVERN-
MENT AND A BODY OF INDIVIDUALS DESIROUS TO FOUND A
COLONY.

PROVISIONAL COMMITTEE

Of the South Australian Land Company.

W. Wolryche Whitmore, Esq., M.P., Chairman.

George Fife Angas, Esq.	W. A. Mackinnon, Esq., M.P.
Dominic Browne, Esq., M.P.	J. A. S. Mackenzie, Esq., M.P.
H. L. Bulwer, Esq., M.P.	Samuel Mills, Esq.
Walter F. Campbell, Esq., M.P.	John Melville, Esq.
Henry Drummond, Esq.	Sir R. Musgrave, Bart., M.P.
Captain Gowan.	Richard Norman, Esq.
Richard Heathfield, Esq.	J. E. Strickland, Esq.
Samuel Hoare, Esq.	Colonel Torrens, M.P.
William Hutt, Esq.	George Trail, Esq., M.P.
J. Jephson, Esq., M.P.	R. Throckmorton, Esq., M.P.
C. Shaw Lefevre, Esq., M.P.	Sir H. Williamson, Bart., M.P.
Lord Lumley, M.P.	

*Copy of a Letter from Mr. R. W. Hay, Under-Secretary of State
for the Colonies, to Mr. Wolryche Whitmore, M.P. for Bridge-
north.*

Downing-Street, 30th May, 1832.

Sir,

Lord Goderich has received the note which you addressed to him
on the 28th instant, with its enclosure, containing " A Proposal for
founding a British Colony in South Australia, between the degrees
of longitude 132 and 141, both inclusive, to extend northward to
latitude 20, inclusive, and to include Kangaroo Island and the other
islands on the south coast, under a royal charter ;" and I am directed
to acquaint you that after having given to the subject his best consideration, he has come to the determination of withholding the sanction of his majesty's government to the undertaking.†

* During the late session of Parliament, Mr. Hutt, one of the members for
Hull, requested Lord Howick to agree to a motion for a return of the *whole* of
this correspondence. His lordship said that he should oppose the motion, on
account of the expense of printing. On the same account, I can give here only
a part of the correspondence : but this part of it is enough to show the *animus*
on both sides ; and it leaves the government with the last word.

† It would appear by the terms of this paragraph, as if Lord Goderich had
decided the question in two days, between the 28th, the date of Mr. Whitmore's

Independently of the objections which he should feel himself called on to make to several of the propositions which are brought forward, as well from their novelty as from the difficulty which he foresees in regard to their practical operation, he cannot but consider that great public inconvenience would arise from the circumstance of a new colony being placed so near to the penal settlements at Sydney and in Van Dieman's Land, as that proposed.

I have the honour to be, sir,

Your most obedient servant,

(Signed) R. W. HAY.

W. W. Whitmore, Esq., M.P., &c., &c.

Copy of a MEMORIAL addressed to Viscount Goderich, his majesty's principal Secretary of State for the Colonies; in answer to the above.

Office of the South Australian Land Company, ⎱
8, Regent-Street, June 4, 1832. ⎰

The undersigned, being members of a Provisional Committee formed for the purpose of founding a colony on the south coast of Australia, persons desirous to settle in the proposed colony, and others taking a deep interest in the matter, have perused, with surprise and sorrow, a letter addressed by Mr. Hay to Mr. Whitmore, dated May 30 ; wherein it is stated, that " Lord Goderich has come to the determination of withholding the sanction of his majesty's government from their undertaking :" and they now take the liberty of submitting to Viscount Goderich a statement of the grounds on which they are led to hope and trust that his lordship will be pleased to reconsider his decision in this matter, confident that, when all the circumstances of the case shall be examined, Viscount Goderich will not persist in his present determination.

I. That the proposal submitted to Viscount Goderich by Mr. Whitmore, as chairman of the Provisional Committee, on the 28th ultimo, is not a new proposal, but was submitted to Viscount Goderich in much greater detail, and in a printed form,* during the autumn of last year ; when a deputation, consisting of Colonel Torrens, Mr. Bacon, Mr. Gouger, and Mr. Graham, waited upon Viscount Goderich for the purpose of ascertaining his lordship's opinion of that proposal. That the members of the deputation were so well pleased with the opinion which Viscount Goderich expressed of their undertaking, that they thought it needless to ask for any written reply to

letter, and the 30th, the date of Mr. Hay's. Let us do his lordship justice : the subject had been before him for a whole year, as will be seen further on ; but why should Mr. Hay omit all notice of the fact, and write as if Lord Goderich had never heard of the subject till the 28th of May, 1832 ?

* Proposal to his majesty's government for founding a colony on the southern coast of Australia. 1831.

their proposal, but advised the persons whom they represented to proceed with the undertaking, by submitting the intended charter to the law-officers of the crown, and raising the necessary capital.

II. That a notice of the proposed colony having appeared in a newspaper, in which it was stated that his majesty's government had given their unqualified sanction to the undertaking, Viscount Howick, Under-Secretary of State for the colonies, then superintending the Australian department,* addressed to Mr. Bacon a memorandum in the following words:—

Colonial-Office, 13th October, 1831.

"I was surprised to see in the Spectator newspaper of yesterday, an assertion that the government had given its sanction to the plan for the establishment of a chartered colony in Australia. This statement is not strictly correct. It is a mistake to suppose that any official sanction has been given to the plan. The only approbation which has been expressed was conveyed by myself,† verbally, to Major Bacon; and in the conversation I had with him, I distinctly informed him that I was *authorized* to promise nothing; and that I merely expressed my own opinion, being ignorant of that which Lord Goderich might entertain,‡ as I did not consider the scheme sufficiently matured for his decision.

"The substance of what I said in this unofficial manner was this, that I myself thought very favourably of the project; and that doing so, I was anxious that it should be laid before Lord Goderich in such a shape as to be most likely to meet with his approbation.§ For this purpose, I advised the modification in the original project, with respect to the number of inhabitants who should be considered sufficient for the introduction of a representative government, and with respect to the nomination of the governor, which have since been made.‖ I further suggested that the draft of the charter, which it was desired to obtain, should be prepared and submitted to the attorney-general;¶ and I stated that if this draft, approved by him

* The Australian department was soon afterward taken from Lord Howick, and given to Mr. Hay.

† This is not strictly correct. The deputation had had a long interview with Lord Goderich, whom they found reading their printed proposal, and who suggested two alterations in it, which were immediately adopted. What Lord Goderich said of the plan at that interview, and how far he spoke officially, will be seen further on.

‡ Just so; but Lord Goderich had very distinctly expressed his own opinion, unknown to Lord Howick; and the notice in the Spectator referred, not to the opinion of the under-secretary, but to that of his chief.

§ It had been already, unknown to Lord Howick, laid before Lord Goderich, in the shape of a printed pamphlet of 31 pages.

‖ Both these alterations were also suggested by Lord Goderich to the deputation which waited on his lordship; and it was these suggestions, by the principal secretary of state, which, among other things, led the deputation to conclude that he approved of their enterprise.

¶ Lord Goderich himself had made the very same suggestion.

and accompanied by a respectable list of subscribers, were brought
under the consideration of Lord Goderich ; and if it should be clearly
made to appear that the government would be put to no expense, I
had little doubt that Lord Goderich would recommend that the
charter should be issued.* With respect to the difficulty that was
stated to exist about obtaining subscriptions without having received
the sanction of government to the scheme, I said that, in my opinion,
what would be the fairest for all parties would be, that the draft of
the charter should be submitted to Lord Goderich, with a list of
subscriptions *conditional* upon the sanction of the government being
granted ; and that, upon the draft being approved by Lord Goderich,
the sum subscribed for should be actually paid up, or at least a certain proportion, before the charter should actually issue ; that thus
the subscribers would run no risk of being drawn in to contribute to
an unsanctioned project, and the government would equally avoid
all danger of giving their countenance to a scheme which there were
not funds to support.

(Signed)   H."

III. That the document recited above was considered as confirm-
atory of the opinion of the undertaking expressed by Viscount Goderich to the deputation which had waited on his lordship, and as intended only to provide that the conditions, on which the sanction of
his majesty's government had been required, should be strictly fulfilled before such sanction should be officially expressed.

IV. That on the 16th of April last, a deputation, headed by Mr.
Whitmore, waited upon Viscount Goderich for the purpose of ascertaining whether his lordship continued to entertain a favourable
opinion of the enterprise ; and that the impression left on the minds
of the deputation by Lord Goderich's reception of them was, that his
lordship continued to entertain a favourable opinion of the project
generally, though there might be points of detail requiring modification.

V. That the parties interested in the undertaking further held
several conversations with Viscount Howick and other gentlemen
of the Colonial Department, and especially with Mr. Stephen, the
counsel of that department, whereby they were led to believe that
his majesty's government viewed their undertaking, not merely with
approbation, but with a very warm interest.†

VI. That in consequence of the belief arising from Viscount Goderich's reception of the deputations above-mentioned, from Viscount

---

* This caution and modesty were very becoming in a young nobleman new
to office ; but Lord Goderich, an experienced statesman, had already spoken for
himself in decisive terms ; one of the grounds on which he thought so well of
the plan being that, upon the face of it, the government was not to be put to the
expense of a single shilling for any purpose whatever.

† Thus far Mr. Hay had not been concerned with this affair.

Howick's memorandum, and from the conversations just alluded to, the parties interested in the undertaking have been constantly occupied, for great part of a year, in measures, having for object the fulfilment of conditions which they conceived to be required by his majesty's government; such as circulating pamphlets, with a view to bring the subject before the public, raising the necessary capital, procuring evidence as to the soil and climate of the south coast of Australia, preparing a draft of the proposed charter, and forming the company under whose auspices the proposed colony was to be founded.

VII. That their progress in these measures was greatly retarded, and on two occasions entirely suspended, by the votes of the House of Lords on the reform-bill; but that by dint of the constant labour of a considerable number of persons, the whole of whose time has been devoted to this object, they had, as they imagined, overcome every difficulty; and that the late communication from Mr. Whitmore to Viscount Goderich, whereby the original proposal* was briefly repeated, was made for the purpose of informing his lordship of their success,† and of obtaining that official sanction to their enterprise, without which it was impossible that they should adopt any final step.

VIII. That, though the want of an official expression of the sanction of his majesty's government necessarily prevented them from opening shares to the public, still that, of the 500,000l. which it is proposed to raise, the persons who intended to settle in the colony proposed to subscribe 100,000l.; and that many of them, in order to carry this their purpose into effect, as well as to provide themselves with capital for use in the colony, have disposed of real and other property in this country to a considerable amount; that several of them have abandoned trades and professions in which they were engaged; have purchased outfits and other goods for exportation to the colony; and will be subject to a very serious loss of property (not to mention the loss of their time) in case the hope on which they have acted should, at the eleventh hour, be frustrated by his majesty's government.

IX. That persons, who do not propose settling in the colony, have intimated their intention of subscribing 100,000l. of the capital.

X. That, with reference to Mr. Hay's letter to Mr. Whitmore of the 30th ultimo, it must be acknowledged that the proposal submitted to Viscount Goderich is distinguished by some novelty; since never before did a body of capitalists offer to any government so

---

* With the alterations that Lord Goderich had suggested.

† After this, Mr. Hay's mention of the proposal, as if it had been entirely new, seems unaccountable. Was it a joke? or, as the proposal was indeed new to Mr. Hay, did he speak sincerely enough, meaning himself when he said " Lord Goderich?"

large a sum as 125,000*l.* for 500,000 acres of land, completely waste and in a country absolutely desert.

XI. That in two other respects the plan is distinguished by novelty: in the first place, as it promises a continually increasing fund for the purpose of pauper-emigration; and secondly, as it provides, though but in one case, against the evils which, in all the colonies of modern times, have resulted from the want of any fixed or rational system in the disposal of waste land.*

XII. That in other respects, the proposal submitted to his majesty's government, instead of being distinguished by novelty, is founded on precedent; the English government having invariably, it is believed, except in the case of the late Swan River colony, adopted the principle of self-government in the formation of colonies. That in the case of every colony, properly so called, founded by this country, the home government gave its sanction to that compact among the first settlers, which led to the foundation of the colony; a compact of which the essence was, that the colonists should govern themselves in local matters, and provide for the expenses of local self-government.†

XIII. That although no public announcement has yet been given of the intention of the proposed company to convey poor settlers to Australia, a mere rumour of that intention has led poor persons (nearly all of them without employment, and many of them in a state of great destitution), who together with their families amount to upwards of six thousand, to apply for the benefit which the mere sanction of his majesty's government would enable the company to bestow on them.‡

XIV. That the proposed undertaking is not open to the objection against the establishment of colonies, which is held by many enlightened persons; viz. an objection to the expense which colonies often occasion to the mother country, and to the great amount of patronage which they place at the disposal of a minister at home: since, in the present case, it is provided that all the public expenses attendant on the colony should be borne by the colonists themselves; and that the officers, so to be paid for administering the government

---

* These gentlemen may have known how to found a colony; but it is evident that they did not know how to deal with a corrupt old government. Their *naïveté* in dwelling on two points, which would have rendered impossible all jobbing with new land, or with the purchase-money of it, is almost laughable.

† Here, again, the simplicity of Mr. Whitmore and his coadjutors is almost amusing. Governments love precedent, when it makes in their favour: in this case it could not but be offensive to notice those precedents, of which the memory is held in dislike at the English colonial office; and to notice them, too, for the purpose of getting the best of the argument with a minister.

‡ One of these, having been told that the government had changed its mind, and that the scheme was at an end, said, What! the reform government? Yes, was the answer; even the *reform* government!

of the colony, should not, the governor excepted, be appointed by the secretary of state.*

XV. That, with reference to Mr. Hay's letter to Mr. Whitmore of the 30th ultimo, in which it is stated that " Great public inconvenience would arise from the circumstance of a new colony being placed so near to the penal settlements of Sydney and Van Dieman's Land," it is acknowledged that the proposed colony would present a remarkable contrast with the penal settlements of Australia ; a contrast of all that is good in colonization with all that is bad ; local self-government instead of arbitrary rule ; a rational and fixed system in the disposal of waste land (one of the elements of colonization), instead of a system which, though based on the plan devised by the projectors of the proposed colony,† is rendered almost nugatory by previous want of system, and is dependant for its duration on the pleasure of the secretary of state for the time being ; a society concentrated by that rational system in the disposal of waste land, and enabled to employ their capital and labour with the greatest advantage, instead of a society dispersed by the profusion of the government in granting waste land, and so prevented from raising commodities which require combination of capital and labour ; a moral society, or at least a society placed under circumstances the most favourable to morality, instead of a society pre-eminently vicious, in which the most disgusting depravity prevails, and in which such vices are becoming national habits.   The contrast would, no doubt, have been most striking.   But the undersigned are at a loss to see in what way the establishment of so much good by the side of so much evil could be productive of " public inconvenience."   On the contrary, they submit to Viscount Goderich, that the want of a costless, concentrated, and civilized colony in Australia, furnishes a very strong reason why the home government, not being called on to incur any expense or to create any patronage,‡ should enable the undersigned to establish such a settlement in that part of the world ; so that there may be one British colony at least, in a favourable climate, to which persons of all classes may resort, without incurring political, social, or moral degradation.

XVI. That the only " public inconvenience" which the undersigned can imagine to be alleged as likely to result from the establishment of a self-governed colony in Australia, is, that the settlers in the penal colonies, not being convicts, would thereby be led to ask of the home government the advantage of self-government in local matters.   But in answer to this supposed allegation, the under-

* Worse and worse.   What else could they expect, but to be treated as they were ?   Why did they not rather dwell on their confidence in the secretary of state, as shown in their having given up to him, at his own suggestion, the appointment of the governor ?
† The plan of the *Colonization Society*, just then adopted by the government, as to New South Wales and Van Dieman's Land.
‡ There again : always touching the sore place.

signed venture to remark, that already the free settlers of the penal colonies earnestly beg for, and are bent on obtaining, the advantage in question; that, for any thing that has been stated to the contrary, they are entitled to this advantage; and that they might enjoy it without hinderance to the penal system. If, however, it were clear that the establishment of a self-governed colony near to the penal colonies, would *create* a demand for self-government among the settlers of those penal colonies; and if it were further proved that self-government, in local matters, is incompatible with the penal system, still the undersigned would take the liberty of reminding Viscount Goderich, that the whole system of penal transportation is condemned by some jurists and politicians as being not less costly than ineffectual as a punishment; and that in all probability, and in accordance too with the views of the present government, that system of pretended punishment and colonial depravity will not much longer be followed. Consequently, it appears to the undersigned that, if the objection which they presume to be alleged by Mr. Hay's letter to Mr. Whitmore were not removed, it would amount, on the part of his majesty's government, to a decision, That, because some public inconvenience might by possibility arise, and, if at all, for but a short time, by contrasting the best with the worst mode of colonization in Australia, therefore, none but the worst system should be adopted in any part of that vast region.

That the vicinity of the proposed colony to the penal settlements is calculated to remove an objection, which was stated by Viscount Goderich to the deputation headed by Mr. Whitmore on the 16th of April; namely, that the establishment of a colony at *such a distance* from the penal colonies might be injurious, by extending the line to be protected in case of war. But, if the latter objection should be urged, the undersigned would observe that since the formation of the Swan River colony, the whole of the south coast of Australia ought to be defended in case of war; and that the establishment of a colony in the centre of that coast, midway between Van Dieman's Land and the Swan River, would greatly facilitate such defence.

XVII. That if the above considerations should not remove Viscount Goderich's objection to the new colony, which is founded on the possibility of public inconvenience, the undersigned would further point out to his lordship, that a British settlement, not penal,* and one to which it appears inevitable that the advantage of self-government, in local matters, will be accorded as soon as the settlers are sufficiently numerous, already exists in Australia; namely, the Swan River colony, which extends to King George's Sound.

XVIII. Finally, the undersigned submit to Viscount Goderich, that when a number of persons are disposed to incur the risks and hardships of planting a colony in a desert country, the social arrangements under which they shall exist are, and have always been con-

---

* But costly, they did well not to add.

sidered by the British government, matters in which the settlers alone are deeply interested, and of which they are the best judges; that, in the present case, the intended settlers have formed a plan of colonization, which, if it succeed, must inevitably be productive of great advantage, not merely to themselves, but to this nation at large, by opening a great field for the employment of our surplus labour and capital; and that, in order to carry into effect this purpose of unqualified good, the utmost extent of their request to his majesty's government is, that it will exercise one of the functions for which governments exist, by binding, under a charter from the crown, the compact into which those individuals are desirous to enter.

(Signed)
W. W. Whitmore, M.P.
Robert Torrens, M.P.
J. E. Strickland.
Richard Heathfield.
W. A. Mackinnon, M.P.
J. A. Stewart Mackenzie, M.P.
Wm. Gowan, Upper Baker-street.
J. Melville, Upper Harley-street.
F. Place, Charing-cross.
William Hutt, 54 Conduit-street.
Thomas Hoskyns, M.P.
Thomas Rudge, Hereford.
Robert Gouger, Castle-street, Falcon-square.
Benjamin Hanson, Bruton-street.
D. Elston, Bridge-House, Limehouse.
Robert Price, M.P.
Henry Drummond, Charing-cross.
Samuel Hoare, Lombard-street.
C. Lushington, Edgeware.
G. Long, Tanfield-court, Temple.
Samuel Mills, 20 Russel-square.
L. Thomas, Cheapside.
A. Bacon, North-Bank.
R. Sadlier, Fulham.
D. Munro, Kensington.
D. Wakefield, Gray's Inn.
G. A. Angas, Jeffrey-square, St. Mary Axe.
G. S. Tucker, Birchin-lane.
G. J. Graham, Gray's Inn.
R. Phillips, M.P., Portland-place.
George Vardon, Charles-street, Westminster.
H. L. Bulwer, M.P., Albany.
Samuel Brookes, Islington.
R. D. Hanson, Hackney.
Richard Borrow, Stepney.
William Borrow,　do
William Currie.

John Cobden, Canterbury.
J. Rhodes, Bankside.
J. Evans.
G. Morrison, Soho-square.
E. C. Richards, George-yard, Lombard-street.
D. Browne, M.P.
Charles Hanson, Hackney.
John Cunnold.
R. Throckmorton, M.P.
R. Heathfield, jun., Lincoln's Inn.
H. Surman, Lincoln's Inn.
W. H. Surman,   do.
Erskine Humphreys, Lincoln's Inn.
J. H. Rice, North-Bank, Regent's Park.
J. Harding.
M. Racster.
Alex. M'Math.
Andrew Smith, Birchin-lane.
Joshua Storrs.
F. B. Robinson.
W. Hanson, Hackney.
Joshua Brookes.
George Drury.
John Bowes, 54 Conduit-street.
G. S. Rutherford, Welbeck-street.
G. C. Hawkins, Regent-street.
J. S. Lumley, M.P., Park-street.

To the above memorial, no answer was returned. Two interviews, however, took place between Lord Goderich and deputations from the society.

At the first of these meetings, Lord Goderich urged several new objections to the undertaking. The letter, accordingly, of which a copy follows, was addressed to his lordship by Mr. Strickland, who, during Mr. Whitmore's absence from town, acted as chairman of the Provisional Committee.

South Australian Land Company's Committee-Room, } 8 Regent-street, June 18, 1832.

MY LORD,

As chairman of a meeting of the South Australian Land Company, held this day, I have the honour to address your lordship on the subject which was discussed between your lordship and a deputation from that committee on Friday last.*

---

* At this meeting there were present, besides the Provisional Committee, a considerable number of the gentlemen who had made arrangements for settling in the proposed colony. They were in a state of anxious excitement, such as can be imagined by him only who knows after how painful a struggle people, having strong ties at home, make up their minds to emigrate ; and how earnestly, when they have come to that decision, they think, to the exclusion of all

Before noticing the objections to the proposed colony which were urged by your lordship on that occasion, I would venture once more to remind your lordship, that the proposal now before you is by no means a new one ; but that it was submitted to you so long as nearly twelve months ago. This assertion will be borne out by the following relation of facts.

Early in the month of June last year, Mr. Gouger, in consequence of a conversation with Viscount Howick, delivered to his lordship a paper, entitled *Proposal for establishing a new colony in South Australia.* On the 11th of the same month, Viscount Howick addressed a letter to Mr. Gouger, of which I have the honour to enclose a copy marked A, and by which Mr. Gouger was directed to renew the proposal in a different form. Consequently, another proposal was drawn up, printed, and forwarded to Viscount Howick, who submitted the same to your lordship; and your lordship was pleased to appoint a time when you would receive a deputation from the persons interested in forming the intended colony, for the purpose of giving them some answer to the proposal in question. The deputation, which consisted of Colonel Torrens, Mr. Bacon, Mr. Graham, and Mr. Gouger, waited on your lordship, and read a paper, containing the heads of the printed proposal, which, however, they found in your lordship's hands, and of which you were pleased to say that you had read it with much interest, and that its subject matter was of so much importance as to deserve your immediate and serious attention. One objection* your lordship made to the proposal, viz. to the proposed appointment of the governor by the company.† In all other respects it appeared to the deputation, not merely that your lordship assented to the proposal generally, but that you felt a considerable interest in the undertaking, which, if successful, was calculated to effect so much good. So satisfied were the deputation with your lordship's feeling on the subject, that, upon subsequent consultation among the parties interested, they recommended that your lordship should not be asked for any written answer to the proposal ; on the ground that such a request would be ungracious to your lordship, as

other thoughts, upon their prospects of happiness in the new country. It was a scene for Wilkie to have painted : the minister seated, cross-legged, with an air of official gravity and importance ; the under-secretary standing behind a high desk, a sort of apology for not being seated in the presence of his chief; the petitioners watching every expression of the great man's face ; their own faces lighted up when he uttered a word that seemed favourable to them, and pulled lengthwise when he spoke of objections ; the little-great man suggesting objections from behind the high desk ; and when the would-be settlers stared as if they would eat him, looking down steadily upon a bundle of papers tied with red tape.

* This is a mistake : there were *two* objections ; one to the appointment of the governor by the colonists ; the other to the number of people (5,000 male adults) who, it was proposed, should have a legislative assembly. Both points were conceded : Lord Goderich was to appoint the governor ; and for 5,000 male adults, 10,000 was substituted by Lord Goderich's desire.

† The appointment of the governor was vested in the colonists by the charters of Massachusetts Bay, Connecticut, Rhode-Island, Virginia, Pennsylvania, and Maryland.

savouring of a suspicion, which was most distant from the thoughts
of the deputation, that your lordship's favourable reception of them
might not have been sincere.*

Within a few days of the interview in question, Mr. Bacon, who
happened to be at the Colonial-Office on other business, was called
aside by Viscount Howick (who at that time, it should be remembered, conducted the Australian department), when a conversation
occurred, of which a minute in writing was immediately made by
Mr. Bacon, and communicated to the persons with whom he was
acting. Of that paper I have the honour to enclose a copy, marked
B. The next communication between the Colonial-Office and the
intended colonists was made by Viscount Howick's memorandum,
dated October 31st, 1831, which was copied into the memorial presented to your lordship on the 4th instant.

After this long, and I fear, tiresome recital, your lordship will, I
trust, acknowledge, that I am correct in representing the proposal
before your lordship as by no means a new one, but as one which
was formally submitted to you, in a complete shape, last year, and
which did then obtain your serious attention. If this had not been
the conviction of the intended colonists, or if they had imagined that
your lordship had entertained any one serious objection to their
project, instead of occupying themselves, as they have done, with
other measures for carrying the project into effect, they would either
have sought to convince your lordship that any objections held by
you were ungrounded, or would have requested your lordship to
suggest alterations in their place, calculated to make it entirely agreeable to you. Indeed, on the two points which did occur to your
lordship as objectionable, viz. the appointment of the governor by the
company, and the amount of population which should be entitled to
local self-government, they immediately altered their plan to meet
your lordship's views; and all their subsequent publications have
contained those alterations.

Your lordship will, therefore, be able to appreciate the great disappointment which they have suffered at finding that now, when
they have laboured for a year to fulfil the conditions on which they
had every reason to be confident that a charter would be given to
them, numerous and grave objections have been for the first time
mentioned; objections which, had they occurred last year, would

* There can be no doubt that Lord Goderich's favourable reception of these
gentlemen was perfectly sincere. But it may be doubted whether, at that time,
he had looked to the consequences which might result from *the example* of a very
cheap colony in Australia. One, who is well acquainted with the English
government, having been told of the success of this deputation, said, "They do
not understand your plan: as soon as they understand it they will oppose it.
If you want the sanction of government, you must put a good deal of patronage
into your plan : this plan is too cheap, altogether too good, ever to be liked by
our government. Instead of 5,000l. a year for governing the colony, say
20,000l. a year; and give all the appointments to the Colonial-Office. If you
do this, you will get the charter without trouble : if you hold to the present plan,
you will never get a charter, except by appealing to the House of Commons;
and not then until there shall have been two or three elections under the reform
bill."

either have been removed, or would have saved the trouble, the loss of time, the loss of property, and the pain of frustrated hopes, which must ensue unless they be now removed.

I proceed to notice the objections which were stated by your lordship on Friday last, or at the interview on the 16th of April last.

First in importance is that which supposes, that a number of intelligent men should have wildly neglected to ascertain whether the spot on which they desire to settle and pass the remainder of their lives be sufficiently fertile for the purposes of colonization. On this head, I have to remark that your lordship never so much as hinted at any doubt concerning the fertility of the soil, until such a doubt was expressed by Mr. Whitmore on the 16th of April last; that the doubt which had occurred to Mr. Whitmore has been entirely removed, as is shown by a resolution of the Provisional Committee,* passed unanimously on the 21st of May last (of which I have the honour to enclose a copy maked C); that this is a point which, if his majesty's government had been about to found the colony, they ought to have ascertained from the beginning; but that, whereas, in point of fact, the colony, if founded, will be altogether (according to ancient and most successful practice) the work of individuals, not his majesty's government, but the individuals concerned are deeply interested in the question : that the individuals concerned have examined this question with the deepest anxiety, and have arrived at the conclusion, that they run no risk of meeting with a soil not fit for colonization : that, even if such risk existed, it would involve no greater possible evil than the disappointment of those individuals, since the vicinity of the site of the proposed settlement to the settlements of New South Wales and Van Dieman's Land, where food is not merely plentiful but superabundant, puts out of question the privations which have occurred to the founders of many new colonies ; the proposed settlement being, as relates to food, not a new colony, but a new settlement in an old colony over-supplied with food ;† and, finally, that the objection urged by your lordship would, if maintained, be an objection to the foundation of a colony anywhere ;

* "At a meeting of the Provisional Committee, 21st May, 1832 ; present,

W. Wolryche Whitmore, Esq., in the chair.

Colonel Torrens, M.P.	G. Fife Angas, Esq.
William Hutt, Esq.	J. Jephson, Esq., M.P.
Samuel Mills, Esq.	John Melville, Esq.

After considering the evidence contained in the printed pamphlet, entitled— *Evidence relating to the soil, climate, and productions of the south coast of Australia*; hearing the evidence of Dr. Rutherford and Mr. Riley ; reading that of Mr. Mearing ; reading a *Sydney Gazette*, wherein is set forth the contract prices of meat and bread in Sydney, viz. beef, *d.* per lb., mutton, 1½*d.* per lb., and bread, 1¼*d.* per lb ; also reading extracts from Captain Stuart's Journal : it was resolved, unanimously, That the evidence this day submitted to the committee, in respect of the soil, climate, and productions of Kangaroo Island, and the shores of the Murray River, and Lake Alexandrina, is sufficient to warrant the formation of a colony on those lands with all possible despatch."

† With animal food, which is become a drug in New South Wales and Van Dieman's Land, as it is in Buenos Ayres.

since it would be hard to obtain a body of evidence as to the soil of any desert country so favourable as that of which I have the honour to enclose a copy marked D.* Of the capacity of any desert soil for colonization there must always exist a doubt until the experiment be made: but to say that the existence of such a doubt furnishes a reason for not making the experiment, appears directly contrary to reason.†

And here I venture to request your lordship's particular attention to a point which has been made prominent in every step taken by the projectors of the colony; which appears in the proposal submitted to your lordship last year, in the published plan of the company, and in the prospectus lately submitted to your lordship; viz. that the first outlay of the company is to be *by way of experiment*, the sum to be employed not to exceed 5*l.* on each share of the capital subscribed, or, in the whole, 50,000*l.* In confirmation of this statement, I venture to quote the following passage from the published plan of the company. " The plan pursued by it will be to send out in the first instance a small expedition, for the purpose of examining whether the site proposed for the new colony offers the advantages which have been supposed to attach to it. This may be done at a moderate expense. If the result should be favourable, the agents of the company will select for the first settlement the spot which seems to them the most suitable." Thus your lordship will see, that the doubt, which must exist in every case as to the fertility of the soil of a desert country has not been lost sight of in the present instance, but has led to arrangements which render the first intended expedition nothing more than a sufficient experiment.

Nevertheless, as those who have the deepest interest in the experiment trust and believe that it will prove successful, so were they bound to provide for its success. The case of failure is provided for by the vicinity of other settlements superabounding in land, in food, and in demand for labour. The case of success is provided for by the proposed charter; in order that if a colony be founded, it may not be left without any social regulations; in order that if a settlement be planted on the shores of Spencer's Gulf, the settlers paying for the land, those first settlers may not be ruined by subsequent gifts of land to others who may follow them; in order, briefly, that if the first settlement succeed, as to the question of soil, it may not prove a miserable failure in all other respects.

The next objection urged by your lordship was, the evils that might arise from the resort to the new colony of run-away convicts from the penal settlements. Now, the fact is, that Kangaroo Island has been for many years, and is at this time, a place of refuge for run-away convicts; that in that island such persons have formed a society remarkable for existing without any social ties, and for the prevalence of the most horrid crimes; that convicts in the penal settlements are thus invited to escape, no power existing to prevent

---

* This is a printed pamphlet.

† If for a doubt as to the soil, we read a doubt as to the convenience of self-government and extreme cheapness of government, this objection, coming from the colonial minister, will seem rational enough.

them from inhabiting the south coast of Australia; and that if a
settlement were formed on that coast, instead of any evil so to be
caused, an effectual stop would be put to the evil which already
exists.* In illustration of the state of the people who are settled on
Kangaroo Island, I venture to mention the following fact, which is
stated by Dr. Barnes, a gentlemen of great respectability, now resident in London.

Dr. Barnes, being in New Zealand, met with an Englishman who
some years before had, in a fit of madness, attempted to destroy
himself. His lower jaw was shot away in the attempt. Recovering
his senses, ashamed of what he had done and of his frightful appearance, he sought to hide himself from the sight of civilized men, and
to pass the remainder of his life in a state of savage excitement.
With this view he selected as a place of refuge Kangaroo Island,
where he could obtain the society of men more degraded than himself. It should be further remarked, that the savage settlers of
Kangaroo Island seize native women from the mainland, whom they
treat as slaves, and by whom they have children; so that there is
every prospect, unless some counter measure be adopted, of the
existence of a band of dangerous pirates in the spot, which it is
now proposed to convert into a civilized colony.

The third objection, which appeared to weigh with your lordship,
was the apparent want of any motive for founding a new settlement
in Australia, when three settlements are already established there.
In answer to this objection, if it may be so termed, I am requested
to refer your lordship to the signatures appended to our memorial
of the 4th instant, and to say, that many of the gentlemen who
signed that document intend to settle in the proposed colony; but
that no consideration would induce them to settle in New South
Wales, where, such is the state of society, there are, allowing for
the difference of population, 325 public executions for one in England; and where, moreover, nameless crimes prevail, and are becoming, as in Turkey, national habits. Those gentlemen also request me to say, that the accounts which they have received of the
Swan River settlement, of the ruin and misery which have befallen
the more wealthy emigrants to that colony, render it impossible that
they should settle in a colony where, by the profusion of the government in granting land, the people are dispersed and pauperised;
and where there is no security for the inestimable advantage of local
self-government.

Finally, your lordship was pleased to dwell on the responsibility which his majesty's government might incur, by giving its
sanction to the proposed undertaking. To this objection there would
be no answer, if his majesty's government had originated the undertaking, or were called upon to take active measures for promoting
and conducting it. But the fact is, that, as in the case of our oldest

---

* Acting upon this lesson, the government has, I am told, ordered a crown
settlement to be made on this coast, where it was proposed to found a chartered
colony. If it be so, and they should now be asked to enable individuals to
found a colony there, without expense to the mother-country, the reform government may say, Oh, dear, no : the country is already settled.

and most successful colonies, as in the case, it is believed, of every colony founded by Englishmen, the Swan River colony only excepted, the undertaking originates with, and is to be wholly conducted by, certain individuals deeply interested in every step that they may take, fully conversant with the subject, and influenced by the strongest sense of responsibility; which body of individuals ask no more of his majesty's government than that it will enable them to carry into effect their own purpose, by their own means, and on their own responsibility. For the partial failure of the Swan River settlement, the government, who founded the settlement without any provision for success, is no doubt responsible; but the Plymouth Company and William Penn, not the governments of the time, were responsible for the success of the colonies of Virginia and Pennsylvania. And it may be said further, recurring to principles which have often been eloquently advocated by your lordship, that the two last named colonies flourished so greatly, because, not a distant government, but the individuals most deeply concerned, were responsible for every act performed. It is true that, in the present case, the individuals concerned can perform no act without a charter from the crown; but your lordship will allow me to observe, that the crown is impowered to grant charters for the express purpose of enabling bodies of men to act in concert in matters which involve no evil to the public. Consequently, it appears to me, and in saying so I speak the expressed opinion of many of my coadjutors, that unless there be upon the face of the proposed undertaking some prospect of evil, such as it is the business of government to prevent, his majesty's government could not incur any responsibility by merely enabling a number of men to act in concert, for the accomplishment of their own purposes, by their own means, and, I repeat, on their own responsibility.

But I venture humbly to suggest to your lordship, that the responsibility of frustrating so great and good an object, by refusing so small a boon, is one deserving consideration.

Referring to what fell from your lordship as to the propriety of submitting so important a question to his majesty's ministers, I have to state, that, except on the score of delay and suspense which are most distressing to many of the persons interested in this question, we should be gratified to learn that your lordship had laid the question before the cabinet; confident that the·more our plan shall be examined, the more will it be thought worthy of support by an enlightened and liberal administration.*

In conclusion, I am instructed to say, that if there be any modification of the plan which would render it more agreeable to your lordship, the parties concerned will readily adopt the same, unless it would interfere with the main principles of their scheme : but they are unable to suggest any alteration, because no part of the plan has

---

* Like the hungry workman, who had set his heart on getting fat in the new colony, these gentlemen seem to have placed too much dependance on a *reform* government.

been adopted by them without much inquiry and reflection; nor could any part of it, in their sincere opinion, be changed without an alteration for the worse.

(Signed)   J. E. STRICKLAND.

To the Right Honourable Lord Viscount Goderich,
His Majesty's Principal Secretary of State for the Colonies,
&c., &c., &c.

To the above letter no answer was returned; but Lord Goderich intimated his wish that any further discussion should be carried on verbally. At the interview, when the objections were made to which the above letter was intended as an answer, Mr. Hay was present, and suggested most of the objections. An interview now took place, at which Mr. Hay was not present, between Lord Goderich and a deputation from the committee. On this occasion (of which a particular account has been preserved) Lord Goderich suggested some alterations in the plan, and these being agreed to by the deputation, appeared to abandon all his objections. His manner was courteous, and he appeared to feel for the many families then waiting in the most painful suspense for his decision. He desired that a draft of the proposed charter, with the alterations then proposed and agreed to might be forwarded to him without delay; and the deputation reported to their constituents that, as far as they could judge from his lordship's manner and language, the charter would be speedily granted. On the 9th of July, accordingly, a draft of the proposed charter was delivered at the colonial-office, together with a letter from Colonel Torrens to Lord Goderich. To this letter, the following curious answer was returned by Mr. Hay:—

Downing-street, 17th July, 1832.

SIR,

I am directed by Lord Goderich to acknowledge the receipt of your letter dated the 9th instant, enclosing the draft of a charter for the incorporation of the South Australian Land Company, and to acquaint you, for the information of the gentlemen of the Provisional Committee, that his lordship has bestowed the most careful attention upon the various provisions of that instrument. As the transmission of the proposed charter affords the first occasion which has presented itself during the discussions on this subject, for taking a clear and comprehensive view of the plan of the company in all its bearings,* Lord Goderich has entered on the inquiry with a full conviction, that nothing which has hitherto occurred can be supposed by the parties more immediately concerned to preclude his majesty's government from their free and unfettered discretion on the general principles and the particular details of the scheme.† Whatever de-

---

* The great convenience of making this mistake may be some excuse for having made so great a one.

† That is, translating these fine gilt-paper terms into plain English, all which had gone before was to be counted for nothing. This, certainly, was not "supposed by the parties more immediately concerned." From the tone of the government, *after Mr. Hay became its organ,* one should be led to suppose, that these petitioners, instead of asking for a piece of parchment, had been requesting Mr. Hay and Lord Goderich to emigrate along with them.

liberations may have intervened between the original suggestion of the measure and the delivery at this office of the draft of a charter, they have all taken place upon the assumption, that the proposal, when drawn out in its ultimate form, would be found compatible with the fundamental principles, to which it is the duty of the king's government to adhere in every grant which they may advise his majesty to pass under the great seal; and it is of course obvious that this condition must at all times have been distinctly understood.*

On examining the draft which you have transmitted, Lord Goderich finds that in many important particulars it goes far beyond the proposition as he originally understood it to be conceived;† that it would virtually transfer to this company the sovereignty‡ of a vast unexplored territory, equal in extent to one of the most considerable kingdoms of Europe;§ that it would encroach on the limits of the existing colonies of New South Wales and Western Australia;‖ that it is proposed to throw open the settlement to foreigners as well as to British subjects, in such a manner as at once to place them upon a complete equality;¶ that the objects of the corporation are defined with such latitude of expression as to exclude no conceivable employment of their capital;** that the actual investment of that capital, or any part of it even, is not necessarily to precede the issuing of the charter;†† that the charter would invest the company with a power of legislation, and would even enable them to delegate to others the exercise of that trust, without taking the very least

* Of course : but it was also understood that, when Lord Goderich expressed his approval of the fundamental principles, &c., he knew what they were, and really meant what he said.

† "Beyond ;" in which direction? towards liberalism or toryism? The draft of a charter imbodied the *less* liberal provisions as to the governor and the legislative assembly, which Lord Goderich had suggested.

‡ It had always been proposed that the company should govern the colony until the settlers were numerous enough to govern themselves.

§ This is a mistake. The only creatures, over which sovereignty could be transferred, are a few savages and a great many kangaroos and emues. It is true, that the space within which all waste land was to be sold, and the colonists were to govern themselves in local matters as soon as there should be colonists, was very large. But the charter mentioned exactly the same space as the original proposal.

‖ This is a mistake : those colonies have no defined limits. The nearest part of the outside of the proposed colony to any settlement in Australia would have been some hundreds of miles distant.

¶ I am not aware that "foreigners" were ever mentioned either in writing or verbally by any one connected with the colony ; but it was certainly provided in the charter, that all the poor people taken to the colony with the purchase-money of waste land should be British subjects.

** What the company should do with its capital was stated distinctly. Would Mr. Hay have had the charter recite all the things which the company should *not* do with its capital.

†† The committee had been imploring Lord Goderich to promise, only to promise, the charter officially, in order that subscriptions for the capital might be received. Lord Goderich had been told, too, that the intended settlers were ready to subscribe 100,000*l.* of that capital, and that they had disposed of real and other property with that view.

security against the possible abuse of so high an authority ;* that the company would enjoy the right of erecting courts, and of appointing and removing judges and other officers ;† that they claim the power of raising and commanding the militia ; that they would exclude the king from the exercise of that power of imposing duties of customs which parliament has entrusted to him throughout the Eastern colonies ;‡ that a freedom of trade is claimed, to which the navigation and trade acts, as they now stand, are opposed ;§ that all the powers of the company, extensive as they are, and involving in their practical effect the sovereign dominion of the whole territory, are ultimately to be transferred to a popular assembly,‖ which would be to erect in the British monarchy a government purely republican ;¶ and that the company would be the receivers of large sums of public money,** for the due application of which they do not propose to give any security.††

Other objections might be stated to the plan proposed in this draft ; but for the present Lord Goderich forbears to enter on any discussion of them. His lordship deems it sufficient to have pointed out those which I have already referred to ; and directs me to say that, if the various departments of government which must be consulted should concur in a scheme involving such extensive consequences, as would follow from the adoption of that which is proposed,‡‡ they could not legally carry it into effect without the express sanction of parliament ;§§ but his majesty's government could not

* In this respect, the draft of a charter was a copy from the charters, under which companies founded colonies in America. At one of the interviews with Lord Goderich, his lordship had been requested to examine those charters, copies of which probably exist in the colonial-office. A printed copy of them was in the hands of the committee.

† Of course, if the company were to govern for a time, like the London Company, and the Plymouth Company, and William Penn, and even the company which founded a colony at Sierra Leone, it was, during that time, to have the authority necessary for governing.

‡ Not the king, but the clerks in Downing-street, who legislate for New South Wales and the Swan River. Every provision, however, as to trade, was subject to existing laws ; and of course a charter could not affect an act of parliament. That very power which parliament has given to the king, his majesty was requested to exercise in this case.

§ A great mistake. This charter could not have applied to any ports, save those of the colony ; and even there, could not have interfered with any act of parliament.

‖ Of course ; since one chief object of the plan was, according to ancient and approved practice, to establish local self-government in the colony.

¶ If the company should revive their project, they would do well to put a House of Lords into it ; with a Baron Blackswan. a Viscount Kangaroo, a Marquis of Morrumbidgee, and a Bishop of Ornithoryncus.

** Only for repayment of their private money, with which they proposed to defray all the cost of government and defence, until the colony should be able to repay them.

†† The application of the money was clearly defined : it was to be applied in repayment to the company of their advances for the government and defence of the colony.

‡‡ The admission is worth notice, that the plan was calculated to accomplish the objects of those who formed it.

§§ Very many English colonies have been founded by charter : not one, it is believed, by act of parliament.

recommend to parliament a measure so entirely subversive, in one part of his majesty's dominions* of those royal prerogatives, which, for the common benefit of all his subjects, it is his majesty's duty to maintain.†

I am, sir,
Your obedient humble servant,

Colonel Torrens, M.P.   (Signed)   R. W. HAY.

Extract from the Morning Chronicle of September 23d, 1832.

" We invite attention to a letter of Mr. Gouger upon the subject of the South Australian Land Company, which will be found in another column.   Upon the merits of the proposed company we shall abstain from remarking at large now ; as, it seems, a pamphlet is to be published, containing the whole of the correspondence with government upon the subject, accompanied by a sketch of the original plan.   It is, however, clear that any proposition supported by such men as formed the provisional committee, and of which the object was to provide a place of refuge for six thousand poor persons, ought not to have been rejected by the colonial office without very good reasons.   No one will say that the committee was not sufficiently influential, and high in character, to support any wise measure they chose to commence : neither are they men from whom we should be led to expect any other than a practical and attainable project.

" From the fact of the difficulties occurring only after the Australian colonies were placed under the control of Mr. Hay, the *tory* under-secretary of state for the colonies, it may be inferred that the plan was opposed by Mr. Hay, and was therefore abandoned.   We have more than once had occasion to reprobate the practice of the present ministry, in keeping about them men whose principles are diametrically at variance with their own.   A tory of principle and honour will naturally object to measures founded upon liberal principles : an unprincipled tory will lose no opportunity to serve his party, by *bringing his opponents in politics into disrepute ;* although he may, at the same time, be eating the bread of liberal employers.   Both classes, therefore, should be avoided equally.   Mr. Hay is a tory.   Educated in the school of Lord Melville, he has been the constant attendant of all succeeding ministers.   If it should turn out that a spice of liberalism, in the shape of self-government, appeared in the plan of the company or colony, we have no doubt the ministers will have to thank their tory under-secretary for any odium or unpopularity they may experience from the rejection of the measure in question."

* A complete desert, save as to the runaway convicts, over whom, certainly, his majesty exercises no dominion.
† Fudge !

THE END.